Web Engineering

Emilia Mendes · Nile Mosley (Eds.)

Web Engineering

With 143 Figures and 70 Tables

Springer

Editors
Emilia Mendes

Computer Science Department
University of Auckland
Private Bag 92019
Auckland, New Zealand
emilia@cs.auckland.ac.nz

Nile Mosley

MetriQ (NZ) Ltd.
19A Clairville Crescent
Wai-O-Taiki Bay
Auckland, New Zealand
nile@metriq.biz

Library of Congress Control Number: 2005936101

ACM Computing Classification (1998): D.2, C.4, K.6

ISBN-10 3-540-28196-7 Springer Berlin Heidelberg New York
ISBN-13 978-3-540-28196-2 Springer Berlin Heidelberg New York

Springer is a part of Springer Science+Business Media

springeronline.com

Printed in Germany

Typeset by the authors using a Springer TEX macro package
Production: LE-TEX Jelonek, Schmidt & Vöckler GbR, Leipzig
Cover design: KünkelLopka Werbeagentur, Heidelberg

Printed on acid-free paper 45/3142/YL - 5 4 3 2 1 0

To: Pai, Mãe; Ma, Pa

Preface

Since its original inception the Web has changed into an environment employed for the delivery of many different types of applications, ranging from small-scale information-dissemination-like applications, typically developed by writers and artists, to large-scale commercial, enterprise-planning and scheduling, collaborative-work applications. Numerous current Web applications are fully functional systems that provide business-to-customer and business-to-business e-commerce, with numerous services to numerous users.

As the reliance on larger and more complex Web applications increases so does the need for using methodologies/standards/best practice guidelines to develop applications that are delivered on time, within budget, have a high level of quality and are easy to maintain. To develop such applications Web development teams need to use sound methodologies, systematic techniques, quality assurance, rigorous, disciplined and repeatable processes, better tools, and baselines. Web engineering aims to meet such needs.

The focus of this book is to provide its audience with the fundamental concepts necessary to better engineer Web applications, and also present a set of case studies where these concepts are applied to real industrial scenarios. Chapter 1 provides an introduction to Web engineering and discusses its differences and similarities to software engineering. Ten chapters are used to introduce concepts (e.g. cost estimation, productivity assessment, usability measurement) and details on how to apply each concept to a practical situation. Another three chapters provide readers with introductions to statistical techniques and empirical methods.

There is no other book in the market that examines Web engineering in such breadth and with a practical emphasis. In terms of its audience, this book is of considerable benefit for Web practitioners and graduate students. Practitioners can immediately grasp the usefulness and benefits of Web engineering principles since all case studies describe real situations that can also be similar to their own practices. Graduate students and researchers are provided a great opportunity to study Web engineering and to see its application relative to concrete examples.

Table of Contents

List of Contributors

Abrahão, S., Assistant Professor
Department of Information Systems and Computation,
Valencia University of Technology
Camino de Vera, 46071 Valencia
Spain

Andreolini, M., Dr.
Dipartimento di Ingegneria dell'Informazione,
Università di Modena e Reggio Emilia
Via Vignolese 905
41100 Modena, Italy

Baresi, L., Associate Professor
Dipartimento di Elettronica e Informazione,
Politecnico di Milano, Italy
Via Giuseppe Ponzio, 34/5 - 20133 Milano
Italy

Carughi, G.T., BEng.
Dipartimento di Elettronica e Informazione,
Politecnico di Milano
Via Giuseppe Ponzio, 34/5 - 20133 Milano
Italy

Colajanni, M., Professor
Dipartimento di Ingegneria dell'Informazione,
Università di Modena e Reggio Emilia
Via Vignolese 905
41100 Modena, Italy

Colazzo, S.
HOC- Hypermedia Opcn Center,
Politecnico di Milano
Via Ponzio 34/5, 20133 Milano
Italy

Counsell, S., Dr.
School of Information Systems and Computing,
Brunel University
St John's Building, Uxbridge, UB8 3PH
UK

Covella, G., Assistant Professor
Engineering Faculty,
National University of La Pampa
Calle 9 esq. 110 – (6360) General Pico, La Pampa
Argentina

Di Lucca, G.A., Dr.
RCOST-Research Centre on Software Technology
Department of Engineering,
University of Sannio
Via Traiano Palazzo ex Poste, 82100 Benevento
Italy

El-Emam, K, Associate Professor
Faculty of Medicine, University of Ottawa,
CHEO RI 401 Smyth Road, Ottawa, Ontario K1H 8L1
Canada

Fasolino, A.R., Associate Professor
Dep. 'Informatica and Sistemistica',
University of Naples Federico II
Via Claudio 21, 80125 Naples
Italy

Fons, J., Assistant Professor
Department of Information Systems and Computation,
Valencia University of Technology
Camino de Vera, 46071 Valencia
Spain

Henningsson, K., Dr.
Dept. of Systems and Software Engineering,
School of Engineering
Blekinge Institute of Technology, Box 520, SE-372 25 Ronneby
Sweden

Höst, M., Dr.
Dept. of Communication Systems,
Lund Institute of Technology
Lund University, Box 118, SE-221 00 Lund
Sweden

Kitchenham, B.A., Professor
National ICT Australia,
Locked Bag 9013, Alexandria, NSW 1435,
Australia
Dept. of Computer Science, Keele University
Staffordshire ST5, 5BG
UK

Lancellotti, R., Dr.
Dipartimento di Ingegneria dell'Informazione,
Università di Modena e Reggio Emilia
Via Vignolese 905
41100 Modena, Italy

Mainetti, L., Associate Professor
Dip. Elettronica e Informazione,
Politecnico di Milano
Via Ponzio 34/5, 20133 Milano
Italy

Matera, M., Assistant Professor
Dipartimento di Elettronica e Informazione,
Politecnico di Milano
Via Ponzio 34/5, 20133 - Milano
Italy

Maxwell, K., Dr.
Datamax
7 bis bld. Marechal Foch, 77300 Fontainebleau,
France

Mendes, E., Dr.
Department of Computer Science,
The University of Auckland
Science Centre, 38 Princes Street, Auckland
New Zealand

Morasca, S., Professor
Dipartimento di Scienze della Cultura,
Politiche e dell'Informazione
Università degli Studi dell'Insubria
Via Valleggio 11, I-22100 Como
Italy

Mosley, N., Dr.
MetriQ (NZ) Limited
19 Clairville Crescent, Glendowie, Auckland
New Zealand

Olsina, L., Associate Professor
Engineering Faculty,
National University of La Pampa
Calle 9 esq. 110 - (6360) General Pico, La Pampa
Argentina

Pastor, O., Professor
Department of Information Systems and Computation,
Valencia University of Technology
Camino de Vera, 46071 Valencia
Spain

Pelechano, V., Associate Professor
Department of Information Systems and Computation,
Valencia University of Technology
Camino de Vera, 46071 Valencia
Spain

Rizzo, F., Dr.
Human Computer Interaction Laboratory,
Politecnico di Milano
Via Ponzio 34/5, 20133 Milano
Italy

Rossi, G., Professor
LIFIA, National University of La Plata
calle 50 y 115, Primer Piso, La Plata
Argentina

Schwabe, D., Associate Professor
Computer Science Department,
Catholic University of Rio de Janeiro
Rua Marquês de São Vicente, 225 RDC, CEP 22453-900 Gávea,
Rio de Janeiro RJ
Brazil

Wohlin, C., Professor
Dept. of Systems and Software Engineering,
School of Engineering
Blekinge Institute of Technology,
Box 520, SE-372 25 Ronneby
Sweden

1 The Need for Web Engineering: An Introduction

Emilia Mendes, Nile Mosley, Steve Counsell

Abstract: The objective of this chapter is three-fold. First, it provides an overview of differences between Web and software development with respect to their development processes, technologies, quality factors, and measures. Second, it provides definitions for terms used throughout the book. Third, it discusses the need for empirical investigations in Web engineering and presents the three main types of empirical investigations – surveys, case studies, and formal experiments.

Keywords: Web engineering, Empirical Investigation, Case studies, Surveys, Formal experiment, Scientific principles, Engineering.

1.1 Introduction

The World Wide Web (Web) was originally conceived in 1989 as an environment to allow for the sharing of information (e.g. research reports, databases, user manuals) amongst geographically dispersed individuals. The information itself was stored on different servers and was retrieved by means of a single user interface (Web browser). The information consisted primarily of text documents inter-linked using a hypertext metaphor[1] [23].

Since its original inception the Web has changed into an environment employed for the delivery of many different types of applications. Such applications range from small-scale information-dissemination-like applications, typically developed by writers and artists, to large-scale commercial,[2] enterprise-planning and scheduling, collaborative-work applications. The latter are developed by multidisciplinary teams of people with diverse skills and backgrounds using cutting-edge, diverse technologies [10,12,23]. Numerous current Web applications are fully functional systems that provide business-to-customer and business-to-business e-commerce, and numerous services to numerous users [23].

---

1 http://www.zeltser.com/web-history/.

2 The increase in the use of the Web to provide commercial applications has been motivated by several factors, such as the possible increase of an organisation's competitive position, and the opportunity for small organisations to project their corporate presence in the same way as that of larger organisations [29].

Industries such as travel and hospitality, manufacturing, banking, education, and government utilised Web-based applications to improve and increase their operations [12]. In addition, the Web allows for the development of corporate intranet Web applications, for use within the boundaries of their organisations [15]. The remarkable spread of Web applications into areas of communication and commerce makes it one of the leading and most important branches of the software industry [23].

To date the development of Web applications has been in general ad hoc, resulting in poor-quality applications, which are difficult to maintain [22]. The main reasons for such problems are unsuitable design and development processes, and poor project management practices [11]. A survey on Web-based projects, published by the Cutter Consortium in 2000, revealed a number of problems with outsourced large Web-based projects [11]:

- 84% of surveyed delivered projects did not meet business needs.
- 53% of surveyed delivered projects did not provide the required functionality.
- 79% of surveyed projects presented schedule delays.
- 63% of surveyed projects exceeded their budget.

As the reliance on larger and more complex Web applications increases so does the need for using methodologies/standards/best practice guidelines to develop applications that are delivered on time, within budget, have a high level of quality and are easy to maintain [29,27,20]. To develop such applications Web development teams need to use sound methodologies, systematic techniques, quality assurance, rigorous, disciplined and repeatable processes, better tools, and baselines. Web engineering[3] aims to meet such needs [12].

Web engineering is described as [21]:

> *"the use of scientific, engineering, and management principles and systematic approaches with the aim of successfully developing, deploying and maintaining high quality Web-based systems and applications".*

This is a similar definition to that used to describe software engineering; however, both disciplines differ in many ways. Such differences are discussed in Sect. 1.2.

Section 1.3 provides an introduction to measurement principles and three widely used methods of investigation – surveys, case studies, and formal experiments [7]. Finally, conclusions are presented in Sect. 1.4.

---

[3] The term "Web engineering" was first published in 1996 in a conference paper by Gellersen et al. [9]. Since then this term has been cited in numerous publications, and numerous activities devoted to discussing Web engineering have taken place (e.g. workshops, conference tracks, entire conferences).

1.2 Web Applications Versus Conventional Software

An overview of differences between Web and software development with respect to their development processes, technologies, quality factors, and measures is presented here. In addition, this section also provides definitions and terms used throughout the book (e.g. Web application).

1.2.1 Web Hypermedia, Web Software, or Web Application?

The Web is the best known example of a hypermedia system. To date, numerous organisations world-wide have developed a vast array of commercial and/or educational Web applications. The Web literature uses numerous synonyms for a Web application, such as Web site, Web system, Internet application. The IEEE Std 2001-2002 uses the term Web site defined as [17]:

> *"A collection of logically connected Web pages managed as a single entity."*

However, using Web site and Web application interchangeably does not allow one to differentiate between the physical storage of Web pages and their application domains.

The Web has been used as the delivery platform for three types of applications: Web hypermedia applications, Web software applications, and Web applications [4].

- *Web hypermedia application* – a non-conventional application characterised by the authoring of information using nodes (chunks of information), links (relations between nodes), anchors, access structures (for navigation), and delivery over the Web. Technologies commonly used for developing such applications are HTML, XML, JavaScript, and multimedia. In addition, typical developers are writers, artists, and organisations who wish to publish information on the Web and/or CD-ROM without the need to know programming languages such as Java. These applications have unlimited potential in areas such as software engineering, literature, education, and training.
- *Web software application* – a conventional software application that relies on the Web or uses the Web's infrastructure for execution. Typical applications include legacy information systems such as databases, booking systems, knowledge bases, etc. Many e-commerce applications fall into this category. Typically they employ development technologies (e.g. DCOM, ActiveX, etc.), database systems, and development solutions (e.g. J2EE). Developers are in general young programmers fresh

from a Computer Science or Software Engineering degree course, managed by a few more senior staff.
- *Web application* – an application delivered over the Web that combines characteristics of both Web hypermedia and Web software applications.

1.2.2 Web Development vs. Software Development

Web development and software development differ in a number of areas, which will be detailed later. However, of these, three such areas seem to provide the greatest differences and to affect the entire Web development and maintenance processes. These areas encompass the people involved in development, the intrinsic characteristics of Web applications, and the audience for which they are developed.

The development of conventional software remains dominated largely by IT professionals where a sound knowledge of programming, database design, and project management is necessary. In contrast, Web development encompasses a much wider variety of developers, such as amateurs with no programming skills, graphics designers, writers, database experts, and IT professionals, to name but a few. This is possible as Web pages can be created by anyone without the necessity for programming knowledge [3].

Web applications by default use communications technology and have multi-platform accessibility. In addition, since they employ a hypermedia paradigm, they are non-sequential by nature, using hyperlinks to interrelate Web pages and other documents. Therefore, navigation and pluralistic design become important aspects to take into account. Finally, the multitude of technologies available for developing Web applications means that developers can build a full spectrum of applications, from a static simple Web application using HTML to a fully fledged distributed e-commerce application [29]. Conventional software can be developed using several programming languages running on a specific platform, components off the shelf (COTS), etc. It can also use communications technology to connect to and use a database system. However the speed of implementing new technology is faster for Web development relative to non-Web-based applications.

Web applications are aimed at wide-ranging groups of users. Such groups may be known ahead of time (e.g. applications available within the boundaries of the intranet). However, it is more often the case that Web applications are devised for an unknown group of users, making the development of aesthetically pleasing applications more challenging [5]. In contrast, conventional software applications are generally developed for a known user group (e.g. department, organisation) making the explicit identification of target users an easier task.

For the purpose of discussion, we have grouped the differences between Web and software development into 12 areas, which are as follows:

1. Application Characteristics
2. Primary Technologies Used
3. Approach to Quality Delivered
4. Development Process Drivers
5. Availability of the Application
6. Customers (Stakeholders)
7. Update Rate (Maintenance Cycles)
8. People Involved in Development
9. Architecture and Network
10. Disciplines Involved
11. Legal, Social, and Ethical Issues
12. Information Structuring and Design

(1) Application Characteristics

Web applications are created by integrating numerous distinct elements, such as fine-grained components (e.g. DCOM, OLE, ActiveX), interpreted scripting languages, components off the shelf (COTS) (e.g. customised applications, library components, third-party products), multimedia files (e.g. audio, video, 3D objects), HTML/SGML/XML files, graphical images, mixtures of HTML and programs, and databases [5,23,26]. Components may be integrated in many different ways and present different quality attributes. In addition, their source code may be proprietary or unavailable, and may reside on and/or be executed from different remote computers [23]. Web applications are in the main platform-independent (although there are exceptions, e.g. OLE, ActiveX) and Web browsers in general provide similar user interfaces with similar functionality, freeing users from having to learn distinct interfaces [5]. Finally, a noticeable difference between Web applications and conventional software applications is in the use of navigational structures. Web applications use a hypermedia paradigm where content is structured and presented using hyperlinks. Navigational structures may also need to be customised, i.e. the dynamic adaptation of content structure, atomic hypermedia components, and presentation styles [8].

Despite the initial attempt by the hypermedia community to develop conventional applications with a hypermedia-like interface, the large amounts of conventional software applications do not employ this technique.

Again in contrast, conventional software applications can also be developed using a wide variety of components (e.g. COTS), generally developed using conventional programming languages such as C++, Visual Basic, and Delphi. These applications may also use multimedia files, graphical images, and databases. It is common that user interfaces are customised depending on the hardware, operating system, software in use, and the target audience [5]. There are programming languages on the market (e.g. Java) that are intentionally cross-platform; however, the best part of conventional software applications tend to be monolithic running on a single operating system.

(2) Primary Technologies Used

Web applications are developed using a wide range of diverse technologies such as the many flavoured Java solutions (Java servlets, Enterprise JavaBeans, applets, and JavaServer Pages), HTML, JavaScript, XML, UML, databases, and much more. In addition, there is an increasing use of third-party components and middleware. Since Web technology is an area that changes quickly, some authors suggest it may be difficult for developers and organisations to keep up with what is currently available [23].

The primary technology used to develop conventional software applications is mostly represented by object-oriented methods, generators, and languages, relational databases, and CASE tools [26]. The pace with which new technologies are proposed is slower than that for Web applications.

(3) Approach to Quality Delivered

Web companies that operate their business on the Web rely heavily on providing applications and services of high quality so that customers return to do repeat business. As such, these companies only see a return on investment if customers' needs have been fulfilled. Customers who use the Web for obtaining services have very little loyalty to the companies they do business with. This suggests that new companies providing Web applications of a higher quality will most likely displace customers from previously established businesses. Further, that quality is the principal factor that will bring repeated business. For Web development, quality is often considered as higher priority than time to market, with the mantra "later and better" as the mission statement for Web companies who wish to remain competitive [23].

Within the context of conventional software development, software contractors are often paid for their delivered application regardless of its quality. Return on investment is immediate. Ironically, they are also often paid for fixing defects in the delivered application, where these failures principally exist because the developer did not test the application thoroughly. This has the knock-on effect that a customer may end up paying at least twice (release and fixing defects) the initial bid in order to make the application functional. Here time to market takes priority over quality since it can be more lucrative to deliver applications with plenty of defects sooner than high-quality applications later. For these companies the "sooner but worse" rules applies [23].

Another popular mechanism employed by software companies is to fix defects and make the updated version into a new release, which is then resold to customers, bringing in additional revenue.

(4) Development Process Drivers
The dominant development process drivers for Web companies are composed of three quality criteria [23]:

- Reliability,
- Usability, and
- Security.

Followed by:

- Availability,
- Scalability,
- Maintainability, and
- Time to market.

Reliability: applications that work well, do no crash, do not provide incorrect data, etc.

Usability: an application that is simple to use. If a customer wants to use a Web application to buy a product on-line, the application should be as simple to use as the process of physically purchasing that product in a shop. Many existing Web applications present poor usability despite the extensive range of Web usability guidelines that have been published. A Web application with poor usability will quickly be replaced by another more usable application as soon as its existence becomes known to the target audience [23].

Security: the handling of customer data and other information securely so that problems such as financial loss, legal consequences, and loss of credibility can be avoided [23].

With regards to conventional software development, the development process driver is time to market and not quality criteria [23].

(5) Availability of the Application
Customers who use the Web expect applications to be operational throughout the whole year (24/7/365). Any downtime, no matter how short, can be detrimental [23].

Except for a few application domains (e.g. security, safety critical, military, banking) customers of conventional software applications do not expect these applications to be available 24/7/365.

(6) Customers (Stakeholders)
Web applications can be developed for use within the boundaries of a single organisation (intranet), a number of organisations (extranets), or for use by people anywhere in the world. The implications are that stakeholders may come from a wide range of groups where some may be clearly identified (e.g. employees within an organisation) and some may remain unknown,

which is often the case [23,5,6,28]. As a consequence, Web developers are regularl aced with the challenge of developing applications for unknown users, whose expectations (requirements) and behaviour patterns are also unknown at development time [5]. In this case new approaches and guidelines must be devised to better understand prospective and unknown users such that quality requirements can be determined beforehand to deliver high-quality applications [6]. Whenever users are unknown it also becomes more difficult to provide aesthetically pleasing user interfaces, necessary to be successful and stand out from the competition [5].

Some stakeholders can reside locally, in another state/province/county, or overseas. Those who reside overseas may present different social and linguistic backgrounds, which increases the challenge of developing successful applications [5,28]. Whenever stakeholders are unknown it is also difficult to estimate the number of users an application will service, so applications must also be scalable [23].

With regards to conventional software applications, it is usual for stakeholders be explicitly identified prior to development. These stakeholders often represent groups confined within the boundaries of departments, divisions, or organisations [5].

(7) Update Rate (Maintenance Cycles)

Web applications are updated frequently without specific releases and with maintenance cycles of days or even hours [23]. In addition, their content and functionality may also change significantly from one moment to another, and so the concept of project completion may seem unsuitable in such circumstances. Some organisations also allow non-information-systems experts to develop and modify Web applications and in such environments it is often necessary to provide an overall management of the delivery and modification of applications to avoid confusion [28].

The maintenance cycle for conventional software applications complies with a more rigorous process. Upon a product's release software organisations usually initiate a cycle whereby a list of requested changes/adjustments/improvements (either from customers or from its own development team) is prepared over a set period of time, and later incorporated as a specific version or release for distribution to all customers simultaneously. This cycle can be as short as a week and as long as several years. It requires more planning as it often entails other, possibly expensive activities such as marketing, sales, product shipping, and occasionally personal installation at a customer's site [12,23].

(8) People Involved in Development

The Web provides a broad spectrum of different types of Web applications, varying in quality, size, complexity, and technology. This variation is also applicable to the range of skills represented by those involved in Web development projects. Web applications can be created, for example, by artists and writers using simple HTML code or more likely one of the many commercially available Web authoring tools (e.g. Macromedia Dreamweaver, Microsoft Frontpage), making the authoring process available to those with no prior programming experience [28]. However, Web applications can also be very large and complex, requiring a team of people with diverse skills and experience. Such teams consist of Web designers and programmers, graphic designers, librarians, database designers, project managers, network security experts, and usability experts [23].

Web designers and programmers are necessary to implement the application's functionality using the necessary programming languages and technology. In particular they also decide on the application's architecture and technologies applicable, and to design the application taking into account its documents and links [5]. Graphic designers, usability experts, and librarians provide applications pleasing to the eye, easy to navigate, and provide good search mechanisms to obtain the required information. This is often the case where such expertise is outsourced, and used on a project-by-project basis.

Large Web applications most likely use database systems for data storage making it important to have a team member with expertise in database design and the necessary queries to manipulate the data. Project managers are responsible for managing the project in a timely manner and allocating resources adequately such that applications are developed on time, within budget, and are of high quality. Finally, network security experts provide solutions for various security aspects [11].

Conversely, the development of conventional software remains dominated by IT professionals where a sound knowledge of programming, database design, and project management is necessary.

(9) Architecture and Network

Web applications are typically developed using a simple client–server architecture (two-tier), represented by Web browsers on client computers connecting to a Web server hosting the Web application, to more sophisticated configurations such as three-tier or even *n*-tier architecture [23]. The servers and clients within these architectures represent computers that may have a different operating system, software, hardware configurations, and may be connected to each other using different network settings and bandwidth.

The introduction of more than two tiers was motivated by limitations of the two-tier model (e.g. implementation of an application's business logic on the client machine, increased network load as any data processing is only carried out on the client machine). In such architectures the business logic is moved to a separate server (middle-tier), which services client requests for data and functionality. The middle-tier then requests and sends data to and from a (usually) separate database server. In addition, the type of networks used by the numerous stakeholders may be unknown, so assumptions have to be made while developing these Web applications [5].

Conventional software applications either run in isolation on a client machine or use a two-tier architecture whenever applications use data from database systems installed on a separate server. The type of networks used by the stakeholders is usually known in advance since most conventional software applications are limited to specific places and organisations [5].

(10) Disciplines Involved

To develop large and complex Web applications adequately a team of people with a wide range of skills and expertise in different areas is required. These areas reflect distinct disciplines such as software engineering (development methodologies, project management, tools), hypermedia engineering (linking, navigation), requirements engineering, usability engineering, information engineering, graphics design, and network management (performance measurement and tuning) [6,11,12].

Building a conventional software application involves contributions from a smaller number of disciplines than those used for developing Web applications, such as software engineering, requirements engineering, and usability engineering.

(11) Legal, Social, and Ethical Issues

The Web as a distributed environment enables a vast amount of structured (e.g. database records) and unstructured (e.g. text, images, audio) content to be easily available to a multitude of users worldwide. This is often cited as one of the greatest advantages of using the Web. However, this environment is also used for the purpose of dishonest actions, such as copying content from Web applications without acknowledging the source, distributing information about customers without their consent, infringing copyright and intellectual property rights, and even, in some instances, identity theft [5]. The consequences that follow from the unlawful use of the Web are that Web companies, customers, entities (e.g. W3C), and government agencies must apply a similar paradigm to the Web as those applied to publishing, where legal, social, and ethical issues are taken into consideration [6].

Issues referring to accessibility offered by Web applications should also take into account special user groups such as the handicapped [5].

Conventional software applications also share a similar fate to that of Web applications, although to a smaller extent, since these applications are not so readily available for such a large community of users, compared to Web applications.

(12) Information Structuring and Design

As previously mentioned, Web applications present structured and unstructured content, which may be distributed over multiple sites and use different systems (e.g. database systems, file systems, multimedia storage devices) [8]. In addition, the design of a Web application, unlike that of conventional software applications, includes the organisation of content into navigational structures by means of hyperlinks. These structures provide users with easily navigable Web applications. Well-designed applications should allow for suitable navigation structures [6],]as well as the structuring of content, which should take into account its efficient and reliable management [5].

Another difference between Web and conventional applications is that Web applications often contain a variety of specific file formats for multimedia content (e.g. graphics, sound, and animation). These files must be integrated into any current configuration management system, and their maintenance routine also needs to be organised as is likely that it will differ from the maintenance routine used for text-based documents [3]. Conventional software applications present structured content that uses file or database systems. The structuring of such content has been addressed by software engineering in the past so the methods employed here for information structuring and design are well known by IT professionals [5].

Reifer [26]presents a comparison between Web-based and traditional approaches that takes into account measurement challenges for project management (see Table 1.1). Table 1.2 summarises the differences between Web-based and conventional development contexts.

Table 1.1. Comparison between Web-based and traditional approaches

	Web-based approach	Traditional approach
Estimating process	Ad-hoc costing of work, centred on input from the developers.	More formal costing of work based on past experience from similar projects and expert opinion.
Size estimation	No agreement upon a standard size measure for Web applications within the community.	Lines of code or function points are the standard size measures used.
Effort estimation	Effort is estimated using a bottom-up approach based on input from developers. Hardly any historical data is available from past projects.	Effort is estimated using equations built taking into account project characteristics and historical data from past projects.
Quality estimation	Quality is difficult to measure. Need for new quality measures specific for Web-based projects.	Quality is measurable using known quality measures (e.g. defect rates, system properties).

Table 1.2. Web-based versus traditional approaches to development

	Web-based approach	Traditional approach
Application characteristics	Integration of numerous distinct components (e.g. fine-grained, interpreted scripting languages, COTS, multimedia files, HTML/SGML/XML files, databases, graphical images), distributed, cross-platform applications, and structuring of content using navigational structures with hyperlinks.	Integration of distinct components (e.g. COTS, databases, graphical images), monolithic single-platform applications.
Primary technologies used	Variety of Java solutions (Java servlets, Enterprise JavaBeans, applets, and JavaServer Pages), HTML, JavaScript, XML, UML, databases, third-party components and middleware, etc.	Object-oriented methods, generators, and languages, relational databases, and CASE tools.
Approach to quality delivered	Quality is considered as of higher priority than time to market.	Time to market takes priority over quality.
Development process drivers	Reliability, usability, and security.	Time to market.
Availability of the application	Throughout the whole year (24/7/365).	Except for a few application domains, no need for availability 24/7/365.
Customers (stakeholders)	Wide range of groups, known and unknown, residing locally or overseas.	Generally groups confined within the boundaries of departments, divisions, or organizations.
Update rate (maintenance cycles)	Frequently without specific releases, maintenance cycles of days or even hours.	Specific releases, maintenance cycles ranging from a week to several years.
People involved in development	Web designers and programmers, graphic designers, librarians, database designers, project managers, network security experts, usability experts, artists, writers.	IT professionals with knowledge of programming, database design, and project management.
Architecture and Network	Two-tier to *n*-tier clients and servers with different network settings and bandwidth, sometimes unknown.	One to two-tier architecture, network settings, and bandwidth are likely to be known in advance.

	Web-based approach	Traditional approach
Disciplines involved	Software engineering, hypermedia engineering, requirements engineering, usability engineering, information engineering, graphics design, and network management.	Software engineering, requirements engineering, and usability engineering.
Legal, social, and ethical issues	Content can be easily copied and distributed without permission or acknowledgement of copyright and intellectual property rights. Applications should take into account all groups of users including those handicapped.	Content can also be copied infringing privacy, copyright, and IP issues, albeit to a smaller extent.
Information structuring and design	Structured and unstructured content, use of hyperlinks to build navigational structures.	Structured content, seldom use of hyperlinks.

As we have seen, there are several differences between Web development and applications and conventional development and applications. However, there are also similarities that are more evident if we focus on the development of large and complex applications. Both need quality assurance mechanisms, development methodologies, tools, processes, techniques for requirements elicitation, effective testing and maintenance methods, and tools [6].

The next section will provide an introduction to the measurement principles used throughout the book. It also provides an introduction to empirical assessment.

1.3 The Need for an Engineering Approach

Engineering is widely taken as a disciplined application of scientific knowledge for the solution of practical problems. A few definitions taken from dictionaries confirm that:

> *"Engineering is the application of science to the needs of humanity. This is accomplished through knowledge, mathematics, and practical experience applied to the design of useful objects or processes." [30]*

> *"Engineering is the application of scientific principles to practical ends, as the design, manufacture, and operation of structures and machines." [15]*

> *"The profession of applying scientific principles to the design, construction, and maintenance of engines, cars, machines, etc. (mechanical engineering), buildings, bridges, roads, etc. (civil engineering), electrical machines and communication systems (electrical engineering), chemical plant and machinery (chemical engineering), or aircraft (aeronautical engineering)." [14]*

In all of the above definitions, the need for "the application of scientific principles" has been stressed, where scientific principles are the result of applying a scientific process [13]. A process in this context means that our current understanding, i.e. our theory of how best to develop, deploy, and maintain high-quality Web-based systems and applications, may be modified or replaced as new evidence is found through the accumulation of data and knowledge. This process is illustrated in Fig. 1.1 and described below [13]:

- *Observation*: To observe or read about a phenomenon or set of facts. In most cases the motivation for such observation is to identify cause and effect relationships between observed items, since these entail predictable results. For example, we can observe that an increase in the development of new Web pages seems also to increase the corresponding development effort.
- *Hypothesis*: To formulate a hypothesis represents an attempt to explain an *Observation*. It is a tentative theory or assumption that is believed to explain the behaviour under investigation [7]. The items that participate in the *Observation* are represented by variables (e.g. number of new Web pages, development effort) and the hypothesis indicates what is expected to happen to these variables (e.g. there is a linear relationship between number of Web pages and development effort, showing that as the number of new Web pages increases so does the effort to develop these pages). These variables first need to be measured and to do so we need an underlying measurement theory.
- *Prediction*: To predict means to predict results that should be found if the rationale used in the hypothesis formulation is correct (e.g. Web applications with a larger number of new Web pages will use a larger development effort).
- *Validation*: To validate requires experimentation to provide evidence either to support or refute the initial hypothesis. If the evidence refutes the hypothesis then the hypothesis should be revised or replaced. If the evidence is in support of the hypothesis, then many more replications of the experiment need to be carried out in order to build a better understanding of how variables relate to each other and their cause and effect relationships.

The scientific process supports knowledge building, which in turn involves the use of empirical studies to test hypotheses previously proposed, and to ensure if current understanding of the discipline is correct. Experimentation in Web engineering is therefore essential [1,2].

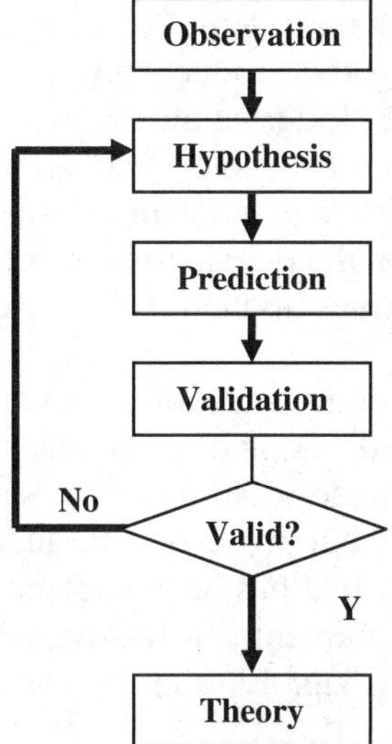

Fig. 1.1. The scientific process

The extent to which scientific principles are applied to developing and maintaining Web applications varies among organisations. More mature organisations generally apply these principles to a larger extent than less mature organisations, where maturity reflects an organisation's current development processes [7]. Some organisations have clearly defined processes that remain unchanged regardless of the people who work on the projects. For such organisations, success is dictated by following a well-defined process, where feedback is constantly obtained using product, process and resource measures. Other organisations have processes that are not so clearly defined (ad hoc) and therefore the success of a project is often determined by the expertise of the development team. In such a scenario product, process, and resource measures are rarely used and each project represents a potential risk that may lead an organisation, if it gets it wrong, to bankruptcy [25].

The variables used in the formulation of hypotheses represent the attributes of real-world entities that we observe. An entity represents a process, product, or resource. A process is defined as a software-related activity. Examples of processes are Web development, Web maintenance, Web design, Web testing, and Web project. A product is defined as an artefact, deliverable, or document that results from a process activity. Examples of products are Web application, design document, testing scripts, and fault reports. Finally, a resource represents an entity required by a process activity. Examples of resources are Web developers, development tools, and programming languages [7].

In addition, for each entity's attribute that is to be measured, it is also useful to identify if the attribute is *internal* or *external*. Internal attributes can be measured by examining the product, process, or resource on its own, separate from its behaviour. External attributes can only be measured with respect to how the product, process, or resource relates to its environment [7]. For example, usability is in general an external attribute since its measurement often depends upon the interaction between user and application.

The classification of entities applied to the case study in Chap. 2 is presented in Table 1.3.

The measurement of an entity's attributes generates quantitative descriptions of key processes, products, and resources, enabling us to understand behaviour and result. This understanding lets us select better techniques and tools to control and improve our processes, products, and resources [24].

The measurement theory that has been adopted in this book is the representational theory of measurement [7]. It drives the definition of measurement scales, presented in Chap. 12, and the measures presented in all remaining chapters.

Table 1.3. Classification of process, product, and resources for Tukutuku[4] dataset

ENTITY	ATTRIBUTE	Description
PROCESS ENTITIES		
PROJECT		
	TYPEPROJ	Type of project (new or enhancement).
	LANGS	Implementation languages used.
	DOCPROC	If project followed defined and documented process.
	PROIMPR	If project team involved in a process improvement programme.
	METRICS	If project team part of a software metrics programme.
	DEVTEAM	Size of project's development team.

[4] The Tukutuku project collects data on industrial Web projects, for the development of effort estimation models and to benchmark productivity across and within Web companies. See http://www.cs.auckland.ac.nz/tukutuku.

ENTITY	ATTRIBUTE	Description
WEB DEVELOPMENT		
	TOTEFF	Actual total effort used to develop the Web application.
	ESTEFF	Estimated total effort necessary to develop the Web application.
	ACCURACY	Procedure used to record effort data.
PRODUCT ENTITY		
WEB APPLICATION		
	TYPEAPP	Type of Web application developed.
	TOTWP	Total number of Web pages (new and reused).
	NEWWP	Total number of new Web pages.
	TOTIMG	Total number of images (new and reused).
	NEWIMG	Total number of new images your company created.
	HEFFDEV	Minimum number of hours to develop a single function/feature by one experienced developer that is considered high (above average).
	HEFFADPT	Minimum number of hours to adapt a single function/feature by one experienced developer that is considered high (above average).
	HFOTS	Number of reused high-effort features/functions without adaptation.
	HFOTSA	Number of adapted high-effort features/functions.
	HNEW	Number of new high-effort features/functions.
	FOTS	Number of low-effort features off the shelf.
	FOTSA	Number of low-effort features off the shelf adapted.
	NEW	Number of new low-effort features/functions.
RESOURCE ENTITY		
DEVELOPMENT TEAM		
	TEAMEXP	Average team experience with the development language(s) employed.

1.4 Empirical Assessment

Validating a hypothesis or research question encompasses experimentation, which is carried out using an empirical investigation. Investigations can be organised as a survey, case study or formal experiment [7].

- *Survey*: a retrospective investigation of an activity in order to confirm relationships and outcomes [7]. It is also known as "research-in-the-large" as it often samples over large groups of projects. A survey should always be carried out after the activity under focus has occurred [18]. When performing a survey, a researcher has no control over the situation at hand, i.e. the situation can be documented, compared to other similar situations, but none of the variables being investigated can be manipulated [7]. Within the scope of software and Web engineering, surveys are often used to validate the response of organisations and developers to a new development method, tool, or technique, or to reveal trends or relationships between relevant variables [7]. For example, a survey can be used to measure the success of changing from Sun's J2EE to Microsoft's ASP.NET throughout an organisation, because it can gather data from numerous projects. The downside of surveys is time. Gathering data can take many months or even years, and the outcome may only be available after several projects have been completed [18].
- *Case study*: an investigation that examines the trends and relationships using as its basis a typical project within an organisation. It is also known as "research-in-the-typical" [18]. A case study can investigate a retrospective event, but this is not the usual trend. A case study is the type of investigation of choice when wishing to examine an event that has not yet occurred and for which there is little or no control over the variables. For example, if an organisation wants to investigate the effect of an object-oriented language on the quality of the resulting Web application but cannot develop the same project using numerous object-oriented languages simultaneously, then the investigative choice is to use a case study. If the quality of the resulting Web application is higher than the organisation's baseline, it may be due to many different reasons (e.g. chance, or perhaps bias from enthusiastic developers). Even if the object-oriented language had a legitimate effect on quality, no conclusions outside the boundaries of the case study can be drawn, i.e. the results of a case study cannot be generalised to every possible situation. Had the same application been developed several times, each time using a different object-oriented language[5] (as a formal experiment) then it would be possible to have better understanding of the relationship between language and quality, given that these variables were controlled. A case study samples *from the variables*, rather than over them. This means that, in relation to the variable object-oriented language, a value that represents the object-oriented language usually used on most projects

[5] The values for all other attributes should remain the same (e.g. developers, programming experience, development tools, computing power, type of application).

will be the one chosen (e.g. J2EE). A case study is easier to plan than a formal experiment, but its results are harder to explain and, as previously mentioned, cannot be generalised outside the scope of the study [18].

- *Formal experiment*: rigorous and controlled investigation of an event where important variables are identified and manipulated such that their effect on the outcome can be validated [7]. It is also known as "research-in-the-small" since it is very difficult to carry out formal experiments in software and Web engineering using numerous projects and resources. A formal experiment samples *over the variable that is being manipulated*, such that all possible variable values are validated, i.e. there is a single case representing each possible situation. If we use the same example used for case studies above, this means that several projects would be developed, each using a different object-oriented programming language. If one aims to obtain results that are largely applicable across various types of projects and processes, then the choice of investigation is a formal experiment. This type of investigation is most suited to the Web engineering research community. Despite the control that needs to be exerted when planning and running a formal experiment, its results cannot be generalised outside the experimental conditions. For example, if an experiment demonstrates that J2EE improves the quality of e-commerce Web applications, one cannot guarantee that J2EE will also improve the quality of educational Web applications [18].

There are other concrete issues related to using a formal experiment or a case study that may impact the choice of study. It may be feasible to control the variables, but at the expense of a very high cost or high degree of risk. If replication *is* possible but at a prohibitive cost, then a case study should be used [7]. A summary of the characteristics of each type of empirical investigation is given in Table 1.4.

Table 1.4. Summary characteristics of the three types of empirical investigations

Characteristic	Survey	Case study	Formal experiment
Scale	Research-in-the-large	Research-in-the-typical	Research-in-the-small
Control	No control	Low level of control	High level of control
Replication	No	Low	High
Generalisation	Results representative of sampled population	Only applicable to other projects of similar type and size	Can be generalised within the experimental conditions

There are a set of steps broadly common to all three types of investigations, and these are described below.

Define the Goal(s) of Your Investigation and Its Context
Goals are crucial for the success of all activities in an investigation. Thus, it is important to allow enough time to fully understand and set the goals so that each is clear and measurable. Goals represent the research questions, which may also be presented by a number of hypotheses. By setting the research questions or hypotheses it becomes easier to identify the dependent and independent variables for the investigation [7]. A dependent variable is a variable whose behaviour we want to predict or explain. An independent variable is believed to have a causal relationship with, or have influence upon, the dependent variable [31]. Goals also help determine what the investigation will do, and what data is to be collected. Finally, by understanding the goals we can also confirm if the type of investigation chosen is the most suitable type to use [7].

Each hypothesis of an investigation will later be either supported or rejected. An example of hypotheses is given below [31]:

H_0 Using J2EE produces the same quality of Web applications as using ASP.NET.

H_1 Using J2EE produces a different quality of Web applications than using ASP.NET.

H_0 is called the null hypothesis, and assumes the quality of Web applications developed using J2EE is similar to that of Web applications developed using ASP.NET. In other words, it assumes that data samples for both come from the same population. In this instance, we have two samples, one representing quality values for Web applications developed using J2EE, and the other, quality values for Web applications developed using ASP.NET. Here, quality is our dependent variable, and the choice of programming framework (e.g. J2EE or ASP.NET), the independent variable.

H_1 is called the alternative or research hypothesis, and represents what is believed to be true if the null hypothesis is false. The alternative hypothesis assumes that samples do not come from the same sample population. Sometimes the direction of the relationship between dependent and independent variables is also presented as part of an alternative hypothesis. If H_1 also suggested a direction for the relationship, it could be described as:

H_1 Using J2EE produces a better quality of Web applications than using ASP.NET.

To confirm H_1 it is first necessary to reject the null hypothesis and, second, show that quality values for Web applications developed using J2EE are significantly higher than quality values for Web applications developed using ASP.NET.

We have presented both null and alternative hypotheses since they are both equally important when presenting the results of an investigation, and, as such, both should be documented.

In addition to defining the goals of an investigation, it is also important to document the context of the investigation [19]. One suggested way to achieve this is to provide a table (see Table 1.3) describing the entities, attributes, and measures that are the focus of the investigation.

Prepare the Investigation

It is important to prepare an investigation carefully to obtain results from which one can draw valid conclusions, even if these conclusions cannot be scaled up. For case studies and formal experiments it is important to define the variables that can influence the results, and once defined, decide how much control one can have over them [7].

Consider the following case study which would represent a *poorly prepared investigation.*

The case study aims to investigate, within a given organisation, the effect of using the programming framework J2EE on the quality of the resulting Web application. Most Web projects in this organisation are developed using ASP.NET, and all the development team has experience with this language. The type of application representative of the majority of applications this organisation undertakes is in electronic commerce (e-commerce), and a typical development team has two developers. Therefore, as part of the case study, an e-commerce application is to be developed using J2EE by two developers. Because we have stated this is a poorly executed case study, we will assume that no other variables have been considered, or measured (e.g. developers' experience, development environment).

The e-commerce application is developed, and the results of the case study show that the quality of the delivered application, measured as the number of faults per Web page, is worse than that for the other similar Web applications developed using ASP.NET. When questioned as to why these were the results obtained, the investigator seemed puzzled, and without a clear explanation.

What is missing?

The investigator should have anticipated that other variables can also have an effect on the results of an investigation, and should therefore be taken into account. One such variable is developers' programming experience. Without measuring experience prior to the case study, it is impossible to discern if the lower quality is due to J2EE or to the effects of learning J2EE as the investigation proceeds. It is possible that one or both developers did not have experience with J2EE, and lack of experience has interfered with the benefits of its use.

Variables such as developers' experience should have been anticipated and if possible controlled, or risk obtaining results that will be incorrect.

To control a variable is to determine a subset of values for use within the context of the investigation from the complete set of possible values for that variable. For example, using the same case study presented above, if the investigator had measured developers' experience with J2EE (e.g. low, medium, high), and was able to control this variable, then (s)he could have determined that two developers experienced with J2EE should participate in the case study. If there were no developers with experience in J2EE, two would be selected and trained.

If, when conducting a case study, it is not possible to control certain variables, they should still be measured, and the results documented.

If, however, all variables are controllable, then the type of investigation to use is a formal experiment.

Another important issue is to identify the population being studied and the sampling technique used (see Chap. 12 for further details on sampling). For example, if a survey was designed to investigate the extent to which project managers use automatic project management tools, then a data sample of software programmers is not going to be representative of the population that has been initially specified.

With formal experiments, it is important to describe the process by which experimental subjects and objects are selected and assigned to treatments [19[, where a treatment represents the new tool, programming language, or methodology you want to evaluate. The experimental object, also known as experimental unit, represents the object to which the treatment is to be applied (e.g. development project, Web application, code). The control object does not use or is not affected by the treatment [7]. In software and Web engineering it is difficult to have a control in the same way as in, say, formal medical experiments. For example, if you are investigating the effect of a programming framework on quality, and your treatment is J2EE, you cannot have a control that is "no programming framework" [19]. Therefore, many formal experiments use as their control a baseline representing what is typical in an organisation. Using the example given previously, our control would be ASP.NET since it represents the typical programming framework used in the organisation. The experimental subject is the "who" applying the treatment [7].

As part of the preparation of an investigation we also include the preparation and validation of data collection instruments. Examples are questionnaires, automatic measurement tools, timing sheets, etc. Each has to be prepared carefully such that it clearly and unambiguously identifies what is to be measured. For each variable it is important also to identify its measurement scale and measurement unit. So, if you are measuring effort, then you should also document its measurement unit (e.g. person hours, person months) or else obtain incorrect and conflicting data. It is also important to document at which stage during the investigation the data collection takes place. If an investigation gathers data on developers' programming experience (before they develop a Web application), size and effort used to design the application, and size and effort used to implement the application, then a diagram, such as the one in Fig. 1.2, may be provided to all participants to help clarify what instrument(s) to use and when to use them.

It is usual for instruments to be validated using pilot studies. A pilot study uses similar conditions to those planned for the real investigation, such that any possible problems can be anticipated.

Finally, it is also important to document the methods used to reduce any bias.

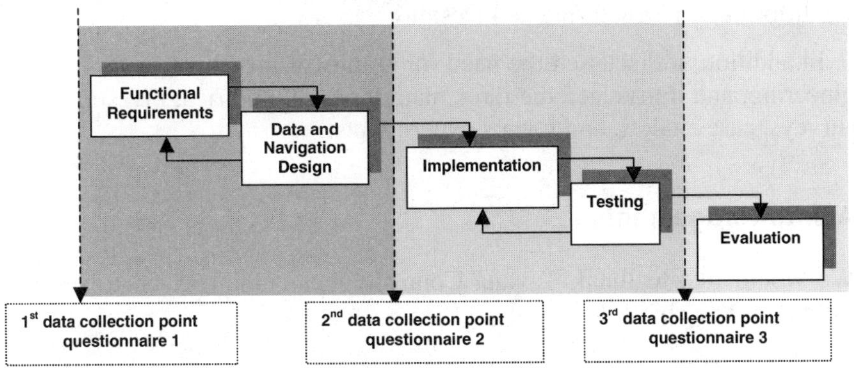

Fig. 1.2. Plan detailing when to apply each instrument

Analysing the Data and Reporting the Results

The main aspect of this final step is to understand the data collected and to apply statistical techniques that are suitable for the research questions or hypotheses of the investigation. For example, if the data was measured using a nominal or ordinal scale then statistical techniques that use the mean cannot be applied as this would violate the principles of the representational theory of measurement. If the data is not normally distributed then it is possible to use non-parametric or robust techniques, or transform the data to conform to the normal distribution [7]. Further details on empirical evaluations are provided in Chap. 13. In addition, several statistical techniques to analyse and report the data are presented throughout this book and further detailed in Chap. 12.

1.5 Conclusions

This chapter discussed differences between Web and software applications, and their development processes based on the following 12 areas:

1. Application Characteristics
2. Primary Technologies Used
3. Approach to Quality Delivered
4. Development Process Drivers
5. Availability of the Application
6. Customers (Stakeholders)
7. Update Rate (Maintenance Cycles)
8. People Involved in Development
9. Architecture and Network
10. Disciplines Involved
11. Legal, Social, and Ethical issues
12. Information Structuring and Design

In addition, it discussed the need for empirical investigation in Web engineering, and introduced the three main types of empirical investigation – surveys, case studies, and formal experiments.

Acknowledgements

We would like to thank Tayana Conte for her comments on a previous version of this chapter.

References

1 Basili VR (1996) The role of experimentation in software engineering: past, current, and future. In: Proceedings of the 18th International Conference on Software Engineering, 25–30 March, pp 442–449

2 Basili VR, Shull F, Lanubile F (1999) Building knowledge through families of experiments. IEEE Transactions on Software Engineering, July–Aug, 25(4):456–473

3 Brereton P, Budgen D, Hamilton G (1998) Hypertext: the next maintenance mountain, Computer, December, 31(12):49–55

4 Christodoulou SP, Zafiris PA, Papatheodorou TS (2000) WWW2000: The developer's view and a practitioner's approach to Web engineering. In: Proceedings of the 2nd ICSE Workshop on Web Engineering, pp 75–92

5 Deshpande Y, Hansen S (2001) Web engineering: creating a discipline among disciplines, IEEE Multimedia, April–June, 8(2):8–87

6 Deshpande Y, Murugesan S, Ginige A, Hansen S, Schwabe D, Gaedke M, White B (2002) Web engineering. Journal of Web Engineering, October, 1(1):3–17

7 Fenton NE, Pfleeger SL (1997) Software metrics: a rigorous and practical approach, 2nd edn. PWS Publishing Company

8 Fraternali P, Paolini P (2000) Model-driven development of Web applications: the AutoWeb system. ACM Transactions on Information Systems (TOIS), October , 18(4):1–35

9 Gellersen H, Wicke R, Gaedke M (1997) WebComposition: an object-oriented support system for the Web engineering lifecycle. Journal of Computer Networks and ISDN Systems, September, 29(8–13):865–1553. Also (1996) In: Proceedings of the Sixth International World Wide Web Conference, pp 429–1437

10 Gellersen H-W, Gaedke M (1999) Object-oriented Web application development. IEEE Internet Computing, January/February, 3(1):60–68

11 Ginige A (2002) Workshop on web engineering: Web engineering: managing the complexity of Web systems development. In: Proceedings of the 14th International Conference on Software Engineering and Knowledge Engineering, July, pp 72–729

12 Ginige A, Murugesan S (2001) Web engineering: an introduction. IEEE Multimedia, January/March, 8(1):14–18

13 Goldstein M, Goldstein IF (1978) How we know: an exploration of the scientific process, Plenum Press, New York

14 Harper Collins Publishers (2000) Collins English Dictionary

15 Houghton Mifflin Company (1994) The American Heritage Concise Dictionary, 3rd edn.

16 Horowitz E (1998) Migrating software to the World Wide Web. IEEE Software, May/June, 15(3):18–21

17 IEEE Std. 2001–2002 (2003) Recommended Practice for the Internet Web Site Engineering, Web Site Management, and Web Site Life Cycle, IEEE.

18 Kitchenham B, Pickard L, Pfleeger SL (1995) Case studies for method and tool evaluation. IEEE Software, 12(4):52–62

19 Kitchenham BA, Pfleeger SL, Pickard LM, Jones PW, Hoaglin DC, El Emam K, Rosenberg J (2002) Preliminary guidelines for empirical research in software engineering. IEEE Transactions on Software Engineering, August, 28(8):721–734

20 Lee SC, Shirani AI (2004) A component based methodology for Web application development. J of Systems and Software, 71(1–2):177–187

21 Murugesan S, Deshpande Y (2001) Web Engineering, Managing Diversity and Complexity of Web Application Development, Lecture Notes in Computer Science 2016, Springer Verlag, Heidelberg

22 Murugesan S, Deshpande Y (2002) Meeting the challenges of web application development: the web engineering approach. In: Proceedings of the 24th International Conference on Software Engineering, May, pp 687–688

23 Offutt J (2002) Quality attributes of Web software applications. IEEE Software, March/April, 19(2):25–32

24 Pfleeger SL, Jeffery R, Curtis B, Kitchenham B (1997) Status report on software measurement. IEEE Software, March/April, 14(2):33–43

25 Pressman RS (1998) Can Internet-based applications be engineered? IEEE Software, September/October, 15(5):104–110

26 Reifer DJ (2000) Web development: estimating quick-to-market software. IEEE Software, November/December:57–64

27 Ricca F, Tonella P (2001) Analysis and testing of Web applications. In: Proceedings of the 23rd International Conference on Software Engineering, pp 25–34

28 Standing C (2002) Methodologies for developing Web applications. Information and Software Technology, 44(3):151–160

29 Taylor MJ, McWilliam J, Forsyth H, Wade S (2002) Methodologies and website development: a survey of practice. Information and Software Technology, 44(6):381–391

30 Wikipedia, http://en.wikipedia.org/wiki/Main_Page (accessed on 25 October 2004)

31 Wild C, Seber G (2000) Chance Encounters: a First Course in Data Analysis and Inference, John Wiley & Sons, New York

Authors' Biographies

Dr. **Emilia Mendes** is a Senior Lecturer in Computer Science at the University of Auckland (New Zealand), where she leads the WETA (Web Engineering, Technology and Applications) research group. She is the principal investigator in the Tukutuku Research project,[6] aimed at developing and comparing Web effort models using industrial Web project data, and benchmarking productivity within and across Web companies. She has active research interests in Web measurement and metrics, and in particular Web cost estimation, Web size measures, Web productivity and quality measurement, and Web process improvement. Dr. Mendes is on the programme committee of numerous international conferences and workshops, and on the editorial board of the International Journal of Web Engineering and Technology and the Journal of Web Engineering. She has collaborated with Web companies in New Zealand and overseas on Web cost estimation and usability measurement. Dr. Mendes worked in the software industry for ten years before obtaining her PhD in Computer Science from the University of Southampton

6 http://www.cs.auckland.ac.nz/tukutuku/.

(UK), and moving to Auckland. She is a member of the New Zealand and Australian Software Measurement Associations.

Dr. **Nile Mosley** is the Technical Director of a software development company. He has active research interests in software measurement and metrics, and object-oriented programming languages. He obtained his PhD in Pure and Applied Mathematics from Nottingham Trent University (UK).

Steve Counsell obtained a BSc (Hons) in Computer Studies from the University of Brighton and an MSc in Systems Analysis from the City University in 1987 and 1988, respectively. After spending some time in industry as a developer, he obtained his PhD in 2002 from the University of London and is currently a Lecturer in the Department of Information Systems and Computing at Brunel University. Prior to 2004, he was a Lecturer in the School of Computer Science and Information Systems at Birkbeck, University of London and between 1996 and 1998 was a Research Fellow at the University of Southampton. In 2002, he was a BT Short-term Research Fellow. His research interests are in software engineering, more specifically metrics and empirical studies.

2 Web Effort Estimation

Emilia Mendes, Nile Mosley, Steve Counsell

Abstract: Software effort models and effort estimates help project managers allocate resources, control costs, and schedule and improve current practices, leading to projects that are finished on time and within budget. In the context of Web development and maintenance, these issues are also crucial, and very challenging, given that Web projects have short schedules and a highly fluidic scope. Therefore this chapter has two main objectives. The first is to introduce the concepts related to effort estimation and in particular Web effort estimation. The second is to present a case study where a real effort prediction model based on data from completed industrial Web projects is constructed step by step.

Keywords: Web effort estimation, Manual stepwise regression, Effort models, Web size measures, Prediction accuracy, Data analysis.

2.1 Introduction

The Web is used as a delivery platform for numerous types of Web applications, ranging from complex e-commerce solutions with back-end databases to on-line personal static Web pages. With the sheer diversity of Web application types and technologies employed, there exists a growing number of Web companies bidding for as many Web projects as they can accommodate. As usual, in order to win the bid, companies estimate unrealistic schedules, leading to applications that are rarely developed within time and budget.

Realistic effort estimates are fundamental for the successful management of software projects; the Web is no exception. Having realistic estimates at an early stage in a project's life cycle allows project managers and development organisations to manage their resources effectively.

To this end, prediction is a necessary part of an effective process, whether it be authoring, design, testing, or Web development as a whole. A prediction process involves:

- The identification of measures (e.g. number of new Web pages, number of new images) that are believed to influence the effort required to develop a new Web application.
- The formulation of theories about the relationship between the selected measures and effort (e.g. the greater the number of new static Web pages, the greater the development effort for a new application).

- The capturing of historical data (e.g. size and actual effort) about past Web projects or even past development phases within the same project.
- The use of this historical data to develop effort estimation models for use in predicting effort for new Web projects.
- The assessment of how effective those effort estimation models are, i.e. the assessment of their prediction accuracy.

Cost and effort are often used interchangeably within the context of effort estimation (prediction) since effort is taken as the main component of project costs. However, given that project costs also take into account other factors such as contingency and profit [20]we will use the word "effort" and not "cost" throughout this chapter.

Numerous effort estimation techniques have been proposed and compared over the last 20 years. A classification and description of such techniques is introduced in Sect. 2.2 to help provide readers with a broader overview. To be useful, an effort estimation technique must provide an effort estimate for a new project that is not widely dissimilar from the *actual* effort this project will need to be finished. The effectiveness of effort estimation techniques to provide accurate effort estimates is called prediction power. Section 2.3 presents the four most commonly used measures of prediction power and, in Section 2.4, the associated prediction accuracy. Finally, Sect. 2.5 details a case study building an effort estimation model using data from world-wide industrial Web projects.

2.2 Effort Estimation Techniques

The purpose of estimating effort is to predict the amount of effort to accomplish a given task, based on knowledge of other project characteristics that are believed to be related to effort. Project characteristics (independent variables) are the input, and effort (dependent variable) is the output we wish to predict (see Fig. 2.1). For example, a given Web company may find that to predict the effort necessary to implement a new Web application, it will require the following input: estimated number of new Web pages, total number of developers who will help develop the new Web application, developers' average number of years of experience with the development tools employed, and the number of functions/features (e.g. shopping cart) to be offered by the new Web application.

A task to be estimated can be as simple as developing a single function (e.g. creating a table on the database) or as complex as developing a large application, and in general the one input (independent variable) assumed to have the strongest influence on effort is size. Other independent variables may also be influential (e.g. developers' average experience, number of tools employed) and these are often identified as cost drivers. Depending on the techniques employed, we can also use data on past finished projects to help estimate effort for new projects.

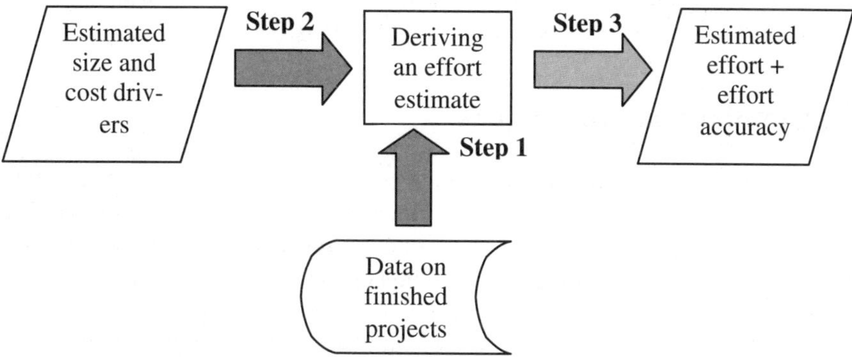

Fig. 2.1. Components of a cost model

Several techniques for effort estimation have been proposed over the past 30 years in software engineering. These fall into three general categories [37]: expert opinion, algorithmic models and artificial intelligence techniques.

2.2.1 Expert Opinion

Expert opinion represents the process of estimating effort by subjective means, and is often based on previous experience from developing/managing similar projects. It has been and still is widely used in software and Web development.

The drawback of this technique is that it is very difficult to quantify and to determine those factors that have been used to derive an estimate, making it difficult to repeat. However, studies show that this technique can be an effective estimating tool when used in combination with other less subjective techniques (e.g. algorithmic models) [11,30,31].

In terms of the diagram presented in Fig. 2.1, the sequence occurs as follows:

a) An expert looks at the estimated size and cost drivers related to a new project for which effort needs to be estimated.
b) Based on the data obtained in a) (s)he remembers or retrieves data on past finished projects for which actual effort is known.
c) Based on the data from a) and b) (s)he subjectively estimates effort for the new project. Deriving an accurate effort estimate is more likely to occur when there are completed projects similar to the one having its

effort estimated. The sequence described corresponds to steps 2, 1, and 3 in Fig. 2.1. The knowledge regarding the characteristics of a new project is necessary to retrieve, from either memory or a database, knowledge on finished similar projects. Once this knowledge is retrieved, effort can be estimated.

2.2.2 Algorithmic Techniques

To date, the most popular techniques described in the effort estimation literature are algorithmic techniques. Such techniques attempt to formalise the relationship between effort and one or more project characteristics. The result is an algorithmic model. The central project characteristic used in such a model is usually taken to be some notion of software size (e.g. the number of lines of source code, number of Web pages, number of links). This formalisation is often translated as an equation such as that shown by Eq. 2.1, where *a* and *b* are parameters that also need to be estimated. Equation 2.1 shows that size is the main factor contributing to effort, and can be adjusted according to an Effort Adjustment Factor (*EAF*), calculated from cost drivers (e.g. developers, experience, tools). An example of an algorithmic model that uses Eq. 2.1 is the COnstructive COst MOdel (COCOMO) model [2], where parameters *a* and *b* are based on the type of project under construction, and the *EAF* is based on 15 cost drivers that are calculated and then summed.

$$Estimated\quad Effort = a\ EstSizeNewproj^{b}\ EAF \tag{2.1}$$

where:
a, *b* are parameters chosen based on certain criteria, such as the type of software project being developed. *EstSizeNewproj* is the estimated size for the new project. *EAF* is the Effort Adjustment Factor.

Equations 2.2 and 2.3 are different examples of algorithmic equations (models), where both are obtained by applying regression analysis techniques [33]on data sets of past completed projects. Equation 2.2 assumes a linear relationship between effort and its size/cost drivers whereas Equation 2.3 assumes a non-linear relationship. In Equation 2.3, when the exponent is < 1 we have economies of scale, i.e., larger projects use less effort comparatively than smaller projects. The opposite situation (exponent > 1) gives diseconomies of scale, i.e. larger projects use more effort comparatively than smaller projects.

$$EstimatedEffort = C + a_0 EstSizeNewproj + a_1\, CD_1 + \cdots + a_n CD_n \tag{2.2}$$

$$EstimatedEffort = C\ EstSizeNewproj^{a_0}\ CD_1{}^{a_1} \cdots CD_n{}^{a_n} \tag{2.3}$$

where:
C is a constant denoting the initial estimated effort (assuming size and cost drivers to be zero) derived from past data.
$a_0 \ldots a_n$ are parameters derived from past data.
$CD_1 \ldots CD_n$ are other project characteristics, other than size, that have an impact on effort.

The COCOMO model is an example of a *generic algorithmic model*, believed to be applicable to any type of software project, with suitable calibration or adjustment to local circumstances. In terms of the diagram presented in Fig. 2.1, the model uses parameter values that are based on past project data; however, for anyone wishing to use this model, the steps to use are 1, 2, and 3. Step 1 is used only once to calculate the initial values for its parameters, which are then fixed from that point onwards. The single use of step 1 makes this model a *generic algorithmic model.*

Regression-based algorithmic models are most suitable to local circumstances such as "in-house" analysis as they are derived from past data that often represents projects from the company itself. Regression analysis, used to generate regression-based algorithmic models, provides a procedure for determining the "best" straight-line fit to a set of project data that represents the relationship between effort (the response or dependent variable) and project characteristics (e.g. size, experience, tools, the predictor or independent variables) [33]. The regression line is represented as an equation, such as those given by Eqs. 2.1 and 2.2. The effort estimation models we will create in Sect. 2.5 fall into this category.

Regarding the regression analysis itself, two of the most widely used techniques are multiple regression (MR) and stepwise regression (SWR). The difference between both is that MR obtains a regression line using all the independent variables at the same time, whereas SWR is a technique that examines different combinations of independent variables, looking for the best grouping to explain the greatest amount of variation in effort. Both use least squares regression, where the regression line selected is the one that reflects the minimum values of the sum of the squared errors. Errors are calculated as the difference between actual and estimated effort and are known as the residuals [33].

The sequence followed here is as follows:

a) Past data is used to generate a cost model.
b) This model then receives, as input, values for the new project characteristics.
c) The model generates estimated effort. The sequence described herein corresponds to steps 1, 2, and 3 from Fig. 2.1, in contrast to that for expert opinion.

A description of regression analysis is presented in Chap. 12.

2.2.3 Artificial Intelligence Techniques

Artificial intelligence techniques have, in the last decade, been used as a complement to, or as an alternative to, the previous two categories. Examples include fuzzy logic [22[, regression trees [34[, neural networks [38], and case-based reasoning [37]. We will cover case-based reasoning (CBR) and regression trees (CART) in more detail as they are currently the most popular machine learning techniques employed for Web cost estimation. A useful summary of numerous machine learning techniques can also be found in [10].

Case-Based Reasoning

Case-based reasoning (CBR) provides estimates by comparing the current problem to be estimated against a library of historical information from completed projects with a known effort (case base). It involves [1]:

i. Characterising a new project *p*, for which an estimate is required, with attributes (features) common to those completed projects stored in the case base. In terms of software cost estimation, features represent size measures and cost drivers which have a bearing on effort. Feature values are normally standardized (between 0 and 1) such that they have the same degree of influence on the result.
ii. Use of this characterisation as a basis for finding similar (analogous) completed projects, for which effort is known. This process can be achieved by measuring the "distance" between two projects, based on the values of the number of features (*k*) for these projects. Although numerous techniques can be used to measure similarity, nearest neighbour algorithms using the unweighted Euclidean distance measure have been the most widely used to date in software and Web engineering.
iii. Generation of a predicted value of effort for project *p* based on the effort for those completed projects that are similar to *p*. The number of similar projects will depend on the size of the case base. For small case bases (e.g. up to 90 cases), typical values are 1, 2, and 3 closest neighbours (analogies). For larger case bases no conclusions have been reached regarding the best number of similar projects to use. The calculation of estimated effort is obtained using the same effort value as the closest neighbour, or the mean of effort for two or more analogies. This is the common choice in Web and software engineering.

The sequence of steps used with CBR is as follows:

a) The estimated size and cost drivers relating to a new project are used to retrieve similar projects from the case base, for which actual effort is known.
b) Using the data from a) a suitable CBR tool retrieves similar projects and calculates estimated effort for the new project. The sequence just described corresponds to steps 2, 1, and 3 in Fig. 2.1, similar to that employed for expert opinion. The characteristics of a new project must be known in order to retrieve finished similar projects. Once similar projects are retrieved, then effort can be estimated.

When using CBR there are six parameters to consider [35]:

- Feature Subset Selection
- Similarity Measure
- Scaling
- Number of Analogies
- Analogy Adaptation
- Adaptation Rules

Feature Subset Selection
Feature subset selection involves determining the optimum subset of features that yield the most accurate estimation. Some existing CBR tools, e.g. ANGEL [36]optionally offer this functionality using a brute force algorithm, searching for all possible feature subsets. Other CBR tools (e.g. CBR-Works) have no such functionality, and therefore to obtain estimated effort, we must use all of the known features of a project to retrieve the most similar cases.

Similarity Measure
The similarity measure measures the level of similarity between different cases, with several similarity measures proposed in the literature. The most popular in the current Web/software engineering literature [1,24,35]are the unweighted Euclidean distance, the weighted Euclidean distance, and the maximum distance. Other similarity measures are presented in [1].

Unweighted Euclidean distance: The unweighted Euclidean distance measures the Euclidean (straight-line) distance d between the points (x_0,y_0) and (x_1,y_1), given by the equation:

$$d = \sqrt{(x_0 - x_1)^2 + (y_0 - y_1)^2} \qquad (2.4)$$

This measure has a geometrical meaning as the shortest distance between two points in an *n*-dimensional Euclidean space [1].

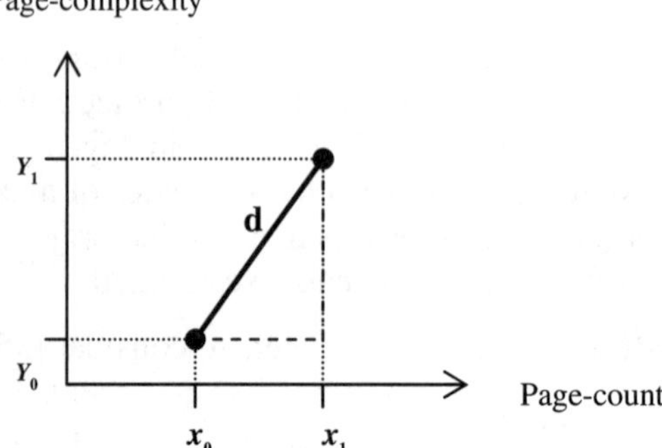

Fig. 2.2. Euclidean distance using two size attributes

Figure 2.2 illustrates this distance by representing coordinates in a two-dimensional space, E2. The number of features employed determines the number of dimensions, E*n*.

Weighted Euclidean distance: The weighted Euclidean distance is used when features vectors are given weights that reflect the relative importance of each feature. The weighted Euclidean distance *d* between the points (x_0,y_0) and (x_1,y_1) is given by the following equation:

$$d = \sqrt{w_x(x_0 - x_1)^2 + w_y(y_0 - y_1)^2} \tag{2.5}$$

where w_x and w_y are the weights of *x* and *y* respectively.

Maximum distance: The maximum distance computes the highest feature similarity, i.e. the one to define the closest analogy. For two points (x_0,y_0) and (x_1,y_1), the maximum measure *d* is equivalent to the formula:

$$d = \sqrt{\max((x_0 - x_1)^2, (y_0 - y_1)^2)} \tag{2.6}$$

This effectively reduces the similarity measure down to a single feature, although this feature may differ for each retrieval episode. So, for a given "new" project P_{new}, the closest project in the case base will be the one that has at least one size feature with the most similar value to the same feature in project P_{new}.

Scaling

Scaling (also known as standardisation) represents the transformation of attribute values according to a defined rule, such that all attributes present values within the same range and hence have the same degree of influence on the results [1]. A common method of scaling is to assign zero to the minimum observed value and one to the maximum observed value [15]. This is the strategy used by ANGEL.

Number of Analogies

The number of analogies refers to the number of most similar cases that will be used to generate the estimation. With small sets of data it is reasonable to consider only a small number of analogies [1]. Several studies in software engineering have restricted their analysis to the closest analogy ($k = 1.0$) [3,30], while others have used two and three analogies [1,13,14,24,25,27,32].

Analogy Adaptation

Once the similar cases have been selected the next step is to decide how to generate the estimation for project P_{new}. Choices of analogy adaptation techniques presented in the literature vary from the nearest neighbour [3,14], the mean of the closest analogies [36], the median [1], inverse distance weighted mean and inverse rank weighted mean [15], to illustrate just a few. The adaptations used to date for Web engineering are the nearest neighbour, mean of the closest analogies [24,25], and the inverse rank weighted mean [26,27].

Each adaptation is explained below:

Mean: The average of k analogies, when $k > 1$. This is a typical measure of central tendency, often used in the software and Web engineering literature. It treats all analogies as being equally influential on estimated effort.

Median: The median of k analogies, when $k > 2$. This is also a measure of central tendency, and has been used in the literature when the number of closest projects increases [1].

Inverse rank weighted mean: Allows higher ranked analogies to have more influence than lower ones. If we use three analogies, for example, the closest analogy (*CA*) would have weight = 3, the second closest (*SC*) weight = 2, and the third closest (*LA*) weight = 1. The estimation would then be calculated as:

$$InverseRankWeighedMean = \frac{3CA + 2SC + LA}{6} \tag{2.7}$$

Adaptation Rules

Adaptation rules are used to adapt estimated effort, according to a given criterion, such that it reflects the characteristics of the target project more closely. For example, in the context of effort prediction, the estimated effort to develop an application would be adapted such that it would also take into consideration the application's size values.

Classification and Regression Trees

The objective of a Classification and Regression Tree (CART) model is to develop a simple tree-structured decision process for describing the distribution of a variable *r* given a vector of predictors *vp [*5]. A CART model represents a binary tree where the trees' leaves suggest values for *r* based on existing values of *vp*. For example, assume the estimated effort to develop a Web application can be determined by an estimated number of pages (WP), number of images (IM), and number of functions (FN). A regression tree such as the one shown in Fig. 2.3 is generated from data obtained from past finished Web applications, taking into account their existing values of effort, WP, IM, and FN. These are the predictors that make up the vector *vp*. Once the tree has been built it is used to estimate effort for a new project. So, to estimate effort for a new project where WP = 25, IM = 10, and FN = 4 we would navigate down the tree structure to find the estimated effort. In this case, 45 person hours.

Whenever predictors are numerical the CART tree is called a *regression tree* and whenever predictors are categorical the CART tree is called a *classification tree.*

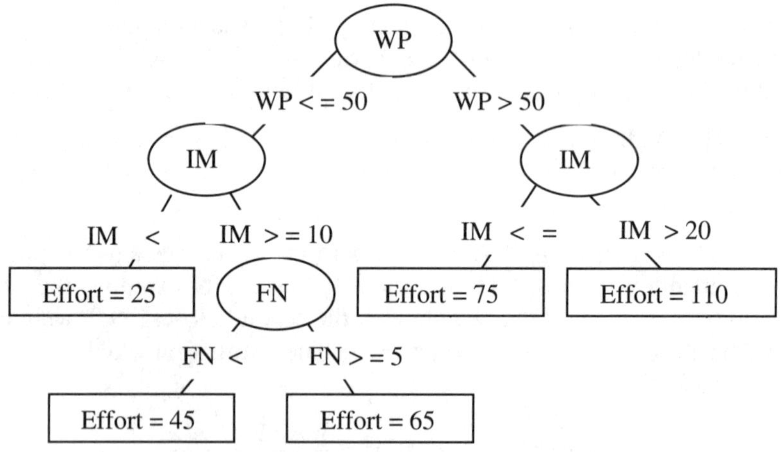

Fig. 2.3. Example of a regression tree for Web cost estimation

A CART model constructs a binary tree by recursively partitioning the predictor space (set of values of each of the predictors in vector *vp*) into subsets where the distribution of values for the response variable (effort) is successively more uniform. The partition itself is determined by splitting rules associated with each of the non-leaf nodes.

A "purity" function calculated from the predictor data is employed to split each node. There are numerous types of "purity" functions where the choice is determined by the software tool used to build the CART model, the type of predictors employed, and the goals for using a CART model (e.g. using it for cost estimation). The sequence used with CART is as follows:

a) Past data is used to generate a CART model.
b) This model is then traversed manually in order to obtain estimated effort, using as input values for the new project characteristics.
c) The sequence described corresponds to steps 1, 2, and 3 from Fig. 2.1, in contrast to that for expert opinion and CBR.

2.3 Measuring Effort Prediction Power and Accuracy

An effort estimation model *m* uses historical data of finished projects to predict the effort of a new project. Some believe this is enough to provide accurate effort estimates. However, to gauge the accuracy of this model we need to measure its predictive accuracy.

To measure a model's predictive accuracy first calculate the predictive power for each of a set of new projects p_1 to p_n that used the effort estimation model *m*. Once predictive power for p_1 to p_n has been obtained, their values are aggregated, which gives the predictive power of model *m* and hence its corresponding predictive accuracy.

This section describes how to measure the predictive power of a model, and how to measure a model's predictive accuracy.

2.3.1 Measuring Predictive Power

The most common approaches to date for measuring predictive power of effort estimation models are:

- The Mean Magnitude of Relative Error (MMRE) [37]
- The Median Magnitude of Relative Error (MdMRE) [30]
- The Prediction at level *n* (Pred(*n*)) [36]

The basis for calculating MMRE and MdMRE is to use the Magnitude of Relative Error (MRE) [16], defined as:

$$MRE = \frac{|e - \hat{e}|}{e} \quad (2.8)$$

where e is the actual effort and $\hat{e}$ is the estimated effort.

The mean of all MREs is the MMRE, calculated as:

$$MMRE = \frac{1}{n}\sum_{i=1}^{i=n}\frac{|e_i - \hat{e}_i|}{e_i} \quad (2.9)$$

As the mean is calculated by taking into account the value of every estimated and actual effort from the data set employed, the result may give a biased assessment of a model's predictive power when there are several projects with large MREs.

An alternative to the mean is the median, which also represents a measure of central tendency, as it is less sensitive to the existence of several large MREs. The median of MRE values for the number *i* of observations (data values) is called the MdMRE.

Another indicator which is commonly used is the prediction at level *l*, also known as Pred(*l*). This measures the percentage of effort estimates that are within *l%* of their actual values.

MMRE, MdMRE, and Pred(*l*) are taken as the *de facto* standard evaluation criteria to measure the predictive power of effort estimation models [39].

2.3.2 Measuring Predictive Accuracy

In order to calculate the predictive accuracy of a given effort estimation model *m*, based on a given data set of finished projects *d*, we do the following:

1. Divide the data set *d* into a training set *t* and a validation set *v*. It is common to create training sets that use 66% of the projects from the complete data set, leaving 34% for the validation set.
2. Using *t*, produce an effort estimation model *m* (if applicable).
3. Using *m*, predict the effort for each of the projects in *v*, simulating new projects for which effort is unknown.

Once done, we will have, for each project in *v*, an *estimated* effort $\hat{e}$, calculated using the model *m*, and also the *actual* effort *e* that the project actually used. We are now able to calculate the predictive power (MRE) for each project in the validation set *v*. The final step, once we have obtained the predictive power for each project, is to aggregate these values to obtain MMRE, MdMRE, and Pred(25) for *v*, which is taken to be the same for *m*.

Calculated MMREs and MdMREs with values up to 0.25, and Pred(25) at 75% or above, indicate good prediction models [6].

This splitting of a data set into training and validation sets is also known as cross-validation. An *n*-fold cross-validation means the original data set is divided into *n* subsets of training and validation sets. When the validation set has only one project the cross-validation is called "leave-one-out" cross-validation. This is an approach commonly used when assessing prediction accuracy using CBR.

2.4 Which Is the Most Accurate Prediction Technique?

Section 2.2 introduced numerous techniques for obtaining effort estimates for a new project, and all have been used, each with a varying degree of success. Therefore the question that is often asked is: Which of the techniques provides the most accurate prediction?

To date, the answer to this question has been simply "it depends".

Algorithmic models have some advantages over machine learning and expert opinion, such as:

1. Allowing users to see how a model derives its conclusions, an important factor for verification as well as theory building and understanding of the process being modelled [10].
2. The need to be specialised relative to the local environment in which they are used [21,7].

Despite these advantages, no convergence on which effort estimation technique has the best predictive power has yet been reached, even though comparative studies have been carried out over the last 15 years (e.g. [1,3,4,8–10,12–16,30,32,35–37]).

One justification is that these studies have used data sets with differing characteristics (e.g. number of outliers,[1] amount of collinearity,[2] number of variables, number of projects) and different comparative designs.

Shepperd and Kadoda [35]presented evidence for the relationship between the success of a particular technique and training set size, nature of the "effort estimation" function (e.g. continuous[3] or discontinuous[4]), and

---

[1] An outlier is a value which is far from the others.

[2] Collinearity represents the existence of a linear relationship between two or more independent variables.

[3] A continuous function is one in which "small changes in the input produce small changes in the output" (http://e.wikipedia.org/wiki/Continuous_function).

characteristics of the data set. They concluded that the "best" prediction technique that can work on any type of data set may be impossible to obtain.

Mendes et al. [28]investigated three techniques for Web effort estimation (stepwise regression, case-based reasoning, and regression trees) by comparing the prediction accuracy of their respective models. Stepwise regression provided the best results overall. This trend has also been confirmed using a different data set of Web projects [29]. This is therefore the technique to be used in Sect. 2.5 to build an effort estimation model for estimating effort for Web projects.

2.5 Case Study

The case study we present here describes the construction and further validation of a Web effort estimation model using data on industrial Web projects, developed by Web companies worldwide, from the Tukutuku database [29].[5] This database is part of the ongoing Tukutuku project,[6] which collects data on Web projects, for the development of effort estimation models and to benchmark productivity across and within Web companies.

The database contains data on 87 Web projects: 34 and 13 come from 2 single Web companies respectively and the remaining 40 projects come from another 23 companies. The Tukutuku database uses 6 variables to store specifics about each company that volunteered projects, 10 variables to store particulars about each project, and 13 variables to store data about each Web application (see Table 2.1). Company data is obtained once and both project and application data are gathered for each volunteered project.

All results presented were obtained using the statistical software SPSS 10.1.3 for Windows. Further details on the statistical methods used throughout this case study are given in Chap. 12. Finally, all the statistical tests set the significance level at 95% ($\alpha = 0.05$).

---

4 "If small changes in the input can produce a broken jump in the changes of the output, the function is said to be discontinuous (or to have a discontinuity)" (http://e.wikipedia.org/wiki/Continuous_function).

5 The raw data cannot be displayed here due to a confidentiality agreement with those companies that have volunteered data on their projects.

6 http://www.cs.auckland.ac.nz/tukutuku.

Table 2.1. Variables for the Tukutuku database

NAME	SCALE[7]	DESCRIPTION
COMPANY DATA		
COUNTRY	Categorical	Country company belongs to.
ESTABLISHED	Ordinal	Year when company was established.
SERVICES	Categorical	Type of services company provides.
NPEOPLEWD	Ratio	Number of people who work on Web design and development.
CLIENTIND	Categorical	Industry representative of those clients to whom applications are provided.
ESTPRACT	Categorical	Accuracy of a company's own effort estimation practices.
PROJECT DATA		
TYPEPROJ	Categorical	Type of project (new or enhancement).
LANGS	Categorical	Implementation languages used.
DOCPROC	Categorical	If project followed defined and documented process.
PROIMPR	Categorical	If project team involved in a process improvement programme.
METRICS	Categorical	If project team part of a software metrics programme.
DEVTEAM	Ratio	Size of project's development team.
TEAMEXP	Ratio	Average team experience with the development language(s) employed.
TOTEFF	Ratio	Actual total effort used to develop the Web application.
ESTEFF	Ratio	Estimated total effort necessary to develop the Web application.
ACCURACY	Categorical	Procedure used to record effort data.
WEB APPLICATION		
TYPEAPP	Categorical	Type of Web application developed.
TOTWP	Ratio	Total number of Web pages (new and reused).
NEWWP	Ratio	Total number of new Web pages.
TOTIMG	Ratio	Total number of images (new and reused).
NEWIMG	Ratio	Total number of new images created.
HEFFDEV	Ratio	Minimum number of hours to develop a single function/feature by one experienced developer that is considered high (above average).[8]
HEFFADPT	Ratio	Minimum number of hours to adapt a single function/feature by one experienced developer that is considered high (above average).[9]

[7] The different types of measurement scale are described in Chap. 12.

[8] This number is currently set to 15 hours based on the collected data.

NAME	SCALE[7]	DESCRIPTION
HFOTS	Ratio	Number of reused high-effort features/functions without adaptation.
HFOTSA	Ratio	Number of reused high-effort features/functions adapted.
HNEW	Ratio	Number of new high-effort features/functions.
FOTS	Ratio	Number of reused low-effort features without adaptation.
FOTSA	Ratio	Number of reused low-effort features adapted.
NEW	Ratio	Number of new low-effort features/functions.

The following sections describe our data analysis procedure, adapted from [23], which consists of:

1. Data validation
2. Variables and model selection
3. Model inspection
4. Extraction of effort equation
5. Model validation

2.5.1 Data Validation

Data validation (DV) performs the first screening of the collected data. It generally involves understanding what the variables are (e.g. purpose, scale type, see Table 2.1) and also uses descriptive statistics (e.g. mean, median, minimum, maximum) to help identify any missing or unusual cases.

Table 2.2 presents summary statistics for numerical variables. None of the numerical variables seem to exhibit unusual or missing values, although this requires careful examination. For example, one would find it strange to see *zero* as minimum value for Total Images (TOTIMG) or *one* as minimum value for Total Web Pages (TOTWP). However, it is possible to have either a Web application without any images or a Web application that provides all its content and functionality within a single Web page. Another example relates to the maximum number of Web pages, which is 2000 Web pages. Although it does not seem possible at first to have such large number of pages we cannot simply assume this has been a data entry error. We were unable to obtain confirmation from the source company. However, further investigation revealed that 1980 pages were developed from scratch, and numerous new functions/features (five high-effort and seven low-effort) were also implemented. In addition, the development team consisted of two people who had very little experience with the six

[9] This number is currently set to 4 hours based on the collected data.

programming languages used. The total effort was 947 person hours, which can correspond to a three-month project assuming both developers worked at the same time. If we only consider number of pages and effort, the ratio of number of minutes per page is 27:1, which seems reasonable given the lack of experience of the development team and the number of different languages they had to use.

Table 2.2. Descriptive statistics for numerical variables

Variables	N	Min.	Max.	Mean	Median	Std. dev.
DEVTEAM	87	1	8	2.37	2	1.35
TEAMEXP	87	1	10	3.40	2	1.93
TOTWP	87	1	2000	92.40	25	273.09
NEWWP	87	0	1980	82.92	7	262.98
TOTIMG	87	0	1820	122.54	40	284.48
NEWIMG	87	0	800	51.90	0	143.25
HEFFDEV	87	5	800	62.02	15	141.25
HEFFADPT	87	0	200	10.61	4	28.48
HFOTS	87	0	3	.08	0	.41
HFOTSA	87	0	4	.29	0	.75
HNEW	87	0	10	1.24	0	2.35
FOTS	87	0	15	1.07	0	2.57
FOTSA	87	0	10	1.89	1	2.41
NEW	87	0	13	1.87	0	2.84
TOTEFF	87	1	5000	261.73	43	670.36
ESTEFF	34	1	108	14.45	7.08	20.61

Once we have checked the numerical variables our next step is to check the categorical variables using their frequency tables as a tool (see Tables 2.4 to 2.7).

Tables 2.4 to 2.6 show that most projects followed a defined and documented process, and that development teams were involved in a process improvement programme and/or part of a software metrics programme. These positive trends are mainly due to the two single companies that together volunteered data on 47 projects (54% of our data set). They have answered "yes" to all three categories. No unusual trends seem to exist.

Table 2.7 shows that the majority of projects (83%) had the actual effort recorded on a daily basis, for each project and/or project task. These numbers are inflated by the two single companies where one chose category "good" (11 projects) and the other chose category "very good" (34 projects). The actual effort recording procedure is not an adequate effort estimator per se, being used here simply to show that the effort data gathered seems to be reliable overall.

Table 2.3. Frequency table for type of project

Type of project	Frequency	%	Cumulative %
New	39	44.8	44.8
Enhancement	48	55.2	100.0
Total	87	100.0	

Table 2.4. Frequency table for documented process

Documented process	Frequency	%	Cumulative %
no	23	26.4	26.4
yes	64	73.6	100.0
Total	87	100.0	

Table 2.5. Frequency table for process improvement

Process improvement	Frequency	%	Cumulative %
no	28	32.2	32.2
yes	59	67.8	100.0
Total	87	100.0	

Table 2.6. Frequency table for metrics programme

Metrics programme	Frequency	%	Cumulative %
no	36	41.4	41.4
yes	51	58.6	100.0
Total	87	100.0	

Table 2.7. Frequency table for companies' effort recording procedure

Actual effort recording procedure	Frequency	%	Cumulative %
Poor	12	13.8	13.8
Medium	3	3.4	17.2
Good	24	27.6	44.8
Very good	48	55.2	100
Total	87	100.0	

Once the data validation is complete, we are ready to move on to the next step, namely variables and model selection.

2.5.2 Variables and Model Selection

The second step in our data analysis methodology is sub-divided into two separate and distinct phases: preliminary analysis and model building.

Preliminary analysis allows us to choose which variables to use, discard, modify, and, where necessary, sometimes create. Model building determines an effort estimation model based on our data set and variables.

Preliminary Analysis

This important phase is used to create variables based on existing variables, discard unnecessary variables, and modify existing variables (e.g. joining categories). The net result of this phase is to obtain a set of variables that are ready to use in the next phase, model building. Since this phase will construct an effort model using stepwise regression we need to ensure that the variables comply with the assumptions underlying regression analysis, which are:

1. The input variables (independent variables) are measured without error. If this cannot be guaranteed then these variables need to be normalised.
2. The relationship between dependent and independent variables is linear.
3. No important input variables have been omitted. This ensures that there is no specification error associated with the data set. The use of a prior theory-based model justifying the choice of input variables ensures this assumption is not violated.
4. The variance of the residuals is the same for all combinations of input variables (i.e. the residuals are homoscedastic rather than heteroscedastic)[10].
5. The residuals must be normally distributed.
6. The residuals must be independent, i.e. not correlated.[11]
7. The independent variables are not linearly dependent, i.e. there are no linear dependencies among the independent variables.

The first task within the preliminary analysis phase is to examine the entire set of variables and check if there is a significant amount of missing values (> 60%). If yes, they should be automatically discarded as they prohibit the use of imputation methods[12] and will further prevent the identification of useful trends in the data. Table 2.2 shows that only ESTEFF presented missing values greater than 60%. ESTEFF was gathered to give

[10] Further details are provided in Chap. 12.

[11] Further details are provided in Chap. 12.

[12] Imputation methods are methods used to replace missing values with estimated values.

an idea of each company's own prediction accuracy; however, it will not be included in our analysis since it is not an effort predictor per se. Note that a large number of zero values on certain size variables do not represent missing or rounded values.

Next we present the analyses for numerical variables first, followed by the analyses for categorical variables.

Numerical Variables: Looking for Symptoms

Our next step is to look for symptoms (e.g. skewness[13], heteroscedasticity[14], and outliers[15]) that may suggest the need for variables to be normalised, i.e. having their values transformed such that they resemble more closely a normal distribution. This step uses histograms, boxplots, and scatter plots.

Histograms, or bar charts, provide a graphical display, where each bar summarises the frequency of a single value or range of values for a given variable. They are often used to check if a variable is normally distributed, in which case the bars are displayed in the shape of a bell-shaped curve. Histograms for the numerical variables (see Figs. 2.4 to 2.6) suggest that all variables present skewed distributions, i.e. values not symmetrical about a central value.

Next we use boxplots to check the existence of outliers. Boxplots (see Fig. 2.7) use the median, represented by the horizontal line in the middle of the box, as the central value for the distribution. The box's height is the inter-quartile range, and contains 50% of the values. The vertical (whiskers) lines up or down from the edges contain observations which are less than 1.5 times inter-quartile range. Outliers are taken as values greater than 1.5 times the height of the box. Values greater than 3 times the box's height are called extreme outliers [19].

---

[13] Skewness measures to what extent the distribution of data values is symmetrical about a central value.

[14] Heteroscedasticity represents unstable variance of values.

[15] Outliers are unusual values.

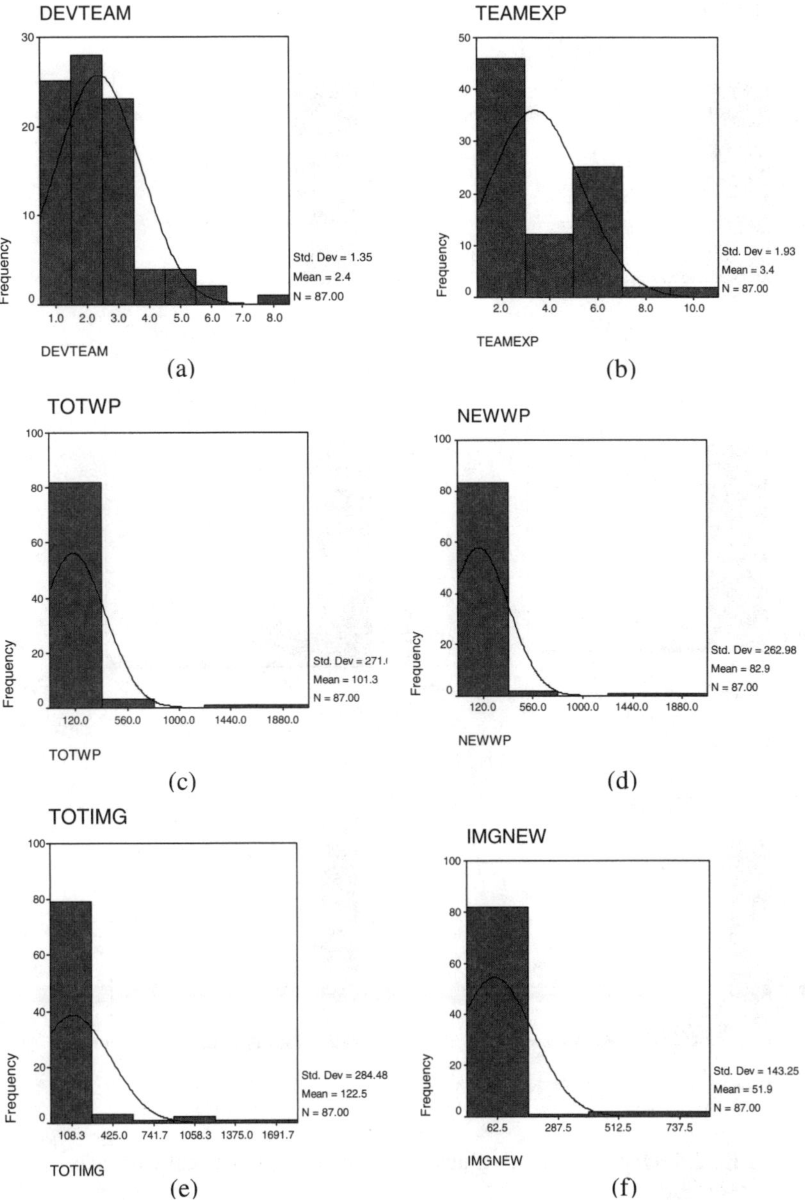

Fig. 2.4. Distribution of values for six numerical variables

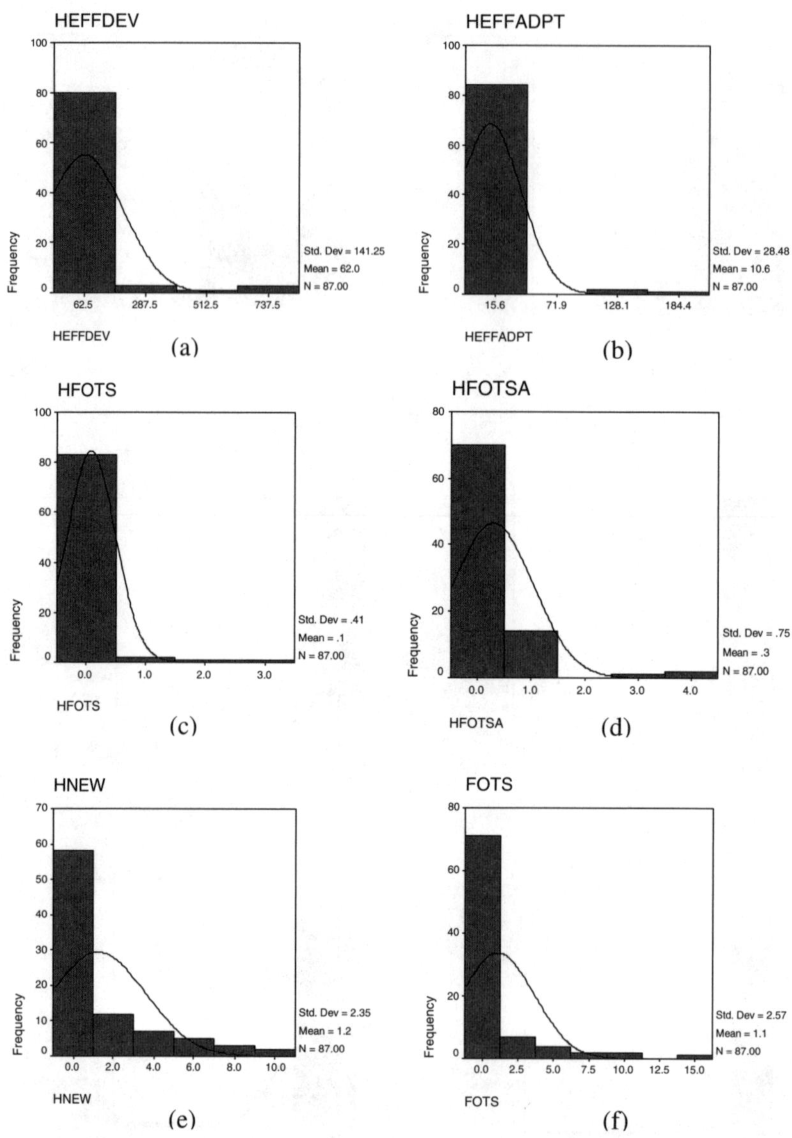

Fig. 2.5. Distribution of values for another six numerical variables

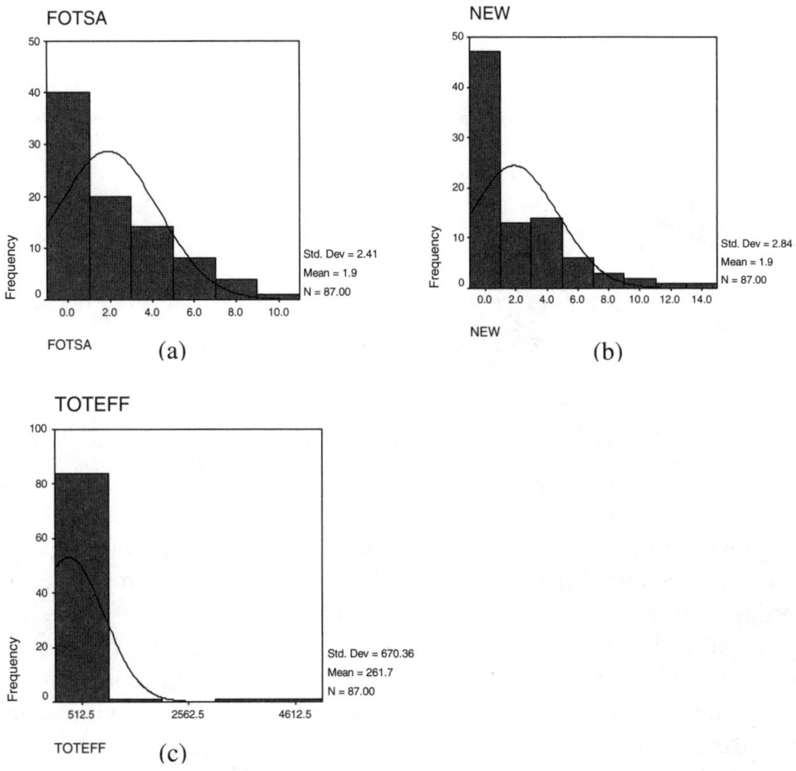

Fig. 2.6. Distribution of values for three numerical variables

When upper and lower tails are approximately equal and the median is in the centre of the box, the distribution is symmetric. If the distribution is not symmetric the relative lengths of the tails and the position of the median in the box indicate the nature of the skewness. The length of the box relative to the length of the tails gives an indication of the shape of the distribution. So, a boxplot with a small box and long tails represents a very peaked distribution, whereas a boxplot with a long box represents a flatter distribution [19].

The boxplots for numerical variables (see Fig. 2.8) indicate that they present a large number of outliers and peaked distributions that are not symmetric.

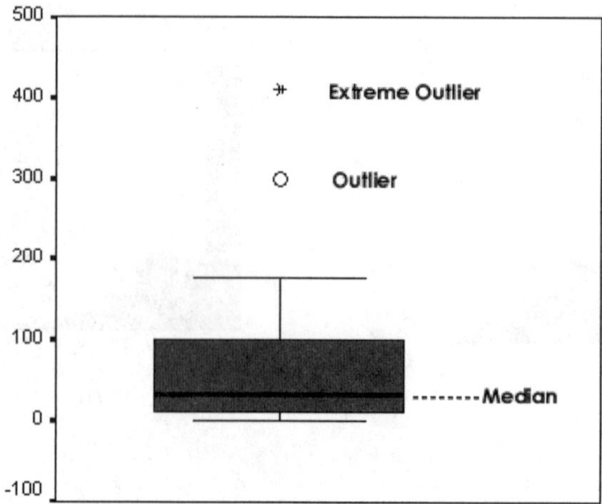

Fig. 2.7. Main components of a boxplot

Whenever outliers are present they should be investigated further, since they may be a result of data entry error. In our study we looked at all cases, in particular in relation to projects that exhibited very large effort values, but did not find anything in the data to suggest they should be removed from the data set. Note that when there are doubts about the correctness of the data, the best solution is to contact the data source for confirmation. Only if the source is not available should an assessment be based on consistency with other variables.

The histograms and boxplots both indicate symptoms of skewness and outliers. When this situation arises it is common practice to normalise the data, i.e. to transform the data trying to approximate the values to a normal distribution. A common transformation is to take the natural log (ln), which makes larger values smaller and brings the data values closer to each other [23]. This is the transformation applied in our case, to all numerical variables. For consistency, all variables with a value of zero had one added to their values prior to being transformed, as there is no natural log of zero.

The Tukutuku database uses six variables to record the number of features/functions for each application. Their histograms (Fig. 2.5(c)–(f), Fig. 2.6(a)–(b)) indicate that each has a large number of zeros, reducing their likelihood of being selected by the stepwise procedure. We therefore decided to group their values by creating two new variables – TOTHIGH (summation of HFOTS, HFOTSA, and HNEW) and TOTNHIGH (summation of FOTS, FOTSA, and NEW). Their histograms are presented in Fig. 2.9(a)–(b).

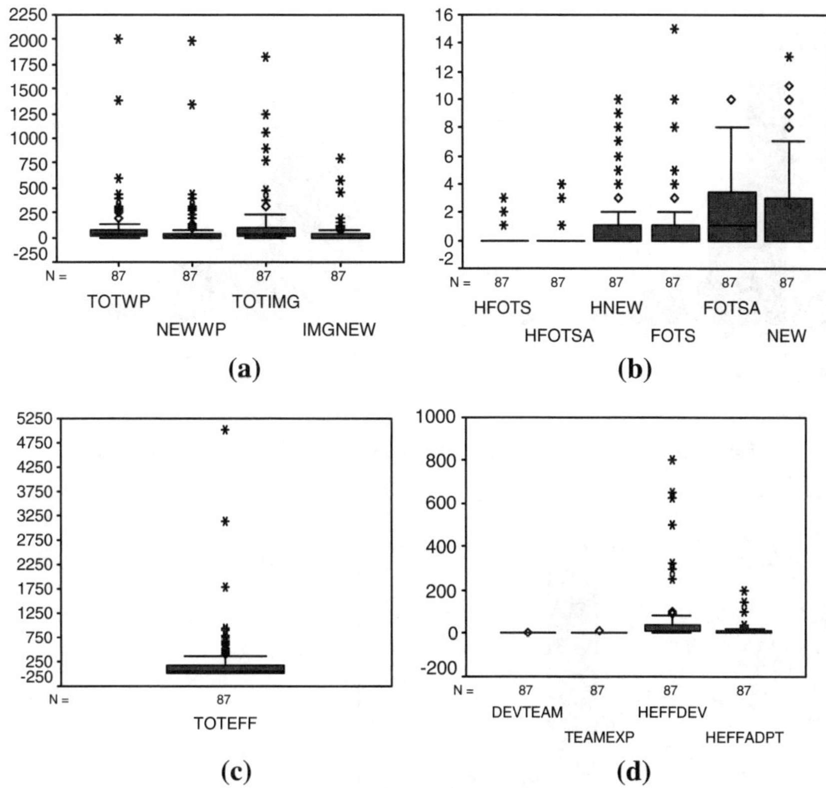

Fig. 2.8. Boxplots for numerical variables

Finally, we created a variable called NLANG, representing the number of different implementation languages used per project, replacing the original multi-valued variable that stored the names of the different implementation languages. The histogram is presented in Fig. 2.10.

TOTHIGH, TOTNHIGH, and NLANG were also transformed since they presented skewness and outliers.

In the following sections, any variables that have been transformed have their names identified by an uppercase L, followed by the name of the variables they originated from.

The last part of the preliminary analysis is to check if the relationship between the dependent variable (LTOTEFF) and the independent variables is linear. The tool used to check such relationships is a scatter plot. Further details on scatter plots are provided in Chap. 12.

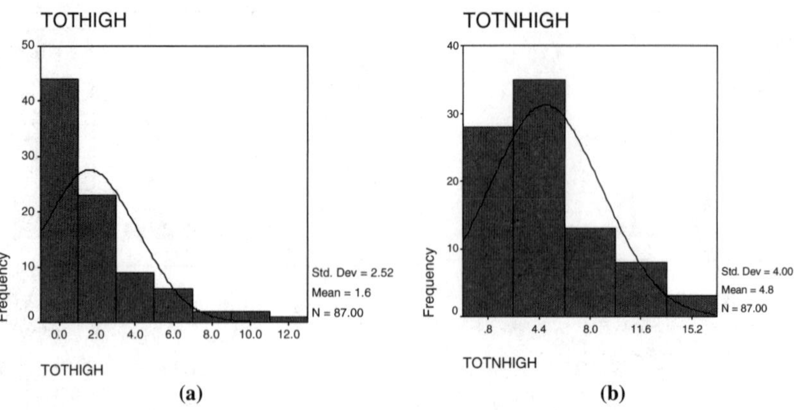

Fig. 2.9. Distribution of values for TOTHIGH and TOTNHIGH

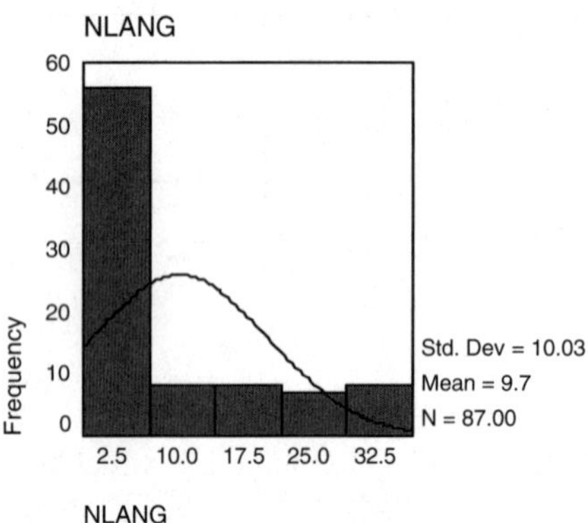

Fig. 2.10. Distribution of values for number of different implementation languages

Numerical Variables: Relationship with Total Effort

Scatter plots are used to explore possible relationships between numerical variables. They also help to identify strong and weak relationships between two numerical variables. A strong relationship is represented by observations (data points) falling very close to or on the trend line. Examples of such relationships are shown in Fig. 2.11(a)–(f), Fig. 2.12(d)–(f), and Fig. 2.13(a)–(d). A weak relationship is shown by observations that do not form a clear pattern, which in our case is a straight line. Examples of such relationships are shown in Fig. 2.12(a)–(c), and Fig. 2.13(e).

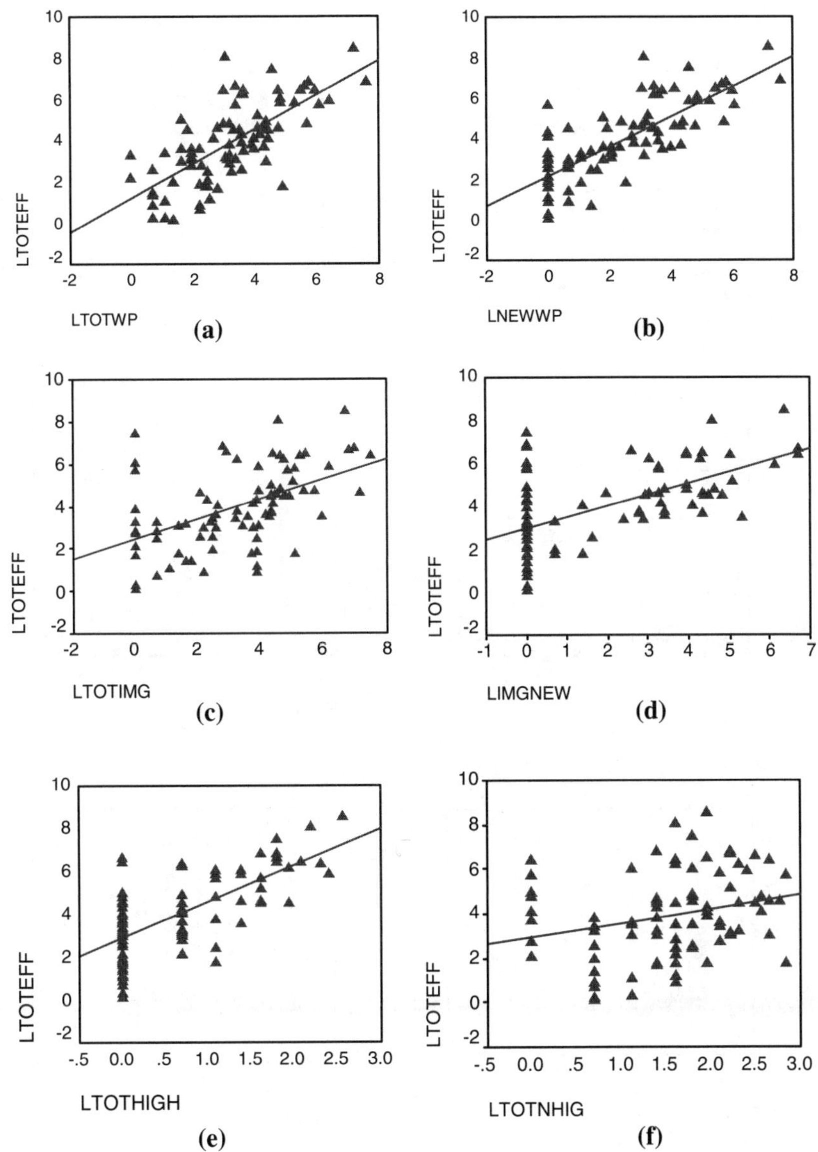

Fig. 2.11. Scatter plots showing strong relationships between ltoteff and several size variables

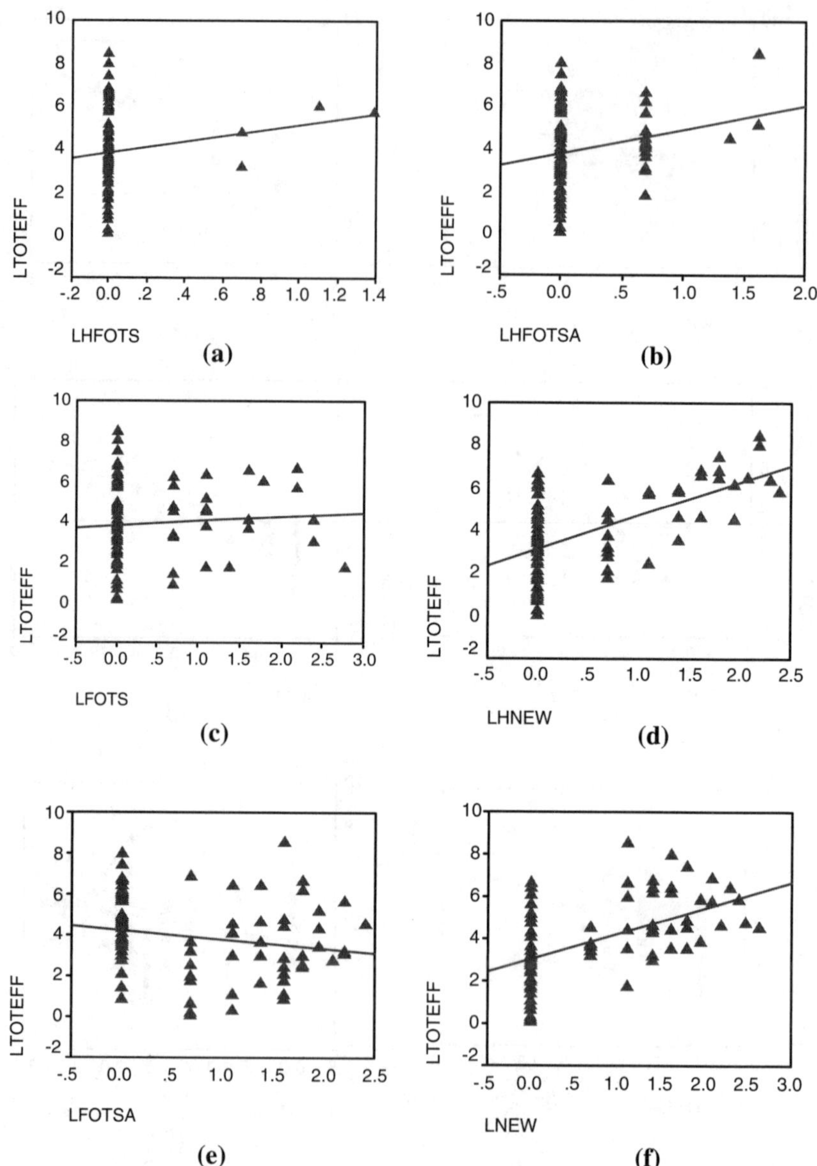

Fig. 2.12. Scatter plots for strong (d,e,f) and weak (a,b,c) relationships between ltoteff and several size variables

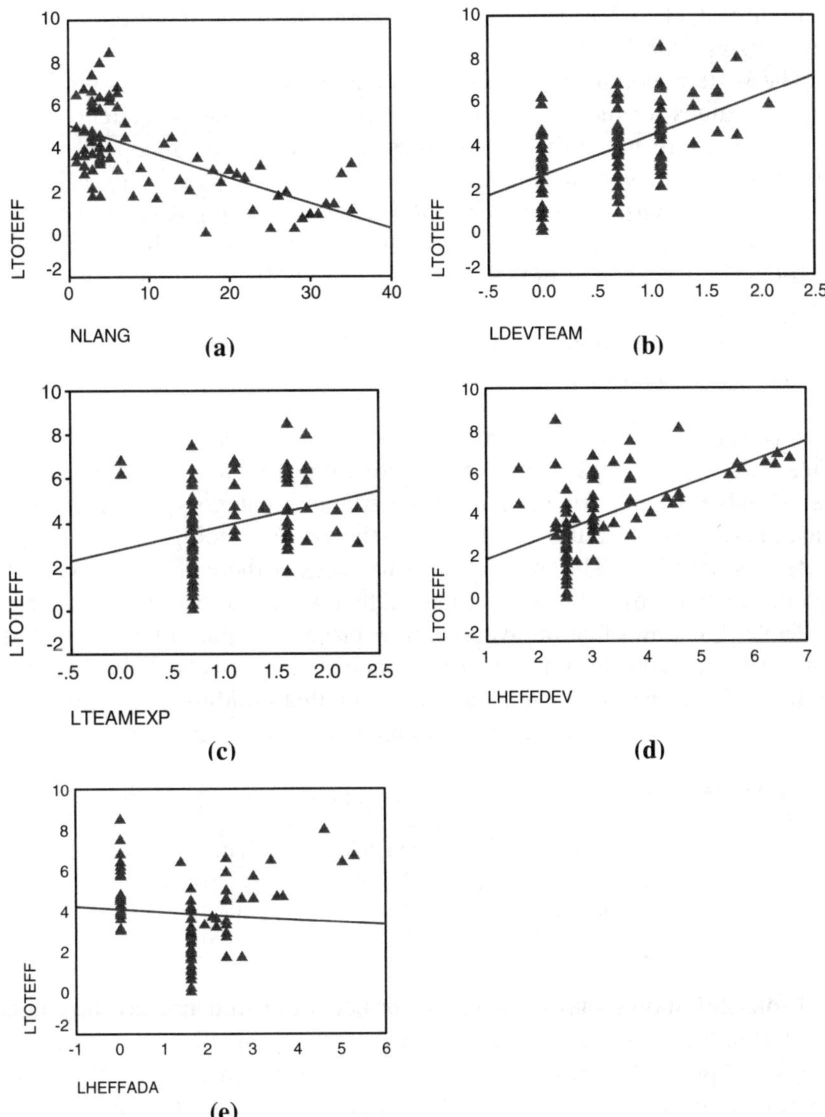

Fig. 2.13. Scatter plots for strong (a–d) and weak (e) relationships between ltoteff and independent variables

We can also say that a relationship is positively associated when values on the y-axis tend to increase with those on the x-axis (e.g. Fig. 2.11(a)–(f)). When values on the y-axis tend to decrease as those on the x-axis increase we say that the relationship is negatively associated (e.g. Fig. 2.12(e) and Fig. 2.13(a)).

Figures 2.11 to 2.13 show that most variables seem to present a positive relationship with LTOTEFF.

The scatter plots in Fig. 3.12(a)–(f) clearly show that the large number of zero values for the independent variables causes the dependent variable to exhibit more variability at the zero point, i.e. when independent variables have zero values, compared with non-zero values. This behaviour violates the fourth assumption underlying linear regression. Therefore within the context of this case study, we will exclude LHFOTS, LHFOSTA, LHNEW, LFOTS, LFOTSA, and LNEW from any subsequent analysis.

Our preliminary analyses for numerical variables is finished. Now we can move on and look at our categorical variables.

Categorical Variables: Relationship with Total Effort

This part of the analysis involves the creation of a table for each categorical variable where, for each of this variable's category, we display the mean and median values of effort and the corresponding number of projects it is based on. The motivation is to check if there is a significant difference in effort by category. If there is, then we need to understand why.

Table 2.8 shows that on average, new projects required more effort, despite being smaller in number than enhancement projects. This should not come as a surprise since we generally know that building an application of size *s* from scratch takes longer than enhancing such application.

Table 2.8. Mean, median effort, and number of projects per type of project category

TYPEPROJ	N	Mean effort	Median effort
New	39	329.8	100.0
Enhancement	48	206.4	18.7
Total	87	261.7	43.0

Table 2.9 shows that on average, projects that did not use any documented process used higher effort, despite being smaller in number than projects that used a documented process. Further inspection of the data revealed that 70% of the 23 projects that did not use any documented process are new, and that 64% of the 64 projects that used a documented process are enhancement projects. These results are in line with those shown in Table 2.8.

Table 2.9. Mean, median effort, and number of projects per documented process category

DOCPROC	N	Mean effort	Median effort
no	23	307.5	50.0
yes	64	245.3	36.2
Total	87	261.7	43.0

Table 2.10. Mean, median effort, and number of projects per process improvement category

PROIMPR	N	Mean effort	Median effort
no	28	508.1	100.0
yes	59	144.8	25.2
Total	87	261.7	43.0

Table 2.11. Mean, median effort, and number of projects per metrics programme category

METRICS	N	Mean effort	Median effort
no	36	462.9	112.5
yes	51	119.7	21.0
Total	87	261.7	43.0

A similar pattern is observed in Tables 2.10 and 2.11, where, on average, projects that are not part of a process improvement or metrics programme required higher effort despite being smaller in size (61% of the 28 projects that are not part of a process improvement programme are new projects).

For projects that are not part of a metrics programme this percentage is also 61% of 36 projects. In both cases the majority of projects that are part of a process improvement or metrics programme are enhancement projects (63% of 59 and 67% of 51 respectively).

Our next step is to check the relationship between categorical variables and effort. Note that we cannot use scatter plots as categorical variables are not numerical. Therefore we use a technique called the one-way ANOVA (see Chap. 12 for details). Table 2.12 summarises the results for the one-way ANOVA.

Table 2.12. Results for the one-way ANOVA

Categorical variables	LTOTEFF
TYPEPROJ	Yes
DOCPROC	No
PROIMPR	Yes
METRICS	Yes

DOCPROC is the only categorical variable not significantly related to LTOTEFF; however, it will not be removed from further analysis as its relationship with LTOTEFF may be concealed at this stage [18].

Next we build the effort model using a two-step process. The first step is to use a manual stepwise regression based on residuals to select the categorical and numerical variables that jointly have a statistically significant effect on the dependent variable, LTOTEFF. The second step is to use these selected variables to build the final effort model using multivariate regression, i.e. linear regression using more than one independent variable.

The size measures used in our case study represent early Web size measures obtained from the results of a survey investigation [29], using data from 133 on-line Web forms aimed at giving quotes on Web development projects. In addition, the measures were validated by an established Web company, and a second survey involving 33 Web companies in New Zealand. Consequently it is our belief that the size measures identified are plausible effort predictors, not an ad-hoc set of variables with no underlying rationale.

Building the Model Using a Two-Step Process

This section describes the use of a manual stepwise regression based on residuals to build the effort model. This technique, proposed by Kitchenham [18], enables the use of information on residuals to handle relationships amongst independent variables. In addition, it only selects the input variables that jointly have a statistically significant effect on the dependent variable, thus avoiding any multi-collinearity problems.

The input variables to use are those selected as a result of our preliminary analyses, which are: LTOTWP, LNEWWP, LTOTIMG, LIMGNEW, LTOTHIGH, LTOTNHIG, TYPEPROJ, DOCPROC, PROIMPR, and METRICS.

Note: the distinct values of a categorical variables are called *levels*. For example, the categorical variable DOCPROC has two levels – Yes and No.

The manual stepwise technique applied to categorical variables comprises the following steps [18]:

Step 1. Identify the categorical variable that has a statistically significant effect on LTOTEFF and gives the smallest error term (mean square within groups). This is obtained by applying simple analysis of variance (ANOVA) using each categorical variable in turn (CV1).

Step 2. Remove the effect of the most significant categorical variable to obtain residuals (ResC1). This means that for each level of the most significant categorical variable, subtract the mean effort from the project effort values. Note that effort represents the normalised effort – LTOTEFF.

Step 3. Apply ANOVA using each remaining categorical variable in turn, this time measuring their effect on ResC1.

Step 4. Any categorical variables that had a statistically significant effect on LTOTEFF (in step 1), but have no statistically significant effect on ResC1, are variables related to CV1 and offer no additional information about the dependent variable. They can therefore be eliminated from the stepwise regression.

Step 5. Identify the next most significant categorical variable from step 4 (CV2). Again, if there are several statistically significant variables, choose the one that minimises the error term.

Step 6. Remove the effect of CV2 to obtain residuals (ResC2).

Step 7. Apply ANOVA using each remaining categorical variable in turn, this time measuring their effect on ResC2.

Step 8. Any categorical variables that had a statistically significant effect on ResC1, but have no statistically significant effect on ResC2, are variables related with CV2 and offer no additional information about the dependent variable. They can therefore be eliminated from the stepwise regression.

Step 9. Repeat the stepwise process until all statistically significant categorical variables are removed or none of the remaining variables have a statistically significant effect on the current residuals.

The initial level means for the four categorical variables to be used in our manual stepwise process are presented in Table 2.13.

Numerical variables can also be added to this stepwise procedure. Their impact on the dependent variable can be assessed using linear regression, and obtaining the mean squares for the regression model and residual. Whenever a numerical variable is the most significant, its effect has to be removed, i.e. the obtained residuals are the ones further analysed.

To construct the full regression model, apply a multivariate regression using only the variables that have been selected from the manual stepwise procedure. At each stage of the stepwise process we also need to verify the stability of the model. This involves identifying large residual and high–influence data points (i.e. projects), and also checking if residuals are homoscedastic and normally distributed. Several types of plots (e.g. residual, leverage, probability) and statistics are available in most statistics tools to accomplish such task.

Table 2.13. Initial level means for categorical variables

Variable/Level	No. projects	Total LTOTEFF	Mean LTOTEFF
TYPEPROJ/New	39	186.7	4.8
TYPEPROJ/Enhancement	48	154.1	3.2
DOCPROC/Yes	64	244.3	3.8
DOCPROC/No	23	96.5	4.2
PROIMPR/Yes	59	204.4	3.5
PROIMPR/No	28	136.4	4.9
METRICS/Yes	51	163.2	3.2
METRICS/No	36	177.6	4.9

The plots we have employed here are:

- A residual plot showing residuals vs. fitted values. This allows us to investigate if the residuals are random and normally distributed. For numerical variables the plotted data points should be distributed randomly about zero. They should not exhibit patterns such as linear or non-linear trends, or increasing or decreasing variance. For categorical variables the pattern of the residuals should appear "as a series of parallel, angled lines of approximately the same length" [18].
- A normal P–P plot (probability plots) for the residuals. Normal P–P plots are generally employed to verify if the distribution of a variable is consistent with the normal distribution. When the distribution is normal, the data points are close to linear.
- Cook's D statistic to identify projects that exhibited jointly a large influence and large residual [23]. Any projects with D greater than $4/n$, where n represents the total number of projects, are considered to have a high influence on the results. When there are high-influence projects the stability of the model is tested by removing these projects and observing the effect their removal has on the model. If the coefficients remain stable and the adjusted R^2 increases, this indicates that the high-influence projects are not destabilising the model and therefore do not need to be removed.

First Cycle

Table 2.14 shows the results of applying ANOVA to categorical and numerical variables. This is the first cycle in the stepwise procedure. The numerical variable LNEWWP is the most significant, since it results in the smallest error term, represented by a within-groups mean square value of 1.47.

Table 2.14. ANOVA for each categorical and numerical variable for first cycle

Variable	Levels	Mean	No. projs	Between-groups MS	Within-groups MS	F test level of significance
TYPEPROJ	New	4.79	39	53.56	3.05	17.56
TYPEPROJ	Enhancement	3.20	48			$p < 0.01$
DOCPROC	Yes	3.82	64	2.44	3.65	0.42
DOCPROC	No	4.20	23			n.s.
PROIMPR	Yes	3.46	59	37.38	3.24	11.64
PROIMPR	No	4.87	28			$p = 0.001$
METRICS	Yes	3.20	51	63.54	2.93	21.67
METRICS	No	4.93	36			$p < 0.01$
LTOTWP	LTOTEFF = 1.183 + 0.841LTOTWP			158.22	1.82	86.97 $p < 0.01$
LNEWWP	**LTOTEFF = 2.165 + 0.731LNEWWP**			**188.21**	**1.47**	**128.36 $p < 0.01$**
LTOTIMG	LTOTEFF = 2.428 + 0.471LTOTIMG			78.55	2.76	28.50 $p < 0.01$
LIMGNEW	LTOTEFF = 2.98 + 0.524LIMGNEW			104.35	2.45	42.54 $p < 0.01$
LTOTHIGH	LTOTEFF = 2.84 + 1.705LTOTHIGH			143.04	2.00	71.61 $p < 0.01$
LTOTNHIG	LTOTEFF = 2.954 + 0.641LTOTNHIG			21.12	3.43	6.15 $p = 0.015$

The single variable regression equation with LTOTEFF as the dependent/response variable and LNEWWP as the independent/predictor variable gives an adjusted R^2 of 0.597. Two projects are identified with Cook's D > 0.045; however, their removal did not seem to destabilise the model, i.e. after their removal the coefficients remained stable and the adjusted R^2 increased. Furthermore, there was no indication from the residual and P–P plots that the residuals were non-normal. The residuals resulting from the linear regression are used for the second cycle in the stepwise procedure.

Second Cycle

Table 2.15 shows the results of applying ANOVA to categorical and numerical variables. This is the second cycle in the stepwise procedure. The numerical variable LTOTHIGH is the most significant, since it results in the smallest error term, represented by a within-square value of 1.118. The linear regression equation with the residual as the dependent/response variable and LTOTHIGH as the independent/predictor variable gives an adjusted R^2 of 0.228. This time five projects are identified with Cook's D > 0.045; however, their removal did not destabilise the model. In addition, the residual and P–P plots found no evidence of non-normality.

Table 2.15. ANOVA for each categorical and numerical variable for second cycle

Variable	Levels	Mean	No. projs	Between-groups MS	Within-groups MS	F test level of significance
TYPEPROJ	New	-0.0181	39	0.023	1.466	0.016
TYPEPROJ	Enhancement	0.0147	48			n.s.
DOCPROC	Yes	0.0385	64	0.359	1.462	0.246
DOCPROC	No	-0.1072	23			n.s.
PROIMPR	Yes	-0.1654	59	5.017	1.407	3.565
PROIMPR	No	0.3486	28			n.s.
METRICS	Yes	-0.2005	51	4.954	1.408	3.519
METRICS	No	0.2840	36			n.s.
LTOTWP	LTOTEFF = -0.474 + 0.146LTOTWP			4.749	1.410	3.367 n.s.
LTOTIMG	LTOTEFF = -0.417 + 0.132LTOTIMG			6.169	1.394	4.427 p = 0.038
LIMGNEW	LTOTEFF = -0.33 + 0.184LIMGNEW			12.915	1.314	9.826 p = 0.002
LTOTHIGH	**LTOTEFF = -0.49 + 0.775LTOTHIGH**			**29.585**	**1.118**	**26.457 p < 0.01**
LTOTNHIG	LTOTEFF = -0.593 + 0.395LTOTNHIG			8.015	1.372	5.842 p = 0.018

Table 2.15 also shows that TYPEPROJ, PROIMPR, METRICS, and LTOTWP have no further statistically significant effect on the residuals obtained in the previous cycle. Therefore they can all be eliminated from the stepwise procedure.

Once this cycle is complete the remaining input variables are DOCPROC, LTOTIMG, LIMGNEW, and LTOTNHIG.

Third Cycle

Table 2.16 shows the results of applying ANOVA to the four remaining categorical and numerical variables. This is the third cycle in the stepwise procedure. As shown in Table 2.16 none of the four remaining variables have any statistically significant effect on the current residuals, and as such the procedure finishes.

Finally, our last step is to construct the effort model using a multivariate regression analysis with only the input variables selected using the manual stepwise procedure – LNEWWP and LTOTHIGH. The coefficients for the effort model are presented in Table 2.17. Its adjusted R^2 is 0.717 suggesting that LNEWWP and LTOTHIGH can explain 72% of the variation in LTOTEFF.

Table 2.16. ANOVA for each categorical and numerical variable for third cycle

Variable	Levels	Mean	No. projs	Between-groups MS	Within-groups MS	F test level of significance
DOCPROC	Yes	0.0097	64	0.023	1.118	0.021 n.s.
DOCPROC	No	-0.0272	23			
LTOTIMG	LTOTEFF = -0.109 + 0.034 LTOTIMG			0.419	1.113	0.376 n.s.
LIMGNEW	LTOTEFF = -0.162 + 0.091 LIMGNEW			3.126	1.081	2.89 n.s.
LTOTNHIG	**LTOTEFF = -0.192 + 0.128 LTOTNHIG**			**0.837**	**1.108**	**0.755 n.s.**

Table 2.17. Coefficients for the effort model

Variable	Coeff.	Std. error	t	P>|t|	[95% conf.	interval]
(Constant)	1.959	0.172	11.355	0.000	1.616	2.302
LNEWWP	0.553	0.061	9.003	0.000	0.431	0.675
LTOTHIGH	1.001	0.164	6.095	0.000	0.675	1.328

Four projects had Cook's D > 0.045 (see Table 2.18) and so we followed the procedure adopted previously. We repeated the regression analysis after excluding these four projects from the data set. Their removal did not result in any major changes to the model coefficients and the adjusted R^2 improved (0.757). Therefore we assume that the regression equation is reasonably stable for this data set and it is not necessary to omit these four projects from the data set.

Table 2.18. Four projects that presented high Cook's distance

ID	NEWWP	TOTHIGH	TOTEFF	Cook's D
20	20	0	625	0.073
25	0	4	300	0.138
32	22	8	3150	0.116
45	280	0	800	0.078

Figure 2.14 shows three different plots all related to residuals. The histogram (see Fig. 2.14(a)) suggests that the residuals are normally distributed, which is further corroborated by the P–P plot (see Fig. 2.14(b)). In addition, the scatter plot of standardised residuals versus standardised predicted values does not show any problematic patterns in the data.

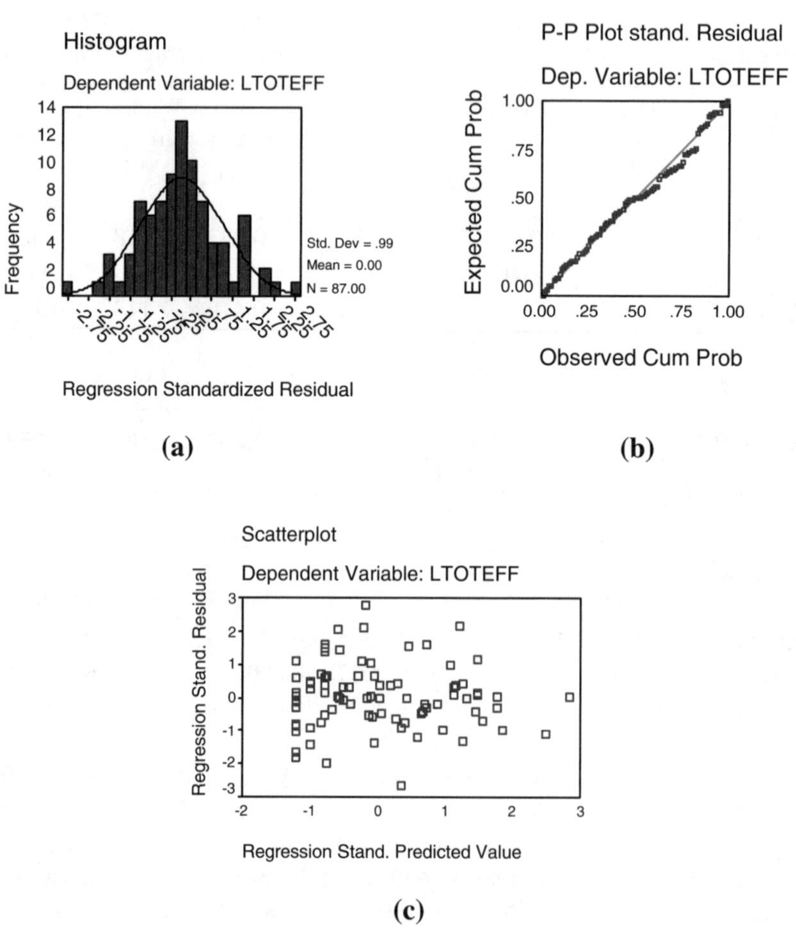

Fig. 2.14. Several residual plots

Once the residuals and the stability of the regression model have been checked, we are in a position to extract the equation that represents the model.

2.5.3 Extraction of effort Equation

The equation that is obtained from Table 2.17 is the following:

$$LTOTEFF = 1.959 + 0.553 LNEWWP + 1.001 LTOTHIGH \qquad (2.10)$$

This equation uses three variables that had been previously transformed, therefore we need to transform it back to its original state, which gives the following equation:

$$TOTEFF = 7.092\,(NEWWP + 1)^{0.553}\,(TOTHIGH + 1)^{1.001} \qquad (2.11)$$

In Eq. 2.11, the multiplicative value 7.092 can be interpreted as the effort required to develop one Web page.

Obtaining a model that has a good fit to the data and can alone explain a large degree of the variation in the dependent variable is not enough to assume this model will provide good effort predictions. To confirm this, it also needs to be validated. This is the procedure explained in Sect. 2.5.4.

2.5.4 Model Validation

As described in Sect. 2.3.2, to validate a model we need to do the following:

Step 1. Divide data set *d* into a training set *t* and a validation set *v*.
Step 2. Use *t* to produce an effort estimation model *te* (if applicable).
Step 3. Use *te* to predict effort for each of the projects in *v*, as if these projects were new projects for which effort was unknown.

This process is known as cross-validation. For an *n*-fold cross-validation, *n* different training/validation sets are used. In this section we will show the cross-validation procedure using a one-fold cross-validation, with a 66% split. This split means that 66% of our project data will be used for model building, the remaining 34% to validate the model, i.e. the training set will have 66% of the total number of projects and the validation set will have the remaining 34%.

Our initial data set had 87 projects. At step 1 they are split into training and validation sets containing 58 and 29 projects respectively. Generally projects are selected randomly.

As part of step 2 we need to create an effort model using the 58 projects in the training set. We will create an effort model that only considers the variables that have been previously selected and presented in Eq. 2.10. These are: LNEWWP and LTOTHIGH. Here we do not perform the residual analysis or consider Cook's D since it is assumed these have also been done using the generic equation, Eq. 2.10. The model's coefficients are presented in Table 2.19, and the transformed equation is presented in Eq. 2.12. The adjusted R^2 is 0.619.

Table 2.19. Coefficients for effort model using 58 projects

Variable	Coeff.	Std. error	t	P>|t|	[95% conf. interval]	
(Constant)	2.714	0.264	10.290	0.000	2.185	3.242
LNEWWP	0.420	0.073	5.749	0.000	0.273	0.566
LTOTHIGH	0.861	0.160	5.389	0.000	0.675	1.328

$$TOTEFF = 15.089\,(NEWWP+1)^{0.420}\,(TOTHIGH+1)^{0.861} \quad (2.12)$$

To measure this model's prediction accuracy we obtain the MMRE, MdMRE, and Pred(25) for the validation set. The model presented as Eq. 2.12 is applied to each of the 29 projects in the validation set to obtain estimated effort, and MRE is computed. Having the calculated estimated effort and the actual effort (provided by the Web companies), we are finally in a position to calculate MRE for each of the 29 projects, and hence MMRE, MdMRE, and Pred(25) for the entire 29 projects. This process is explained in Fig. 2.15.

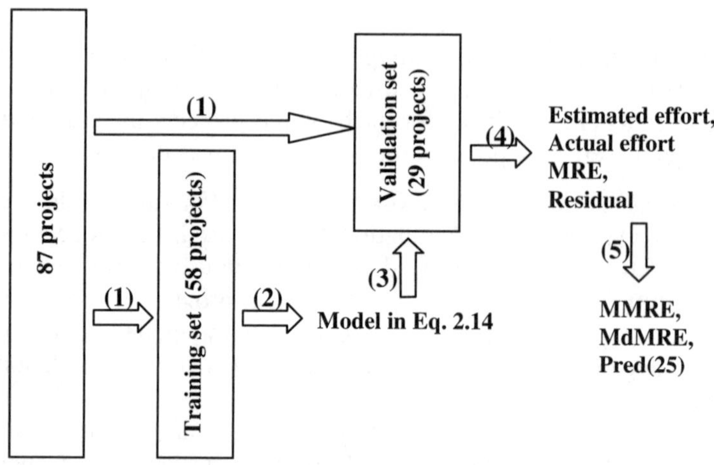

Fig. 2.15. Steps used in the cross-validation process

Table 2.20 shows the measures of prediction accuracy, calculated from the validation set, and is assumed to represent the entire set of 87 projects.

Table 2.20. Prediction accuracy measures using model-based estimated effort

Measure	%
MMRE	129
MdMRE	73
Pred(25)	17.24

If we assume a good prediction model has an MMRE less than or equal to 25% and Pred(25) greater than or equal to 75% then the values presented in Table 2.20 suggest the accuracy of the effort model used is poor. However, if instead we were to use the average actual effort (average = 261) or the median actual effort for the 87 projects (median = 43) accuracy would be considerably worse. One viable approach for a Web company would be to use the effort model described above to obtain an estimated effort, and adapt the obtained values, taking into account factors such as previous experience with similar projects and the skills of the developers.

Table 2.21. Prediction accuracy measures based on average and median effort

	Average effort as estimated effort	Median effort as estimated effort
MMRE	4314%	663%
MdMRE	1413%	149%
Pred(25)	6.89%	3.44%

Table 2.21 presents the results for a one-fold cross-validation. However, research on effort estimation suggests that to have unbiased results for a cross-validation we should actually use at least a 20-fold cross-validation analysis [17]. This would represent for the data set presented here, the selection of 20 different training/validation sets and the aggregation of the MMREs, MdMREs, and Pred(25)s after accuracy for all 20 groups has been calculated.

2.6 Conclusions

This chapter introduced the concepts related to effort estimation, and described techniques for effort estimation using three general categories: expert opinion, algorithmic models and artificial intelligence (AI) techniques. In addition, it discussed how to measure effort prediction power and accuracy of effort estimation models.

This chapter also presented a case study that used data from industrial Web projects held in the Tukutuku database, to construct and validate an effort estimation model. The size measures used in the case study represent early Web size measures obtained from the results of a survey investigation [29], using data from 133 on-line Web forms aimed at giving quotes for Web development projects. In addition, the measures were validated by an established Web company, and by a second survey involving 33 Web companies in New Zealand. Consequently we believe that the size measures identified are plausible effort predictors, not an ad-hoc set of variables with no underlying rationale.

Furthermore, a detailed analysis of the data was provided, with details of a manual stepwise procedure [18] used to build an effort estimation model. The two variables that were selected by the effort estimation model were the total number of new Web pages and the total number of high-effort features/functions in the application. Together they explained 76% of the variation in total effort. Note that the effort model constructed and the selected variables are applicable only to projects belonging to the data set on which they were constructed.

The case study details the mechanism that can be used by any Web company to construct and validate its own effort estimation models. Alternatively, Web companies that do not have a data set of past projects may be able to benefit from the cross-company effort estimation models provided within the context of the Tukutuku project, provided they are willing to volunteer data on three of their past finished projects.

References

1 Angelis L, Stamelos I (2000) A Simulation Tool for Efficient Analogy Based Cost Estimation. Empirical Software Engineering, 5:35–68

2 Boehm B (1981) Software Engineering Economics. Prentice-Hall, Englewood Cliffs, NJ

3 Briand LC, El-Emam K, Surmann D, Wieczorek I, Maxwell KD (1999) An Assessment and Comparison of Common Cost Estimation Modeling Techniques. In: Proceedings of ICSE 1999, Los Angeles, USA, pp 313–322

4 Briand LC, Langley T, Wieczorek I (2000) A Replicated Assessment and Comparison of Common Software Cost Modeling Techniques. In: Proceedings of ICSE 2000, Limerick, Ireland, pp 377–386

5 Brieman L, Friedman J, Olshen R, Stone C (1984) Classification and Regression Trees. Wadsworth, Belmont.,CA

6 Conte S, Dunsmore H, Shen V (1986) Software Engineering Metrics and Models. Benjamin/Cummings, Menlo Park, CA

7 DeMarco T (1982) Controlling Software Projects: Management, Measurement and Estimation. Yourdon, New York

8 Finnie GR, Wittig GE, Desharnais J-M (1997) A Comparison of Software Effort Estimation Techniques: Using Function Points with Neural Networks, Case-Based Reasoning and Regression Models. Journal of Systems and Software, 39:281–289

9 Gray A, MacDonell S (1997) Applications of Fuzzy Logic to Software Metric Models for Development Effort Estimation. In: Proceedings of IEEE Annual Meeting of the North American Fuzzy Information Processing Society - NAFIPS, Syracuse, NY, USA, pp 394–399

10 Gray AR, MacDonell SG (1997) A comparison of model building techniques to develop predictive equations for software metrics. Information and Software Technology, 39:425–437

11 Gray R, MacDonell SG, Shepperd MJ (1999) Factors Systematically associated with errors in subjective estimates of software development effort: the stability of expert judgement. In: Proceedings of the 6th IEEE Metrics Symposium

12 Hughes RT (1997) An Empirical investigation into the estimation of software development effort. PhD thesis, Dept. of Computing, University of Brighton

13 Jeffery R, Ruhe M, Wieczorek I (2000) A Comparative study of two software development cost modelling techniques using multi-organizational and company-specific data. Information and Software Technology, 42:1009–1016

14 Jeffery R, Ruhe M, Wieczorek I (2001) Using Public Domain Metrics to Estimate Software Development Effort. In: Proceedings of the 7th IEEE Metrics Symposium, London, UK, pp 16–27

15 Kadoda G, Cartwright M, Chen L, Shepperd MJ (2000) Experiences Using Case-Based Reasoning to Predict Software Project Effort. In: Proceedings of the EASE 2000 Conference, Keele, UK

16 Kemerer CF (1987) An Empirical Validation of Software Cost Estimation Models, Communications of the ACM, 30(5):416–429

17 Kirsopp C, Shepperd M (2001) Making Inferences with Small Numbers of Training Sets, January, TR02-01, Bournemouth University

18 Kitchenham BA (1998) A Procedure for Analyzing Unbalanced Datasets. IEEE Transactions on Software Engineering, April, 24(4):278–301

19 Kitchenham BA, MacDonell SG, Pickard LM, Shepperd MJ (2001) What accuracy statistics really measure. IEE Proceedings Software, June, 148(3):81–85

20 Kitchenham BA, Pickard LM, Linkman S, Jones P (2003) Modelling Software Bidding Risks. IEEE Transactions on Software Engineering, June, 29(6):54–554

21 Kok P, Kitchenham BA, Kirakowski J (1990) The MERMAID Approach to software cost estimation. In: Proceedings of the ESPRIT Annual Conference, Brussels, pp 296–314

22 Kumar S, Krishna BA, Satsangi PS (1994) Fuzzy systems and neural networks in software engineering project management. Journal of Applied Intelligence, 4:31–52

23 Maxwell K (2002) Applied Statistics for Software Managers. Prentice Hall PTR, Englewood Cliffs, NJ

24 Mendes E, Counsell S, Mosley N (2000) Measurement and Effort Prediction of Web Applications. In: Proceedings of the 2nd ICSE Workshop on Web Engineering, June, Limerick, Ireland, pp 57–74

25 Mendes E, Mosley N, Counsell S (2001) Web Metrics – Estimating Design and Authoring Effort. IEEE Multimedia, Special Issue on Web Engineering, January/March:50–57

26 Mendes E, Mosley N, Counsell S (2002) The Application of Case-Based Reasoning to Early Web Project Cost Estimation. In: Proceedings of COMPSAC 2002, Oxford, UK

27 Mendes E, Mosley N, Counsell S (2003) Do Adaptation Rules Improve Web Cost Estimation?. In: Proceedings of the ACM Hypertext conference 2003, Nottingham, UK

28 Mendes E, Mosley N, Counsell S (2003) A Replicated Assessment of the Use of Adaptation Rules to Improve Web Cost Estimation. In: Proceedings of the ACM and IEEE International Symposium on Empirical Software Engineering. Rome, Italy, pp 100–109

29 Mendes E, Mosley N, Counsell S (2003) Early Web Size Measures and Effort Prediction for Web Costimation. In: Proceedings of the IEEE Metrics Symposium. Sydney, Australia, September, pp 18–29

30 Myrtveit I, Stensrud E (1999) A Controlled Experiment to Assess the Benefits of Estimating with Analogy and Regression Models. IEEE Transactions on Software Engineering, July/August, 25(4):510–525

31 Ruhe M, Jeffery R, Wieczorek I (2003) Cost Estimation for Web Applications. In: Proceedings of ICSE 2003. Portland, USA

32 Schofield C (1998) An empirical investigation into software estimation by analogy. PhD thesis, Dept. of Computing, Bournemouth University

33 Schroeder L, Sjoquist D, Stephan P (1986) Understanding Regression Analysis: An Introductory Guide, No. 57. In: Quantitative Applications in the Social Sciences, Sage Publications, Newbury Park, CA

34 Selby RW, Porter AA (1998) Learning from examples: generation and evaluation of decision trees for software resource analysis. IEEE Transactions on Software Engineering, 14:1743–1757

35 Shepperd MJ, Kadoda G (2001) Using Simulation to Evaluate Prediction Techniques. In: Proceedings of the IEEE 7th International Software Metrics Symposium, London, UK, pp 349–358

36 Shepperd MJ, Schofield C (1997) Estimating Software Project Effort Using Analogies. IEEE Transactions on Software Engineering, 23(11):736–743

37 Shepperd MJ, Schofield C, Kitchenham B (1996) Effort Estimation Using Analogy. In: Proceedings of ICSE-18. Berlin

38 Srinivasan K, Fisher D (1995) Machine Learning approaches to estimating software development effort. IEEE Transactions on Software Engineering, 21:126–137

39 Stensrud E, Foss T, Kitchenham BA, Myrtveit I (2002) An Empirical validation of the relationship between the magnitude of relative error and project size. In: Proceedings of the IEEE 8th Metrics Symposium. Ottawa, pp 3–12

Authors' Biographies

Dr. **Emilia Mendes** is a Senior Lecturer in Computer Science at the University of Auckland (New Zealand), where she leads the WETA (Web Engineering, Technology and Applications) research group. She is the principal investigator in the Tukutuku Research project,[16] aimed at developing and comparing Web effort models using industrial Web project data, and benchmarking productivity within and across Web companies. She has active research interests in Web measurement and metrics, and in particular Web cost estimation, Web size measures, Web productivity and quality measurement, and Web process improvement. Dr. Mendes is on the programme committee of numerous international conferences and workshops, and on the editorial board of the International Journal of Web Engineering and Technology and the Journal of Web Engineering. She has collaborated with Web companies in New Zealand and overseas on Web cost estimation and usability measurement. Dr. Mendes worked in the software industry for ten years before obtaining her PhD in Computer Science from the University of Southampton (UK), and moving to Auckland. She is a member of the Australian Software Measurement Association.

Dr. **Nile Mosley** is the Technical Director of a software development company. He has active research interests in software measurement and metrics, and object-oriented programming languages. He obtained his PhD in Pure and Applied Mathematics from Nottingham Trent University (UK).

Steve Counsell obtained a BSc (Hons) in Computer Studies from the University of Brighton and an MSc in Systems Analysis from the City University in 1987 and 1988, respectively. After spending some time in industry as a developer, he obtained his PhD in 2002 from the University of London and is currently a Lecturer in the Department of Information Systems and Computing at Brunel University. Prior to 2004, he was a Lecturer in the School of Computer Science and Information Systems at Birkbeck, University of London and between 1996 and 1998 was a Research Fellow at the University of Southampton. In 2002, he was a BT Short-term Research Fellow. His research interests are in software engineering, more specifically metrics and empirical studies.

[16] http://www.cs.auckland.ac.nz/tukutuku/.

3 Web Productivity Measurement and Benchmarking

Emilia Mendes, Barbara Kitchenham

Abstract: Project managers use software productivity measures to assess software development efficiency. Productivity is commonly measured as the ratio of output to input. Within the context of software development, output is often assumed to be product size and input to be effort. However, Web applications are often characterised using several different size measures and there is no standard model for aggregating those measures into a single size measure. This makes it difficult to measure Web application productivity.

In this chapter, we present a productivity measurement method, which allows for the use of different size measures. An advantage of the method is that it has a built-in interpretation scale. It ensures that each project has an expected productivity value of one. Values between zero and one indicate lower than expected productivity; values greater than one indicate higher than expected productivity. We demonstrate how to use the method by analysing the productivity of Web projects from the Tukutuku database.

Keywords: Web productivity measurement, Productivity measure, Manual stepwise regression, Size-based effort model, Data analysis.

3.1 Introduction

Productivity is commonly measured as the ratio of output to input. The more output per unit of input, the more productive a project is assumed to be. Within the context of software development the output of the software production process is often taken to be product size and the input to the process to be effort. Therefore, productivity is represented by the following equation:

$$Productivity = Size/Effort \quad (3.1)$$

Equation 3.1 is simple to apply when product size is represented by a single dominant size measure (e.g. product size measured in lines of code or function points). However, there are circumstances when there are several different effort-related size measures and there is no standard model for aggregating these measures. When we have more than one size measure related to effort and no theoretical model for aggregating those measures, it is difficult to construct a single size measure. In these circumstances,

Eq. 3.1 cannot be used to measure productivity. This is exactly the problem we face when attempting to measure Web application productivity. The majority of studies published in the Web sizing literature have identified the need to use a variety of different measures to adequately characterise the size of a Web application, but there is no widely accepted method for aggregating the measures into a single size measure.

In this chapter we describe a case study that analyses the productivity of 87 Web projects from the Tukutuku database. This is the same subset of projects used in Chap. 2. We adopt the productivity measurement method suggested in Kitchenham and Mendes [2], which allows for the use of several effort-related size measures, and also provides a productivity baseline of one. Thus, productivity values between zero and one indicate lower than expected productivity, values greater than one indicate higher than expected productivity.

Section 3.2 presents the method used to build the productivity measure and the assumptions underlying the productivity measure. The results of our productivity analysis using the new productivity measurement method are described in Sect. 3.3, followed by our conclusions in Sect. 3.4.

3.2 Productivity Measurement Method

The productivity measurement method employed in this chapter allows for the use of multiple effort-related size measures. It is based on the idea that any *size-based effort estimation model* constructed using the stepwise regression technique is *by definition* a function of effort-related size measures. Thus the *size-based effort estimation model* can be regarded as an *AdjustedSize measure*, and used in the following equation to represent productivity [2]:

$$\text{Productivity} = \text{AdjustedSize/Effort} \tag{3.2}$$

The *AdjustedSize* measure contains only size measures that *together* are strongly associated with effort. In addition, the relationship between these size measures and effort does not need to be linear.

The benefits of using this method for measuring productivity are as follows [2]:

- The standard value of productivity is one, since it is obtained using the ratio of estimated to actual effort.
- A productivity value greater than one suggests above-average productivity.
- A productivity value smaller than one suggests below-average productivity.

- The stepwise regression technique used to build a regression model that represents the *AdjustedSize* measure can also be employed to construct upper and lower bounds on the productivity measure. These bounds can be used to assess whether the productivity achieved by a specific project is significantly better or worse than expected.
- The productivity measure automatically allows for diseconomies (or economies) of scale before being used in a productivity analysis. This means that an investigation of factors that affect productivity will only select factors that affect the productivity of all projects. If we ignore the impact of diseconomies (or economies) or scale, we run the risk of detecting factors that differ between large and small projects rather than factors that affect the productivity of all projects.

3.3 Case Study

The case study presented in this section describes the construction of a productivity measure and its use to analyse the productivity of Web projects from the Tukutuku database.[1]

The database used in our analysis has data on 87 Web projects where 13 and 34 come from 2 single Web companies, respectively, and the remaining 40 projects come from another 23 companies. The Tukutuku database uses 6 variables to store data on companies which volunteered projects, 10 variables to store data on each project and 13 variables to store data on each Web application2 (see Table 3.1). Company data is obtained once and both project and application data are gathered for each volunteered project.

Table 3.1. Variables for the Tukutuku database

NAME	SCALE	DESCRIPTION
Company data		
COUNTRY	Categorical	Country company belongs to.
ESTABLISHED	Ordinal	Year when company was established.
SERVICES	Categorical	Type of services company provides.
NPEOPLEWD	Ratio	Number of people who work on Web design and development.
CLIENTIND	Categorical	Industry representative of those clients to whom applications are provided.
ESTPRACT	Categorical	Accuracy of a company's own effort estimation practices.

[1] The raw data cannot be displayed here due to a confidentiality agreement with those companies that have volunteered data on their projects.

[2] A definition of Web application is given in Chap. 1.

NAME	SCALE	DESCRIPTION
Project data		
TYPEPROJ	Categorical	Type of project (new or enhancement).
LANGS	Categorical	Implementation languages used.
DOCPROC	Categorical	If project followed defined and documented process.
PROCIMPR	Categorical	If project team involved in a process improvement programme.
METRICS	Categorical	If project team part of a software metrics programme.
DEVTEAM	Ratio	Size of project's development team.
TEAMEXP	Ratio	Average team experience with the development language(s) employed.
TOTEFF	Ratio	Actual total effort in person hours used to develop the Web application.
ESTEFF	Ratio	Estimated total effort in person hours necessary to develop the Web application.
ACCURACY	Categorical	Procedure used to record effort data.
Web application		
TYPEAPP	Categorical	Type of Web application developed.
TOTWP	Ratio	Total number of Web pages (new and reused).
NEWWP	Ratio	Total number of new Web pages.
TOTIMG	Ratio	Total number of images (new and reused).
NEWIMG	Ratio	Total number of new images created.
HEFFDEV	Ratio	Minimum number of hours to develop a single function/feature by one experienced developer that is considered high (above average).[3]
HEFFADPT	Ratio	Minimum number of hours to adapt a single function/feature by one experienced developer that is considered high (above average).[4]
HFOTS	Ratio	Number of reused high-effort features/functions without adaptation.
HFOTSA	Ratio	Number of adapted high-effort features/functions.
HNEW	Ratio	Number of new high-effort features/functions.
FOTS	Ratio	Number of low-effort features off the shelf.
FOTSA	Ratio	Number of low-effort features off the shelf adapted.
NEW	Ratio	Number of new low-effort features/functions.

[3] This number is currently set to 15 hours based on the collected data.

[4] This number is currently set to 4 hours based on the collected data.

All results presented here were obtained using the statistical software SPSS 10.1.3 for Windows. Finally, all the statistical significance tests used $\alpha = 0.05$.

Two main steps are used in this case study. The first step is to build the productivity measure using the productivity measurement method proposed in [2]. The second step is to use the productivity values (including lower and upper bounds) obtained from step 1 to carry out a productivity analysis.

3.3.1 Productivity Measure Construction

To build the productivity measure we will employ the same technique used in Chap. 2, a manual stepwise regression. However, here the attributes of interest are only size and effort measures. We will use the following steps to carry out our data analysis [4]:

1. Data validation
2. Variables and model selection
3. Model building and inspection
4. Extraction of *AdjustedSize* equation

Each of these steps will be detailed below.

Data Validation

Data validation represents a first screening of the data set to become familiar with it and also to identify any missing or unusual values. It generally involves understanding what the variables are (e.g. purpose, scale type) and also using descriptive statistics that will help identify any unusual cases.

Table 3.2 presents a set of results that show summary values for the size and effort variables. It might be considered unusual to see "zero" as minimum value for TOTIMG, or "one" as minimum value for TOTWP; however, it is possible to have a Web application without any images or an application that provided all its information and functionality using only one Web page.

The average size of applications is around 82 new Web pages and 51 new images. However, their corresponding medians are 7 and 0 respectively, which indicates that half the Web applications in the data set construct no more than seven new Web pages, and no new images.

Our summary statistics also show that there is least one very large application with 2000 Web pages. Although this value is atypical for our data set, we cannot simply assume that this has been a data entry error. Best practice in such circumstances is to ask the data provider to check

Table 3.2. Descriptive statistics for numerical variables

Variables	N	Minimum	Maximum	Mean	Median	Std. deviation
TOTWP	87	1	2000	92.40	25	273.098
NEWWP	87	0	1980	82.92	7	262.982
TOTIMG	87	0	1820	122.54	40	284.482
IMGNEW	87	0	800	51.90	0	143.254
HFOTS	87	0	3	.08	0	.410
HFOTSA	87	0	4	.29	0	.746
HNEW	87	0	10	1.24	0	2.352
FOTS	87	0	15	1.07	0	2.574
FOTSA	87	0	10	1.89	1	2.413
NEW	87	0	13	1.87	0	2.836
TOTEFF	87	1	5000	261.73	43	670.364

the value. However, we were unable to obtain confirmation from the source company. If the data providers are unavailable, it is customary to investigate whether the data is internally consistent. In this case, the developers produced 1980 pages from scratch, and constructed numerous new functions/features (five high-effort and seven low-effort). The development team consisted of two people who had very little experience with the six programming languages used. The total effort was 947 person hours, which corresponds to a three-month project, assuming both developers worked full time, and in parallel. Considering only the number of Web pages and effort, the project delivered just over 2 Web pages per hour compared with an average of about 0.4 Web pages per hour for the other projects. Thus, the results cast some doubt on the internal consistency of the project values, particularly given the lack of experience of the development team and the number of different languages they had to use. However, for the purpose of illustrating the data analysis method we have not removed this project from the data set.

In terms of TOTEFF, the average person hours is around 261 and its median is 43 person hours, indicating that half the applications on the data set are relatively small with a duration close to a working week. Further investigation of the data revealed that more than half of the projects are enhancements of existing Web applications, which may explain the small median for TOTEFF, NEWWP and IMGNEW.

Once the data validation is finished we are ready to move on to the next step, namely variables and model selection.

Variables and Model Selection

The second step in our data analysis methodology is sub-divided into two separate and distinct phases: preliminary analyses and model building.

A Preliminary analyses allows us to choose which variables to use, discard, modify and sometimes create. Model building determines the best size-based effort estimation model based on our data set and set of variables.

Preliminary Analyses

Our aim is to build an *AdjustedSize* measure using manual stepwise regression. The assumptions underlying stepwise regression are as follows:

1. The input variables (independent variables) are measured without error. If this cannot be guaranteed then these variables need to be normalised.
2. The relationship between dependent and independent variables is linear.
3. No important input variables have been omitted. This ensures that there is no specification error associated with the data set. The use of a prior theory-based model justifying the choice of input variables helps to ensure this assumption is not violated.
4. The variance of the residuals is the same for all combinations of input variables (i.e. the residuals are homoscedastic rather than heteroscedastic).
5. The residuals are normally distributed.
6. The residuals are independent, i.e. not correlated.
7. The independent variables are not linearly dependent, i.e. there are no linear dependencies among the independent variables.

The first task is to look at the set of variables (size measures and effort) and see if they have a large number of missing values (> 60%). If they do, they should be automatically discarded. Without sufficient values it is not possible to identify useful trends and a large number of missing values also prohibits the use of imputation methods. Imputation methods are methods used to replace missing values with estimated values.

Table 3.2 shows that there are no variables with missing values. Even though we have a large number of zero values on certain size variables, these zeros do not represent a missing value or a rounded-down value. However, a problem with many zero values is that they may cause heteroscedasticity at the zero point (see Fig. 3.6), i.e. the dependent variable exhibits more variability when the input variable is zero. It is not possible to correct this form of heteroscedasticity by normalising the corresponding variables.

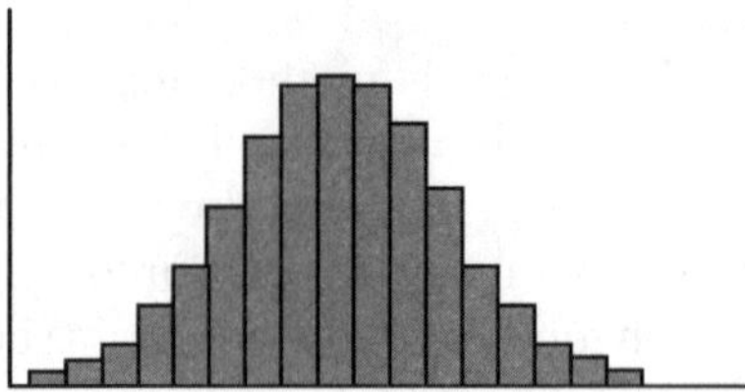

Fig. 3.1. Example of a histogram representing a normal distribution

Our next step is to look for symptoms (e.g. skewness,[5] heteroscedasticity,[6] and outliers[7]) that may suggest the need for variables to be normalised, i.e. to have their values transformed such that they resemble more closely a normal distribution. This step uses histograms, boxplots and scatter plots. Histograms, or bar charts, provide a graphical display where each bar summarises the frequency of a single value/range of values for a given variable. They are often used to check whether a variable is normally distributed, in which case the bars are displayed according to a bell-shaped curve (see Fig. 3.1). Figure 3.2 confirms that all variables have skewed distributions since their data values are not symmetrical about a central value.

Next, we use boxplots to check the existence of outliers. Boxplots (see Fig. 3.3) use the median value as the central value for the distribution. The median is represented by the horizontal line in the middle of the box. The length of the box corresponds to the inter-quartile range, and contains 50% of the values. The vertical (whiskers) lines up or down from the edges contain observations which are less than 1.5 times inter-quartile range. Outliers are taken as values greater than 1.5 times the length of the box. If a value is greater than 3 times the length of the box it is called an extreme outlier [3].

When upper and lower tails are approximately equal and the median is in the centre of the box, the distribution is symmetric. If the distribution is not symmetric the relative lengths of the tails and the position of the median in the box indicate the extent of the skewness. The length of the box relative to the length of the tails gives an indication of the shape of the distribution. A boxplot with a small box and long tails represents a very peaked distribution, whereas a boxplot with a long box represents a flatter distribution [3].

---

5 Skewness measures to what extent the distribution of data values is symmetrical about a central value.

6 Heteroscedasticity represents unstable variance of values.

7 Outliers are unusual values.

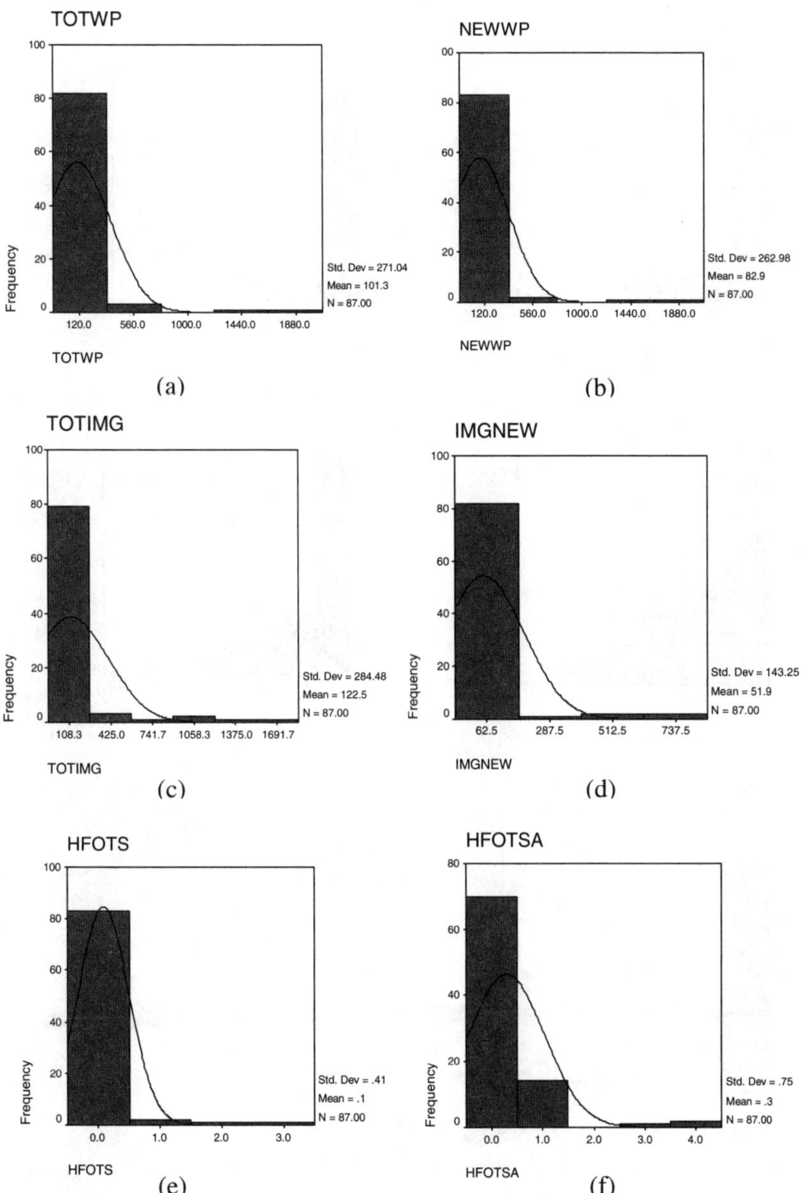
TOTWP
Frequency
Std. Dev = 271.04
Mean = 101.3
N = 87.00
120.0 560.0 1000.0 1440.0 1880.0
TOTWP
(a)
NEWWP
Std. Dev = 262.98
Mean = 82.9
N = 87.00
120.0 560.0 1000.0 1440.0 1880.0
NEWWP
(b)
TOTIMG
Frequency
Std. Dev = 284.48
Mean = 122.5
N = 87.00
108.3 425.0 741.7 1058.3 1375.0 1691.7
TOTIMG
(c)
IMGNEW
Frequency
Std. Dev = 143.25
Mean = 51.9
N = 87.00
62.5 287.5 512.5 737.5
IMGNEW
(d)
HFOTS
Frequency
Std. Dev = .41
Mean = .1
N = 87.00
0.0 1.0 2.0 3.0
HFOTS
(e)
HFOTSA
Frequency
Std. Dev = .75
Mean = .3
N = 87.00
0.0 1.0 2.0 3.0 4.0
HFOTSA
(f)

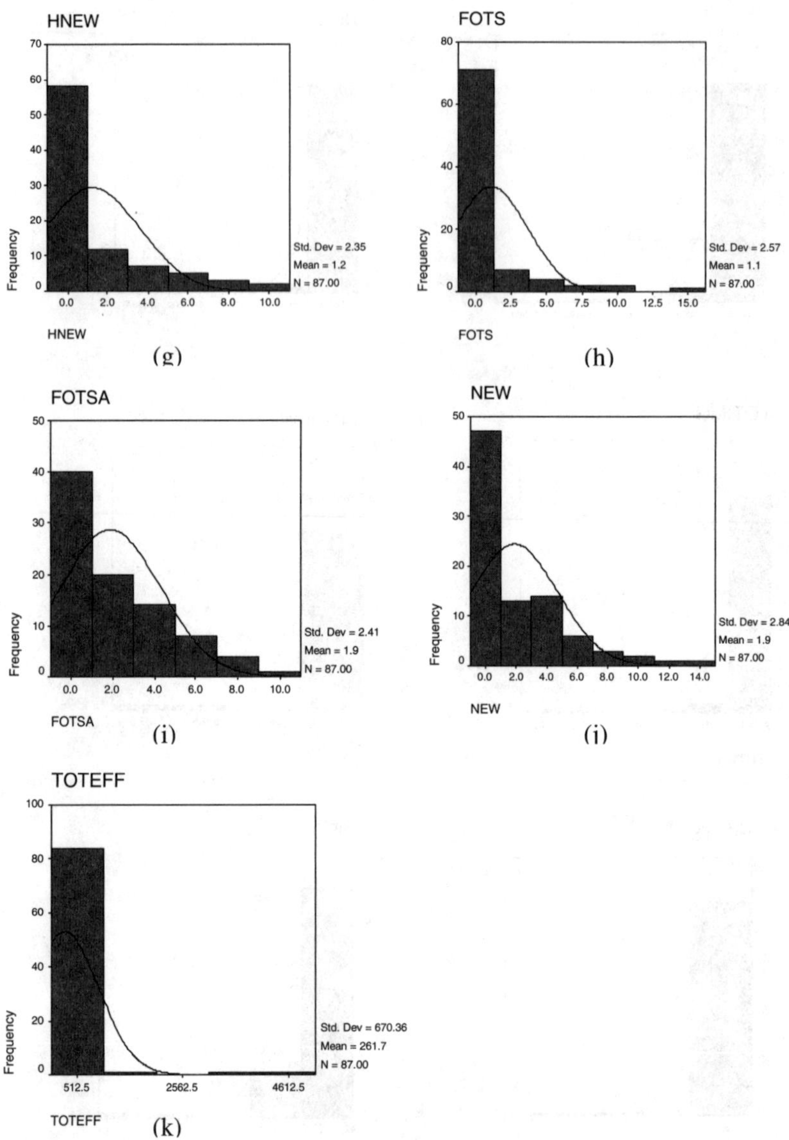

Fig. 3.2. Distribution of values for size and effort variables

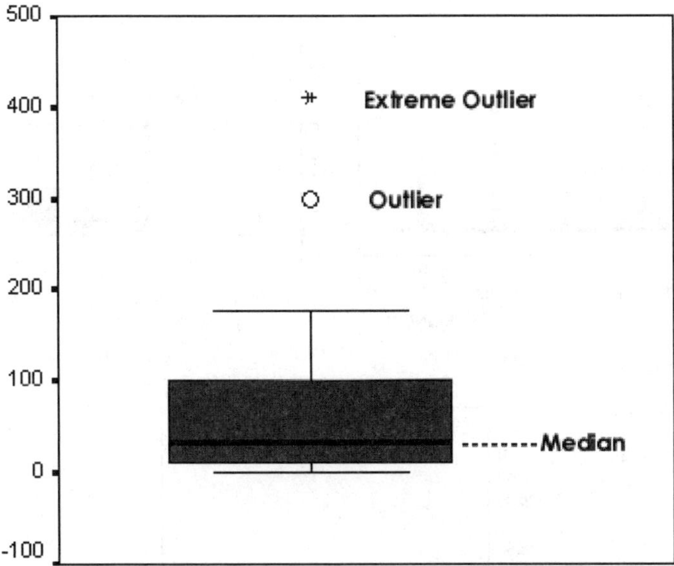

Fig. 3.3. Main components of a boxplot

The boxplots for size and effort measures (see Fig. 3.4) confirm that each variable has a large number of outliers, and a peaked distribution that is not symmetric.

Whenever outliers are present they need to be investigated since they may be a result of data entry error. In our study, we looked at all these cases, in particular in relation to projects that exhibited very large effort values, and did not find anything on the data suggesting that they should be removed from the data set. As we said earlier, whenever there are doubts about the correctness of the data the best solution is to contact the data provider for confirmation. Only if the source is not available should an assessment be based on consistency with other variables.

The histograms and boxplots both show symptoms of skewness and outliers. When this situation arises, it is common practice to normalise the data, i.e. to apply a functional transformation to the data values to make the distribution closer to a normal distribution. A common transformation is to take the natural log (ln), which makes larger values smaller and brings the data values closer to each other [4]. This is the procedure we have adopted, i.e. we created new variables representing the natural log for each of our size and effort variables. Whenever a numerical variable had zero values, we added one to all values before applying the transformation. In the subsequent sections, we refer to logarithmical transformed variables as Lvarname, e.g. LTOTHIGH is the variable obtained by transforming TOTHIGH.

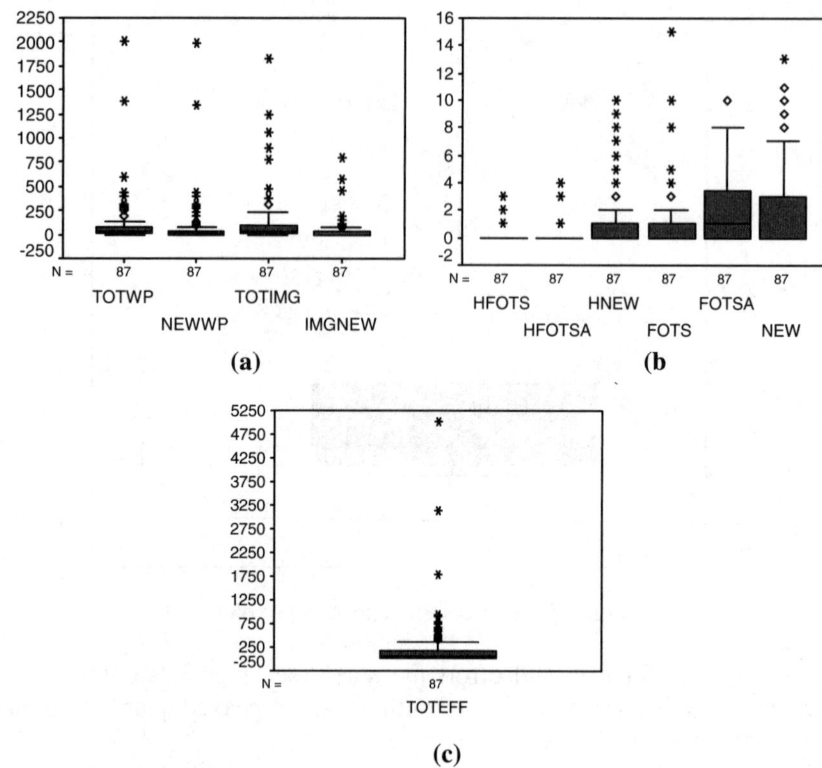

Fig. 3.4. Boxplots for size and effort variables

The Tukutuku database uses six variables to record the number of features/functions for each Web application. Their histograms (see Fig. 3.2(e)–(j)) indicate that each has a large number of zeros. We therefore decided to construct two new variables, one related to high-effort functions/features, the other related to low-effort functions/features: TOTHIGH and TOTNHIGH. TOTHIGH is the sum of HFOTS, HFOTSA and HNEW, and TOTNHIGH is the sum of FOTS, FOTSA and NEW. Their histograms are shown in Fig. 3.5(a)–(b).

Finally, we created two new variables: RWP and RIMG. RWP is the difference between TOTWP and NEWWP, and RIMG is the difference between TOTIMG and IMGNEW. RWP represents the number of reused Web pages and RIMG the number of reused images. The motivation for their creation was twofold: first, to be consistent with the criteria used regarding the features/functions variables; second, to enable us to check the effect of reused Web pages and reused images on total effort. Their histograms are shown in Fig. 3.5(c)–(d). All four new variables were also transformed since they exhibit both skewness and outliers.

It is important to note that creating new variables as linear combinations of existing variables places a constraint on subsequent analyses. One assumption of multiple regression is that there are no linear combinations in the model. This means that we must not attempt to include a constructed variable and all the variables used to construct it in the same model, e.g. we can attempt to include in a model only three of the following four variables: TOTHIGH, HFOTS, HFOSTA and HNEW. In fact, since the variable TOTHIGH was constructed because of problems of multiple zeros, the best approach is to exclude HFOTS, HFOSTA and HNEW from any subsequent analysis.

Our next step is to check if the relationships between the dependent variable (LTOTEFF, the natural logarithm of TOTEFF) and the independent variables are linear. The tool used to check such relationships is a scatter plot.

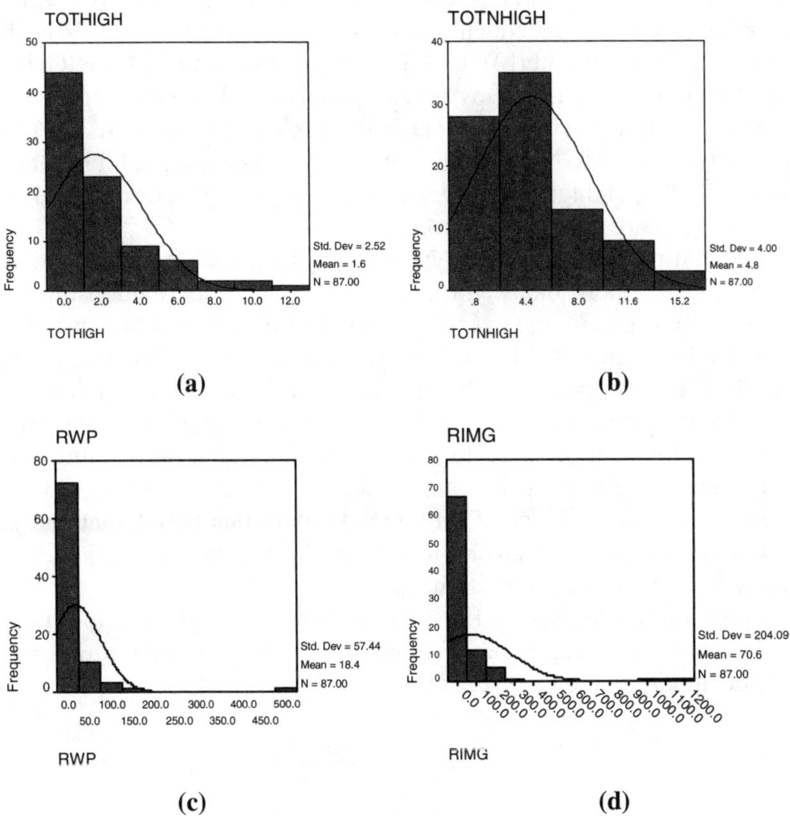

Fig. 3.5. Distribution of values for TOTHIGH, TOTNHIGH, RWP and RIMG

A scatter plot is used to visualise possible relationships between numerical variables. A relationship is said to be positive when values on the y-axis tend to increase with those on the x-axis. When values on the y-axis tend to decrease as those on the x-axis increase the relationship is negative. Adding a simple regression line to a scatter plot helps identify the strength of the relationship between two numerical variables. A strong relationship is represented by observations (data points) all falling very close to the linear trend line.

Scatter plots of LTOTEFF against each of the independent variables are shown in Fig. 3.6. They demonstrate very clearly that zero values are a problem for this data set. Figure 3.6(l) shows a negative trend line between LFOTSA and LTOTEFF. This is counterintuitive in the sense that including more functions that need adaptation (even if the adaptation effort is low) should not reduce total production effort. The effect occurs because the projects with zero values have distorted the underlying relationship. Nonetheless, there are several reasonably strong relationships between LTOTEFF and the independent variables, in particular LTOTWP (Fig. 3.6(a)), LNEWW (Fig. 3.6(b)), LHNEW (Fig. 3.6(i)) and LTOTHIGH (Fig 3.6(j)). Some other relationships appear quite strong but are being distorted by the large number of zeros, in particular LRWP (Fig. 3.6(c)), TOTIMG (Fig. 3.6(d)) and LIMGNEW (Fig. 3.6(e)). Other variables exhibit relationships that look as though they are solely due to multiple zero value distortions, see Fig. 3.6(g) and Fig 3.6(m).

A potential problem with this type of analysis is that the more variables you measure the more likely you are to detect spurious relationships. For this reason, best practice is to include only those variables that are "a priori" plausible predictors. The size measures used in our case study represent early Web size measures obtained from the results of a survey investigation [5], using data from 133 on-line Web forms aimed at giving quotes on Web development projects. In addition, the measures were validated by an established Web company, and a second survey involving 33 Web companies in New Zealand. Consequently it is our belief that the size measures identified are plausible effort predictors, not an ad hoc set of variables with no underlying rationale.

Our preliminary analysis is finished. Now we are ready to build the *AdjustedSize* measure using manual stepwise regression. Assumptions 4 to 7 will be dealt with in the next section.

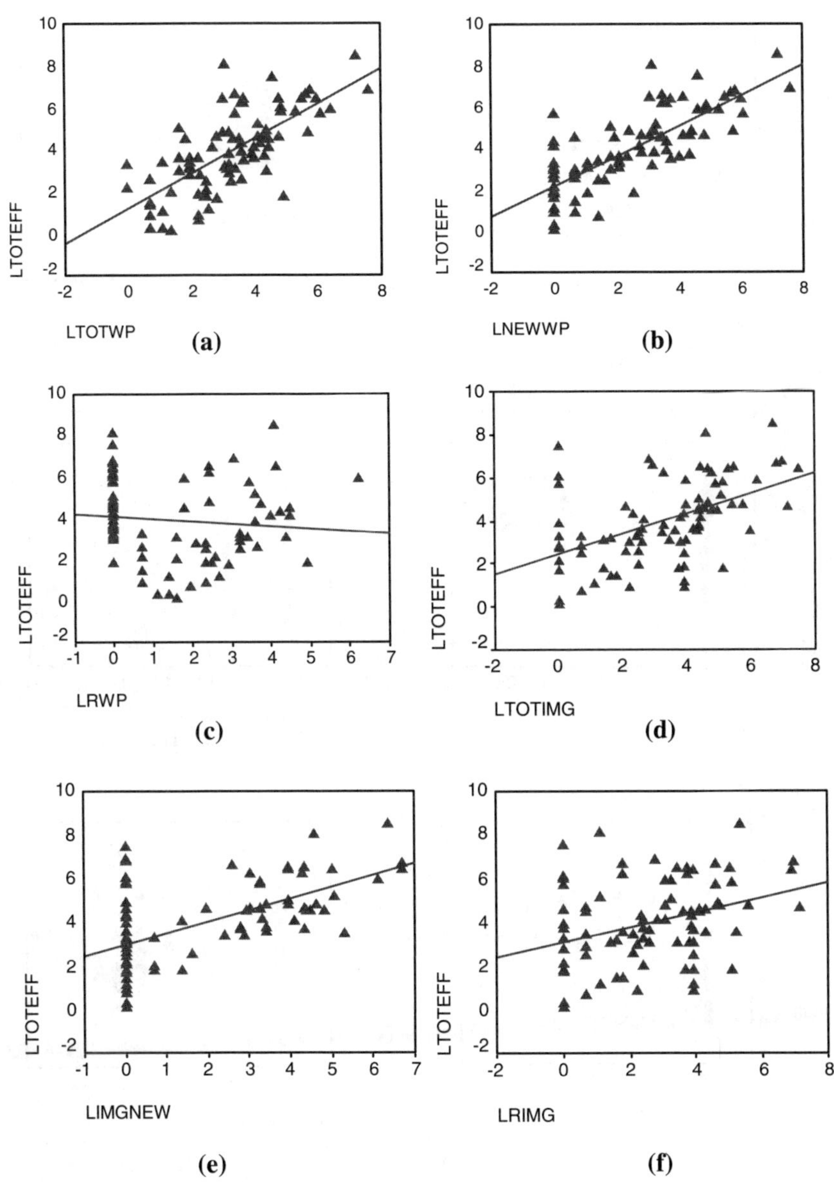
LTOTEFF
LTOTWP
(a)
LNEWWP
(b)
LRWP
(c)
LTOTIMG
(d)
LIMGNEW
(e)
LRIMG
(f)

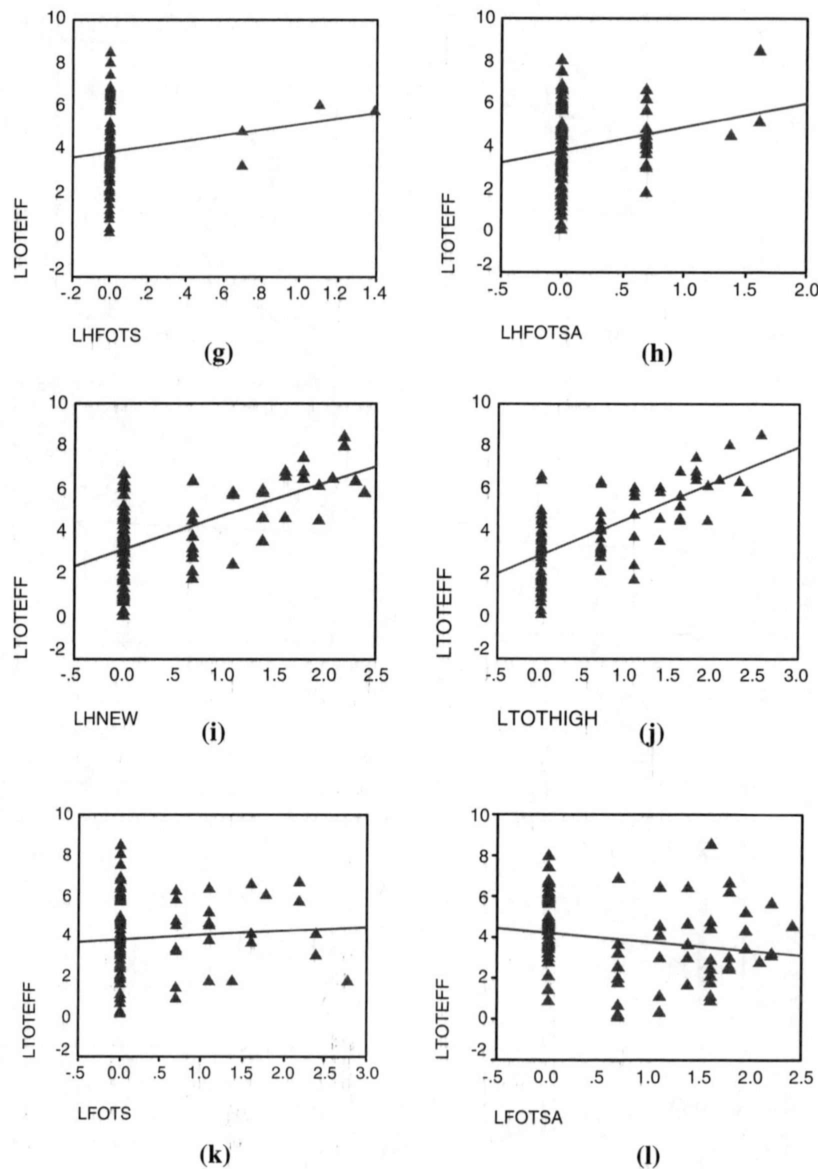

(g) (h) (i) (j) (k) (l)

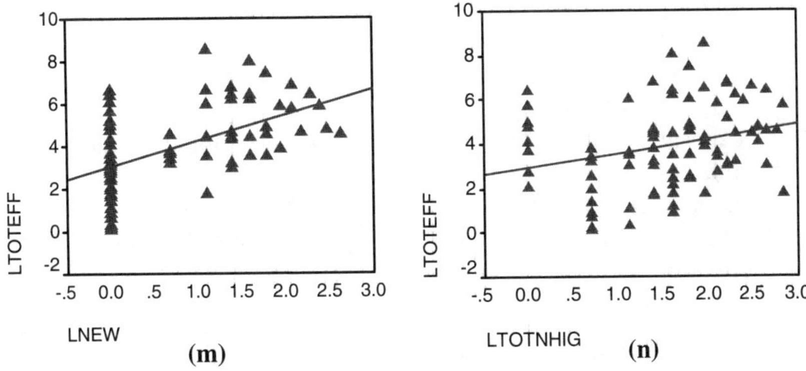

Fig. 3.6. Scatter plots for LTOTEFF versus transformed independent variables

Model Building and Inspection

This section describes the use of a manual stepwise regression based on residuals to build the *AdjustedSize* model. This technique, proposed by Kitchenham [1], enables the use of information on residuals to handle relationships among independent variables. In addition, it only selects the input variables that jointly have a statistically significant effect on the dependent variable, thus avoiding any multi-collinearity problems.

The input variables to use are those selected as a result of our preliminary analyses, which are: LTOTWP, LNEWWP, LRWP, LTOTIMG, LIMGNEW, LRIMG, LHFOTS, LHFOTSA, LHNEW, LTOTHIGH, LFOTS, LFOTSA, LNEW, and LTOTNHIG.

The manual stepwise technique comprises the following steps:

Step 1. Construct the single variable regression equation with effort as the dependent variable using the most highly (and significantly) correlated input variable (IV1).
Step 2. Calculate the residuals (Res1).
Step 3. Correlate the residuals with all the other input variables.
Step 4. Any input variables that were initially significantly correlated with effort but are not significantly correlated with the residual are significantly correlated with IV1 and offer no additional information about the dependent variable. They can therefore be eliminated from the stepwise regression.
Step 5. Construct a single variable regression with the residuals (Res1) as the dependent variable and the variable (IV2), of the remaining input variables, that is most highly (and significantly) correlated with Res1.
Step 6. Calculate residuals Res2.

Step 7. Correlate the residuals Res2 with the remaining input variables. Any variables that were correlated with Res1 in step 5 but are not correlated with Res2 are eliminated from the analysis. They are variables that are highly correlated with IV2.

Step 8. Continue in this way until there are no more input variables available for inclusion in the model or none of the remaining variables are significantly correlated with the current residuals.

Step 9. The simplest way to construct the full regression model is then to use simple multivariate regression with only the selected input variables.

We also need to verify the stability of the regression model. This involves identifying large residual and high-influence data points (i.e. projects), and also checking whether residuals are homoscedastic and normally distributed. Several types of plots (e.g. residual, leverage, probability) and statistics are available in most statistics tools to accomplish such task. The ones we have employed here, which are available in SPSS v10.1.3, are:

- A residual plot showing residuals vs. fitted values to investigate if the residuals are random and normally distributed. The plotted data points should be distributed randomly about zero. They should not exhibit patterns such as linear or non-linear trends, or increasing or decreasing variance.
- A normal P–P plot (probability plots) for the residuals. Normal P–P plots are generally employed to verify whether the distribution of a variable is consistent with the normal distribution. If the distribution is Normal, the data points are close to linear.
- Cook's D statistic to identify projects that exhibited jointly a large influence and large residual [4]. Any projects with D greater than $4/n$, where n represents the total number of projects, are considered to have high influence on the results. When there are high-influence projects the stability of the model needs to be tested by removing these projects, and observing the effect their removal has on the model. If the coefficients remain stable and the adjusted R^2 increases, this indicates that the high-influence projects are not destabilising the model and therefore do not need to be removed.

LNEWWP is the most highly and significantly correlated variable with LTOTEFF, therefore it is the first input variable to be selected. The single variable regression equation, with LTOTEFF as the dependent/response variable and LNEWWP as the independent/predictor variable, gives an adjusted R^2 of 0.597 (see Table 3.3). Two projects are identified with Cook's D > 0.045, but their removal did not seem to destabilise the model, i.e. after their removal the coefficients remained stable and the adjusted R^2

increased. Furthermore, there was no indication from the residual and P–P plots that the residuals were non-normal.

The correlation between the residual and the remaining input variables reveals that LTOTWP, LRIMG and LNEW are no longer significantly correlated with the residual, therefore they are eliminated from the stepwise procedure. Since we have a linear relationship among the variables RWP, TOTWP and NEWWP, it is appropriate that LTOTWP is removed from the list of candidate variables once LNEWWP is selected.

Once this step is finished the remaining input variables are LRWP, LTOTIMG, LIMGNEW, LHFOTS, LHFOTSA, LHNEW, LTOTHIGH, LFOTS, LFOTSA and LTOTNHIG.

The next highly and significantly correlated variable with the residual is LTOTHIGH. The single variable regression equation, with the residual as the dependent/response variable and LTOTHIGH as the independent/predictor variable, gives an adjusted R^2 of 0.228 (see Table 3.3). This time five projects are identified with Cook's D > 0.045, but their removal did not destabilise the model. In addition, the residual and P–P plots found no evidence of non-normality. The correlation between the residual and the remaining input variables reveals that LRWP, LTOTIMG, LIMGNEW, LHFOTS, LHFOTSA, LHNEW and LTOTNHIG are no longer significantly correlated with the residual, therefore they are eliminated from the stepwise procedure. Again, since we have a relationship among the variables, TOTHIGH, HFOTS, HFOTSA and HNEW, after selecting LTOTHIGH, it is appropriate that LFOTS, LFOTSA and LHNEW are all removed from the list of candidate variables.

Neither of the two remaining variables, LFOTS and LFOTSA, are significantly correlated with the current residuals, therefore the procedure finishes.

Finally, our last step is to construct the *AdjustedSize* model using a multivariate regression analysis with only the input variables selected using the manual stepwise procedure. The coefficients for the *AdjustedSize* model are presented in Table 3.4. Its adjusted R^2 is 0.717 suggesting that LNEWWP and LTOTHIGH can explain 72% of the variation in LTOTEFF.

Table 3.3. Summary of the manual stepwise procedure

Variable	Effect	Adj. R^2	Comments
LNEWWP	+	0.597	Variables removed after correlation with residuals: LTOTWP, LRIMG, LNEW
LTOTHIGH	+	0.228	Variables removed after correlation with residuals: LRWP, LTOTIMG, LIMGNEW, LHFOTS, LHFOTSA, LHNEW and LTOTNHIG

Table 3.4. Coefficients for the *AdjustedSize* model

Variable	Coeff.	Std. error	t	P>|t|	[95% conf. interval]	
(Constant)	1.959	0.172	11.355	0.000	1.616	2.302
LNEWWP	0.553	0.061	9.003	0.000	0.431	0.675
LTOTHIGH	1.001	0.164	6.095	0.000	0.675	1.328

Four projects had Cook's D > 0.045 (see Table 3.5), therefore we followed the procedure adopted previously. We repeated the regression analysis after excluding these four projects from the data set. Their removal did not result in any major changes to the model coefficients and the adjusted R^2 improved (0.757). Therefore, we assume that the regression equation is reasonably stable for this data set, and it is not necessary to omit these four projects from the data set.

Table 3.5. Four projects that presented high Cook's distance

ID	NEWWP	TOTHIGH	TOTEFF	Cook's D
20	20	0	625	0.073
25	0	4	300	0.138
32	22	8	3150	0.116
45	280	0	800	0.078

Figure 3.7 shows three different plots all related to residuals. The histogram (see Fig. 3.7(a)) suggests that the residuals are normally distributed, corroborated by the P–P plot (see Fig. 3.7(b)). In addition, the scatter plot of standardised residuals versus standardised predicted values does not show any problematic patterns in the data.

Once the residuals and the stability of the regression model have been checked, we are in a position to extract the equation that represents the model.

However, before continuing, it is necessary to consider whether the accuracy of the multiple regression model is good enough to be the basis of a subsequent productivity analysis. This is not a simple case of statistical significance. It is possible to have a statistically significant equation that accounts for such a small amount of the variation in the data that further analysis would be valueless. However, there is no clear guideline on how accurate the model needs to be. Our model has an R^2 value of 0.72; is this good enough? In our opinion, models need to account for at least 70% of the variation before it can be considered viable for subsequent productivity analysis. However, it is also important to consider the size of the data set. We are more likely to detect spurious results with a large number of variables and a small number of data points. As a rule of thumb, in addition to achieving an R^2 value of more than 0.7, the basic data set should

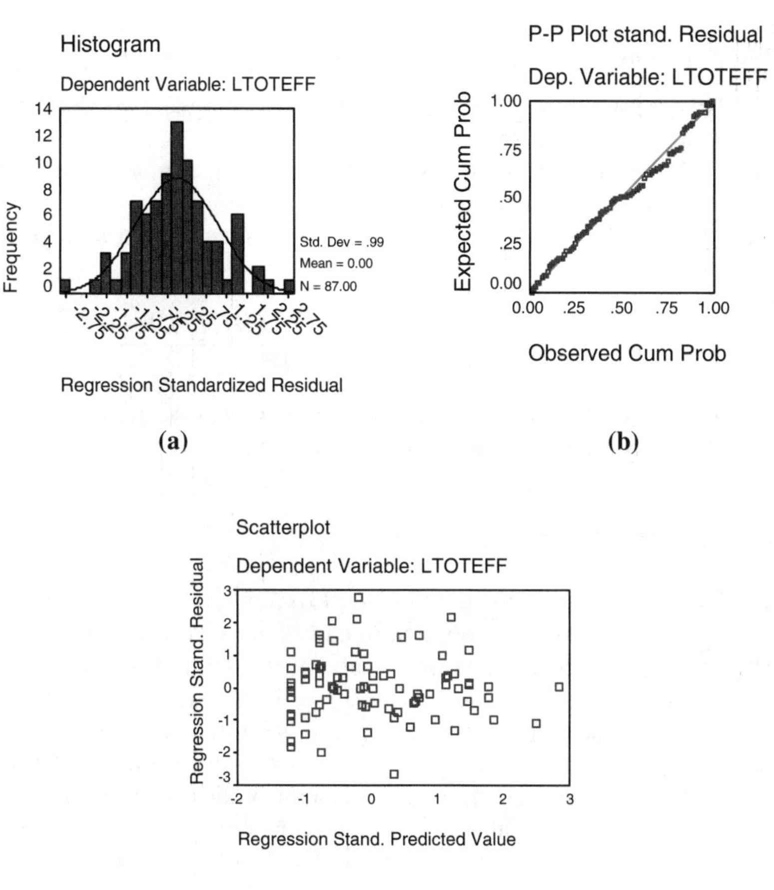

(a) (b)

(c)

Fig. 3.7. Several residual plots

include more than 30 data points per independent variable before the model is used for further analysis.[8] Thus, our model is on the borderline for use in a productivity analysis and we need to treat any results with caution.

Extraction of AdjustedSize Equation

The equation that is obtained from Table 3.4 is the following:

$$LTOTEFF = 1.959 + 0.553LNEWWP + 1.001LTOTHIGH \tag{3.3}$$

[8] This is an area where simulation studies are needed to provide evidence-based guidelines.

This equation uses three variables that had been previously transformed, therefore we need to transform it back to its original state, which gives the following equation:

$$TOTEFF = 7.092\,(NEWWP + 1)^{0.553}\,(TOTHIGH + 1)^{1.001} \tag{3.4}$$

In Eq. 3.4, the multiplicative value 7.092 can be interpreted as the effort required to develop one Web page.

Treating Eq. 3.4 as an *AdjustedSize* function, we can construct a productivity measure:

$$Productivity = \frac{7.092\,(NEWWP + 1)^{0.553}\,(TOTHIGH + 1)^{1.001}}{TOTEFF} \tag{3.5}$$

Once the productivity measure has been constructed we are able to carry out a productivity analysis as explained in the next section

3.3.2 Productivity Analysis

The productivity values constructed using Eq. 3.5 varied from a minimum of 0.06 to a maximum of 14.66. The mean value was 1.61, the standard deviation was 2, and the median was 1. The distribution of the productivity values is shown in Fig. 3.8 using boxplots (see Fig. 3.8(a)) and a histogram (see Fig. 3.8(b)). The histogram shows that 45% of the productivity values are between 0.5 and 1.5, representing a range of values similar to the baseline of 1. The boxplots also show a number of outliers, which may be an indication of productivity values significantly different from one.

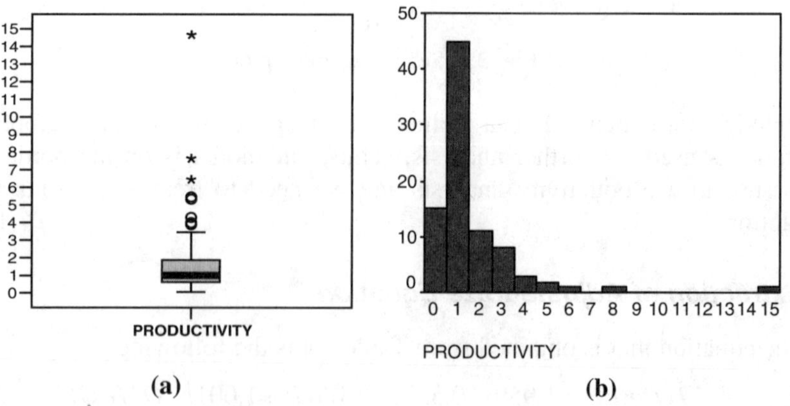

Fig. 3.8. Distribution of productivity values

The mechanism used to check the existence of productivity values significantly different from one is to use the upper and lower bounds of the *AdjustedSize* model to construct upper and lower bounds for the productivity values. The steps employed to obtain these upper and lower bounds are the following:

Step 1. During the construction of the *AdjustedSize* model using a multivariate regression analysis also obtain the prediction intervals for each individual value of the *AdjustedSize* measure, for a corresponding effort. SPSS creates two new variables (LICI_1 and UICI_1), each with 87 values.

Step 2. The variables LICI_1 and UICI_1 have lower and upper values for a predicted value LTOTEFF, therefore we need to transform them back to the raw data scale by creating two new variables:

$$\text{LICI\_1\_new} = e^{\text{LICI\_1}} \tag{3.6}$$

$$\text{UICI\_1\_new} = e^{\text{UICI\_1}} \tag{3.7}$$

Step 3. Finally, divide the upper and lower bounds by total effort to get the upper and lower productivity bounds, i.e. LICI_1_new/TOTEFF and UICI_1_new/TOTEFF. This gives the upper and lower bounds for the productivity value.

Once these bounds are obtained, the next step is to check whether there are any productivity values either smaller than their lower bound or greater than their upper bound. Figure 3.9 shows a line chart with lines representing values for productivity (PRODUCTI), lower productivity bound (LOWER)

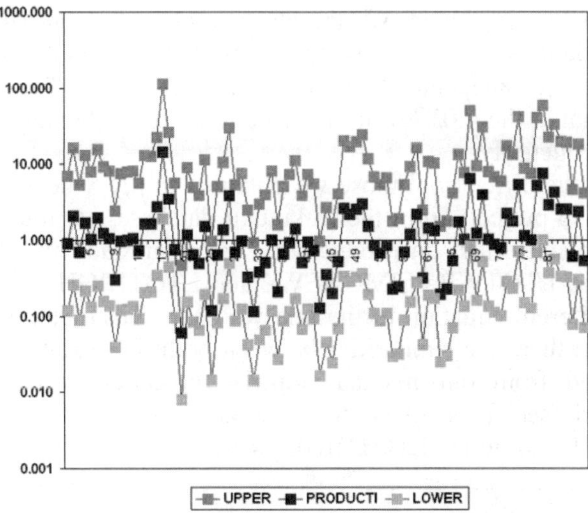

Fig. 3.9. Productivity values and their corresponding lower and upper bounds

and upper productivity bound (UPPER). We used a logarithmic scale to display the (Y) axis values to illustrate better that productivity values, represented by black squares, consistently remain in between their lower and upper bounds, represented by light grey and grey squares, respectively. This means that we did not find any productivity values significantly different from one.

After calculating suitable productivity values for each of the 87 Web projects, we can carry out standard productivity analyses. The issues to be investigated as part of this case study are:

Issue #1. The impact of reuse of Web pages on productivity.
Issue #2. The impact of team size on productivity.
Issue #3. The impact of number of programming languages on productivity.
Issue #4. The impact of average team experience with the programming languages on productivity.

The Impact of Reuse of Web Pages on Productivity

We created a dummy variable to differentiate between projects that reused Web pages and those that did not. Then we investigated the productivity differences between the two groups of projects. The mean and median productivity for the 48 projects that reused Web pages are 1.79 and 1.2, respectively. The remaining 39 projects have mean and median of 1.4 and 0.92, respectively.

Figure 3.10 shows boxplots of the productivity distribution for each group. Both distributions are not symmetric and exhibit outliers. Since none of these distributions are normally distributed, we have to compare their productivity values using a statistical test that does not assume the data is normally distributed. We therefore employed a non-parametric test called the Mann–Whitney U test to assess if the difference between the two groups (two independent samples) was significant. The results were not significant at the 0.05 level, therefore reuse is not having a significant effect on productivity.

These results differ from those we obtained in [2], where, using a subset of 54 Web projects from the Tukutuku database, we found that reuse had a significant effect on productivity. For that study the *AdjustedSize* equation used LTOTWP,[9] LIMGNEW[10] and LTOTHIGH as its variables. This is a different equation to the one we have constructed in this chapter; however, there are similarities between both. For example, LTOTWP was removed from our manual stepwise procedure when LNEWWP was selected (see Table 3.3), thus showing that it is a surrogate for LNEWWP. In addition, LTOTHIGH is present in both equations. The

[9] ln(TOTWP).

[10] ln(IMGNEW +1).

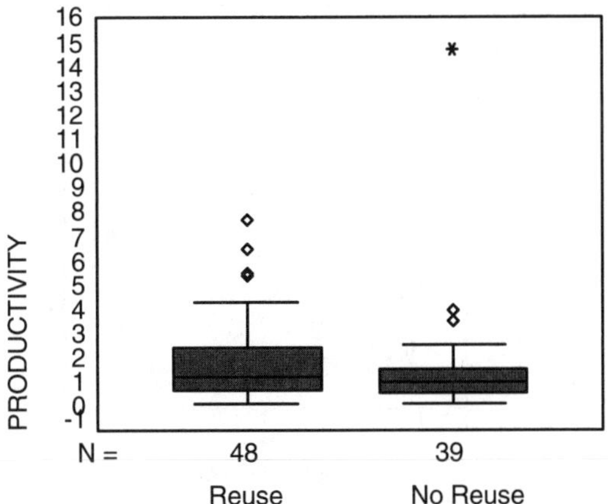

Fig. 3.10. Boxplots of the productivity of projects that reused Web pages and those that did not

best fitting equations are likely to change when more data is gathered. However, the similarities between both equations suggest that they are capturing a genuine underlying phenomenon. Whenever that is the case, some variables are included in most equations, and surrogate variables are selected in different equations. Note that, despite the similarity between both equations, the productivity measures obtained and the corresponding productivity analyses carried out are dependent on the data set employed.

The Impact of Team Size on Productivity

We created a dummy variable to differentiate between the seven team-size values we observed in the data set. Next, we investigated the productivity differences between the projects in each of the seven groups. Figure 3.11 shows boxplots of the productivity distribution for each group. Except for one, all remaining distributions are not symmetric and three exhibit outliers.

In order to compare their productivity values, we used the Kruskal-Wallis test. This is a non-parametric test that allows more than two groups to be compared. The Kruskal-Wallis test suggests that productivity is significantly different between groups (chi-squared = 14.82 with 6 degrees of freedom, $p = 0.022$).

The boxplots suggest that projects with a team size of 1 person presented the best productivity overall, with the median productivity above the baseline of 1.

In addition to using boxplots, we also used a scatter plot to further investigate the relationship between productivity and team size. Figure 3.12(a) shows a scatter plot of productivity and team size, which suggests a linear relationship.

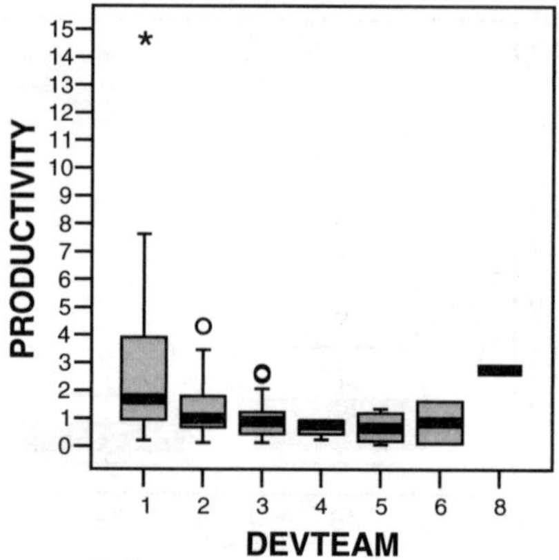

Fig. 3.11. Boxplots of productivity for different team sizes

Since both productivity and team size are skewed and present outliers, they were transformed. Figure 3.12(b) shows the scatter plot for the transformed variables. Both scatter plots indicate that, as productivity values decrease, team size increases, which represents a relationship that is negatively associated.

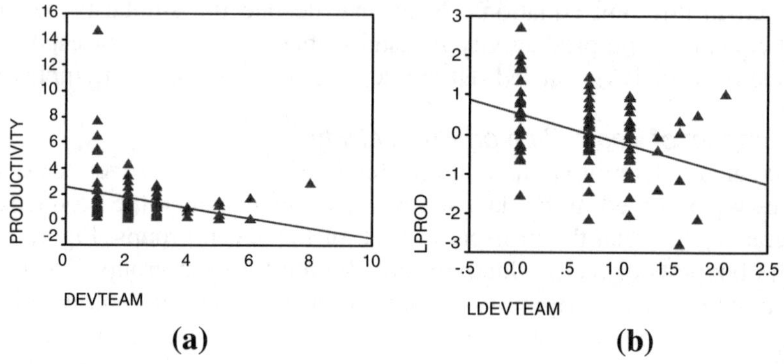

Fig. 3.12. Scatter plots of productivity and team size before and after transforming variables

We performed a linear regression analysis using LPROD as the dependent variable and LDEVTEAM as the independent variable (see Table 3.6). This analysis confirms that there is a statistically significant negative relationship between productivity and team size.[11] This means that productivity

[11] Kitchenham and Mendes 2 demonstrate that LPROD is mathematically equivalent to using the residual values of the original regression model (multiplied by –1).

decreases as team size increases. These results are supported by another study, where, using data from European space and military projects, Briand et al. [1] provide evidence that smaller teams result in substantially higher productivity.

Table 3.6. Coefficients for productivity model based on team size

Variable	Coeff.	Std. Error	t	P>|t|	[95% conf. interval]	
(Constant)	0.512	0.166	3.094	0.003	0.183	0.841
LDEVTEAM	-0.716	0.185	-3.878	0.000	-1.083	-0.349

The Impact of Number of Programming Languages on Productivity

We created a dummy variable to differentiate between the seven different values for number of programming languages. Next, we investigated the productivity differences between these seven groups. Figure 3.13 shows boxplots of the productivity distribution for each group.

None of the distributions are symmetric and three exhibit outliers. In order to compare their productivity values we used the Kruskal–Wallis test, which suggests that productivity is significantly different between groups (chi-squared = 86 with 6 degrees of freedom, $p < 0.01$).

Boxplots for projects that used six languages presented the highest median, suggesting they were the most productive overall. However, since this group contains only three projects, these results must be interpreted with caution. The group that used seven languages also presented a median above the baseline, but it only contained a single project.

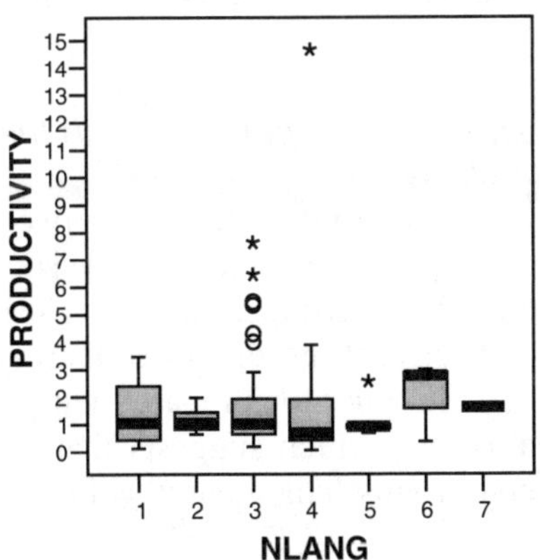

Fig. 3.13. Boxplots of productivity for different number of languages

In addition to using boxplots we also used scatter plots to further investigate the relationship between productivity and number of languages. Figure 3.14(a) shows a scatter plot of productivity and number of languages, which does not suggest a strong linear pattern.

Since both productivity and number of languages are skewed and present outliers they were transformed. Figure 3.14(b) shows the scatter plot for the transformed variables.

None of the scatter plots indicate a significant linear relationship between productivity and number of languages. Linear regression analysis with LPROD as the dependent variable and LNLANG as the independent variable confirms that there is no significant linear relationship between LPROD and LNLANG.

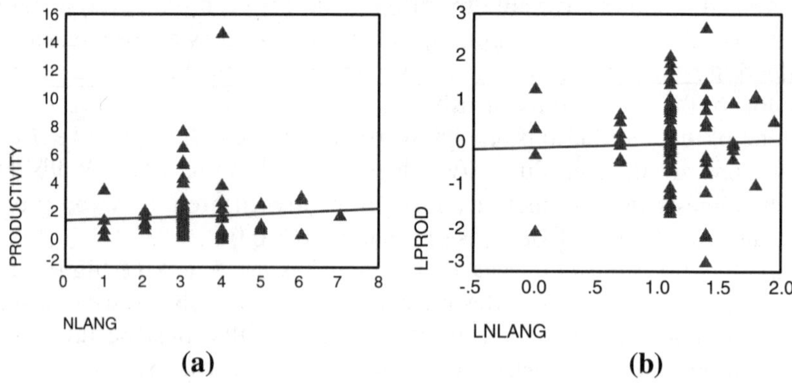

Fig. 3.14. Scatter plots of productivity and team size before and after transforming variables

The Impact of Average Team Experience with the Programming Languages on Productivity

We created a dummy variable to differentiate between the eight different values for average team experience. Next, we investigated the productivity differences between these eight groups. Figure 3.15 shows boxplots of the productivity distribution for each group. Two distributions are symmetric and three exhibit outliers. In order to compare their productivity values we used the Kruskal–Wallis test, which suggests that productivity is significantly different between groups (chi-squared = 86 with 7 degrees of freedom, $p < 0.01$).

Boxplots suggest that two groups, with average team experience of 1 and 10, respectively, are very productive with all, or nearly all, of their data points above the baseline. However, both groups contain only two projects each, therefore these results must be interpreted with care. Two

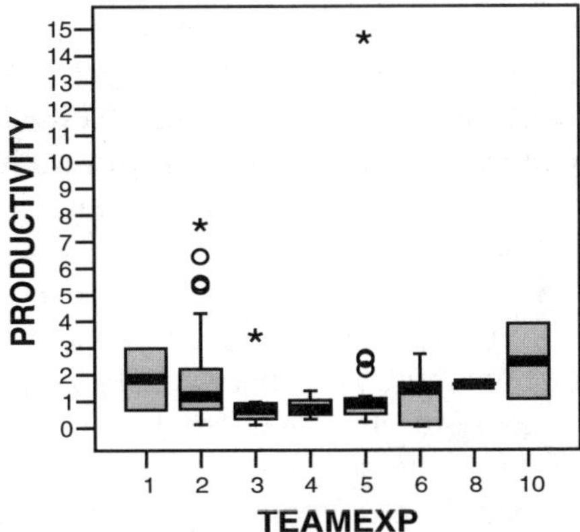

Fig. 3.15. Boxplots of productivity for different average team experiences

other groups, with average team experience of 2 and 6, respectively, also seem to contain productive projects, with a median productivity greater than the productivity baseline. In addition, they contain at least six projects each, which may indicate a more reliable pattern than that provided by the two "very productive" groups.

In addition to using boxplots, we also used a scatter plot to further investigate the relationship between productivity and average team experience. Figure 3.16(a) shows a scatter plot of productivity and average team experience, which does not suggest any linear relationship.

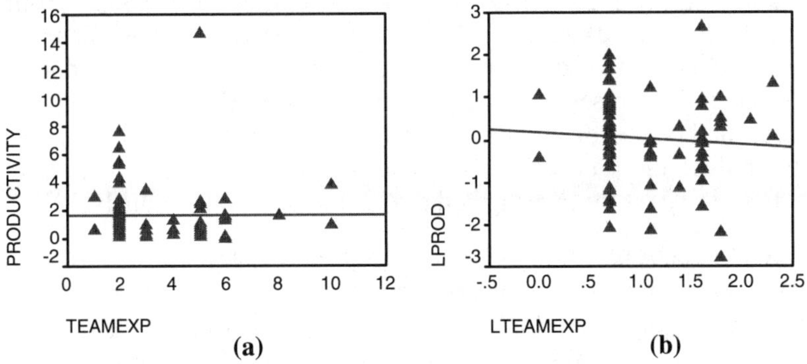

Fig. 3.16. Scatter plots of productivity and average team experience before and after transforming variables

Since both productivity and average team experience are skewed and present outliers, they were transformed. Figure 3.16(b) shows the scatter plot for the transformed variables, which suggests a weak negative association between LPROD and LTEAMEXP. However, regression analysis confirmed that there is no statistically significant relationship between LPROD and LTEAMEXP.

The data set used in this case study comprises data on projects volunteered by individual companies. It was not a random sample of projects from a defined population; thus, we *cannot* conclude that the results of our productivity analysis apply to other Web application projects [2]. The results apply to the specific data set under analysis and may not be stable when more data is added. For example, a previous analysis of a smaller subset of 54 projects from the Tukutuku data set observed a significant reuse effect that is not found in the current data set [2].

3.4 Conclusions

This chapter presented a productivity measurement method, which allows for the use of different size measures. An advantage of the method is that it has a built-in interpretation scale. It ensures that each project has an expected productivity value of one. We have presented a software productivity measure that can be used when there are several size measures jointly significantly related to effort. Such a productivity measure is easy to construct from a regression-based effort estimation model, and it is simple to interpret. In addition, it has a built-in baseline. A value greater than one is a sign of good productivity, and a value less than one is a sign of poor productivity.

We have also presented a case study that used the productivity measurement method to construct a productivity measure, and used this measure to analyse the productivity of Web projects from the Tukutuku database. Four issues were investigated during the productivity analysis:

- The impact of reuse of Web pages on productivity.
- The impact of team size on productivity.
- The impact of number of programming languages on productivity.
- The impact of average team experience with the programming languages on productivity.

Results showed that reuse of Web pages had no impact on productivity, and that different team sizes, number of programming languages and average team experiences could each present significant productivity differences among projects. However, we cannot generalise these results to other Web projects and companies since the data set used is not a random sample from a defined population [2]. Therefore the productivity measure is applicable only to projects belonging to the data set based upon which it was constructed.

References

1 Briand LC, El Emam K, Wieczorek I (1999) Explaining the Cost of European Space and Military Projects. In: Proceedings of the ICSE 99 Conference, May. Los Angeles, CA, pp 303–312

2 Kitchenham BA (1998) A Procedure for Analyzing Unbalanced datasets. IEEE Transactions on Software Engineering, 24(4):278–301

3 Kitchenham BA, Mendes E (2004) Software Productivity Measurement Using Multiple Size Measures. IEEE Transactions on Software Engineering, 30(12):1023–1035

4 Kitchenham BA, MacDonell SG, Pickard LM, Shepperd MJ (2001) What Accuracy Statistics Really Measure. IEE Proceedings Software, June, 148(3):81–85

5 Maxwell K (2002) Applied Statistics for Software Managers. Prentice Hall PTR

6 Mendes E, Mosley N, Counsell S (2003) Investigating Early Web Size Measures for Web Cost Estimation. In: Proceedings of the EASE'2003 Conference, Keele, UK, pp 1–22

Acknowledgements

We would like to thank Associate Professor Guilherme Travassos for his comments on a previous version of this chapter.

Authors' Biographies

Dr. **Emilia Mendes** is a Senior Lecturer in Computer Science at the University of Auckland (New Zealand), where she leads the WETA (Web Engineering, Technology and Applications) research group. She is the principal investigator in the Tukutuku Research project,[12] aimed at developing and comparing Web effort models using industrial Web project data, and benchmarking productivity within and across Web companies. She has active research interests in Web measurement and metrics, and in particular Web cost estimation, Web size measures, Web productivity and quality measurement, and Web process improvement. Dr. Mendes is on the programme committee of numerous international conferences and workshops, and on the editorial board of the International Journal of Web Engineering

[12] http://www.cs.auckland.ac.nz/tukutuku/.

and Technology and the Journal of Web Engineering. She has collaborated with Web companies in New Zealand and overseas on Web cost estimation and usability measurement. Dr. Mendes worked in the software industry for ten years before obtaining her PhD in Computer Science from the University of Southampton (UK), and moving to Auckland. She is a member of the Australian Software Measurement Association.

Barbara Kitchenham is Professor of Quantitative Software Engineering at Keele University and currently has a part-time position as a Senior Principal Researcher with National ICT Australia (NICTA). She has worked in software engineering for over 20 years in both industry and academia. Her main research interest is software metrics and its application to project management, quality control, risk management and evaluation of software technologies. She is particularly interested in the limitations of technology and the practical problems associated with applying measurement technologies and experimental methods to software engineering. She is a Chartered Mathematician and Fellow of the Institute of Mathematics and Its Applications. She is also a Fellow of the Royal Statistical Society. She is a visiting professor at both the University of Bournemouth and the University of Ulster.

4 Web Quality

Luis Olsina, Guillermo Covella, Gustavo Rossi

Abstract: In this chapter we analyse the different quality perspectives of software and Web applications. In particular, we review quality taking into account the ISO (International Organization for Standardization) standards for software product, and discuss the distinction between quality and quality in use, and how different requirements, from different users' standpoints, should be considered as well. Moreover, we also describe Web quality and how it can be measured and evaluated. In order to illustrate the specific procedures and processes of an inspection evaluation methodology, a case study on the external quality of the shopping cart component of two typical e-commerce Web applications is presented.

Keywords: Web quality, quality measurement, Logic Scoring Preference.

4.1 Introduction

The quality of an entity is easy to recognise but hard to define and evaluate. Although the term seems intuitively self-explanatory, there are actually many different perspectives and approaches to measure and evaluate quality as part of a software or Web development, operation, and maintenance processes.

The meaning of quality is not simple and atomic, but a multidimensional and abstract concept. Common practice assesses quality by means of the quantification of lower abstraction concepts, such as attributes of entities. The attribute can be briefly defined as a measurable property of an entity.[1] An entity may have many attributes, though only some of them may be of interest to a given project's measurement and evaluation purposes. Therefore, quality is an abstract relationship between attributes of entities and information needs (measurement goals).[2] Figure 4.1 specifies some of these terms and their relationships.

To illustrate these concepts let us consider the following example. One of the goal's of an organisation's project, within a quality assurance plan, is to "*evaluate the link reliability of a Web application's static pages*". The

---

[1] Types of entities of interest to software and Web engineering are resource, process, product, product in use, and service.

[2] In fact, quality, quality in use, cost, etc., are instances of a computable concept.

purpose is to *evaluate* the *link reliability* calculable concept for *static Web pages* as the product entity, from a user's viewpoint; we can see that the link reliability sub-concept is a sub-characteristic related to the external quality of a product. Considering the level of abstraction, a calculable concept can be composed of other sub-concepts that may be represented by a concept model (e.g. ISO 9126-1 [13]specifies the external quality model based on characteristics and sub-characteristics). A calculable concept combines one or more attributes of entities. Figure 4.2 shows a simple concept model where three attributes are part of the *link reliability* calculable concept.

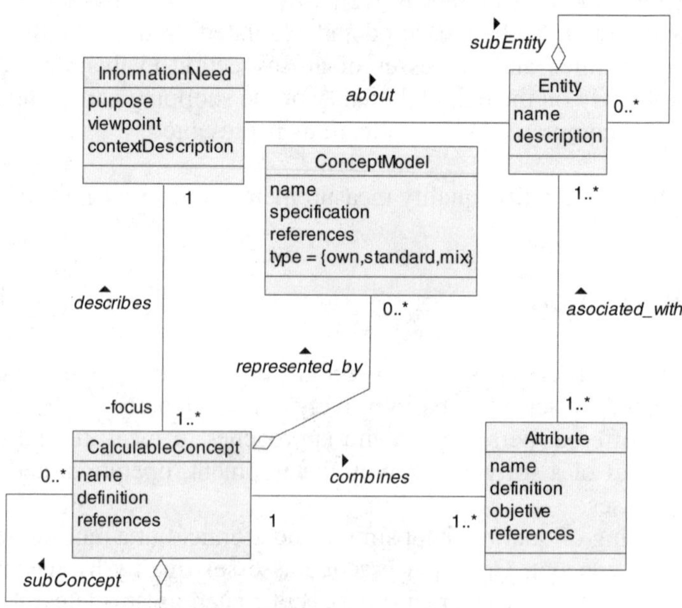

Fig. 4.1. Main terms and relationships related with the calculable concept term where quality or quality in use are instances of it

1. Link Reliability
   1.1 Internal Broken Links (IBL)
   1.2 External Broken Links (EBL)
   1.3 Invalid Links (IL)

Fig. 4.2. A concept model for the link reliability calculable concept

On the other hand, each attribute can be quantified by one or more metrics.[3] The metric contains the definition of the selected measurement method and scale (the conceptual model of metrics and indicators are introduced in Sect. 4.3.2).

The previous example, which does not include other external quality subconcepts, such as efficiency, functionality, and usability, is intended to show that the meaning of quality is not atomic but rather a complex, multidimensional concept. Quality cannot be measured directly, at least not in a trivial and subjective way. On the other hand, the requirements for quality can vary depending on the entity type, user's viewpoint, and context of use. Regarding the entity type (e.g. process, product), quality requirements specified as quality models can differ from one another. Moreover, we can specify different requirements, from different users' standpoints, for the same entity type. In addition, the quality perception for the same software or Web product can vary depending on contexts of use for the same user type!

In Sect. 4.2, we discuss the different perspectives of quality for software. In particular, in Sect. 4.2.1 we review the state of the art of quality according to the ISO standards for software quality; we also address the importance of distinguishing between quality and quality in use (see Sect. 4.2.2); and how different requirements, from diverse users' standpoints, should be considered (see Sect. 4.2.3).

The next section describes Web quality, focusing on the quality of Web products and the perceived quality of real users in a real context of use.

Nowadays, the Web plays a central role in diverse application domains such as business, education, government, industry, and entertainment. The Web's growing importance heightens concerns about Web applications' development and evaluation methods, and requires the systematic use of engineering models, methods, and tools. In particular, we need sound evaluation methods for obtaining reliable information about product quality and quality in use. There are different categories of methods (e.g. inspection, testing, inquiry, simulation) and specific types of evaluation methods and techniques (e.g. heuristic evaluation technique [19,20], the concept model-centred evaluation method [24]). In Sect. 4.3 we present the Web Quality Evaluation Method (WebQEM) as a model-centred evaluation method. Using WebQEM to assess Web applications helps to meet quality requirements in new Web development projects and to evaluate requirements in operational phases. It also helps discover absent attributes or poorly implemented requirements, such as interface-related designs, and implementation drawbacks or problems with navigation, accessibility, search mechanisms, content, reliability and performance, among others.

3 Metric and measure mean the same within the context of this book.

Section 4.4 presents a case study where the external quality of the shopping cart component of two typical e-commerce Web applications is assessed, using the specific models, procedures, and processes of the WebQEM methodology. In Sect. 4.5 concluding remarks to this chapter are drawn.

4.2 Different Perspectives of Quality

The essential purpose-oriented evaluation of quality characteristics and attributes for different entities is not an easy endeavour in either software or Web engineering [18]. It is difficult to consider all the characteristics and mandatory or desirable attributes of a process, or a product (e.g. Web application), without using sound quality frameworks, models, and methods. These allow evaluators to specify systematically goal-oriented quality concepts, sub-concepts, and attributes. An example of a generic quality model is provided by the ISO standards for specifying quality requirements in the form of quality models to software processes and products.

As previously mentioned, quality requirements can vary depending on the entity type, the users' viewpoint, and the context of use. From a software measurement and evaluation point of view, we can identify different entity types at a high level of abstraction, i.e. a resource, a process, a product, a service, a product or a system in use, as well as a software or Web project. Quality requirements can be specified using a concept model representing quality or quality in use. Studies have shown that resource quality can potentially help improve process quality; process quality can help improve product quality, which can help improve quality in use [13]. In the same way, evaluating quality in use can provide feedback to improve product quality; evaluating a product can provide feedback to improve process quality; and evaluating a process can provide feedback to improve resource quality (see Fig. 4.3).

Within the context of this chapter we focus on product quality and quality in use.

4.2.1 Standards and Quality

One standardisation milestone of the software product quality for assessment purposes occurred at the end of 1991, when ISO/IEC issued the quality model and the evaluation process model [9]. Previously, seminal work defined software quality models and frameworks; among these were the quality models specified by McCall, Boehm, and the US Air Force (see [9]). The aim of the ISO/IEC organisation was to reach the required consensus and to encourage international agreement.

The ISO/IEC 9126 standard prescribes six characteristics (sub-concepts) that describe, with minimal overlap, software quality. In addition, it presents a set of quality sub-characteristics for each characteristic. As it also specifies an evaluation process model, the two inputs to the quality requirement definition step are the ISO quality model and stated or implied user needs.

The quality definition in this standard is "*The totality of features and characteristics of a software product that bears on its ability to satisfy stated or implied needs*" ([9]this definition is adopted from the previous ISO 8402 standard entitled "*Quality – Vocabulary*" issued in 1986). The six prescribed characteristics useful to evaluate product quality are *Usability*, *Functionality*, *Reliability*, *Efficiency*, *Portability*, and *Maintainability*. For instance, *Usability* is defined as "*A set of attributes that bear on the effort needed for use, and on the individual assessment of such use, by a stated or implied set of users.*" In turn, usability is broken down into three sub-characteristics, namely: *Understandability*, *Learnability*, and *Operability* (e.g. operability is defined as "*Attributes of software that bear on the users' effort for operation and operation control*").

Other aspects of this standard are as follows:

- The meaning of quality is taken as a complex, multidimensional concept that cannot be measured directly.
- Given the complexity that the quality concept embraces, a quality model to specify software product quality requirements is needed.
- The general-purpose quality model contains a minimum number of characteristics by which every type of software can be evaluated.
- For the quality requirement definition step, the stated or implied user needs are considered. In addition, the term user is acknowledged in some definitions of characteristics and sub-characteristics (e.g. usability and its sub-characteristics).
- ISO 9126 differs from traditional quality approaches that emphasise the need to meet requirements that are primarily functional (e.g. the manufacturing quality approach of ISO 9000).

As observed above, the ISO 9126 definitions acknowledge that the goal of quality is to meet user needs. But what is not clearly stated is that the purpose of software quality is to be "perceived with quality": that is, with degrees of excellence by end users in actual contexts of use. Rather, ISO 9126 suggests that quality is determined by the presence or absence of the attributes, with the implication that these are specific attributes which can be designed into the product. As Bevan [2]says:

> *"Although developers would like to know what attributes to incorporate in the code to reduce the 'effort required for use', presence or absence of predefined attributes cannot assure usability, as there is no reliable way to predict the behaviour of the users of the final product."*

To fill this gap, the ISO 9126 standard has been revised to specify a quality framework that distinguishes among three different approaches to software quality – internal quality, external quality, and quality in use. The ISO/IEC 9126-1 standard, which includes these three approaches to quality, was officially issued in 2001 [13]. The evaluation process model initially included in ISO 9126 was moved to and fully developed in the ISO/IEC 14598 series [11,12]. The three approaches of quality in ISO 9126-1 can be summarised as follows:

- *Internal quality*, which is specified by a quality model (similar to the ISO 9126 model), and can be measured and evaluated by static attributes of documents such as specification of requirements, architecture, or design; pieces of source code; and so forth. In early phases of a software lifecycle, we can evaluate and control the internal quality of these early products, but assuring internal quality is not usually sufficient to assure external quality.
- *External quality*, which is specified by a quality model (similar to the ISO 9126 model), and can be measured and evaluated by dynamic properties of the running code in a computer system, i.e. when the module or full application is executed in a computer or network simulating as close as possible the actual environment. In late phases of a software lifecycle (mainly in different kinds of testing, or even in the acceptance testing, or furthermore in the operational state of a software or Web application), we can measure, evaluate, and control the external quality of these late products, but assuring external quality is not usually sufficient to assure quality in use.
- *Quality in use*, which is specified by a quality model (similar to the ISO 9241-11 model [10]), and can be measured and evaluated by the extent to which the software or Web application meets specific user needs in the actual, specific context of use.

The internal quality definition in ISO 9126-1 is *"the totality of attributes of a product that determines its ability to satisfy stated and implied needs when used under specified conditions"*; the external quality definition is *"the extent to which a product satisfies stated and implied needs when used under specified conditions"*; and the quality in use definition is *"the extent to which a product used by specified users meets their needs to achieve specified goals with effectiveness, productivity and satisfaction in specified context of use*" (note that these definitions are in the ISO/IEC 14598-1 standard [12])

These three slightly different definitions of quality (instead of the unique definition in the previous 9126 standard) refer particularly to the product when it is used under specified conditions and context of use, so making it clear that quality is not an absolute concept, but depends on specific conditions and context of use by specific users.

The same six prescribed quality characteristics have been maintained in the revised internal and external quality models. Moreover, sub-characteristics are now prescriptive. Besides, new sub-characteristics were added and redefined in terms of "*the capability of the software*" to enable them to be interpreted as either an internal or an external perspective of quality. For instance, usability characteristic is defined in [13]as "*The capability of the software product to be understood, learned, used and attractive to the user, when used under specified conditions.*" In turn, usability is subdivided into five sub-characteristics, namely: *Understandability*, *Learnability*, *and Operability*, in addition to *Attractiveness* and *Usability compliance* (see Table 4.1 for the definition of these sub-characteristics).

Table 4.1. Definition of usability sub-characteristics prescribed in ISO 9126-1 [13]for internal and external quality

Sub-characteristic	Definition
Understandability	The capability of the software product to enable the user to understand whether the software is suitable, and how it can be used for particular tasks and conditions of use.
Learnability	The capability of the software product to enable the user to learn its application.
Operability	The capability of the software product to enable the user to operate and control it.
Attractiveness	The capability of the software product to be attractive to the user.
Compliance	The capability of the software product to adhere to standards, conventions, style guides or regulations relating to usability.

External quality is ultimately the result of the combined behaviour of the software component or application and the computer system, while quality in use is the effectiveness, productivity, safety, and satisfaction of specific users when performing representative tasks in a specific, realistic working environment. By measuring and evaluating the quality in use (by means of metrics and indicators) the external quality of the software or Web application can be validated. Quality in use evaluates the degree of excellence, and can be used to validate the extent to which the software or

Web application meets specific user needs. In turn, by measuring and evaluating external quality, a software product's internal quality can be validated. Similarly, taking into account suitable software/Web application attributes for internal quality is a prerequisite to achieve the required external behaviour, and to consider suitable software attributes to external behaviour is a prerequisite to achieve quality in use (this dependency is suggested in Fig. 4.3).

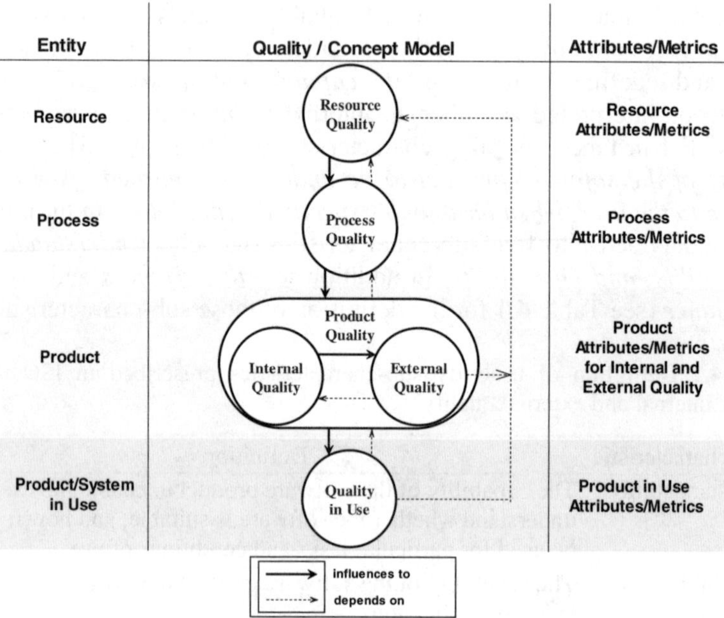

Fig. 4.3. Framework of quality regarding different entity types and potential quality models

The basic example introduced in Figure 4.2 focuses on external quality because we cannot measure such application attributes (i.e. IBL, EBL, IL) without Web server and network infrastructure support.

4.2.2 Quality Versus Quality in Use

While users are becoming more and more mature in the use of IT systems and tools, there is greater demand for the quality of software and Web applications that match real user needs in actual working environments.

The core aim in designing an interactive (software or Web) application is to meet the user needs; that is, to provide degrees of excellence or quality in use by interacting with the application and by performing its tasks comfortably. Within the context of the ISO 9126-1 standard, quality in use is the end user's view of the quality of a running system containing software, and is measured and evaluated in terms of the result of using the software, rather than by properties of the software itself. A software product's internal and external quality attributes are the cause, and quality in use attributes are the effect. According to Bevan [2]:

> *"Quality in use is (or at least should be) the objective, software product quality is the means of achieving it."*

Quality in use is a broader view of the ergonomic concept of usability as for ISO 9241-11 [10]. Quality in use is the combined effect of the internal and external quality characteristics for the end user. It can be measured and evaluated by the extent to which specified users can achieve specified goals with effectiveness, productivity, safety, and satisfaction in specified contexts of use. Table 4.2 shows the definition of these four characteristics, and Fig. 4.4 outlines a partial view of the quality in use (concept) model and associated attributes.

Table 4.2. Definition of the four quality in use characteristics prescribed in ISO 9126-1

Characteristic	Definition
Effectiveness	The capability of the software product to enable users to achieve specified goals with accuracy and completeness in a specified context of use.
Productivity	The capability of the software product to enable users to expend appropriate amounts of resources in relation to the effectiveness achieved in a specified context of use.
Safety	The capability of the software product to achieve acceptable levels of risk of harm to people, business, software, property or the environment in a specified context of use.
Satisfaction	The capability of the software product to satisfy users in a specified context of use. Note [by ISO]. Satisfaction is the user's response to interaction with the product, and includes attitudes towards use of the product.

In order to design and select metrics (and indicators) for assessing quality in use it is first necessary to associate attributes to the effectiveness, productivity, safety, and satisfaction characteristics. Figure 4.4 shows attributes for two characteristics, namely effectiveness and productivity.

Quality in Use
1. Effectiveness
   1.1 *Task Effectiveness* (TE)
   1.2 *Task Completeness* (TC)
   1.3 *Error Frequency* (EF)
2. Productivity
   2.1 *Efficiency related to Task Effectiveness* (ETE)
   2.2 *Efficiency related to Task Completeness* (ETC)

Fig. 4.4. Specifying an instance of the Quality in Use model

Note that effectiveness, productivity, safety, and satisfaction are influenced not only by the usability, functionality, reliability, and efficiency of a software product, but also by two resource components of the context of use. The context of use depends on both the infrastructure (i.e. the computer, network, or even the physical working medium) and the user-oriented goals (i.e. the supported application tasks and the properties of the user type such as level of training, expertise, and cultural issues as well). Care should be taken when generalising the results of any quality in use assessment to another context of use with different types of users, tasks, or environments [2].

As a consequence, when designing and documenting quality in use measurement and evaluation processes, at least the following information is needed:

- Descriptions of the components of the context of use, including user type, equipment, environment, and application tasks (tasks are the steps or sub-goals undertaken to reach an intended goal).
- Quality in use metrics and indicators for the intended purpose and measurement goal(s).

As a final remark, it can be observed that quality is not an absolute concept; there are different quality perspectives both to a product and to a product in a context of use. Internal quality, external quality, and quality in use can then be specified, measured and evaluated. Each of these perspectives has its own added value considering a quality assurance strategy in the overall lifecycle. However, the final objective is the quality in use. How a concept model (quality, quality in use) can be instantiated for different user standpoints is discussed next.

4.2.3 Quality and User Standpoints

In a measurement and evaluation process, the quality requirements specified in the form of a quality model should be agreed upon. The quality model can be a standard-based quality model, a project or organisation's proprietary quality model, or a mixture of both.

Depending on the goal and scope of the evaluation, the concept model and corresponding characteristics and attributes that might intervene should be selected. Moreover, the importance of each characteristic varies depending on the application's type and domain, in addition to the user standpoint taken into account. Therefore, the relative importance of characteristics, sub-characteristics, and attributes depends on the evaluation's goal and scope, the application domain, and the user's viewpoint.

When designing an evaluation process, the assessment purpose and scope may be manifold. For instance, the purpose can be to understand the external quality of a whole software application or one of its components; we might want to predict the external quality by assessing the internal quality of a software specification, or to improve the quality in use of a shopping cart component, or to understand and compare the external quality of two typical e-commerce Web applications to incorporate the best features in a new development project. On the other hand, the type of applications can be at least categorised as mission-critical, or non-mission-critical, and the domain can be diverse (e.g. avionics, e-commerce, e-learning, information-oriented Web applications).

Lastly, the user standpoint for evaluation purposes can be categorised as one of an acquirer, a developer, a maintainer, a manager, or a final (end) user. In turn, a final user can, for instance, be divided into a novice user or an expert user. Thus, final users are mainly interested in using the software or Web application, i.e. they are interested in the effects of the software rather than in knowing the internal aspects of the source code or its maintainability. For this reason, when the external quality requirements are, for example, defined from the end user's standpoint, generally usability, functionality, reliability, and efficiency are the most important. Instead, from the maintainer's viewpoint, analysability, changeability, stability, and testability of application modules are the most important.

As a final comment, we would like to draw the reader's attention to the conceptual model shown in Fig. 4.1. That basic model is a key piece of a set of tools we are currently building for measurement and evaluation projects. Given an *entity* (e.g. e-learning components to support course tasks), it allows us to specify an evaluation *information need:* that is to say, the *purpose* (e.g. understand), the *user viewpoint* (e.g. a novice student), in a given *context* of use (e.g. the software is installed in the engineering school server as support to a preparatory mathematics course for pre-enrolled students, etc.), with the *focus* on a *calculable concept* (quality in use) and *sub-concepts* (effectiveness, productivity, and satisfaction), which can be *represented by* a *concept model* (e.g. the ISO quality in use model) and associated *attributes* (as shown in Fig. 4.4).

The next section describes Web quality. The main focus is on the quality of Web products and the perceived quality of real users in a real context of use.

4.2.4 What is Web Quality?

According to Powell [26]Web applications "*involve a mixture between print publishing and software development, between marketing and computing, between internal communications and external relations, and between art and technology*".

Nowadays, there is a greater awareness and acknowledgement in the scientific and professional communities about the multidimensional nature of Web applications; it encompasses technical computing, information architecture, contents authoring, navigation, presentation and aesthetic, multiplicity of user audiences, legal and ethical issues, network performance and security, and heterogeneous operational environments.

As pointed out in Chap. 1, Web applications, taken as product, or product in use entities (without talking about distinctive features of Web development processes), have their own features, distinct from traditional software [18,26], namely:

- Web applications will continue to be content-driven and document-oriented. Most Web applications, besides the increasing support to functionalities and services, will continue aiming at showing and delivering information. This is a basic feature stemming from the early Web that is currently empowered by the Semantic Web initiative [4].
- Web applications are interactive, user-centred, hypermedia-based applications, where the user interface plays a central role; thus, Web applications will continue to be highly focused on the look and feel. Web interfaces might be easy to use, understand, and operate because thousand of users with different profiles and capabilities interact with them daily.
- The Web embodies a greater bond between art and science than that encountered in software applications. Aesthetic and visual features of Web development are not just a technical skill, but also a creative, artistic skill.
- Internationalisation and accessibility of content for users with various disabilities are real and challenging issues in Web applications.
- Searching and browsing are two basic functionalities used to find and explore documents and information content. These capabilities are inherited from hypermedia-based applications.

- Security is a central issue in transaction-oriented Web applications. Likewise, performance is also critical for many Web applications, although both are also critical features for traditional applications.
- The entire Web application, and its parts, are often evolutionary pieces of information.
- The medium where Web applications are hosted and delivered, is generally more unpredictable than the medium where traditional software applications run. For instance, unpredictability in bandwidth maintenance, or in server availability, can affect the perceived quality that users could have.
- Content privacy and intellectual property rights of materials are current issues too. They involve ethic, cultural, and legal aspects as well. Most of the time it is very difficult to establish legal boundaries due to the heterogeneity of legislation in different countries, or even worse, the absence of them.

Most of the above features make a Web application a particular artefact. However, like a software application, it also involves source and executable code, persistent structured data, and requirements, architecture, design, and testing specifications as well.

Therefore, we argue that the ISO quality framework introduced in previous sections is also applicable to a great extent to intermediate and final lifecycle Web products. A discussion of this statement follows, as well as how we could adapt specific particularities of Web quality requirements into quality models.

Like any software line production, the Web lifecycle involves different stages of its products, whether in early phases as inception and development, or in late phases as deployment, operation, and evolution. To assure the quality of products, we can plan to do it by evaluating and controlling the quality from intermediate products to final products. Thus, if we can apply to the general question the same ISO internal and external quality, and quality in use models, the natural answer is *yes* – we believe this does not need further explanation. However, to the more specific question of whether we can use the same six prescribed quality characteristics for internal and external quality, and the four characteristics for quality in use, our answer is *yes* for the latter, but some other considerations might be taken into account for the former.

In particular, as highlighted at the beginning of this section, the very nature of Web applications is a mixture of information (media) content, functionalities, and services. We argue that the six quality characteristics (i.e. *Usability*, *Functionality*, *Reliability*, *Efficiency*, *Portability*, and *Maintainability*) are not well suited (or they were not intended) to specify requirements for information quality. As Nielsen [19] writes regarding

Web content for informational Web applications: "*Ultimately, users visit your Web site for its contents. Everything else is just the backdrop.*" Hence, to follow the thread of our argument, the central issue is how we can specify and gauge the quality of Web information content from the internal and external quality perspectives.

Taking into account some contributions made in the area of information quality [1,7,8,15,17] we have primarily identified four major sub-concepts for the *Content* characteristic. The following categories can help to evaluate information quality requirements of Web applications:

- *Information accuracy.* This sub-characteristic addresses the very intrinsic nature of the information quality. It assumes that information has its own quality *per se*. Accuracy is the extent to which information is correct, unambiguous, authoritative (reputable), objective, and verifiable. If a particular piece of information is believed to be inaccurate, the Web site will likely be perceived as having little added value and will result in reduced visits.
- *Information suitability.* This sub-characteristic addresses the contextual nature of the information quality. It emphasises the importance of conveying the appropriate information for user-oriented goals and tasks. In other words, it highlights the quality requirement that content must be considered within the context of use and the intended audience. Therefore, suitability is the extent to which information is appropriate (appropriate coverage for the target audience), complete (relevant amount), concise (shorter is better), and current.
- *Accessibility.* This emphasises the importance of technical aspects of Web sites and applications in order to make Web content more accessible for users with various disabilities (see, for instance, the WAI initiative [27]).
- *Legal compliance.* This concerns the capability of the information product to adhere to standards, conventions, and legal norms related to contents and intellectual property rights.

Besides the above categories, sub-concepts of information structure and organisation should be addressed. Many of these sub-characteristics, such as global understandability,[4] learnability, and even internationalisation, can be related to the *Usability* characteristic.

On the other hand, other particular features of Web applications, such as search and navigation functionalities, can be specified in the *Functionality* sub-characteristics (e.g. are the basic and advanced searches suitable for

[4] implemented by mechanisms that help to understand quickly the structure and contents of the information space of a Web site like a table of contents, indexes, or a site map.

the end user, o are they tolerant of mis-spelled words and accurate in retrieving documents?). In the same way, we can represent link and page maturity attributes, or attributes to deficiencies due to browsers' compatibility, in the *Reliability* sub-characteristics.

As a consequence, in order to represent software and Web applications, quality information requirements accordingly, we propose to include the *Content* characteristic in the internal and external quality model of the ISO standard. A point worth mentioning is that in the spirit of the ISO 9126-1 standard it is stated that "*evaluating product quality in practice requires characteristics beyond the set at hand*"; and as far as the requirements for choosing the prescribed characteristics, an ISO excerpt recommended "*To form a set of not more than six to eight characteristics for reasons of clarity and handling*."

Finally, from the "quality in use" perspective, for the *Satisfaction* characteristic, specific items for evaluating the quality of content as well as items for navigation, aesthetics, functions, etc., can be included. In addition, for other quality in use characteristics such as *Effectiveness* and *Productivity*, specific user-oriented evaluation tasks that include performing actions with content and functions can be designed and tested.

4.3 Evaluating Web Quality using WebQEM

As introduced in Sect. 4.1, the Web currently plays a central role in diverse application domains for various types of organisations and even in the personal life of individuals. Its growing importance heightens concerns about Web processes being used for the development, maintenance, and evolution of Web applications, and about the evaluation methods being used for assuring Web quality, and ultimately argues for the systematic use of engineering models, methods, and tools. Therefore, we need sound evaluation methods that support efforts to meet quality requirements in new Web development projects and assess quality requirements in operational and evolutionary phases. It is true that one size does not fit all the needs and preferences, but an organisation might at least adopt a method or technique in order to judge the state of its quality, for improvement purposes. We argue that a method or technique is usually not enough to assess different information needs for diverse evaluation purposes.

In this section we present the Web Quality Evaluation Method (WebQEM) [24] as a model-centred evaluation method for the inspection category; that is, inspection of concepts, sub-concepts, and attributes stemming from a quality or quality in use model. We have used the WebQEM methodology since the late 1990s. The underlying WebQEM strategy is evaluator-driven by domain experts rather than user-driven; quantitative and model-centred rather than qualitative and intuition-centred; and objective rather than subjective. Of course, a global quality evaluation (and eventual comparison), where many characteristics and attributes, metrics, and indicators intervene, cannot entirely avoid subjectivity. Next, a robust and flexible evaluation methodology must properly aggregate subjective and objective components controlled by experts.

The WebQEM process steps are grouped into four major technical phases that are now further described:

1. Quality Requirements Definition and Specification.
2. Elementary Measurement and Evaluation (both Design and Implementation Stages).
3. Global Evaluation (both Design and Implementation Stages).
4. Conclusion and Recommendations.

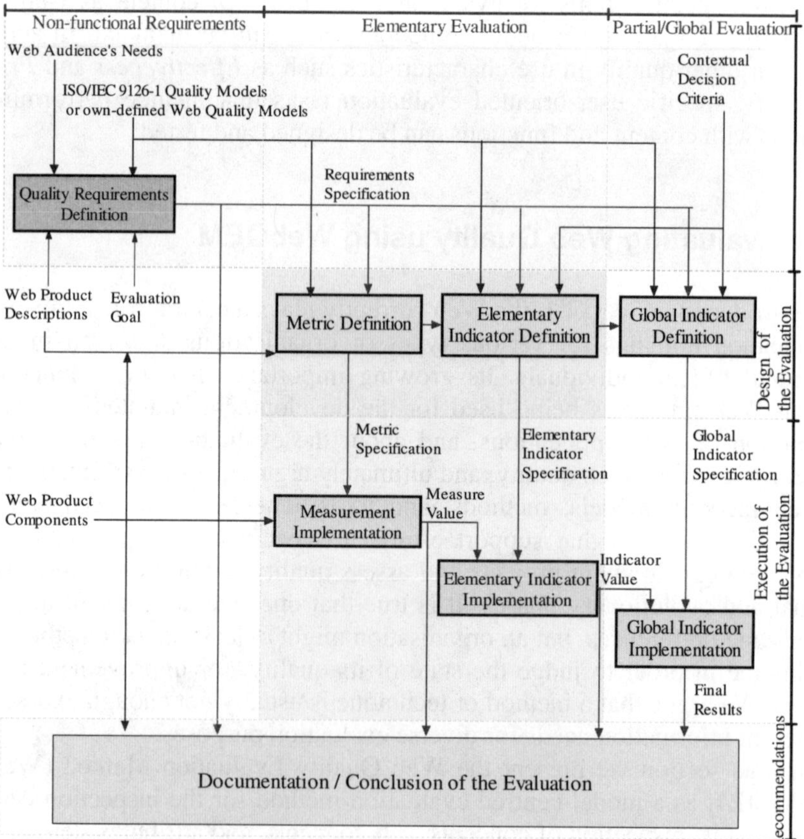

Fig. 4.5. The evaluation processes underlying the WebQEM methodology. The technical phases, main processes, and their inputs and outputs are represented

Figure 4.5 shows the evaluation process underlying the methodology, including the phases, main processes, inputs, and outputs. This model follows to some extent the ISO's process model for evaluators [11]. Next we give an overview of the major technical phases, and some used models.

4.3.1 Quality Requirements Definition and Specification

During the definition and specification of quality requirements, evaluators clarify the evaluation goals and the intended user's viewpoint. They select a quality model, for instance the ISO-prescribed characteristics, in addition to attributes customised to the Web domain. Next, they identify these components' relative importance to the intended audience and the extent of coverage required.

Once the domain and product descriptions, the agreed goals, and the selected user view (i.e. the explicit and implicit user needs) are defined, the necessary characteristics, sub-characteristics, and attributes can be specified in a quality requirement tree (such as that shown in Figs. 4.5 and 4.9). This phase yields a quality requirement specification document.

4.3.2 Elementary Measurement and Evaluation

The elementary measurement and evaluation phase defines two major stages (see Fig. 4.5): elementary evaluation design and execution (implementation). Regarding the elementary evaluation design, we further identify two main processes: (a) *metric definition* and (b) *elementary indicator definition.*

In our previous work [16,25], we have represented the conceptual domain of metrics and indicators from an ontological viewpoint. The conceptual framework of metrics and indicators, which was based as much as possible on the concepts of various ISO standards [12,14], can be useful to support different quality assurance processes, methods, and tools. That is the case for the WebQEM methodology and its supporting tool (WebQEM_Tool [23]), which are based on this framework.

As shown in Fig. 4.6, each attribute can be quantified by one or more metrics. For *the metric definition process* we should select just a metric for each attribute of the quality requirement tree, given a specific measurement project.

The metric contains the definition of the selected measurement and/or calculation method and scale. The metric m represents the mapping m: $A \rightarrow X$, where A is an empirical attribute of an entity (the empirical world), X the variable to which categorical or numerical values can be assigned (the formal world), and the arrow denotes a mapping. In order to perform this mapping a sound and precise definition of measurement activity is needed by specifying explicitly the metric's method and scale (see Fig. 4.6). We can apply an objective or subjective measurement method for direct metrics, and we can perform a calculation method for indirect metrics; that is, when an equation intervenes.

To illustrate this, we examine the following direct metrics, taken from the example shown in Fig. 4.2:

1) *Internal Broken Links Count* (#IBL, for short),
2) *External Broken Links Count* (#EBL), and
3) *Invalid Links Count* (#IL).

In case we need a ratio or percentage, with regard to the *Total of Links Count* (#TL), the next indirect metrics can be defined:

4) %IBL = (#IBL / #TL) * 100, and so forth to
5) %EBL; and
6) %IL.

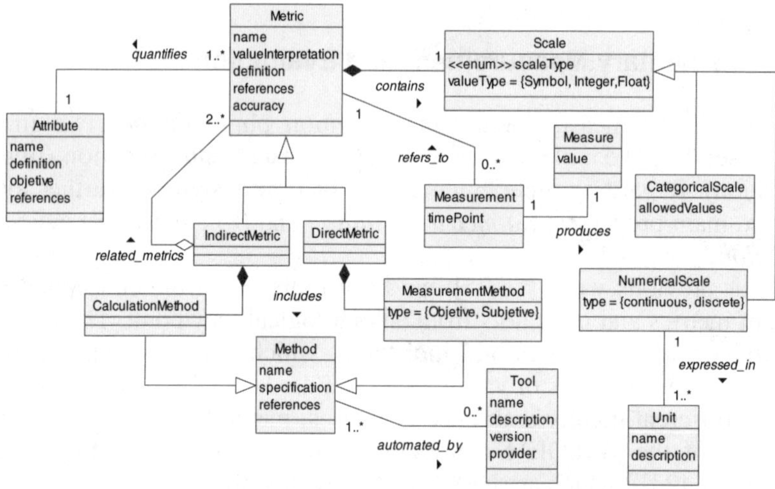

Fig. 4.6. Main terms and relationships with the metric concept

The scale type for the direct metrics presented above is absolute, represented by a numerical scale with integer value type. For the direct metrics 1) and 2), a specific objective measurement method can be applied (e.g. a recursive algorithm that counts each 404 HTTP status code). In addition, to automate the method, a software tool can be utilised; conversely, for the direct metric 3), it is harder to find a tool to automate it. On the other hand, for the indirect metrics 4), 5), and 6), we can use a calculation method in order to perform the specified equation.

However, because the value of a particular metric will not represent the elementary requirement's satisfaction level, we need to define a new mapping that will yield an elementary indicator value.

In [16,25] the indicator term is stated as:

> *"the defined calculation method and scale in addition to the model and decision criteria in order to provide an estimate or evaluation of a calculable concept with respect to defined information needs."*

In particular, we define an elementary indicator as that which does not depend upon other indicators to evaluate or estimate a concept at a lower level of abstraction (e.g. for associated attributes to a concept model); in addition, we define a partial or global indicator as that which is derived from other indicators to evaluate or estimate a concept at a higher level of abstraction (i.e. for sub-characteristics and characteristics). Therefore, the elementary indicator represents a new mapping coming from the interpretation of the metric's value of an attribute (the formal world) into the new variable to which categorical or numerical values can be assigned (the new formal world). In order to perform this mapping, a model and decision criterion for a specific user information need is considered. Figure 4.7 represents these concepts.

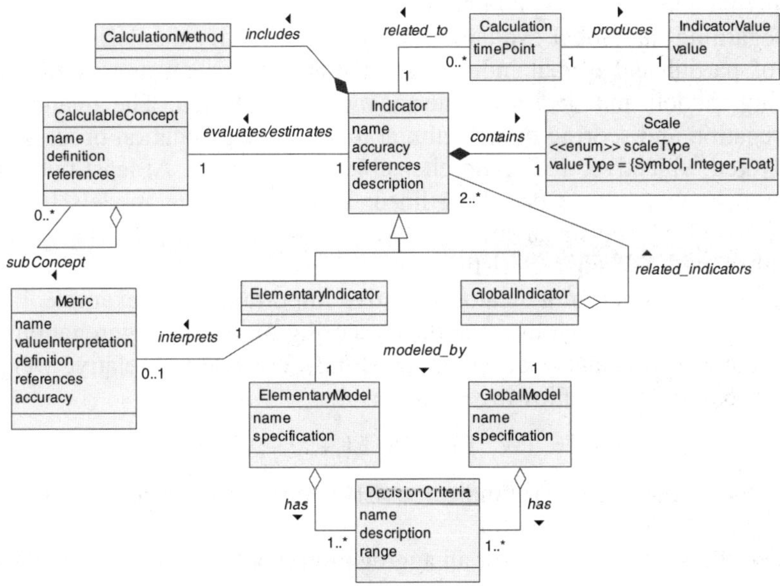

Fig. 4.7. Main terms and relationships with the indicator concept

Hence, an elementary indicator for each attribute of the concept model can be defined. To the 1.1 attribute of Fig. 4.2, the name of the elementary indicator can be for example *Internal Broken Links Preference Level* (IBL_P). The specification of the elementary model can look like this:

IBL_P= 100% if %IBL = 0; IBL_P= 0% if %IBL >= X_{max}
otherwise IBL_P=((X_{max} – %IBL) / X_{max}) * 100
if 0 < %IBL < X_{max} where X_{max} is some agreed upper threshold

The decision criteria that a model of an indicator may have are the agreed acceptability levels in a given scale; for instance, it is *unsatisfactory* if the range is 0 to 40%; *marginal* if it is greater than 40% and less than or equal than 60%; otherwise, *satisfactory.*

One fact worth mentioning is that the selected metrics are useful for a measurement process, as long as the selected indicators are useful for an evaluation process. Indicators are ultimately the foundation for interpretation of information needs and decision-making. Finally, Fig. 4.5 depicts the execution stage for the specified metrics and elementary indicators.

4.3.3 Global Evaluation

The global evaluation phase has two major stages: design and execution of the partial and global quality evaluation.

Regarding the global evaluation design, we identify the definition process of partial and global indicators. In this process, an aggregation and scoring model, and decision criteria, must be selected. The quantitative aggregation and scoring models aim at making the evaluation process well structured, objective, and comprehensible to evaluators. At least two types of models exist: those based on linear additive scoring models [6[, and those based on non-linear multi-criteria scoring models [5], where different attributes and characteristic relationships can be designed. Both use weights to consider an indicator's relative importance. For example, if our procedure is based on a linear additive scoring model, the aggregation and computing of partial/global indicators (P/GI), considering relative weights (W), is based on the following equation:

$$P/GI = (W_1\ EI_1 + W_2\ EI_2 + \ldots + W_m\ EI_m) \tag{4.1}$$

such that, if the elementary indicator (EI) is on a percentage scale, the following holds: $0 <= EI_i <= 100$.

Also the sum of weights for an aggregation block, or group, must fulfil:

$$(W_1 + W_2 + \ldots + W_m) = 1; \text{ if } W_i > 0; \text{ to } i = 1 \ldots m \tag{4.2}$$

where m is the number of sub-concepts at the same level in the aggregation block's tree.

The basic arithmetic aggregation operator for inputs is the plus (+) connector. We cannot use Equation 4.1 to model input simultaneity, or replaceability, among other limitations, as we discuss later.

Therefore, once we have selected a scoring model, the aggregation process follows the hierarchical structure as defined in the quality or quality in use requirement tree (see Fig 4.4), from bottom to top. Applying a stepwise aggregation mechanism, we obtain a global schema. This model lets us compute partial and global indicators in the execution stage. The global quality and 'quality in use' indicator ultimately represents the global degree of satisfaction in meeting the stated requirements, from a user's viewpoint.

4.3.4 Conclusions and Recommendations

The conclusion of the evaluation comprises documenting Web product components, the specification of quality requirements, metrics, indicators, elementary and global models, and decision criteria; and also it records measures and elementary, partial, and global indicator values. Requesters and evaluators can then analyse and understand the assessed product's strengths and weaknesses with regard to established information needs, and suggest, and justify, recommendations.

4.3.5 Automating the Process using WebQEM_Tool

The evaluation and comparison processes require both methodological and technological support. We have developed a Web-based tool (WebQEM_Tool [23]) to support the administration of evaluation projects. It permits editing, relating non-functional requirements, and calculating indicators based on the two aggregation models previously presented. Next, by automatically or manually editing elementary indicators, WebQEM_Tool aggregates the elements to yield a schema and calculates a global quality indicator for each application. This allows evaluators to assess and compare a Web product's quality to quality in use. WebQEM_Tool relies on a Web-based hyperdocument model that supports traceability of evaluation projects. It shows evaluation results using linked pages with textual, tabular, and graphical information, and dynamically generates pages with these results, obtained from tables stored in the data layer.

Currently, we are implementing a more robust measurement and evaluation framework, so-called INCAMI (Information Need, Concept model, Attribute, Metric, and Indicator). Its foundation lies in the ontological specification of metrics and indicators [16,25]. The Web-based tool related to the INCAMI framework is called INCAMI_Tool.

4.4 Case Study: Evaluating the Quality of Two Web Applications

We have used WebQEM to evaluate the quality of Web applications in several domains, which is documented elsewhere [3,21,22]. We discuss here its application in an e-business domain.

4.4.1 External Quality Requirements

Many potential attributes, both general and domain-specific, can contribute to the quality of a Web application. However, an evaluation must be focused, and purpose-oriented for a real information need. Let us establish that the purpose is to understand and compare the external quality of the shopping cart component of two typical e-stores, from a general visitor's viewpoint, in order to incorporate the best features in a new e-bookstore development project. To this end, we chose a successful international application – Amazon (www.amazon.com/books), and a well-known regional application – Cuspide (www.cuspide.com.ar).

Figure 4.8 shows a screenshot of Cuspide's shopping cart page with several highlighted attributes, which intervene in the quality requirements tree of Fig. 4.9. For the definition of the external quality requirements, we considered four main characteristics: *Usability* (1), *Functionality* (2), *Content* (3), and *Reliability* (4), and 32 attributes related to them (see Fig. 4.9). For instance, the *Usability* characteristic splits into sub-characteristics, such as *understandability* (1.1), *learnability* (1.2), *operability* (1.3), and *attractiveness* (1.4). We also consider another two separate characteristics: *Functionality* and *Content*. *Functionality* is decomposed into *function suitability* (2.1) and *accuracy* (2.2). *Content* is decomposed into *information suitability* (3.1) and *content accessibility* (3.2). As the reader can observe (see Fig. 4.9), we relate five measurable attributes to the function suitability sub-characteristic, and three to the function accuracy. In the latter sub-characteristic, we mainly consider precision attributes to recalculate values, after making supported edit operations.

On the other hand, as mentioned in Sect. 4.2.4, information suitability stresses the contextual nature of the information quality. It emphasises the importance of conveying the appropriate information for user-oriented goals and tasks.

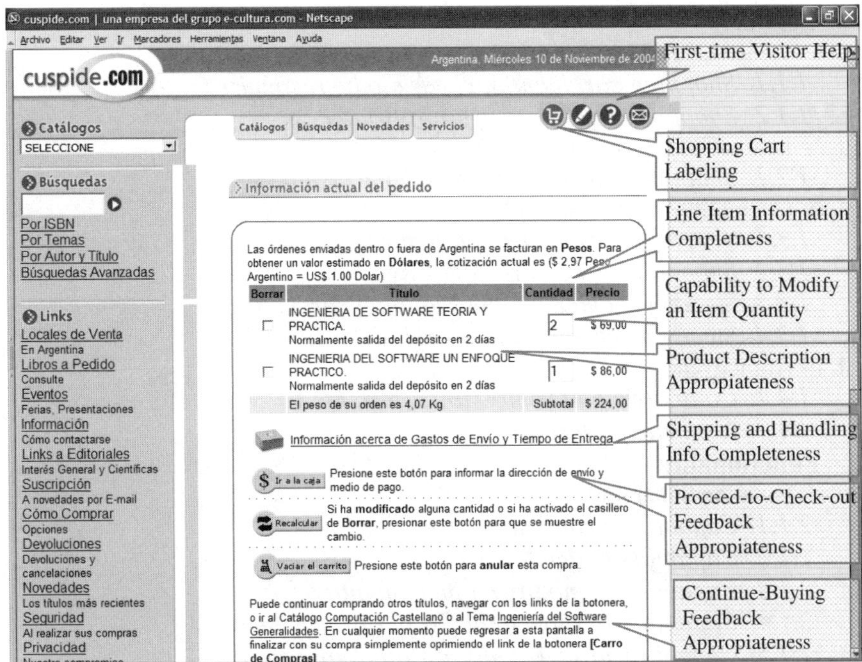

Fig. 4.8. A screenshot of Cuspide's shopping cart page with several attributes

INCAMI_Tool records all the information for an evaluation project. Besides the project data itself, it also saves to the *InformationNeed* class (see Fig. 4.1) the purpose, user viewpoint, and context description metadata; for the *CalculableConcept* and *Attribute* classes, it saves all the names, and definitions, respectively. The *ConceptModel* class permits one to instantiate a specific model, i.e. the external quality model in our case, allowing evaluators to edit and relate specific concepts, sub-concepts, and attributes. The resulting model is similar to that in Fig. 4.9.

4.4.2 Designing and Executing the Elementary Evaluation

As mentioned in Sect. 4.3.2, the evaluators should design, for each measurable attribute of the instantiated external quality model, the basis for the elementary evaluation process, by defining each specific metric and elementary indicator accordingly.

In the design phase we record all the information for the selected metrics and indicators, regarding the conceptual schema of *Metric* and *Elementary Indicator* classes shown in Figs. 4.6 and 4.7, respectively.

1. Usability
- 1.1. Understandability
  - *1.1.1. Shopping cart icon/label ease to be recognized*
  - *1.1.2. Shopping cart labeling appropriateness*
- 1.2. Learnability
  - *1.2.1. Shopping cart help (for first-time visitor)*
- 1.3. Operability
  - *1.3.1. Shopping cart control permanence*
  - *1.3.2. Shopping cart control stability*
  - *1.3.3. Steady behaviour of the shopping cart control*
  - *1.3.4. Steady behaviour of other related controls*
- 1.4. Attractiveness
  - *1.4.1. Color style uniformity (links, text, etc.)*
  - *1.4.2. Aesthetic preference*

2. Functionality
- 2.1. Function Suitability
  - *2.1.1. Capability to add items from anywhere*
  - *2.1.2. Capability to delete items*
  - *2.1.3. Capability to modify an item quantity*
  - *2.1.4. Capability to show totals by performed changes*
  - *2.1.5. Capability to save items for later/move to cart*
- 2.2. Function Accuracy
  - *2.2.1. Precision to recalculate after adding an item*
  - *2.2.2. Precision to recalculate after deleting items*
  - *2.2.3. Precision to recalculate after modifying an item quantity*

3. Content
- 3.1. Information Suitability
  - 3.1.1. Shopping Cart Basic Information
    - *3.1.1.1. Line item information completeness*
    - *3.1.1.2. Product description appropriateness*
  - 3.1.2. Shopping Cart Contextual Information
    - *3.1.2.1. Purchase Policies Related Information*
      - *3.1.2.1.1. Shipping and handling costs information completeness*
      - *3.1.2.1.2. Applicable taxes information completeness*
      - *3.1.2.1.3. Return policy information completeness*
    - *3.1.2.2. Continue-buying feedback appropriateness*
    - *3.1.2.3. Proceed-to-check-out feedback appropriateness*
- 3.2. Content Accessibility
  - 3.2.1. Readability by Deactivating the Browser Image Feature
    - *3.2.1.1. Image title availability*
    - *3.2.1.2. Image title readability*
  - 3.2.2. Support for text-only version

4. Reliability
- 4.1. Nondeficiency (Maturity)
  - 4.1.1. Link Errors or Drawbacks
    - *4.1.1.1. Broken links*
    - *4.1.1.2. Invalid links*
    - *4.1.1.3. Reflective links*
  - 4.1.2. Miscellaneous Deficiencies
    - *4.1.2.1. Deficiencies or unexpected results dependent on browsers*
    - *4.1.2.2. Deficiencies or unexpected results independent on browsers*

Fig. 4.9. Specifying the external quality requirements tree of the shopping cart component for a general visitor standpoint

Table 4.3. Summary of elementary indicators' values of the shopping cart of both applications

Code	Attribute name	Amazon	Cuspide
2.1.1	Capability to add items from anywhere	50.0	50.0
2.1.2	Capability to delete items	66.0	100.0
2.1.3	Capability to modify an item quantity	100.0	100.0
2.1.4	Capability to show totals by performed changes	66.0	66.0
2.1.5	Capability to save items for later/move to cart	100.0	0.0
3.1.1.1	Line item information completeness	100.0	33.0
3.1.1.2	Product description appropriateness	100.0	30.0
3.1.2.1.1	Shipping and handling costs information completeness	100.0	100.0
3.1.2.1.2	Applicable taxes information completeness	100.0	100.0
3.1.2.1.3	Return policy information completeness	100.0	66.0
3.1.2.2	Continue-buying feedback appropriateness	100.0	60.0
3.1.2.3	Proceed-to-check-out feedback appropriateness	100.0	100.0
3.2.1.1	Image title availability	50.0	50.0
3.2.1.2	Image title readability	100.0	50.0
3.2.2	Support for text-only version	0.0	0.0
4.1.1.1	Broken links	100.0	100.0
4.1.1.2	Invalid links	100.0	100.0
4.1.1.3	Reflective links	50.0	50.0
4.1.2.1	Deficiencies or unexpected results dependent on browsers	100.0	66.0
4.1.2.2	Deficiencies or unexpected results independent of browsers	30.0	30.0

In addition, in the execution phase, we record for the *Measurement* and *Calculation* classes' instances the yielded final values for each metric and indicator. Table 4.3 contains calculated elementary indicators' values for the shopping cart component of Amazon and Cuspide. The data collection for the measurement activity was performed from 15 to 20 November 2004.

Once evaluators have designed and implemented the elementary evaluation, they should consider not only each attribute's relative importance, but also whether the attribute (or sub-characteristic) is mandatory, alternative, or neutral. For this task, we need a robust aggregation and scoring model, described next.

4.4.3 Designing and Executing the Partial/Global Evaluation

The design and execution of the partial/global evaluation represents a phase where we select and apply an aggregation and scoring model (see Fig. 4.5). Arithmetic or logic operators will then relate the hierarchically grouped attributes, sub-characteristics, and characteristics accordingly.

As mentioned earlier, we can use a linear additive or a non-linear multi-criteria scoring model (or even others). We cannot use the additive scoring model to model input simultaneity (an *and* relationship among inputs) or replaceability (an *or* relationship), because it cannot express, for example, simultaneous satisfaction of several requirements as inputs. Additivity assumes that insufficient presence of a specific attribute (input) can always be compensated by sufficient presence of any other attribute. Furthermore, additive models cannot model mandatory requirements; that is, a necessary attribute's or sub-characteristic's total absence cannot be compensated by others' presence.

A non-linear multi-criteria scoring model lets us deal with simultaneity, neutrality, replaceability, and other input relationships by using aggregation operators based on the weighted power means mathematical model. This model, called Logic Scoring of Preference [5](LSP), is a generalisation of the additive scoring model, and can be expressed as follows:

$$P/Gl(r) = (W_1 El_1^r + W_2 El_2^r + \cdots + W_m El_m^r)^{\frac{1}{r}} \tag{4.3}$$

where

$$-\infty \leq r \leq +\infty; \quad P/Gl(-\infty) = \min(El_1, El_{2,} \ldots El_m); \qquad \text{and}$$

$$P/Gl(+\infty) = \max(El_1, El_2, \ldots, El_m)$$

The power r is a parameter selected to achieve the desired logical relationship and polarisation intensity of the aggregation function. If *P/GI*(r) is closer to the minimum, such a criterion specifies the requirement for input simultaneity. If it is closer to the maximum, it specifies the requirement for input replaceability. Equation 4.3 is additive when $r = 1$, which models the neutrality relationship; that is, the formula remains the same as in the first additive model. Equation 4.3 is supra-additive for $r > 1$, which models input disjunction or replaceability. And it is sub-additive for $r < 1$ (with $r <> 0$), which models input conjunction or simultaneity.

For our case study we selected this last model and used a 17-level approach of conjunction–disjunction operators, as defined by Dujmovic [5]. Each operator in the model corresponds to a particular value of the r parameter. When $r = 1$ the operator is tagged with A (or the + sign). The C or conjunctive operators range from weak (C–) to strong (C+) quasi-conjunction functions; that is, from decreasing r values, starting from $r < 1$.

In general, the conjunctive operators imply that low-quality input indicators can never be well compensated by a high quality of some other input to output a high-quality indicator (in other words, a chain is as strong as its weakest link). Conversely, disjunctive operators (D operators) imply that low-quality input indicators can always be compensated by a high quality of some other input. Designing an LSP aggregation schema requires answering the following key basic questions (which are part of the *Global Indicator Definition* task in Fig. 4.5):

- What is the relationship between this group of related attributes and sub-characteristics: conjunctive, disjunctive, or neutral? (For instance, when modelling the attributes' relationship for the *Function Suitability* (2.1) sub-characteristic, we can agree that they are neutral or independent of each other.)
- What is the level of intensity of the logic operator, from a weak to strong conjunctive or disjunctive polarisation?
- What is the relative importance or weight of each element in the aggregation block or group?

WebQEM_Tool (which is being integrated into INCAMI_Tool) lets evaluators select the aggregation and scoring model. When using the additive scoring model, the aggregation operator is A for all tree aggregation blocks. If evaluators select the LSP model, they must indicate the operator for each group.

Figure 4.10 shows a partial view of the enacted schema for Amazon.com, as generated by our tool.

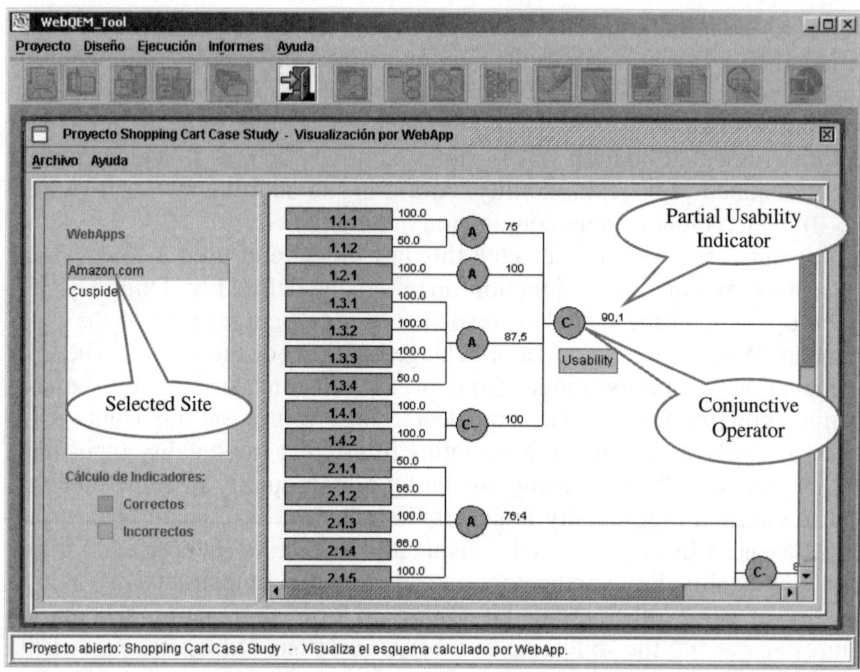

Fig. 4.10. Once the weights and operators were agreed and the schema checked, WebQEM_Tool yields partial and global indicators as highlighted in the right-hand pane

4.4.4 Analysis and Recommendations

Once we have performed the final execution of the evaluation, decision-makers can analyse the results and draw conclusions and recommendations.

As stated in Sect. 4.4.1, one of the primary goals of this study is the understanding and comparison of the current level of fulfilment of required external quality characteristics and attributes (see Fig. 4.9) for the shopping cart of two typical e-commerce applications, from a general visitor's standpoint. In addition, the best features of both shopping carts can be incorporated in a new e-bookstore development project. The underlying assumption of this study is that at the level of characteristics at least they are within the satisfactory acceptability range.

Table 4.4 shows the final values for the *Usability*, *Functionality*, *Content*, and *Reliability* characteristics, and the global quality indicator to both the Amazon and Cuspide shopping carts. The quality bars in Fig. 4.11 indicate the acceptability ranges and the quality level each shopping cart has reached. Amazon scored a higher quality level (84.32%) than Cuspide (65.73%). We suggest that scores between 40% and 60% (marginal acceptance) indicate the need for improvement. An unsatisfactory rating, obtained by a score below 40%, means that improvements must be made very soon, so taking high priority. A score above 60% indicates a satisfactory quality.

Table 4.4. Summary of partial and global indicators' values of the Amazon.com and Cuspide.com shopping carts

Code	Characteristic/Subcharacteristic name	Amazon	Cuspide
	External Quality Indicator	84.32	65.73
1	Usability	90.1	90.1
1.1	Understandability	75.00	75.00
1.2	Learnability	100.00	100.00
1.3	Operability	87.50	87.50
1.4	Attractiveness	100.00	100.00
2	Functionality	87.61	80.05
2.1	Function Suitability	76.40	63.20
2.2	Function Accuracy	100.00	100.00
3	Content	81.61	45.11
3.1	Information Suitability	100.00	47.30
3.1.1	Shopping Cart Basic Information	100.00	31.47
3.1.2	Shopping Cart Contextual Information	100.00	81.17
3.1.2.1	Purchase Policies Related Information	100.00	88.68
3.2	Content Accessibility	56.79	41.91
3.2.1	Readability by Deactivating the Browser Image Feature	67.75	50.00
4	Reliability	75.34	67.61
4.1	Nondeficiency (Maturity)	75.34	67.61
4.1.1	Link Errors or Drawbacks	94.35	94.35
4.1.2	Miscellaneous Deficiencies	58.00	44.40

Looking at the *Usability* and *Functionality* characteristics we see similar scores in both applications, so that we can emulate such attributes in a new development project. We can just highlight that the *Capability to save items for later/move to cart* (2.1.5) desirable attribute is absent in Cuspide, and the *Capability to delete items* (2.1.2) attribute is more suitable in Cuspide, as users can delete several items at once from the shopping cart (see the elementary indicators in Table 4.3).

Nonetheless, the greatest score differences can be observed in the *Content* characteristic (see Tables 4.3 and 4.4). Cuspide must plan changes in the *Shopping Cart Basic Information* sub-characteristic mainly in the 3.1.1.1 and 3.1.1.2 attributes. For instance, the *Line item information completeness* has to have at least the author description besides the title description, because when users add another item with the same starting title (e.g. Software Engineering …) they cannot, looking at the shopping cart, determine who is the author of each title. Even worse, users might navigate back to find out who the authors are because they have no link to a detailed product description.

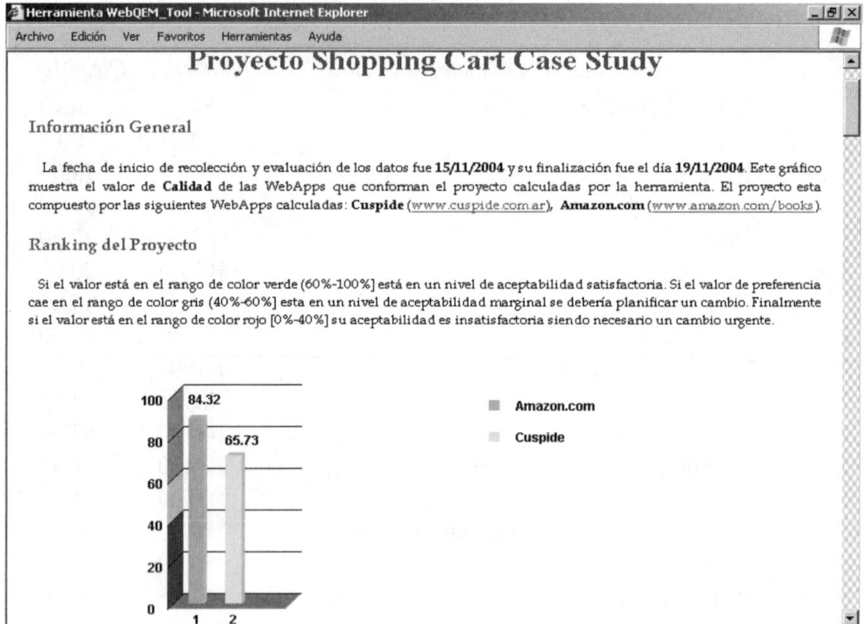

Fig. 4.11. WebQEM_Tool shows diverse information types (as textual, tabular, and graphical). The graph depicts the final shopping cart ranking

With regard to the *Content Accessibility* sub-characteristic, we may not emulate both applications because they are in the marginal acceptability level. On the other hand, we found *Deficiencies or unexpected results independent of browsers* (4.1.2.2) in both shopping carts; that is, there is no input validation in the quantity field so that a user can type decimal numbers or alphanumeric inputs, which can lead to unexpected outcomes.

Finally, we observe that the state of the art of the shopping cart quality on typical e-bookstores, from the visitor's point of view, is rather high, but the wish list is not empty because of some poorly designed or absent attributes. Notice that elementary, partial, and global indicators reflect the results of these specific requirements for this specific audience and should not be regarded as generalised rankings. Moreover, results themselves from a case study are seldom intended to be interpreted as generalisations that can be applicable to any other applications.

4.5 Concluding Remarks

Developing successful Web applications with economic and quality issues in mind requires broad perspectives and the incorporation of a number of principles, models, methods, and techniques from diverse disciplines such as information systems, computer science, hypertext, graphic design, information structuring, knowledge management, and ultimately software engineering as well. Web engineering is therefore an amalgamation of many disciplines, but with its own challenges. It has a very short history compared with other engineering disciplines, but is rapidly evolving. Like any other engineering science, Web engineering is concerned with the establishment and use of sound scientific, engineering, and management principles, and disciplined and systematic approaches to the successful development, deployment, maintenance, and evolution of Web sites and applications within budgetary, calendar, and quality constraints.

As mentioned above, the quality of an entity is easy to recognise but hard to define and evaluate, and sometimes costly to incorporate in the end product. In this chapter we have discussed what quality in general, and what Web quality in particular, is about. We adhere to the ISO approaches of quality: that is, internal quality, external quality, and quality in use. Because quality is not achieved at the end of a development without a carefully designed quality assurance strategy in the early stages, we argue that the three perspectives of quality per se have their own relative importance. However, we also adhere to the saying "*Quality in use is (or at least should be) the objective, software product quality is the means of achieving it*" [2].

We have highlighted that the very nature of Web applications is a mixture of information content, functionalities, and services. Next, we proposed to include *Content* as an extra characteristic in the internal and external quality models to the ISO 9126-1 standard (see Sect. 4.2.4).

On the other hand, regarding Web engineering evaluation approaches, we posed the need for counting with sound evaluation frameworks, methods, and techniques that support efforts to meet quality requirements at different stages of a Web project. We also stated that very often a method or technique is not enough to assess different information needs for diverse evaluation purposes. In this context, we presented WebQEM as a quantitative evaluation method for the inspection category whose underlying strategy is evaluator-driven by domain experts rather than user-driven; quantitative and model-centred rather than qualitative and intuition-centred; and objective rather than subjective. We are aware that a global quality evaluation (and eventual comparison), where many characteristics and attributes, metrics, and indicators intervene, cannot entirely avoid subjectivity. Then a robust and flexible evaluation methodology must properly aggregate subjective and objective components controlled by experts.

In order to illustrate WebQEM and its applicability, we conducted an e-business case study by evaluating the external quality of the shopping cart components of Amazon and Cuspide sites, taking into account a general visitor's standpoint. As a matter of fact, the data collection and evaluation were made by two expert evaluators working simultaneously. Note the important difference between evaluating external quality and quality in use. The former generally involves only experts and the latter always involves real end users. The advantage of using expert evaluation without extensive user involvement is minimising costs, time, and potential misinterpretation of questions (i.e. end users may sometimes interpret instructions and questionnaire items in a different way than they were intended to). The choice of whether to involve end users or not should be carefully planned and justified. Ultimately, without end user participation, it is unthinkable to conduct task testing in a real context of use. Nielsen indicates that commonly up to five subjects in the testing process for a given audience produce meaningful results minimizing costs: "*The best results come from testing no more than 5 users and running as many small tests as you can afford*" [19].

As a last remark, we are currently implementing a more robust measurement and evaluation framework called INCAMI which stands for Information Need, Concept model, Attribute, Metric, and Indicator; its foundation lies in the ontological specification of metrics and indicators [24]. WebQEM_Tool, which is part of this measurement and evaluation framework, allows consistently saving of not only metadata of metrics and indicators but also data for specific evaluation projects. Inter- and intra-project analyses and comparisons can now be performed in a consistent way. This applied research is thoroughly discussed in a follow-up manuscript.

Acknowledgements

This research is supported by the UNLPam-09/F022 project, Argentina. Gustavo Rossi has been partially funded by Secyt's project PICT No 13623.

References

1 Alexander J, Tate M (1999) Web Wisdom: How to Evaluate and Create Information Quality on the Web. Lawrence Erlbaum, Hillsdate, NJ

2 Bevan N (1999) Quality in Use: Meeting User Needs for Quality. Journal of Systems and Software, 49(1):89–96

3 Covella G, Olsina L (2002) Specifying Quality Attributes for Sites with E-Learning Functionality. In: Proceedings of the Ibero American Conference on Web Engineering (ICWE, 02), Santa Fe, Argentina, pp 154–167

4 Davies J, Fensel D, Van Harmelen F (2003) Towards the Semantic Web: Ontology-driven Knowledge Management. John Willey & Sons

5 Dujmovic J (1996) A Method for Evaluation and Selection of Complex Hardware and Software Systems. In: Proceedings of the 22nd International Conference for the Resource Management and Performance Evaluation of Enterprise CS, CMG 96 Proceedings, 1, pp 368–378

6 Gilb T (1976) Software Metrics. Chartwell-Bratt, Cambridge, MA

7 Herrera-Viedma E, Peis E (2003) Evaluating the Informative Quality of Documents in SGML Format from Judgements by Means of Fuzzy Linguistic Techniques Based on Computing with Words. J Information Processing. & Management 39(2):233–249

8 Huang K, Lee YW, Wang RY (1999) Quality Information and Knowledge. Prentice Hall, Englewood Cliffs, NJ

9 ISO/IEC 9126 (1991) Information technology – Software product evaluation – Quality characteristics and guidelines for their use

10 ISO 9241–11 (1998) Ergonomic requirements for office work with visual display terminals (VDT)s – Part 11 Guidance on Usability

11 ISO/IEC 14598–5 (1998) Information technology – Software product evaluation – Part 5: Process for evaluators

12 ISO/IEC 14598–1 (1999) Information technology – Software product evaluation – Part 1: General Overview

13 ISO/IEC 9126–1 (2001) Software Engineering – Product Quality – Part 1: Quality Model

14 ISO/IEC 15939 (2002) Software Engineering – Software Measurement Process

15 Lee YW, Strong DM, Kahn BK, Wang RY (2002) AIMQ: A Methodology for Information Quality Assessment. Information & Management, 40(2):133–146

16 Martín M, Olsina L (2003) Towards an Ontology for Software Metrics and Indicators as the Foundation for a Cataloging Web System. In: Proceedings of the 1st Latin American Web Congress, Santiago de Chile, pp 103–113

17 Mich L, Franch M, Gaio L (2003) Evaluating and Designing the Quality of Web Sites. IEEE MultiMedia, 10(1):34–43

18 Murugesan S, Deshpande Y, Hansen S, Ginige A (2001) Web Engineering: A New Discipline for Development of Web-based Systems. In: Murugesan S, Deshpande Y (eds) Web Engineering: Managing University and Complexity of Web Application Development, LNCS 2016, Springer, Berlin,pp 3–13

19 Nielsen J (1995–2004) The Alertbox column, http://www.useit.com/alertbox/

20 Nielsen J, Molich R, Snyder C, Farrell S (2001) E-Commerce User Experience, NN Group

21 Olsina L, Godoy D, Lafuente G, Rossi G (1999) Assessing the Quality of Academic Web sites: a Case Study. New Review of Hypermedia and Multimedia, 5:81–103

22 Olsina L, Lafuente G, Rossi G (2000) E-commerce Site Evaluation: a Case Study. In: Proceedings of the 1st International Conference on Electronic Commerce and Web Technologies. LNCS 1875, Springer London, UK, pp 239–252

23 Olsina L, Papa MF, Souto ME, Rossi G (2001) Providing Automated Support for the Web Quality Evaluation Methodology. In: Proceedings of the 4th Workshop on Web Engineering, at the 10th International WWW Conference, Hong Kong, pp 1–11

24 Olsina L, Rossi G (2002) Measuring Web Application Quality with WebQEM. IEEE Multimedia, 9(4):20–29

25 Olsina L, Martín M (2004) Ontology for Software Metrics and Indicators. J of Web Engineering. 2(4):262–281

26 Powel TA (1998) Web Site Engineering: Beyond Web Page Design. Prentice Hall

27 WWW Consortium, Web Content Accessibility Guidelines 1.0, http://www.w3.org/TR/WAI-WEBCONTENT/ (accessed on 10th November 2004)

Authors' Biographies

Luis Olsina is an Associate Professor in the Engineering School at National University of La Pampa, Argentina, and heads the Software and Web Engineering R&D group (GIDISWeb). His research interests include Web engineering, particularly Web metrics and indicators, quantitative evaluation methods, and ontologies for the measurement and evaluation domain. He authored the WebQEM methodology. He earned a PhD in software engineering and an MSE from National University of La Plata, Argentina. In the last seven years, he has published over 50 refereed papers, and participated in numerous regional and international events both as programme committee chair and member. He is an IEEE Computer Society member.

Guillermo Covella is an Assistant Professor in the Engineering School at National University of La Pampa, Argentina. He is currently an MSE student in the Informatics School at National University of La Plata, developing his thesis on quality in use evaluation of web applications. His primary research interests are web quality and quality in use, specifically in the field of e-learning.

Gustavo Rossi is Full Professor at Universidad Nacional de La Plata, Argentina, and heads LIFIA, a computer science research lab in the College of Informatics. His research interests include context-awareness and Web design patterns and frameworks. He coauthored the Object-Oriented Hypermedia Design Method (OOHDM) and is currently working on the application of design patterns in context-aware software. He earned a PhD in Computer Science from Catholic University of Rio de Janeiro (PUC-Rio), Brazil. He is an ACM member and IEEE member.

5 Web Usability: Principles and Evaluation Methods

Maristella Matera, Francesca Rizzo, Giovanni Toffetti Carughi

Abstract: Current Web applications are very complex and highly sophisticated software products, whose usability can greatly determine their success or failure. Defining methods for ensuring usability is one of the current goals of Web engineering research. Also, much attention is currently paid to usability by industry, recognising the importance of adopting methods for usability evaluation before and after application deployment. This chapter introduces principles and evaluation methods to be adopted during the whole application lifecycle for promoting usability. For each evaluation method, the main features, as well as the emerging advantages and drawbacks, are illustrated so as to support the choice of an evaluation plan that best fits the goals to be pursued and the available resources. The design and evaluation of a real application is also described for exemplifying the concepts and methods introduced.

Keywords: Web usability, Evaluation methods, Web usability principles, Development process.

5.1 Introduction

The World Wide Web has had a significant impact on access to the large quantity of information available through the Internet. Web-based applications have influenced several domains, by providing access to information and services to a variety of users with different characteristics and backgrounds. Users visit Web applications, and return to previously accessed applications, if they can easily find useful information, organised in a way that facilitates access and navigation, and presented according to a well-structured layout. In other words, the acceptability of Web applications by users relies strictly on the applications' *usability*.

Usability is one relevant factor of a Web application's quality. Recently, it has received great attention, and been recognised as a fundamental property for the success of Web applications. Defining methods for ensuring usability is therefore one of the current goals of Web engineering research. Also, much attention is currently paid to usability by industry, which is recognising the importance of adopting usability methods during the development process, to verify the usability of Web applications before and after their deployment. Some studies have demonstrated how the use of such methods reduces costs, with a high cost benefit ratio, as they reduce the need for changes after the application is delivered [40,50].

5.1.1 Usability in the Software Lifecycle

Traditional software engineering processes do not explicitly address usability within their lifecycles. They suggest different activities, from the initial inception of an idea until the product deployment, where testing is conducted at the end of the cycle to check if the application design satisfies the high-level requirements, agreed by the customer, is complete and internally consistent. To achieve usable applications, it is necessary to extend the standard lifecycle to explicitly address usability issues. This objective does not imply simply adding some activities; rather it requires appropriate techniques which span the entire lifecycle [20].

Given the emergent need for usability, traditional development processes were extended to enable the fulfilment of usability requirements. Evaluation methods have been adopted at all stages within the process, to verify the usability of incremental design artefacts, as well as of the final product. This has resulted in the proposal of the so-called *iterative design* [58,16] for promoting usability throughout the entire development lifecycle.

With respect to more traditional approaches, which suggest the use of a top-down method (such as for example the waterfall model), iterative design prescribes that the development process be complemented by a bottom-up, synthetic approach, in which the requirements, the design, and the product gradually evolve to become well defined. The essence of iterative design is that the only way to be sure about the effectiveness of design decisions is by building and evaluating application prototypes. The design can then be modified, to correct any false assumptions detected during the evaluation activities, or to accommodate new requirements; the cycle represented by design, evaluation, and redesign must be repeated as often as necessary.

In this context, *usability evaluation* is interpreted as an extension of testing, carried out through the use of prototypes with the aim of verifying the application design against usability requirements. Evaluation is central to this model: it is relevant at all the stages in the lifecycle, not just at the end of the product development. All aspects of the application development are in fact subject to constant evaluation, involving expert evaluators and users.

Iterative development is consistent with the real nature of design. It emphasises the role of prototyping and evaluation, the discovery of new requirements, and the importance of involving diverse stakeholders – including users.

What makes iterative development more than merely well-intentioned trial and error? Usability engineering became the banner under which diverse methodological endeavours were carried throughout the 1990s:

- It proposes that iterative development is managed according to explicit and measurable objectives, called "usability specifications", which must be identified early in the development process. Explicit usability goals are therefore incorporated within the design process, emphasising that the least expensive way of obtaining usable products is to consider usability issues early in the lifecycle, reducing the need to modify the design at the end of the process [44,45].
- It suggests the use of "simple usability engineering", which adopts easy- to-apply, and efficient, evaluation techniques, encouraging developers to consider usability issues throughout the whole development cycle [47].

5.1.2 Chapter Organisation

The aim of this chapter is to illustrate usability principles and evaluation methods that, in the context of an iterative design process, can support the production of usable Web applications. After introducing the general concept of usability and its specialisation for the Web, we present usability criteria that support Web usability in two ways: first, they can guide the design process, providing guidelines on how to organise the application by means of usable solutions; second, they drive the evaluation process, providing benchmarks for usability assessment. We will then present evaluation methods to be tackled during the entire development process – both during design and after application deployment based on the intervention of usability specialists, or involvement of real users.

In order to exemplify the concepts introduced, we discuss several important usability issues during the design and evaluation of a real Web application, developed for the Department of Electronics and Information (DEI) at Politecnico di Milano (http://www.elet.polimi.it). The DEI application is a very large, data-intensive application, consisting of:

- A *public area*, publishing information about the Department staff, and their teaching and research activities. It receives about 9000 page requests per day from external users.
- An *intranet area*, supporting some administrative tasks available to 300 DEI members.
- A *content management area*, which provides Web administrators with an easy-to-use user interface front-end for creating or updating content to be published via the Web application.

5.2 Defining Web Usability

Usability is generally taken as a software quality factor that aims to provide the answer to many frustrating problems caused by the interaction between people and technology. It describes the quality of products and systems from the point of view of its users.

Different definitions of usability have been proposed, which vary according to the models they are based on. Part 11 of the international standard ISO 9241 (*Ergonomic Requirements for Office Work with Visual Display Terminals*) provides guidance on usability, introducing requirements and recommendations to be used during application design and evaluation [29]. The standard defines usability as "the extent to which a product can be used by specified users to achieve specified goals with effectiveness, efficiency and satisfaction in a specified context of use". In this definition, *effectiveness* means "the accuracy and completeness with which users achieve specified goals", *efficiency* is "the resources expended in relation to the accuracy and completeness with which users achieve goals", and *satisfaction* is described as "the comfort and acceptability of use". Usability problems therefore refer to aspects that make the application ineffective, inefficient, and difficult to learn and use.

Although the ISO 9241-11 recommendations have become the standard for the usability specialists' community, the usability definition most widely adopted is the one introduced by Nielsen [45]. It provides a detailed model in terms of usability constituents that are suitable to be objectively and empirically verified through different evaluation methods. According to Nielsen's definition, usability refers to:

- *Learnability*: the ease of learning the functionality and behaviour of the system.
- *Efficiency*: the level of attainable productivity, once the user has learned the system.
- *Memorability*: the ease of remembering the system functionality, so that the casual user can return to the system after a period of non-use, without needing to learn again how to use it.
- *Few errors*: the capability of the system to feature a low error rate, to support users making few errors during the use of the system, and, in case they make errors, to help them recover easily.
- *Users' satisfaction*: the measure in which the user finds the system pleasant to use.

The previous principles can be further specialised and decomposed into finer-grained criteria that can be verified through different evaluation methods. The resulting advantage is that more precise and measurable criteria contribute towards setting an engineering discipline, where usability is not just argued, but systematically approached, evaluated, and improved [44,45].

When applying usability to Web applications, refinements need to be applied to the general definitions, to capture the specificity of this application class. Main tasks for the Web include: finding desired information and services by direct search, or the discovery of others by browsing; comprehending the information presented; invoking and executing services specific to certain Web applications, such as the ordering and downloading of products. Paraphrasing the ISO definition, Web usability can therefore be considered as the ability of Web applications to support such tasks with effectiveness, efficiency, and satisfaction. Also, Nielsen's usability principles mentioned above can be interpreted as follows [48]:

- *Web application learnability* must be interpreted as the ease for Web users to understand the contents and services made available through the application, and how to look for specific information using the available links for hypertext browsing. Learnability also means that each page in the hypertext front-end should be composed in a way such that its contents are easy to understand and navigational mechanisms are easy to identify.
- *Web applications efficiency* means that any content can be easily reached by users through available links. Also, when users get to a page, they must be able to orient themselves and understand the meaning of this page with respect to the starting point of their navigation.
- *Memorability* implies that, after a period of non-use, users are still able to orient themselves within the hypertext; for example, by means of navigation bars pointing to landmark pages.
- *Few errors* mean that when users erroneously follow a link, they are able to return to their previous location.
- *Users' satisfaction* refers to the situation in which users feel they are in control with respect to the hypertext, since they comprehend the available content and navigational commands.

In order to be evaluated, the previous criteria can be further refined into more objective and measurable criteria. Section 5.3 will introduce a set of operational criteria for Web application design and evaluation.

5.2.1 Usability and Accessibility

Recently, the concept of usability has been extended to include *accessibility*. Accessibility focuses on application features that support universal access by any class of users and technology [59]. In particular, accessibility focuses on properties of the mark-up code that make page contents "readable" by technologies assisting impaired users. Some literature gives *accessibility* a broader meaning: that is, the ability of an application to support any users identifying, retrieving, and navigating its contents [26,63]. In fact, accessible Web applications are advantageous to any users, especially in specific contexts of use, such as adopting voice-based devices (e.g. cellular phones) while driving. According to this meaning, accessibility can therefore be considered a particular facet of Web usability.

The W3C Web Accessibility Initiative (WAI) acts as the central point for setting accessibility guidelines for the Web. Its work concentrates on the production of Web Content Accessibility Guidelines (WCAG 2.0) [72], which focus on two main goals:

- *Producing contents that must be perceivable and operable*: this implies using a simple and clear language, as well as defining navigation and orientation mechanisms for supporting content access and browsing.
- *Ensuring access alternatives*: this means that pages must be designed and coded so they can be accessed independently from the adopted browsing technologies and devices, and from the usage environment.

The first goal is strictly related to the definition of Web usability; it can be pursued by focusing on usability criteria that enhance the effectiveness and efficiency of navigation and orientation mechanisms. The second goal can be achieved via the page mark-up, and in particular:

- *Separating presentation from content and navigation design*, which enables an application to present the same content and navigational commands according to multiple presentation modalities, suitable for different devices.
- *Augmenting multimedia content with textual descriptions*, so it can be presented through alternative browsing technologies, such as screen readers for assisting impaired users.
- *Creating documents that can be accessed by different types of hardware devices*. For example, it should be possible to interact with page contents even through voice devices, small-size devices, or black and white screens, and when pointing devices are not available.

WCAG recommendations provide 14 guidelines, each specifying how it can be applied within a specific context. For further details the reader is referred to [72].

5.3 Web Usability Criteria

According to the usability engineering approach, a cost-effective way to increase usability is for it to be addressed from the early phases of an application's development. A solution for achieving this goal is to take into account criteria that refine general usability principles (such as those presented in Sect. 5.2), suggesting how the application must be organised to conform to usability requirements [45]. Such criteria drive the design activity, providing guidelines on how to restrict the space of design alternatives, thus preventing designers from adopting solutions that can lead to unusable applications [20]. In addition, they constitute the background for the evaluation activity.

The development of Web applications, according to several methods recently introduced in Web engineering [5,14,57], must focus on three separate dimensions: data, hypertext, and presentation design - each being accompanied by a set criterion. Criteria so far proposed for the design of user interfaces [28,45,53], as well as the W3C-WCAG guidelines for accessibility, work well for organising the presentation layer of Web applications [39,49]. Table 5.1 summarises the ten "golden rules" proposed by Nielsen in 1993 for the design and evaluation of interactive systems.

More specific criteria are, however, needed for addressing the specific requirements, conventions and constraints characteristic of the design of content and hypertext links in Web applications. This section therefore proposes a set of criteria that suggest how Web applications should be organised, at the data and hypertext level, supporting information finding, browsing, and user orientation. These represent the three fundamental aspects we believe have the greatest impact on usability of Web applications. The criteria have been defined in the context of a model-driven design method [14,15]; as such, they take advantage of adopting a few high-level conceptual abstractions for systematically planning the overall structure of the application, avoiding implementation details and mark-up coding of single pages. Our method focuses on the broad organisation of the information content and the hypertext structure ("in-the-large"). In particular, the criteria are based on the assumption that the retrieval and fruition of content by end users is significantly affected by the way in which the content itself is conceived, designed, and later delivered by the hypertext interface. This assumption is also supported by a recommendation coming from the fields of human computer interaction and human factor studies [41,69,70].

Table 5.1. Nielsen's ten heuristics for user interface design and evaluation (http://www.useit.com/papers/heuristic/heuristic_list.html)

HEURISTIC	DESCRIPTION
1. Visibility of system status	The system should always keep users informed about what is going on, through appropriate feedback within reasonable time.
2. Match between system and the real world	The system should speak the users' language, with words, phrases, and concepts familiar to the user, rather than system-oriented terms. Follow real-world conventions, making information appear in a natural and logical order.
3. User control and freedom	Users often choose system functions by mistake and will need a clearly marked "emergency exit" to leave the unwanted state without having to go through an extended dialogue. Support undo and redo.
4. Consistency and standards	Users should not have to wonder whether different words, situations, or actions mean the same thing. Follow platform conventions.
5. Error prevention	Even better than good error messages is a careful design which prevents a problem from occurring in the first place.
6. Recognition rather than recall	Make objects, actions, and options visible. The user should not have to remember information from one part of the dialogue to another. Instructions for use of the system should be visible or easily retrievable whenever appropriate.
7. Flexibility and efficiency of use	Accelerators - unseen by the novice user - may often speed up the interaction for the expert user such that the system can cater to both inexperienced and experienced users. Allow users to tailor frequent actions.
8. Aesthetic and minimalist design	Dialogues should not contain information which is irrelevant or rarely needed. Every extra unit of information in a dialogue competes with the relevant units of information and diminishes their relative visibility.
9. Help users recognise, diagnose, and recover from errors	Error messages should be expressed in plain language (no codes), precisely indicate the problem, and constructively suggest a solution.
10. Help and documentation	Even though it is better if the system can be used without documentation, it may be necessary to provide help and documentation. Any such information should be easy to search, focused on the user's task, list concrete steps to be carried out, and not be too large

The usability of Web applications thus requires the complete understanding and accurate modelling of data resources. As such, and differently from previous proposals [25,48,49], our criteria are organised as general principles later expanded into two sets of more practical guidelines, one suggesting how to structure content, and another proposing the definition of usable navigation and orientation mechanisms for content access and browsing.

5.3.1 Content Visibility

In order to understand the structure of the information offered by the application, and become oriented within hypertext, users must be able to easily identify the main conceptual classes of contents.

Identification of Core Information Concepts

Content visibility can be supported by an appropriate content design, where the main classes of content are identified and adequately structured. To fulfil this requirement, the application design should start from the identification of the information entities modelling the *core concepts* of the application, which act as the application backbones, representing the best answer to users' information requirements [15]. Data design will be centred on such content, and will gradually evolve by detailing its structure in terms of elementary components, and further add access and browsing content.

Hypertext Modularity

The hypertext must be designed to support users to *perceive* where core concepts are located. To this end:

- The hypertext can be organised in *areas,* i.e. modularisation constructs grouping pages that publish homogeneous contents. Each one should refer to a given core concept identified at a data level.
- Areas must be defined as *global landmarks* accessible through links, grouped in *global navigation bars* that are displayed in any page of the application interface.
- Within each area, the most representative pages (e.g. the area entry page, search pages, or any other page from which users can invoke relevant operations) can be defined as *local landmarks*, reachable through *local navigation bars* displayed in any page within the area.

These links supply users with cornerstones to enhance their orientation within the area.

The regular use of hierarchical landmarks within pages enhances learnability and memorability: landmarks indeed provide intuitive mechanisms for highlighting the available content and the location within the hypertext where they are placed. Once learned, they also support orientation and error recovery, as they are available throughout the application as the simplest mechanism for context change.

Content Visibility in the DEI Application

In the DEI application, the core concepts of the public module are the *research areas*, the *teaching activities*, the *industrial projects*, and the *DEI members.* In accordance with this organisation of information content, the hypertext of the Web application is organised into four areas, *Research, Teaching, Industry, and People*, each corresponding to a single core concept (see Fig. 5.1).

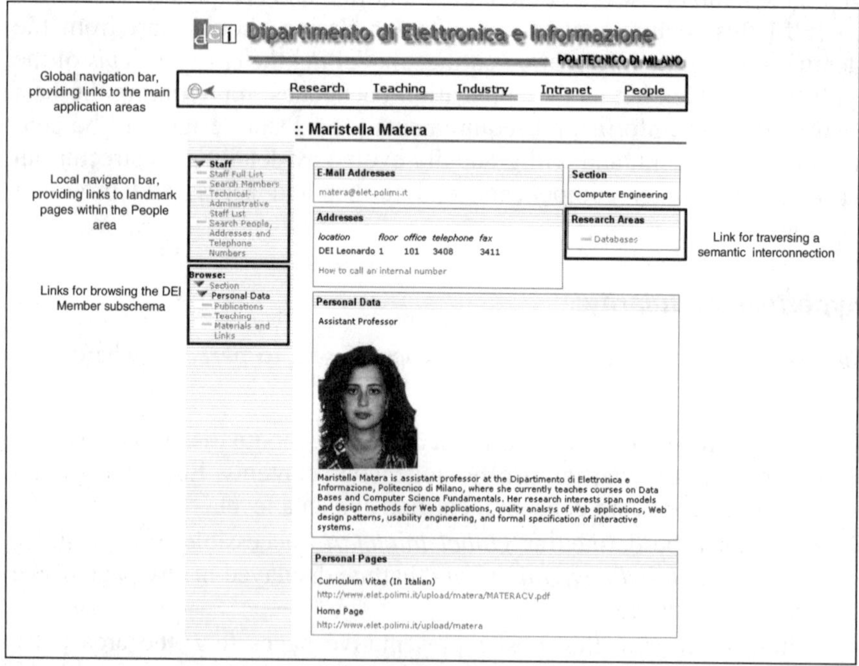

Fig. 5.1. Page organisation, with global and local landmarks, and core, peripheral, and interconnection sections

Each page within the application includes a global navigation bar, grouping links to the four application areas. Also, each page contains a local navigation bar that groups links to local landmarks. Figure 5.1 shows a page from the *People* area, which displays information about a DEI member. The global navigation bar is placed in the top region of the page. The bar also includes a link to the non-public intranet and to the Home Page. Landmarks defined locally for the *People* area are placed in the top region of the left-side bar.

5.3.2 Ease of Content Access

Once users have identified the application's main content classes, they must be provided with "facilities" for accessing the specific content items they are interested in.

Identification of Access Information Concepts

The design of access paths for retrieving core content items can be facilitated if designers augment the application content with *access concepts*, which correspond to classification criteria or context over core concepts. These enable users to move progressively from broader to narrower categories, until they locate the specific core concept of interest [49]. In general, multiple and orthogonal hierarchies of access concepts should be related to every core concept.

Navigational Access and Search-Based Access

In order to facilitate access to specific instances of core concepts, access concepts, defined at data level, should be used to construct *navigational access mechanisms*. These typically consist of multi-level indexes, possibly distributed on several *access pages*, bridging pages with a high visibility (e.g. the Home Page or the entry page of each area), to pages devoted to the publication of core concepts.

Especially in large Web applications, navigational access is often complemented with *direct access*, i.e. keyword-based search mechanisms, which allow users to avoid navigation and to rapidly reach the desired information objects. Direct access mechanisms are essential for interfaces (such as those of mobile devices) that are not able to support multiple navigation steps. In traditional hypertext interfaces, they enhance orientation when users "get lost" while moving along navigational access mechanisms [60,49].

Pairing navigational and direct access with explicit visibility over available categorisations and free text queries, in addition to a regular use of these access mechanisms within the hypertext, can greatly enhance content accessibility.

Content Access in the DEI Application

In the DEI application, each area is provided with navigational and direct access. Figure 5.2 shows the contextual access path defined for the core concept *DEI Member*. It consists of a hierarchy of indexes, developed through different access pages, which let users move from broader *People* categories, presented in the application's Home Page (e.g. academic staff), to pages listing narrower sub-categories (e.g. all the categories of the academic staff). In addition, users can move to the list of members in a selected sub-category, from which they can select a person's name and access her/his corresponding page. Each page also provides direct access, by means of a keyword-based search, for directly reaching single DEI members.

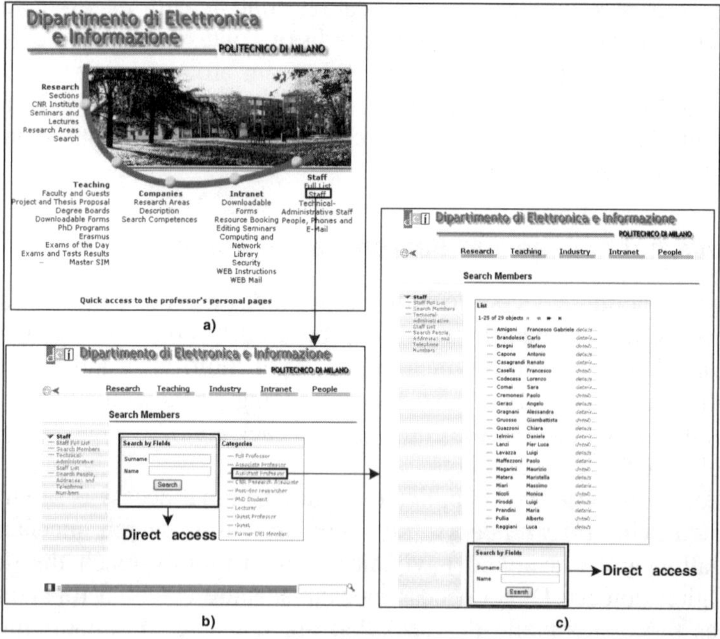

Fig. 5.2. Hierarchy of indexes in the navigational access to the DEI Member, consisting of the Home Page (a), the Member Categories page (b), and the Category Member Index page (c). Pages (b) and (c) also include a keyword-based search for direct access

5.3.3 Ease of Content Browsing

Users must be able to easily identify possible auxiliary content related to each single core concept, as well as the available interconnections between different core concepts.

Core Concepts' Structuring and Interconnection

The ease of use and learnability of a Web application can be enhanced by supporting users' understanding of the content structure and the semantic interconnections defined between different content classes. Therefore, when the core concepts represent a structured and complex concept, it is recommended that they be expanded, using a top-down design, into a composite data structure. Such structure collectively represents the entire core concept, and is characterised by:

- A *central information content* – which expresses the concept's main content and provides to an individual the means to identity each core concept.
- Some other *peripheral information elements*, which complete the concept's description.

Semantic interconnections among core concepts must be established for producing a knowledge network through which users can easily move, and explore the information content [41]. If defined, interconnections allow users to comprehend a Web application's structure and how to navigate through it efficiently.

Organisation of Core Pages

In order to highlight the structure of each core concept, and the interconnections between different concepts, pages devoted to core concept presentation should contain at least three sections:

- A *core section* that clearly conveys the content associated with the core concept.
- A *peripheral* section that highlights auxiliary information – if any – completing the core concept.
- An *interconnection* section that represents links to other pages within the area, or to the core contents of other areas.

The definition of the internal structure of pages by means of these three sections facilitates the understanding of the information in the page. If systematically repeated through the application, it enhances consistency among the components displayed by pages [49]. In addition, it is perceived as a key component in helping users understand the application's hypertextual structure, and to support a conscious shift of focus by users. Finally, if the structure is explicitly annotated on the page mark-up code, it can be used to build intelligent page readers, and thus enable accessibility to any users.

Content Browsing in the DEI Application

As an example of the organisation of content browsing in the DEI application, let us consider the DEI Member page (see Fig. 5.1). The page features as a core section a central region that presents the attributes qualifying a DEI Member (e-mail address, postal address, department section, biography, list of personal pages). The page then includes two link groups:

- The first refers to the page's peripheral section, and points to pages that contain further details about each DEI member (e.g. the list of publications and courses).
- The second represents the page's interconnection section, thus enabling a semantic interconnection, and points to the research area the member belongs to.

Note that such page structure also applies to pages in other application areas.

5.4 Evaluation Methods

Applying principles for the design of usable applications is not sufficient to ensure good usability of the final product. Even though systematic design techniques can be used, it is still necessary to check the intermediate results, and to test the final application to verify if it actually shows the expected features, and meets the user requirements. The role of *evaluation* is to help verify such issues.

The three main goals of an evaluation are, first, to assess the application's functionality; second, to verify the effect of the application's interface on the user; third, to identify any specific problems with the application, such as aspects which show unexpected effects when used within the intended context [20]. In relation to Web applications, an evaluation should verify if the application design allows users to easily retrieve and browse content, and to invoke available services and operations. Therefore, it implies not only to have the appropriate content and services available, but also to make them easily reachable to users by means of adequate hypertext structures.

Depending on the phase in which an evaluation is performed, it is possible to distinguish between *formative evaluation*, which takes place during the design stage, and *summative evaluation*, which takes place after the product has been developed, or when a prototype is ready. During the early design stages, the goal of a formative evaluation is to provide feedback during the design activities by checking the design team's understanding of the users' requirements, and by testing design choices quickly and informally. Later, a summative evaluation can be used to identify users' difficulties using the application, and help improve the final product or prototype.

Within these two broad categories, there are different methods that can be used at different stages of the development cycle of an application. The most commonly adopted methods are *user testing*, where the real users participate, and *usability inspection*, which is conducted by specialists. Recently, *Web usage analysis* has also emerged as a method for studying user behaviour through the computation of access statistics, and the reconstruction of user navigation on the basis of Web access logs.

The remainder of this section illustrates the main features of these three classes of evaluation methods, and also highlights their advantages and drawbacks.

5.4.1 User Testing

User testing aims to investigate real users' behaviour, observed using a representative sample of real users [46]. It requires users to perform a set of tasks using physical artefacts, which can be either prototypes or finished applications, while an investigator observes their behaviour and gathers data about the way users execute assigned tasks [20,55,68]. In general the data gathered during such investigations are user's execution time, number of errors, and user satisfaction. After the user test is complete, the collected data are analysed and used to improve the application's usability.

Usability testing is explicitly devoted to analysing in detail how users interact with the application while accomplishing well-defined tasks. This characteristic differentiates between usability and beta testing, which is largely applied in industry. Beta testing is always carried out using the final product, where after an application's release, end users are asked about their satisfaction with the product. Conversely, usability testing is conducted by observing a sample of users that perform specific tasks while interacting with the application. The test is usually video recorded. The list of detected problems is reported, in addition to specific redesign suggestions.

To avoid unreliable and biased results, the design of a user test evaluation and its execution should be carefully planned and managed. A good usability test should involve the following steps:

1. *Define the goals of the test.* The objective of the evaluation can be generic (e.g. to improve end users' satisfaction with and the design of a product); or it can be specific (e.g. to evaluate the effectiveness of a navigational bar for user orientation, or the readability of labels).
2. *Define the user sample to participate in the test.* The user sample for the test should be representative of the population of end users that will use the application or prototype under scrutiny. Failing to do so will provide results that cannot be generalised to the population of real users. Possible criteria to use to define the sample are: user's experience (experts vs. novices), age, application's frequency of use, and experience with similar applications. The number of participants can vary, depending on the objectives of the test. Nielsen and Molich [52] assert that 50% of the most important usability problems can be identified with three users. Other authors claim that five users enable the discovery of 90% of usability problems [47,64]. Note that the use of very small samples not suggested by the literature on empirical investigations: thus, within the context of this book, they are simply informative.
3. *Select tasks and scenarios.* The tasks to be carried out during the test have to be real, i.e. they have to represent the activities people would normally perform with the application. Task scenarios can be obtained from the requirements phase. In addition, tasks can also be intentionally prepared to test unexpected situations.
4. *Define how to measure usability.* Before conducting a usability test, it is important to define the attributes that will be used to measure the results. Such attributes, or measures, can be qualitative[1] (e.g. user satisfaction, or difficulty of use), or quantitative (e.g. task completion time, number and typology of errors, number of successfully accomplished tasks, the amount of time users invoke help (verbal, on- line help, manual)). Users' anonymity should be guaranteed, and participants should also be provided with the test results. Besides observing, an investigator can also use other techniques for gathering data on task execution. Examples of such techniques are: the *think aloud* protocol, in which a subject is required to talk out loud while executing tasks, explaining the actions (s)he is trying to tackle, their reason, and the expectations; the *co-discovery* (or collaborative) approach, in which two participants execute the tasks together, helping each other; the *active intervention*, in which the investigator asks participants to reflect upon the events of the test session. It is worth noting that such techniques do not provide ways for measuring users' satisfaction. Such subjective measurement can instead be obtained through *survey techniques*, based on the use of questionnaires and interviews [35,58], to be answered by users after the completion of testing.

[1] Qualitative measures are also known to be subjective.

5. *Prepare the material and the experimental environment.* The experimental environment should be organised and equipped with a computer and a video camera for recording user activities. In addition, it is also important to establish the roles of the investigative team members, and prepare any supporting material (e.g. manuals, pencils, paper). Prior to running the test, a pilot trial is necessary to check, and possibly refine, all test procedures. Note that it is not mandatory to execute the test in a laboratory.

5.4.2 Inspection Methods

User testing is considered the most effective way of assessing the use of products and prototypes, from a real user's point of view. However, user testing is an expensive activity. In addition, to be useful, feedback needs to be obtained at earlier stages in the development process, and repeated throughout the process. Such constraints have led to the proposal of usability inspection methods, to be used by developers to predict usability problems that could be detected through user testing.

Usability inspection refers to a set of evaluation techniques that have evolved from inspection methods, used in software engineering, to debug and improve code. Within the context of usability, inspectors examine usability-related aspects of an application, to detect violations of established usability principles [51], and to provide feedback to designers about necessary design improvements. Such inspectors can be usability specialists, designers, and engineers with special expertise (e.g. knowledge of specific domains or standards). To be effective, inspection methods rely upon a good understanding of usability principles, how these principles affect the specific application being analysed, and the skills of the inspector to discover problems where the main violations occur.

Usability inspection methods were proposed as a cost-effective alternative to traditional usability evaluation [8]. The cost of user test studies and laboratory experiments became a central issue, and therefore many usability evaluation techniques were proposed, based on the involvement of specialists to supplement or even replace direct user testing [51,52].

Different methods can be used for inspecting an application [51]. The most commonly used method is *heuristic evaluation* [45,51], in which usability specialists judge if an application's properties conform to established usability principles. Another method is *cognitive walkthrough* [54,67], which uses detailed procedures for simulating users' problem-solving processes, to assess if the functions provided by the application are efficient for users, and can lead them to correct actions. The remainder of this section describes these two methods in more depth.

A detailed description of other inspection techniques is provided in [51].

Heuristic Evaluation

Heuristic evaluation is the most informal of inspection methods. It prescribes having a small set of experts analysing the application against a list of recognised usability principles – the heuristics. This technique is part of the so-called discount usability method. In fact, research has shown that it is a very efficient usability engineering method [32], with a high cost-benefit [47].

During the evaluation session, each evaluator goes through the system interface at least twice. The first step is to obtain an overall understanding of the flow of interaction and the general scope of the application. The second step focuses on specific objects and functionality, evaluating their design and implementation against a list of heuristics. The output of a heuristic evaluation session is a list of usability problems with reference to the violated heuristics (see Table 5.2 for an example). The reporting of problems caused by the violation of heuristics enables an easy generation of a revised design. The revised design is prepared in accordance with what is prescribed by the guidelines underlying the violated principles. Once the evaluation has been completed, the findings of the different evaluators are compared and aggregated.

Table 5.2. An example of table for reporting heuristic violations

Found problem	Violated heuristic	Severity	Suggested improvement
Download time is not indicated	Feedback	High	Use a scrolling bar for representing the time left till the end of download

Heuristic evaluations are especially valuable when time and resources are short, given that skilled evaluators can produce high-quality results in a limited amount of time, without the need for real users' involvement [34]. In principle, heuristic evaluation can be conducted by a single evaluator. However, in an analysis of six studies, it has been found that single evaluators are able to find only 35% of the total number of existing usability problems [43], and that different evaluators tend to find different problems. Therefore, it seems that the more experts involved in the evaluation, the greater the number of different problems that can be identified. Figure 5.3 shows the percentage of usability problems found by number of evaluators, as reflected by a mathematical model defined in [50]. The curve suggests that five evaluators may be able to identify close to 75% of usability problems; however, such results should be interpreted with caution, since they are reliant on the data from which they were obtained.

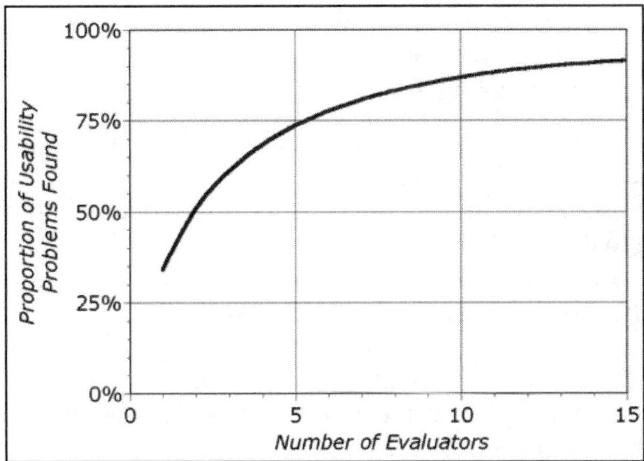

Fig. 5.3. The percentage of usability problems found by heuristic evaluation when using different numbers of evaluators [50]

Heuristic evaluations can have a number of drawbacks, with the major one being a high dependence on the skills and experience of the evaluators [21,33,34]. Nielsen states that novice evaluators with no usability expertise are poor evaluators, that usability experts are 1.8 times as good, and that application domain and usability experts are 2.7 times as good [44,45]. These results suggest that specific experience with a specific category of applications may significantly improve evaluators' performance.

Cognitive Walkthrough

A cognitive walkthrough simulates the user's problem-solving process, i.e. what the user will do in specific situations of use and why [54]. Evaluators go through the interface, step by step, using a task scenario, and discuss the usability issues as they arise. In particular, the method guides evaluators in the analysis of the actions that users would accomplish to reach the objectives defined in the scenario, by means of the identification of the relationship between user goals, actions, and the visible states of the application interface [27]. As such, cognitive walkthrough is particularly suited for the detection of problems affecting an application's learnability.

Cognitive walkthrough is a technique largely applied to evaluating aspects of an application's interface. Its use is recommended in the advanced phases of Web application development, to evaluate high-fidelity prototypes for which the interaction functionalities already work. The typical cognitive walkthrough procedure prescribes that, on the basis of selected scenarios of use, a series of tasks are chosen to be performed by an expert evaluator on the interface. The evaluator executes such tasks, and after the completion of each elementary action (s)he interprets the application's answer, and evaluates the steps forward for the achievement of the end user's goal, by answering the following standard questions:

1. Are the feasible and correct actions sufficiently evident to the user, and do the actions match with her/his intention?
2. Will the user associate the correct action's description with what (s)he is trying to do?
3. Will the user receive feedback in the same place where (s)he has performed her/his action and in the same modality?
4. Does the user interpret the system's response correctly: does (s)he know if (s)he has made a right or wrong choice?
5. Does the user properly evaluate the results: is (s)he able to assess if (s)he got closer to her/his goal?
6. Does the user understand if the intention (s)he is trying to fulfil cannot be accomplished with the current state of the world: does (s)he find alternative goals?

During this interpretation process, it is also possible that the user/evaluator needs to change her/his initial goal because it is impossible to achieve. Each negative answer to the previous questions increments the list of detected problems. At the end of the evaluation session, the list of problems is completed with the indications of possible design amendments, and communicated back to the design team.

Web Usage Analysis

A recent direction in the evaluation of Web applications is called Web usage analysis [30]. It is performed using the recorded users' access to the application's Web pages, stored in a Web server log [61], according to one of the available standard formats [71]. This technique can only be used once a Web application is deployed, and can be used to analyse how users exploit and browse the information provided by the application. For instance, it can help discover navigation patterns that correspond to high Web usage, or those which correspond to early leaving.

Very often, Web logs are analysed with the aim of calculating *traffic statistics*. Such type of analysis can help identify the most accessed pages and content, and may therefore highlight user preferences. These preferences may not have been previously anticipated during the design stage, and may therefore need to be incorporated by restructuring the application's hypertext structure.

Traffic analysis is not able to detect users' navigational behaviour. To allow a deeper insight into users' navigation paths, the research community has investigated techniques to reconstruct user navigation from log files [17,19,22,23]. Most techniques are based on the extensions of Web logging mechanisms, used to record additional semantic information about the content presented in the pages accessed. This information can later be used to understand observed frequent paths and corresponding pages [6]. Such extensions exploit Semantic Web techniques, such as RDF annotations for mapping URLs into a set of ontological entities. Also, recent work [23,56] has proposed conceptual enrichment of Web logs through the integration of information about a page's content and the hypertext structure deriving from the application's conceptual specification. The reconstruction of a user navigation can then be incorporated into automatic tools, which provide designers and evaluators with statistics about identified navigation paths. Such paths can be useful to evaluate and improve an application's organisation with respect to its actual usage.

User navigation paths can also be analysed by means of *Web usage mining* techniques, which apply data mining techniques on Web logs to identify associations between visited pages and content [17,22]. With respect to the simple reconstruction of user navigation, Web usage mining can discover unexpected user behaviour, not foreseen by the application designers. The user behaviour can be a symptom of a poor design, rather than a defect. The aim is to identify possible improvements that accommodate such user needs.

Different techniques can be used to mine Web logs. Mining of *association rules* is probably the one used the most. Association rules [1] are implications of the form `X` ⇒ `Y`, stating that in a given session where the `X` log element (e.g. a page) is found, the `Y` log element is also very likely to be found. Methods for discovering association rules can also be extended to the problem of discovering *sequential patterns*. These are extensions of association rules to the case where the relation between rule items specifies a temporal pattern. The sequential pattern of the form `X.html` ⇒ `Y.html` states that users, who in a session visit page `X.html`, are also likely to next visit page `Y.html` in the same session [62].

The discovery of association rules and sequential patterns is interesting from the Web usage perspective, because the results produced can provide evidence of content or pages that are frequently associated. If this behaviour is not supported by proper navigational structures, connecting such content to pages, then it can suggest possible improvements to ease content browsing.

A drawback of Web usage mining techniques is that they require a substantial amount of pre-processing[2] [17,61]. In particular, user session identification can be very demanding, since requests for pages tracked in

---

2 To extract user navigation sessions containing consistent information, and to format data in a way suitable for analysis.

Web logs may be compromised due to proxy servers, which do not allow the unique identification of users [18]. Solutions to circumvent this problem are illustrated in [18].

Comparison of Methods

User testing provides reliable evaluations, because its results are based on user samples representative of the population of real users. It helps evaluators overcome problems, such as lack of precision of predictive models whenever the application domain is not supported by a strong and detailed theory. User testing, however, has a number of drawbacks. The first is the difficulty to select a sample representative of the population of real users, since the identification of such a population is sometimes not straightforward. A sample that does not represent the correct population provides results unlikely to be of use. The second drawback is that it can be difficult to train users, within a limited amount of time, to master advanced features of a Web application. This can lead to shallow conclusions, in most cases only related to the simple application features. The third drawback is that the limited amount of time available for user tests makes it difficult to mimic real usage scenarios. Such scenarios require the provision of a real environment where the application is to be used, and also the motivations and the goals that users may have in real-life situations [37]. Failure to reproduce such a context may lead to unrealistic results and conclusions. Finally, the fourth drawback is that user observation provides little information about the cause of a problem, since it deals primarily with the symptoms [21]. Not understanding the underlying cause has implications for an application's redesign. In fact, the new design can remove the original symptoms, but if the underlying cause remains, a different symptom may result.

Unlike user testing, inspection methods enable the identification of the underlying cause of a problem. Inspectors know exactly which part of the design violates a usability principle, and how. The main advantage of inspection methods, compared to user testing, is that they can be carried out with a smaller number of people, i.e., they are conducted by usability and human factor experts, who can detect problems and possible future faults of a complex system in a limited amount of time. This is in our view a relevant point, which strongly supports the use of usability evaluations during the design activities. In fact, it constitutes an inexpensive add-on to existing development practices, easily enabling the integration of usability goals into those of the software design and development [21]. Furthermore, inspection techniques can be used early on in the development process lifecycle, using if necessary design specifications, whenever a prototype is not yet available.

The three main disadvantages of inspection methods are, first, the great subjectivity of the evaluation – different inspectors may produce incomparable outcomes; and second, the strong dependency upon inspectors' skills. Third, experts can misjudge the reactions of real users in two ways, i.e. not detecting potential problems, or discovering problems that will not be relevant for real users.

According to Brooks [12], usability inspection methods cannot replace user testing because they are not able to analyse aspects, such as trade-offs, the entire interface acceptability, or the accuracy of a user's mental model. Also, they are not suitable to define the most usable interface out of several, or anything that relates to a preference. However, usability testing cannot predict if an interface will "just do the job" or will "delight the user"; this type of information is, however, important within the context of a competitive user market share. Therefore it may be beneficial also to consider features that can distinguish an interface from good to excellent, rather than to focus solely on its problems, which is what usability inspection does.

The analysis of Web server logs seems to solve a series of problems in usability evaluation, as it may reduce the need for usability testing. Also, with respect to the experimental settings, it offers the possibility of analysing the behaviour of a higher number of users, compared to user tests, increasing the number of attributes that can be measured, and the reliability of the detected errors. However, the use of Web server log files is not without problems of its own. The most severe relates to the meaning of the information collected and how much it describes real users' behaviour. Even when logs are effective in finding patterns in the users' navigation sessions, they cannot be used to infer users' goals and expectations, central for a usability evaluation.

5.5 Automatic Tools To Support Evaluations

Automatic tools have been suggested as the most efficient means to treat repetitive evaluation tasks, without requiring much time and skills from human resources. There are three main categories of Web evaluation tools [11], which cover a large set of tests for usability and accessibility:

- *Tools for accessibility analysis.* Measures that can be automatically collected by these tools correspond to official accessibility criteria (such as those prescribed by W3C), and refer to properties of the HTML page coding, such as browser compatibility, use of safe colours, appropriate colour contrast, etc. Examples are Bobby [10], A-Prompt [3], and LIFT [36].

- *Tools for usability analysis.* These tools verify usability guidelines by analysing an application's design. They operate predominantly at the presentation layer, with the aim of discovering problems, such as the consistency of content presentation and navigation commands (e.g. link labels, colour consistency). They often neglect structural and navigation problems, although recent proposals (see for example [23]) plan to address such issues, by focusing on the identification of structural problems in the hypertext definition. Examples are CWW [9], WebTango [31], and WebCriteria SiteProfile [65].
- *Tools for Web usage analysis.* These tools allow the computation of statistics about an application's activities, and mine data about user behaviour. The majority of commercial tools (see for example [2,4]) are traffic analysers. Their functionality is limited to producing the following reports and statistics [22]:
  - *Site traffic reports*, such as total number of visits, average number of hits, average view time.
  - *Diagnostic statistics*, such as server errors and pages not found.
  - *Referrer statistics*, such as search engines accessing the application.
  - *User statistics*, such as top geographical regions.
  - *Client statistics*, such as users Web browsers and operating systems.

Research has been recently proposed to analyse user navigation paths, and to mine Web usage [7,17,42].

While the adoption of automatic tools for Web log analysis is mandatory, an important observation must be made about the first two categories of tools. Such tools constitute valuable support to reduce the effort required to manually analyse an entire application with respect to all of the possible usability problems. However, they are not able to exhaustively verify usability issues. In particular, they cannot assess any properties that require judgement by a human specialist (e.g. usage of natural and concise language). Also, automatic tools cannot provide answers about the nature of a discovered problem and the design revision that can solve it.

Automatic tools are therefore useful when their use complements the activity of human specialists, since they can execute repetitive evaluation tasks to inspect the application, and highlight critical features that should later be inspected by evaluators.

5.6 Evaluation of the DEI Application

The DEI application has been developed by means of an iterative development process, in which several incremental application versions have been released, evaluated, and improved based upon problems raised by the evaluations. Such a process has been enabled by the ease of prototype generation, due to the adoption of a modelling language, WebML [14], and its accompanying development tool [13,66], offering a visual environment for composing WebML-based specifications of an application's content and hypertext, and a solid XML and Java-based technology for automatic code generation.

The guidelines introduced in Sect. 5.3 have been taken into account during the application design. However, in order to further validate usability, several evaluation sessions, through different evaluation methods, have been conducted. In particular:

- Inspection sessions to examine the hypertext specification have been conducted, using an automatic tool aimed at discovering structural problems related to the definition of erroneous or inconsistent navigation mechanisms.
- After the application delivery, Web logs have been analysed to verify if the application structure envisioned by the application designers matched user needs, or if some unexpected behaviours could occur.
- The released prototypes, as well as the delivered final application, have been analysed through heuristic evaluations, to further identify problems that could not easily be revealed through the analysis of design specifications.

5.6.1 Design Inspection

Design inspections have been carried out over 14 successive versions of the DEI application, by applying different procedures to evaluate structural properties, such as its internal consistency and the soundness of navigation mechanisms.

Thanks to the availability of the XML-based representation of the hypertext specification, generated by the adopted development tool, the inspection was conducted automatically through the adoption of WQA (Web Quality Analyzer) [23], an XSL-based tool able to parse the XML specification for retrieving usability problems. In particular, the tool inspects the application design, looking for configurations that are considered potential sources of problem. Thus, it executes analysis procedures aimed at verifying if any configurations found violate usability.

In the following section we will illustrate two main problems we identified within the content management area used by Web administrators.

Consistency of Operation Design

Some of our inspection procedures aimed to verify the design consistency of content management operations, used to create and modify an application's content, within the content management area. In particular, they had to identify all occurrences of operations within pages, and to verify if their invocation, and the visualisation of results after their execution, was coherent across the entire application.

Fig. 5.4 plots the history of the Modify Termination (MT) evaluation procedure along several releases of the DEI application. Such procedure allowed us to evaluate and measure the consistency of visualisation results for content modification operations, with respect to two possible variants: visualisation of the modified content *(i)* in the same page where the operation was invoked (*Same Page Termination* variant), or *(ii)* in a new page (*Different Page Termination* variant). The procedure thus entailed:

1. To identify all the modification operations specified in the application's hypertext;
2. To compute the statistical variance (a value between 0 and 1) with respect to the occurrences of the two different termination variants, normalised with respect to the best-case variance (see [24] for further details).

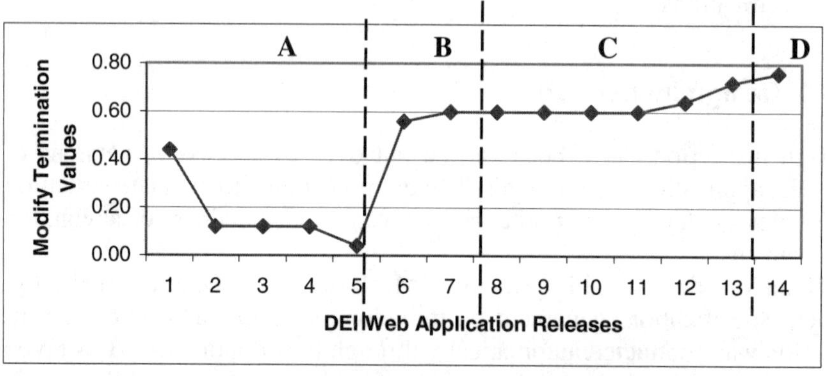

Fig. 5.4. History of the MT computation along the different DEI application releases

The plot in Fig. 5.4 highlights four different phases (from A to D) in the application's development. Phase A is characterised by a limited care regarding the design consistency. The initial high value of the computed measures for release 1 depended on the limited number of modification operations in the application at that time. However, as soon as the number of modification operations in the following releases started to grow, the consistency value for the termination of modification operations decreased, and reached its lowest value (0.04) in release 5. At this point, the evaluators raised the problem. Therefore during phase B, the application designer modified the application, trying to use a single design variant (the Same Page termination variant) in almost every case. Release 6 clearly shows the improvement obtained by the re-engineering activity, with the variance value going from 0.04 to 0.54. Improvement is also noted in relation to the percentages of use of the two variants in releases 5 and 6, as detailed in Table 5.3.

Table 5.3. The percentage of the occurrences of the two different Modify pattern variants within releases 5 and 6

	Different page termination	Same page termination
Release 5	42,86%	57,14%
Release 6	12,5%	87,5%

Starting from release 7 (phase C), the MT measure computation has reached a constant value – no modifications have been applied to the modification operation. From release 12 to 14 (phase D), we have instead assisted with improving the application's consistency. The last computed value for the MT metrics was 0.76, which corresponds to an acceptable level of consistency with respect to the set usability goals.

Identification of Dead-ends

Besides verifying consistency, some inspection tasks were performed to discover structural weaknesses within the application's hypertext. One particular inspection procedure, executed on DEI's hypertext specification, aimed to discover *dead-ends*. Dead-ends are pages reachable by different navigation paths preventing the user from navigating further. The only choice they give to a user is to go back (e.g. by hitting a browser's "back" button). These pages either have no outgoing links, or activate operations that end up where they started, thus making navigation difficult.

While analysing the entire application's structure we identified 20 occurrences of the *dead-end* pattern. A closer look at each occurrence revealed that all *dead-ends* were pages reached whenever a database update operation failed. In such a situation, the user is presented with a page displaying an error message, and is unable to navigate further, to recover from the error. According to the "ease of browsing" usability criterion, the designer should have inserted a link to allow a user to go back to the initial page from which the operation had been invoked.

It is worth noting that dead-end pages would have been difficult to find by means of user testing. The reason is that the investigator would need to induce database-related errors in order to obtain one of these pages. This is therefore an example where the analysis of design specifications (automatic or not) to verify structural properties can support the identification of usability problems that may be difficult to find.

5.6.2 Web Usage Analysis

Once the WEI application was deployed, we carried out a Web usage analysis. To do so, we analysed Web logs to reconstruct user navigation patterns, and to identify possible critical situations that had been encountered by users. In particular, the analysis focused on navigational access mechanisms.

Navigation Sequences for Accessing a DEI Member's Page

The computation of traffic statistics was used to identify that, apart from the application's Home Page, the other most visited URL corresponded to the page showing the details for a single DEI member, with links to the member's publications, personal home page, and research areas. The navigational facilities provided by the application enabled us to examine the means employed by users to reach the page. As can be observed in Fig. 5.2, the page is reachable through a navigational access that takes a user from the Home Page to an index page, thus providing two different ways to reach a single member's page:

- The first using an index of member categories (e.g. professor, lecturer), which allows for the selection of a category and, using a different page, the selection of a specific member from an alphabetically ordered list.
- The second using a search-based direct access.

Given these navigational access facilities, we wanted to monitor their usage, to find out whether they showed any usability problems. In order to identify navigational sequences, we adopted a module of the WQA tool [23], which is able to analyse Web logs and to reconstruct user navigation. The analysis of logs for 15 days showed that the navigational sequence from the index page to the DEI member page was followed about 20,000 times during that period, and that:

- The indexes of categories and members were used less than 900 times.
- Times users went through the search box more than 19,000.

These results suggested either that users did not know which category to use when looking for a DEI member, or that the navigational access was not easy to use and needed improvements. This feedback is currently being taken into account by the application designers, to assess the merits of re-designing the application.

Another problem related to the access to the DEI member pages was identified while carrying out a mining session on the DEI Web logs, to discover possible association rules [42]. The mining query was aimed at discovering the page sequences most frequently visited. Results showed that requests for a "research area" page were later followed by a request to a DEI member page. A possible reason for this behaviour could be that users perceive the "research area" page as an access page for the DEI members. This result supports the view that users are not making use of the navigational access on DEI members, as envisioned by the application designers.

Navigation Sequences for Accessing a DEI Member's Publications

Another problem also identified was related to accessing the DEI member's publication details. The "Publication Details" page[3] can be reached from four distinct pages: "Search Publications,"[4] "All Publications,"[5] "DEI Member Publications"[6], and "Project Publications"[7]. Yet again, our goal was to discover the mostly used path to reach the "Publication Details" page. To do so, we gathered data on all the navigation sequences that contained the "Publication details" page.

The analysis of 15 days of Web logs revealed that the "Publication Details" page had been visited 440 times during that period, organised as follows:

- The "Publication Details" page was reached 420 times from the "DEI Member Publications" page.
- Of the remaining 20 times: the page "Publication Details" was reached 8 times from "Project Publications", 7 times from the "All Publications" page, and twice from the "Search Publications" page.

---

3 Page that shows the full details of a publication.

4 Page that provides a keyword-based search.

5 Page that displays the list of all the publications.

6 Page that shows the publication list for a specific DEI member.

7 Page that displays the publications produced in the context of a specific research project.

To reach the "Publication Details" page the "DEI Member Publications" page seems very likely to occur, therefore the results were not surprising. However, the small number of times that other pages were used to reach the "Publication Details" page was a concern. To understand these results, we inspected the application's hypertext design, to consider all the navigational sequences that reached the "Publication Details" page from pages other than the "DEI Member Publications" page. The inspection results showed that the "All Publications" and "Search Publications" pages were only reachable through links displayed in the "Publication Details" page. Therefore the reason for the low usage of such pages is that they were not visible to users.

Note that a problem such as this could not be identified solely by analysing the design, as this suggests that both pages can be reached using links from "Publication Details" page. The analysis of the design would not therefore take both pages as "unreachable". In addition, this problem could not be identified using a heuristic evaluation as the hypertext structure employed does not violate any usability principles. This is therefore an example that supports the need for observing real users' behaviour.

Heuristic Evaluation of Hypertext Interface

To achieve more complete and reliable evaluation results, design inspection and Web usage analysis were complemented with a heuristic evaluation session, conducted by expert evaluators from outside the design team. The aim of this evaluation was to assess the usability of the hypertext's presentation layer, which had not been addressed by the two previous evaluations.

Nielsen's heuristics were considered as the benchmark criteria. Results indicated problems related to the effectiveness of the language adopted. For example, the DEI Home Page (see Fig. 5.2) shows content categories that are related to the application core concepts. The same content categories are presented within each page using a permanent navigation bar. However, the category "Staff" in the Home Page is displayed as "People" in the navigation bar available in all remaining pages. The solution to the naming inconsistency is always to use the same category name.

Another problem, also related to naming conventions, is related to the inconsistent semantics of the "Details", within a page that shows the publications for a DEI professor (see Fig. 5.5). The link "Details" on the left side of the navigation bar is used as a link to the DEI "Member" page. However, the link "Details" underneath each publication is used as a link to the detailed description of a particular publication. Interpreting the problem in the light of Nielsen's heuristics, we can therefore observe that:

1. A system-oriented language has been employed, rather than a user-orientated language. In fact, "Details" was the term constantly referred to by application designers, during the application's development, to represent the presentation of an information entity's detailed contents (e.g. DEI "Member" and "Publication"). This problem is therefore an example where the interface has not been user-centred. Such a problem can be solved by assigning meaningful names to links clearly indicating the contents to be displayed in the target page.
2. To adopt the same name to denote two different concepts means users have to "remember" the interaction model implemented, rather than allowing them to "recall" such a model. The interface does not make objects, actions, and options visible, thus requiring the user to remember how to reach the content across different application areas, and different interaction sessions.

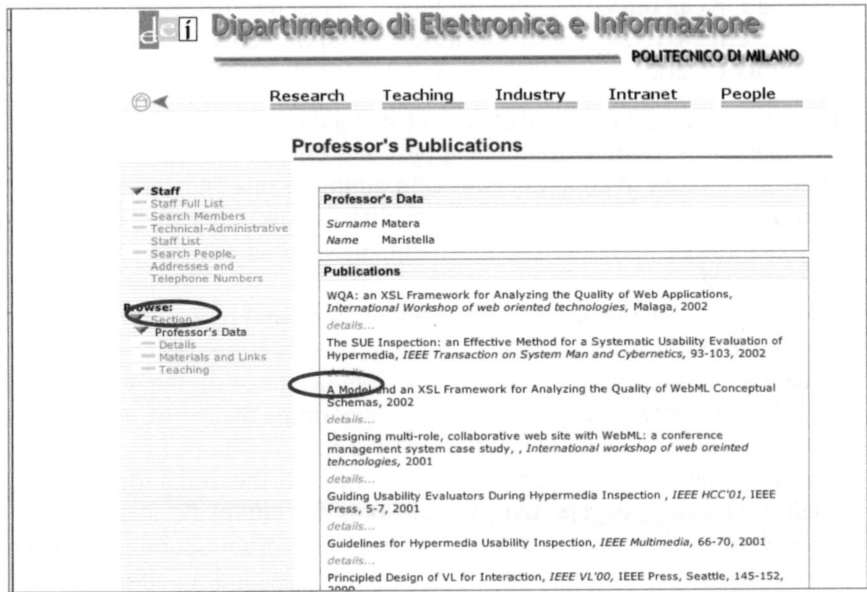

Fig. 5.5. Ambiguous semantics for the "Details" link name

5.7 Concluding Remarks

Web applications are quickly growing in number and complexity, becoming the *de facto* standard for distributed applications that require human interaction. The increasing number of Web users, the diversity of application domains, content, the complexity of hypertext structures and interfaces, all encourage the use and measurement of usability as a determinant factor for the success of such applications.

The process by which engineering principles are applied to developing Web applications started only recently [5,14,57]. Web engineering provides application designers with a collection of tools and languages to accelerate the development process, and to enforce a level of syntactic correctness, allowing for semi or complete, automatic code generation. Syntactic correctness prevents a designer from specifying an application that has defects. However, a quality application is more than a piece of defect-free code.

Applications that incorporate usability engineering into their development process are expected to comply with quality requirements. In particular [38]:

1. Evaluation is the key for assuring quality: the effort devoted to an evaluation can directly determine the quality of the final application.
2. To be effective, an evaluation must rely upon suitable and validated usability criteria.

This chapter provided an overview of methods currently adopted in assessing the usability of Web applications, and criteria that can be applied to the evaluation of Web applications. In addition, this chapter also highlighted the advantages and drawbacks of different usability methods so as to help practitioners choose the most suitable method with respect to the evaluation goals.

Independent of the method chosen, practitioners and researchers suggest that a sound usability evaluation plan should include the use of different, complementary methods, to ensure the completeness of the evaluation results. The characteristics of each method determine their effectiveness in discovering a specific class of usability problems.

The adoption of automatic tools can improve the reliability of the evaluation process. As reported in [11], tools for automatic analysis can address some of the issues that prevent developers from adopting evaluation methods. In particular, tools are systematic, fast, and reliable, and can be effectively adopted for tackling repetitive and time-consuming evaluation tasks. Also, tools may allow developers to code and execute procedures for the verification of in-house guidelines, making them easily enforceable.

However, tools may help verify structural properties, but fail to assess properties that require specialised human judgement, to provide answers explaining the nature of a given problem, and suggestions on how to fix it. Automatic tools are therefore very useful when their use complements the activity of human specialists.

References

1 Agrawal R, Imielinski T, Swami A. 1993) Mining Association Rules Between Sets of Items in Large Databases. In: Proceedings of *ACM-SIGMOD 93*, Washington, DC, May, pp 207–216

2 Analog. (2005) http://www.analog.cx. (accessed on 18th January 2005)

3 A-Prompt Project. (2005) http://aprompt.snow.utoronto.ca/ (accessed 18 January 2005)

4 AWSD-WebLog. (2005) http://awsd.com/scripts/weblog/index.shtml (accessed 18 January 2005)

5 Baresi L, Garzotto F, Paolini P (2001) Extending UML for Modeling Web Applications. In: Proceedings of the 34th Annual Hawaii International Conference on System Sciences, Maui, USA, January

6 Berendt B, Hotho A, Stumme G (2002) Towards Semantic Web Mining. In: Proceedings of the 1st International Semantic Web Conference, Sardinia, Italy, June. Springer, Berlin, LNCC. 2342, pp 264–278

7 Berendt B, Spiliopoulou M (2000) Analysis of Navigation Behaviour in Web Sites Integrating Multiple Information Systems. J Very Large Data Bases, 9(1):56–75

8 Bias RG, Mayhew DJ (1994) Cost-justifying usability. Academic Press, Boston, MA

9 Blackmon MH, Polson PG, Kitajima M, Lewis C (2002) Cognitive Walkthrough for the Web. In: Proceedings of the 2002 International Conference on Human Factors in Computing Systems, Minneapolis, USA, April, pp 463–470

10 Bobby. (2005) http://bobby.watchfire.com/bobby/html/en/index.jsp (accessed 18 January 2005)

11 Brajnik G (2004) Using Automatic Tools in Accessibility and Usability Assurance. In: Proceedings of the 8th International Workshop on User Interface for All, Vienna. June, Springer, Berlin, LNCC 3196, pp 219–234

12 Brooks P (1994) Adding Value to Usability Testing. In: Nielsen J, Mack RL (eds) Usability Inspection Methods. Wiley, New York, pp 255–271

13 Ceri S, Fraternali, P (2003) Architectural Issues and Solutions in the Development of Data-Intensive Web Applications. In: Proceedings of the First Biennial Conference on Innovative Data Systems Research, Asilomar, USA, January

14 Ceri S, Fraternali P, Bongio A, Brambilla M, Comai S, Matera M (2003) Designing Data-Intensive Web Applications, Morgan Kaufmann, San Francisco, CA

15 Ceri S, Fraternali P, Matera M (2002) Conceptual Modeling of Data-Intensive Web Applications. IEEE Internet Computing, 6(4):20–30

16 Conallen J (2002) Building Web Applications with UML, Addison-Wesley, Boston, MA

17 Cooley R (2003) The Use of Web Structures and Content to Identify Subjectively Interesting Web Usage Patterns. ACM Transactions on Internet Technology 3(2):93–116

18 Cooley R, Mobasher B, Srivastava J (1999) Data Preparation for Mining World Wide Web Browsing Patterns. J Knowledge and Information Systems, 1(1):5–32

19 Cooley R, Tan P, Srivastava J (2000) Discovery of Interesting Usage Patterns from Web Data. In: Proceedings of the 1999 International Workshop on Web Usage Analysis and User Profiling, San Diego, USA, August. Springer, Berlin, LNCC 1836, pp 163–182

20 Dix A, Finlay J, Abowd G, Beale R (1998) Human-Computer Interaction, 2nd edn. Prentice Hall, London

21 Doubleday A, Ryan M, Springett M, Sutcliffe A (1997) A Comparison of Usability Techniques for Evaluating Design. In: Proceedings of the 1999 Symposium on Designing Interactive Systems: Processes, Practices, Methods and Techniques, Amsterdam, the Netherlands, August, pp 101–110

22 Eirinaki M, Vazirgiannis M (2003) Web Mining for Web Personalization. J ACM Transactions on Internet Technology, 3(1):1–27

23 Fraternali P, Lanzi PL, Matera M, Maurino A (2004) A Model-Driven Web Usage Analysis for the Evaluation of Web Application Quality. Web Engineering, 3(2):124–152

24 Fraternali P, Matera M, Maurino A (2002) WQA: An XSL Framework for Analyzing the Quality of Web Applications. In: Proceedings of the Second International Workshop on Web-Oriented Software Technologies, Malaga, Spain, June

25 Garzotto F, Matera M (1997) A Systematic Method for Hypermedia Usability Inspection. New Review of Hypermedia and Multimedia, 6(3):39–65

26 Hull L (2004) Accessibility: It's Not Just for Disabilities Any More. ACM Interactions, 41(2):36–41

27 Hutchins EL, Hollan JD, Norman DA (1985) Direct manipulation interfaces. Human-Computer Interaction, 1:311–338

28 IBM (2005) Ease of Use guidelines. http://www-306.ibm.com/ibm/easy/eou_ext.nsf/publish/558 (2005). (accessed 18 January 2005)

29 ISO (1997) ISO 9241: Ergonomics Requirements for Office Work with Visual Display Terminal (VDT) Parts 1–17

30 Ivory MY, Hearst MA (2001) The State of the Art in Automating Usability Evaluation of User Interfaces. ACM Computing Surveys, 33(4):470–516

31 Ivory MY, Sinha RR, Hearst MA (2001) Empirically Validated Web Page Design Metrics. In: Proceedings of the ACM International Conference on Human Factors in Computing Systems, Seattle, USA, April, pp 53–60

32 Jeffries R, Desurvire HW (1992) Usability Testing vs. Heuristic Evaluation: Was There a Context? ACM SIGCHI Bulletin, 24(4):39–41

33 Jeffries R, Miller J, Wharton C, Uyeda KM (1991) User Interface Evaluation in the Real Word: A Comparison of Four Techniques. In: Proceedings of the ACM International Conference on Human Factors in Computing Systems, New Orleans, USA, pp 119–124

34 Kantner L, Rosenbaum S (1997) Usability Studies of WWW Sites: Heuristic Evaluation vs. Laboratory Testing. In: Proceedings of the ACM 1997 International Conference on Computer Documentation, Snowbird, USA, pp 153–160

35 Lewis JR (1995) IBM Computer Usability Satisfaction Questionnaires: Psychometric Evaluation and Instruction for Use. Human-Computer Interaction, 7(1):57–78

36 LIFT. (2005) http://www.usablenet.com (accessed 18 January 2005)

37 Lim KH, Benbasat I, Todd PA (1996) An Experimental Investigation of the Interactive Effects of Interface Style, Instructions, and Task Familiarity on User Performance. ACM Transactions on Computer-Human Interaction, 3(1):1–37

38 Lowe D (2003) Emerging knowledge in Web Development. In Aurum A, Jeffery R, Wohlin C, Handzic M (eds) Managing Software Engineering Knowledge. Springer, Berlin, pp 157–175

39 Lynch P, Horton S (2001) Web Style Guide: Basic Design Principles for Creating Web Sites, 2nd edn. Yale University Press, New Heaven, CT

40 Madsen KH (1999) Special Issue on The Diversity of Usability Practices. J Communications of the ACM, 42(5)

41 Marchionini G, Shneiderman B (1988) Finding Facts vs. Browsing Knowledge in Hypertext Systems. IEEE Computer, 21(1):70–80

42 Meo R, Lanzi PL, Matera M, Esposito R (2004) Integrating Web Conceptual Modeling and Web Usage Mining. In: Proceedings of the 2002 International ACM Workshop on Web Mining and Web Usage Analysis, Seattle, USA, August

43 Molich R, Nielsen J (1990) Improving a Human-Computer Dialogue. Communications of the ACM, 33(3):338–348

44 Nielsen J (1992) The Usability Engineering Lifecycle. J IEEE Computer, 25(3):12–22

45 Nielsen J (1993) Usability Engineering. Academic Press, Cambridge, MA

46 Nielsen J (1994) Special Issue on Usability Laboratories. Behavior and Information Technology, 13(1)

47 Nielsen J (1994) Guerrilla HCI: Using Discount Usability Engineering to Penetrate Intimidation Barrier. In: Proceedings of the Cost-Justifying Usability, Academic Press, Cambridge, MA

48 Nielsen J (1995) Multimedia and Hypertext Internet and Beyond, Academic Press, London

49 Nielsen J (2000) Web Usability. New Riders, New York

50 Nielsen J, Landauer TK (1993) A Mathematical Model of the Finding of Usability Problems. In: Proceedings of the ACM 1993 International Conference on Human Factors in Computing Systems, Amsterdam, Netherlands, April, pp 296–213

51 Nielsen J, Mack RL (1994) Usability Inspection Methods. Wiley, New York

52 Nielsen J, Molich R (1990) Heuristic Evaluation of User Interfaces. In: Proceedings of the ACM 1990 International Conference on Human Factors in Computing Systems, Seattle, USA, April, pp 249–256

53 Norman DA (1991) Cognitive Artifacts. In: Proceedings of the Designing Interaction: Psychology at the Human–Computer Interface. Cambridge University. New York, pp. 17–38

54 Polson P, Lewis C, Rieman J, Wharton C (1992) Cognitive Walkthrough: A Method for Theory-based Evaluation of User Interfaces. Man-Machine Studies, 36:741–773

55 Preece J, Rogers Y, Sharp H, Benyon D, Holland S, Carey T (1994) Human-Computer Interaction. Addison-Wesley, New York

56 Punin JR, Krishnamoorthy MS, Zaki MJ (2002) LOGML: Log Markup Language for Web Usage Mining. In: Proceedings of the Third International Workshop on Web Mining and Web Usage Analysis, San Francisco, USA, August, pp 88–112

57 Schwabe D, Rossi G (1998) An Object Oriented Approach to Web-Based Applications Design. Theory and Practice of Object Ssystems, 4(4):207–225

58 Shneiderman B (1992) Designing the User Interface. Strategies for Effective Human-Computer Interaction. Addison-Wesley, New York

59 Shneiderman B (2000) Universal Usability. Communications of the ACM, 43(5):84–91

60 Shneiderman B, Byrd D, Croft WB (1998) Sorting out searching. Communications of the ACM, 41(4):95–98

61 Srivastava J, Cooley R, Deshpande M, Tan PN (2000) Web Usage Mining: Discovery and Applications of Usage Patterns from Web Data. ACM Special Interest Group on Knowledge Discovery in Data Explorations, 1(2):12.23

62 Stroulia E, Niu N, El-Ramly M (2002) Understanding Web Usage for Dynamic Web-site Adaptation: A Case Study. In: Proceedings of the 4th International Workshop on Web Site Evolution, Montreal, Canada, October, pp 53–64

63 Theofanos MF, Redish J (2003) Bridging the gap between accessibility and usability. ACM Interactions, 10(6):36–51

64 Virzi RA (1992) Refining the Test Phase of Usability Evaluation: How Many Subjects is Enough? Human Factors, 34(4):457–468

65 WebCriteria SiteProfile. (2005) http://www.coremetrics.com (accessed 18 January 2005)

66 WebRatio Site Development Studio. (2005) http://www.webratio.com (accessed 18 January 2005)

67 Wharton C, Rieman J, Lewis C, Polson P (1994) The Cognitive Walkthrough Method: A Practitioner's Guide. In: Nielsen J, Mack RL (eds) Usability Inspection Methods, Wiley, New York, pp 105–140

68 Whiteside J, Bennet J, Holtzblatt K (1988) Usability Engineering: Our Experience and Evolution. In: Helander M (ed.) Handbook of Human-Computer Interaction. Elsevier, Amsterdam pp 791–817

69 Wilson TD (2000) Human Information Behavior. Informing Science, 3(2):49–55

70 Wurman RS (1997) Information Architects, Watson-Guptill, New York

71 W3C Consortium – Extended log file format. (2005) http://www.w3.org/TR/WD-logfile.html. (accessed 18 January 2005)

72 W3C Consortium - WAI-Web Content Accessibility Guidelines 2.0. (2005) W3C-WAI Working Draft. http://www.w3.org/TR/WCAG20/ (accessed 18 January 2005)

Authors' Biographies

Maristella Matera is Assistant Professor at Politecnico di Milano, where she teaches Databases and Computer Science Fundamentals. Her research interests focus on design methods and tools for Web applications, and in particular concentrate on conceptual modelling quality, Web log mining, personalisation of Web applications, context-aware Web applications, multimodal Web interfaces, Web application usability and accessibility. She is author of about 50 papers on the previous topics and of the book Designing Data-Intensive Web Applications, published by Morgan Kaufmann in December 2002. She has served as co-chair for several editions of the "Web Technologies and Applications" track at ACM SAC, and of the CAISE Workshop UMICS (Ubiquitous Mobile Information and Collaboration Systems). She is also regularly a member of the programme committee of several conferences and workshops in the field of Web Engineering.

A more detailed curriculum vitae and list of publications can be found at: http://www.elet.polimi.it/people/matera.

Francesca Rizzo is a junior researcher at Politecnico di Milano, where she is a lecturer for the Human Computer Interaction Laboratory. She obtained her PhD in Telematics and Information Society from the University of Siena in 2003. In the last five years she has taught human computer interaction and interaction design at the University of Siena and at Politecnico di Milano. Her fields of interest are human computer interaction (HCI), user centered design (UCD), usability evaluation and activities analysis. She has worked in many European research projects. Currently, her research is focused on Web application usability and accessibility, e-learning, story telling technologies design and evaluation for children. She is author of about 20 papers on the previous topics. She has served as reviewer for several conferences and journals such as ICWE (International Conference on Web Engineering) and JWE (Journal of Web Engineering).

Giovanni Toffetti Carughi graduated in Information Engineering at Politecnico di Milano in 2001. His thesis work focused on the extension through plugins of the WebML methodology for designing and automatically generating data-intensive Web applications. He worked for three years in the software industry both as a developer for WebRatio and as analyst and consultant in different industrial Web applications such as Acer-Euro portals, ABI-Pattichiari, Nortel-Consip, MetalC.

He is currently a PhD student at Politecnico di Milano and his topics of interest are conceptual modelling, model transformation, Web application engineering, Web log analysis, human computer interaction, rich internet applications, and image compression.

6 Web System Reliability and Performance:

Mauro Andreolini, Michele Colajanni, Riccardo Lancellotti

Abstract: Modern Web applications provide multiple services that are deployed through complex technologies. The importance and the economic impact of consumer-oriented Web applications introduce significant requirements in terms of performance and reliability. This chapter presents several methods to design new, and improve existing, Web applications that, even within a context of unpredictable load variations, must satisfy performance requirements. The chapter also provides a case study that describes the application of the proposed methods to a typical consumer-oriented Web application.

Keywords: Web systems, Performance, Reliability, Design.

6.1 Introduction

The use of Web technologies to deploy many classes of services through the Internet is becoming a *de facto* standard. A large number of software and hardware technologies are available with their pros and cons in terms of complexity, performance and cost. Because of the extreme heterogeneity of Web-related services and technologies, it is impossible to identify, from this universe, the solution which best suits every possible Web application. Multiple issues need addressing during the design and deployment of a Web-based service, which include the efficacy of the presentation, richness of the provided services, guarantee of security. Moreover, system performance and reliability remain key actors for the success of any Web-based services. The popularity of a Web application perceived as too slow or presenting availability problems can decline dramatically if navigation becomes a frustrating experience for the user. There are specific aspects of the design process that focus mainly on data organisation. The interested reader can refer to [24] and to references therein. In this chapter, we focus instead on the architectural design of Web applications that are subject to performance and reliability requirements. Note that we remain in the domain of best-effort Web-based services, with no strict guarantees on the performance levels, similarly to that which characterises QoS-based applications [44,23]. The techniques described in this chapter are hybrid in nature, but there are some major steps that must be followed. These main procedural steps, listed below, are illustrated in Fig. 6.1, and detailed in the following sections.

Step 1. We have first to identify the main classes of services that must be provided by the Web application.

Step 2. As we are interested in serving a large number of users with many *classes* of services, it is important to define the most likely workload models that are expected to access the Web application. Each workload model is characterised by a *workload intensity*, which represents the number of requests admitted in the Web application, and by the *workload mixes*, which denote the number of requests in each class of service.

Step 3. The third step in the design phase is to define the performance and reliability requirements of the Web application. There are many system- and user-oriented performance parameters, as well as many types of reliability goals, the most severe of which is the well known 24/7 attribute (i.e. 24 hours, seven days a week) that aims to deploy Web applications that are always reachable.

Step 4. Once the main characteristics and requirements for the Web application are specified, we have to choose the most appropriate software and hardware technologies to deploy it.

Step 5. After the implementation phase, we have to verify whether the Web application works as expected and whether it respects the performance and reliability requirements. As usual, a test can lead to positive or negative outcomes.

Step 6. In the case of some negative results, an iterative step begins. It aims to understand the causes of violation, remove them, and check again until all expected performance requirements are satisfied. In the most severe cases, a negative outcome may require interventions at the system or implementation level (dashed line in Fig. 6.1)

Step 7. Often, even a positive conclusion of the tests does not conclude the work. If one considers the extreme variability of the user patterns, the frequent updates/improvements of the classes of services, the first deployment may be followed by a *consolidation* phase. It can have different goals, from capacity planning tests to the verification of the performance margins of the system resources.

The remainder of the chapter is organised as follows. Section 6.2 outlines the different types of Web applications and the main design challenges for each class. Section 6.3 describes software technologies and hardware architectures for the deployment of Web applications that must serve mainly dynamic Web resources. Section 6.4 focuses on the testing process of a Web application. Section 6.5 outlines the main countermeasures to be undertaken whenever the deployed system fails to meet performance and reliability

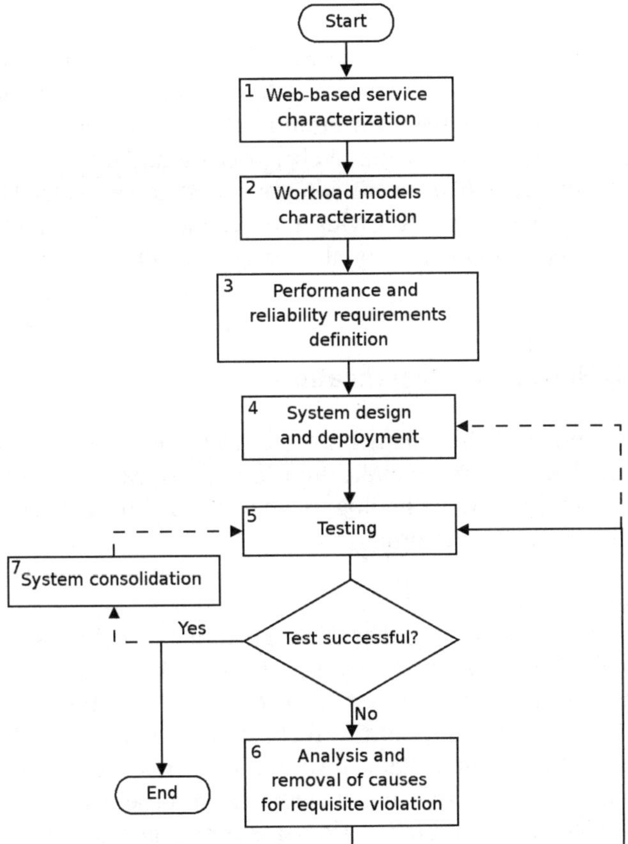

Fig. 6.1. Procedural steps for designing and testing Web applications with performance requirements

requirements. Section 6.6 describes a case study showing how the proposed design and testing methods can be applied to a typical e-commerce Web application of medium size. Section 2.7 concludes the chapter with some final remarks.

6.2 Web Application Services

There are so many services provided through the Web that it is difficult to integrate all of them in a universally accepted taxonomy. We prefer to describe the Web-based services through the following considerations:

- Each class of requests to the Web application involves one or more types of *Web resources*, hence we consider that the first important step is to classify the most important resources that characterise an application.
- Each class of requests has a different impact on the *system resources* of the platform that supports the Web application. The system resources include hardware and software components that are typically based on distributed technologies. Knowing the available technologies and their interactions is fundamental for the design of performance-aware Web applications.

6.2.1 Web Resource Classification

Within the context of this chapter we recognise five basic resource types that are provided by a Web application. Servicing each of these Web resources requires specific technologies, and has a different computational impact on the system's platform.

Static Web Resources
Static Web resources are stored as files. There are dozen of static resource types, from HTML files to images, text files, archive files, etc. They are typically managed by the file system of the same machine that hosts the Web server. In the early days of the Web, static files were the only type of Web resource. Servicing a static resource does not require a significant effort from the Web system, since it is requested through a GET method of the HTTP protocol, then fetched from a storage area or, often, from the disk cache, and then sent to the client through the network interface. Performance problems may occur only when the static resource is very large.[1]

Dynamic Web Resources
Dynamic Web resources are generated "on-the-fly" by the application as a response to a client request. There are many examples of dynamic resources, such as the result Web page from a Web search, a shopping cart virtualisation in a Web store, the dynamic generation of embedded objects or frames. Web resources generated in a dynamic way allow the highest flexibility and personalisation because the page code is generated as a response to each client's request.

There are two main motivations behind the use of dynamic resources. The first is that the traditional dynamic request comes from the necessity to obtain answers from an organised source of information, such as a database. The generation of this type of response requires a significant computational

[1] Based on current technology, large represents Megabytes and up.

effort due to data retrieval from databases, and (optional) information processing and construction of the HTTP output. The computational impact of dynamic requests on a Web application is increased also by the fact that it is quite difficult to take advantage of caching for the dynamic resources. The second is that one of the new trends on the Web is the generation of dynamic content even when this is not strictly necessary. For example, XML- and component-based technologies [19,29] provide mechanisms for separating structure and representation details of a Web document. As a consequence, all the documents (even static pages) are generated dynamically from a template through computationally expensive operations.

Volatile Web Resources

Volatile Web resources are regenerated dynamically on a periodic time basis or when a given event occurs. This type of resource represents information portals that deliver up-to-date news, sport results, stock exchange information, etc. Avoiding frequent re-computation keeps the cost of volatile resource service low, and comparable to that of static resources. On the other hand, the Web application must be equipped with mechanisms that can regenerate resources through automated technologies similar to those used for dynamic Web resources [40,21]. Pushing methods to the clients are sometimes utilised [41].

Secure Web Resources

Secure Web resources are static, dynamic or volatile objects transferred over a ciphered channel, usually through the HTTPS protocol. Secure resources address the need for privacy, non-repudiation, integrity and authentication. They are typically characterised by high CPU processing demands, due to the computational requirements of the cryptographic algorithms [18,25].

Multimedia Resources

Multimedia resources are associated with video and audio content, such as video clips, mp3 audio files, Shockwave Flash animations and movies. There are two main ways to use multimedia resources: download-and-play, or play-during-download. In the former case, multimedia content is usually transferred through the HTTP protocol. The typical size of a multimedia resource is much larger than that of other resources, hence download traffic caused by these files has a deep impact on network bandwidth requirements. In the case of play-during-download, the download service must be integrated with streaming-oriented protocols, such as RTP [21,43], and well-designed technologies that provide content from the Web application without interruption.

6.2.2 Web Application's Bearing on System Resources

Over the years, Web applications have evolved from being simple, static pages to applications that incorporate complex, dynamic and secure services, such as e-commerce and home-banking applications. A complete taxonomy that take into account every type of Web application is outside the context of this chapter. Thus, we focus solely on application designs that takes into account performance and reliability. In such a scenario, it is important to consider the four main hardware resources of a system's platform: CPU, disk, central memory and network interface. Moreover, we suggest it is more important to focus on the classes of requests than on the types of resources offered by a Web application. Indeed, each application comprises a mix of Web resources, but for each workload mix there is a prevalent class of requests that has a major impact on system resources. As an example, if the workload model is predominantly characterised by downloads of multimedia files, the network capacity has a primary impact on system performance; hence it is important to design an architecture able to guarantee high network throughput. For the above reasons we classify Web applications according to their predominant request class.

Predominantly Static Applications
Currently, the design of static Web applications is not considered challenging, as existing Web technologies are able to serve an impressive volume of static requests, even with commodity off-the-shelf hardware and software. The only requirement a static Web application has to meet relates to the network capacity of the outbound link, which must handle the necessary volume of client requests/responses with no risk of bottleneck.

Predominantly Dynamic Applications
Dynamic Web applications offer sophisticated and interactive services, possibly with personalised content. An idiosyncrasy of dynamic applications is the strong interaction between Web technology and information sources (usually, databases) for nearly every client request. To provide adequate performance to serve dynamic resources may prove to be a non-trivial task, as there are several technologies for dynamic content generation, each with advantages and drawbacks. Choosing the wrong technology may lead to poor performance of the entire application. Section 6.3 is dedicated to the analysis of dynamic Web applications and related technologies.

Predominantly Secure Applications
Secure Web applications provide services that are protected due to security and privacy concerns. Examples include on-line shopping, and auction

applications, and home-banking services. Purchase is the most critical operation in secure e-commerce applications, because sensitive information (e.g. credit card number) is exchanged. When users buy, security requirements become significant and include privacy, non-repudiation, integrity and authentication rules. The transactions should be tracked throughout the entire user session and backed up in the case of failures. The largest part of secure applications' content is often generated dynamically; however, even static resources may need a secure transmission.

The maximum computational requirement in secure applications is due to the initial public-key cryptographic challenge, which is needed to perform the authentication phase [18]. This is in accordance with a previous result [25], which confirms that the reuse of cached SSL session keys can significantly reduce client response time (from 15% to 50%) in secure Web-based services.

Predominantly Multimedia Applications
Multimedia Web applications are characterised by a large amount of multimedia content, such as audio and video clips, animations or slide-shows. Examples of multimedia applications include e-learning services, a few e-commerce services specialised in music (e.g. iTunes [28]), on-line radios, and applications that offer a download section with a repository of multimedia files.

We recall that two modes are available for multimedia resources realization: file download or content streaming. In the former case, the primary design challenge is the same as for static Web applications, i.e. to provide enough network bandwidth for downloading large multimedia files. As multimedia resources are orders of magnitude larger than static resources, bandwidth requirements are quite critical. In the latter case, introducing streaming protocols increases the issues in the design of a Web application because streaming-based delivery of multimedia content introduces real-time constraints in packet scheduling [43], and often requires a network resource reservation protocol.

6.2.3 Workload Models and Performance Requirements

Knowing the composition of each service in terms of Web resources gives a precise idea about the functional and software requirements for the design of the Web application, but only a rough approximation for the design of the Web platform. Indeed, service characterisation alone is not enough to quantify the amount of system resources that are needed to meet the requested level of performance. For example, a service requiring many system resources, but represented by infrequent accesses, may not have an impact on the Web application. On the other hand, another service with low resource requirements and frequent accesses may influence the performance of the entire Web system.

For these reason, it is necessary to characterise a set of *workload models* that represent the behaviour of clients when they access each Web application's service. The combined knowledge, obtained from both the service and the workload characterisation, permits us to identify the system and Web resources that will be used most intensively. As we are interested in serving a large number of users with many classes of services, it is important to define the main workload models that are expected to access the Web application. Each workload model is represented by the *workload intensity* that correspond to the typical number of requests admitted in the Web application, and by the *workload mixes* that corresponds to the number of requests in each class of service. Hence, we can consider expected workload models that reflect the typical volume and mix of requests supposed to reach the Web system, and also worst-case workload models that reflect the maximum amount of client requests that are admitted in the Web application.

The next critical step is to quantify the level of adequate performance for the expected set of workload models. Only after this choice is it possible to design and size the components and the system resources of the Web system, according to performance and reliability expectations. The problem here is that it is quite difficult to anticipate the possible offered loads to the Web application without any previous experience. The large number of system- and user-oriented performance parameters (some of which are reported in Section 6.4), as well as the types of reliability goals, make it even more complicated to define exact levels of adequate performance without testing the system under representative workload models. In practice, the definition of the performance expectations is an iterative process. During the design phase, the commissioner can provide a rough idea of workload intensity and mixes to the Web application designers and architects. It should be clear to both parties that the initial proposals do not represent a formal contract. On the other hand, the designers should be aware that it is preferable to choose a Web application architecture that guarantees a safe margin in expected performance (twofold as initially declared by the commissioner is not unusual).

Once the requirements of the Web system are defined in terms of Web resources, workload models and performance expectations, the design and deployment of the Web application become a matter of choosing the right software and hardware technology. For this purpose, it is important to know the main strengths and weaknesses of the most popular technologies. We review in the following section those related to the dynamic-oriented Web applications.

6.3 Applications Predominantly Dynamic

To describe the hardware and software design of a Web application, we consider a system servicing resources that are mainly dynamic. This type of application is highly popular and introduces interesting design challenges, hence we consider it a representative case for describing the proposed methodology of design and testing.

6.3.1 Dynamic Request Service

An abstract view of the main steps for servicing a dynamic request is presented in Fig. 6.2. Three main entities are involved in the request service: the client, the Internet and the Web system. As we are more interested in the server part, we detail the Web system components. There are three main abstract functions that contribute to service a dynamic request: *HTTP interface*, *application logic* and *information source*.

The HTTP interface handles connection requests from the clients through the standard HTTP protocol and serves static content. It is not responsible for the generation of dynamic content. Instead, the functions offered by the *application logic* are at the heart of a dynamic Web system: they define the logic behind the generation of dynamic content and build the HTML documents that will be sent back to the clients. Usually, the construction of a Web page requires the retrieval of further data. The *information source* layer provides functions for storage of critical information that is used in the management of dynamic requests that are passed to the application logic. The final result of the computations is an HTML (or XML) document that is sent back to the HTTP interface for delivery to the client.

The use of three separate levels of functions has its advantages. The most obvious is the *modularity*: if the interfaces among different abstraction levels are kept consistent, changes at one level do not influence other levels. Another advantage is the *scalability*: the separation of abstraction layers makes it easier to deploy them on different nodes. It is even possible

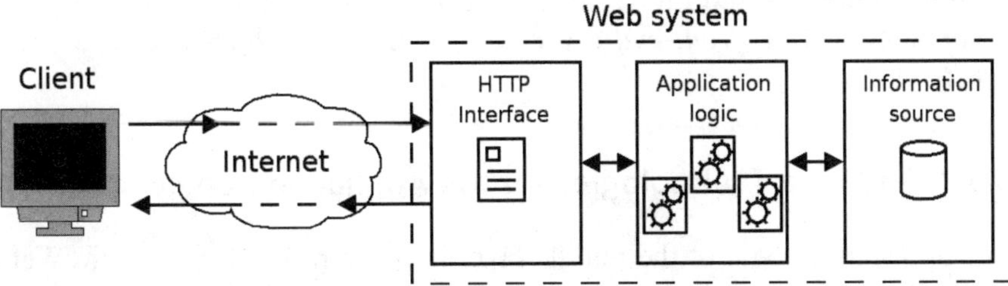

Fig. 6.2. Abstract view of a dynamic request

to deploy a single level over multiple, identical nodes. Section 6.3.3 provides some insights on these possibilities.

The management of a dynamic request is the result of the interaction of multiple and complex functions (see Fig. 6.2). Each of them can be deployed through different software technologies that have their own strengths and weaknesses. Furthermore, they can be mapped in different ways to the underlying hardware. A performance-oriented design must address both issues: choose the right software technologies and the hardware architecture for the Web system. This is a non-trivial task that must be solved through an extensive analysis of the main alternatives at the software and hardware levels.

From the point of view of software technologies, the real design challenge resides in the choice of the appropriate *application logic*, since both the HTTP interface and information source are well established. For the HTTP interface, Apache has become the most popular Web server [35], followed by other products, such as MS Internet Information Services, Sun Java System Web Server, Zeus. All of them provide the main functions of an HTTP server, but differ in the portability and efficiency levels that depend on operating systems and system platforms. Hence, the design of the HTTP interface becomes a simple choice among one of the aforementioned products, as long as it is compatible with the underlying platform and adopted software technologies. Apache works better with other open source products, such as PHP, Perl, Python. MS IIS works better with Microsoft software technologies.

Similar considerations hold for the *information source* layer that handles the storage and retrieval of data. This layer consists of a database management system (DBMS) and storage elements. There are many alternatives in the DBMS world, even if all of them are based on the relational architecture and an SQL dialect. The most common products are MySQL [33] and PostgreSQL [38] on the open source side, and MS SQL Server, Oracle and IBM DB2 on the proprietary side. Hence, choosing the information source basically is a matter of cost, management, operating system constraints, internal competences and taste.

In the following section, we use a notation that is widely adopted in the Web literature. We refer to HTTP interface, application logic and information source also as *front-end layer*, *middle layer* and *back-end layer*, respectively.

6.3.2 Software Technologies for the Application Logic

The application logic of the middle layer is at the heart of a dynamic Web application. This layer computes the information which will be used to construct documents that are sent over a protocol handler. There is a plethora of software technologies which implement different standards. Each of them has its advantages and drawbacks with respect to performance, modularity, scalability. Let us distinguish the *scripting* from the *component-based* technologies.

Scripting Technologies

Scripting technologies are based on a language interpreter that is integrated in the Web server software. The interpreter processes the code that is embedded in the HTML pages and that typically accesses the database. The script code is replaced with its output, and the resulting HTML is returned to the client. Static HTML code (also called *HTML template*) is left unaltered. Examples of scripting technologies include language processors such as PHP [37], ASP [1] and ColdFusion [20].

Scripting technologies are efficient for dynamic content generation, because they are tightly coupled with the Web server. They are ideal for medium-sized, monolithic applications that require an efficient execution environment. Other applications that benefit from scripting technologies are characterised by large amounts of static, template HTML code that embeds a (relatively) small amount of dynamically generated data. An example is the ordinary product description page of an e-commerce application, which has an HTML template that is filled with variable information, retrieved from the database.

On the other hand, the tight coupling between the front-end and the middle layer, which is typical of scripting languages, severely limits their use in Web-related applications that require high scalability. Indeed, to achieve scalability, it may be necessary to add nodes, but scripting technologies often lack integrated, high-level support for coordination and synchronisation of tasks running on different nodes. This support can be implemented through the use of function libraries, provided with the most popular scripting languages. However, this requires an additional, significant programming effort. For this reason, scripting technologies are seldom used to deploy highly distributed Web-based services.

Component-Based Technologies

Component-based technologies use software objects that implement the application logic. These objects are instantiated within special execution environments called *containers*. A popular component-based technology for dynamic Web resource generation is the Java 2 Enterprise Edition (J2EE) [29], which includes specifications for *Java Servlets*, *Java Server Pages* (JSPs), and *Enterprise Java Beans* (EJBs).

Java Servlets are Java classes that implement the application logic for a Web application. They are instantiated within a *Servlet container* (such as Tomcat [44]) that has an interface with the Web server. The object-oriented nature of Java Servlets enforces better modularity in the design, while the possibility to run distinct containers, on different nodes, facilitates a system scalability level that could not be achieved by the scripting technologies. Java Servlets represent the building blocks of the J2EE framework. Indeed, they only provide the low-level mechanisms for servicing dynamic requests. The programmer must take care of many details, such as coding the HTML document template, and organising the communication with external information *sources*. For these reasons, Java Servlets are usually integrated with other J2EE technologies, such as JSP and EJB technologies.

JSPs are a standard extension defined on top of the Java Servlet API that permits the embedding of Java code in an HTML document. Each JSP is automatically converted into a Java Servlet, used to serve future requests. JSPs pages try to preserve the advantages of Java Servlets, without penalising Web pages that contain a large amount of static HTML templates, and a small amount of dynamically generated content. As a consequence, JSP is a better solution for dynamic content generation than plain Java Servlets, which are more suitable to data processing and client request handling. JSP is usually the default choice for dynamic, component-based content generation.

EJBs are Java-based server-side software components that enable dynamic content generation. An EJB runs in a special environment called an *EJB container*, which is analogous to a Java Servlet container. EJB provides native support for atomic transactions that are useful for preserving data consistency through commit and rollback mechanisms. Moreover, they handle persistent information across several requests. These added functions introduce a performance penalty due to their overhead. They should be used only in those services which require user session persistence among different user requests to the same application. Common examples include database transactions and shopping cart services in e-commerce applications.

Technology Comparison

An interesting performance comparison between scripting and component-based technologies is provided in [14]. This study compares the PHP scripting technology against Java Servlets and EJB for the implementation of a simple e-commerce application. Using the same hardware architecture, PHP provides better performance with respect to other component-based technologies. The performance gain is 30% over Java Servlets, and more than double with respect to EJB. On the other hand, Java Servlets outperform the scripting technology when the system platform consists of a sufficient number of nodes.

Figure 6.3 displays a qualitative performance comparison between the two software technologies, which takes system throughput as a function of client traffic volume. From this figure we can see that scripting technologies tend to reach their maximum throughput sooner than component-based technologies, because of their more efficient execution environment. Hence, component-based technologies tend to perform badly on small-to-medium-sized Web applications, but scale better than scripting technologies and can reach even higher throughput. The main motivation lies in their high modularity, which allows for the distribution of the application logic among multiple nodes.

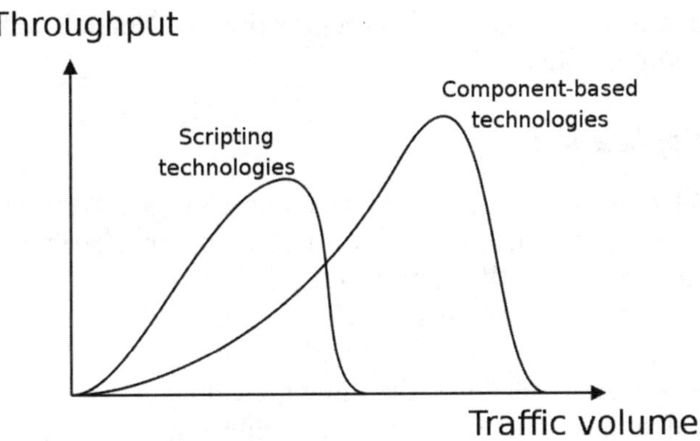

Fig. 6.3. A qualitative comparison of software technologies

6.3.3 System Platforms

Once the logical layers and the proper software technologies needed to implement the Web application are defined, they need to be mapped onto physical nodes. Typically, we do not have a one-to-one mapping because many logical layers may be located on the same physical node, and a single layer may be distributed among different nodes for the sake of performance, modularity and fault tolerance.

There are two approaches to map logical layers over the physical nodes, called *vertical* and *horizontal* replications. In a vertical replication, each logical layer is mapped to at most one physical node. Hence, each node hosts one or more logical layers. In a horizontal replication, multiple replicas of the same layer are distributed across different nodes. Horizontal and vertical replications are usually combined to reach a scalable and reliable platform.

The simplest possible hardware architecture consists of a *single node*, where all logical layers (front-end, middle, back-end) are placed on the same physical node. This architecture represents the cheapest alternative for providing a Web-based service; on the other hand, it suffers from multiple potential bottlenecks. In particular, the system resources can be easily exhausted by a high volume of client requests. Moreover, the lack of hardware component replication prevents the fault tolerance of a single node architecture. Explicit countermeasures, such as RAID storage and hot-swappable redundant hardware, may reduce the risks of single points of failure, but basically there is no reliability opportunity. We should also consider that placing every logical layer on the same node has a detrimental effect on system security because once the node has been corrupted, the entire Web system is compromised. From the above considerations, we can conclude that the single node architecture is not a viable solution for the deployment of a dynamic Web application that intends to ensure performance and reliability.

Vertical Replication

In a vertical replication, logical layers comprising the Web-based service are placed into different nodes. The most common distributions for dynamic resource-oriented Web applications lead to the vertical architectures that are based on *two-node*, *three-node* and *four-node* schemes. Figure 6.4 shows the three examples of vertical replication.

In the two-node architecture, the three logical layers are distributed over two physical nodes. There are three possible mappings between logical layers and physical nodes. However, the typical solution is to have the back-end layer on one node, and the front-end and middle layers on another. There are two main motivations for this choice. First, the tasks performed by a DBMS can easily exhaust the system resources of a single node. Second, front-end and application logic may be tightly coupled, as in the case of the scripting technologies; this makes separation of the logical layers very hard (if not impossible). The distribution over two nodes generally improves the performance of the Web system, with respect to the single node architecture. Fault tolerance still remains a problem, because a failure in any of the two nodes causes a crash of the entire Web system.

In the three-node architecture, each logical layer is placed on a distinct node. Due to the tight coupling between front-end and middle layer in scripting technologies, an architecture based on at least three nodes is the best choice for component-based technologies. For example, the J2EE specification provides inter-layer communication mechanisms that facilitate the distribution of the front-end and the middle layer among the nodes. Scripting technologies do not natively have similar mechanisms; hence they have to be entirely implemented if the distribution of the layers, over more than two nodes, is a primary concern of the architectural design. Fault tolerance is still not guaranteed by three-node architectures, since a failure in any node hinders the generation of dynamic Web content. However, the three-node solution helps improve performance and reliability, with respect to the two-node architecture, as shown in [14].

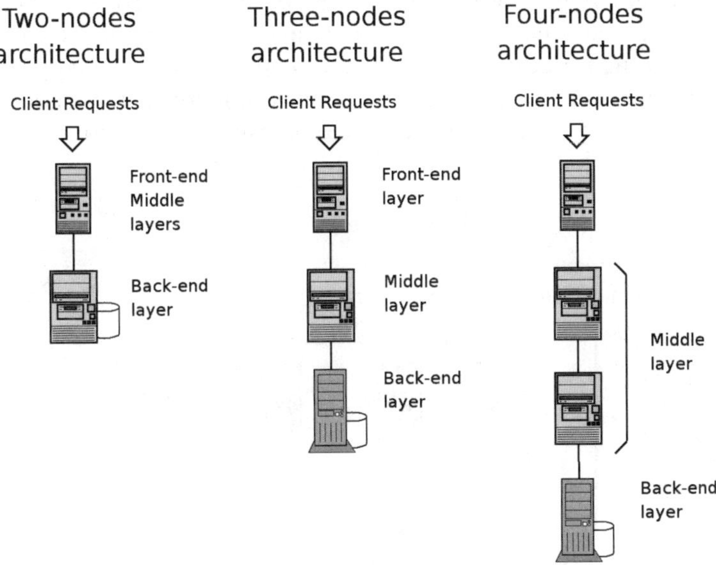

Fig. 6.4. Vertical replication

Four-node architectures are usually the choice for J2EE systems that distribute the middle layer between two physical nodes: one hosting the business logic, encapsulated into the EJB container, and the others hosting the application functions through the JSP Servlet Engine. It is convenient to adopt this architecture due to overheads caused by the EJB component.

Vertical replication is widely adopted, not just for performance reasons. When security is a primary concern, this hardware architecture is useful because it allows the deployment of a secure platform between the nodes through the use of firewalls. The possibility of controlling and restricting communication among the nodes of a Web system aids in detecting security breaches, and in reducing the consequences of a compromised system. In fact, the multi-layered architectures presented in Fig. 6.4 are a simplification of real systems that include network switches, authentication servers and other security-oriented components.

Vertical and Horizontal Replications

Higher performance and reliability purposes motivate the replication of nodes at one or more logical layers, which is called *horizontal replication*. This replication type is usually combined with vertical replication. Figure 6.5 shows the combination of horizontal and vertical replication. In particular, it shows a three-layer system, where each of the three logical levels is hosted over a cluster of identical nodes, each connected through a high-speed LAN, and running the same components. Initial distribution is achieved through a component called *Web switch*, which may be implemented in hardware or software. To achieve horizontal replication, other mechanisms are needed for distributing requests among the nodes of each layer.

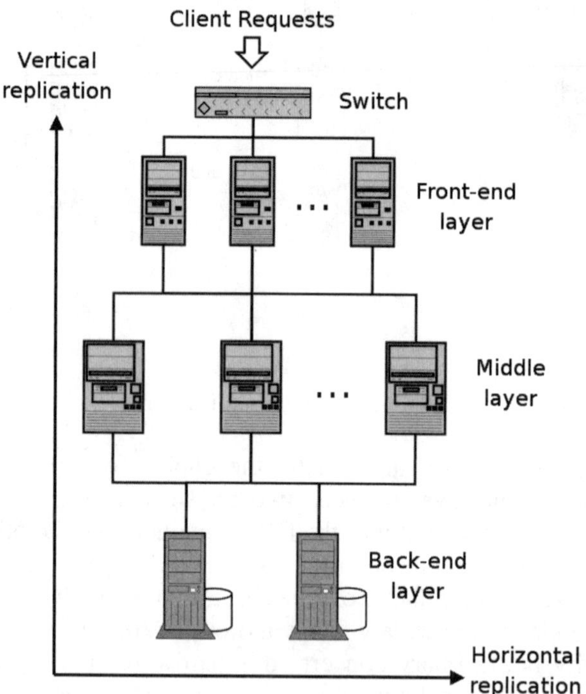

Fig. 6.5. Vertical and horizontal replication

When choosing a Web system's architecture, it is important to know that the horizontal replication requires different efforts depending on the layer concerned. For example, the replication of the front-end layer causes fewer problems because the HTTP protocol is stateless and different HTTP requests may be handled independently by different nodes [11].

The replication of the middle layer is rather complex due to two main factors: first, the use of user session information by most applications; and second, the type of software technology that is adopted for the implementation. Web-based services that use session information must be equipped with mechanisms that guarantee data consistency. Scripting technologies usually do not support such mechanisms natively; some rely on external modules, others are forced to store session information in the back-end, with risks of serious slowdowns. Even in component-based technologies, the implementation of data consistency is not always immediate. For example, Java Servlets do not provide native persistent data support, while this is one of the strong attributes of EJB.

It is generally difficult to replicate horizontally, even the back-end layer, because it introduces data consistency issues that must be addressed through difficult and onerous solutions [26]. Modern DBMSs are equipped with the necessary mechanisms that guarantee horizontal replication of databases, but this replication is limited to a few units.

The combination of vertical and horizontal replication helps to improve important design objectives, such as scalability and fault tolerance, which are crucial for obtaining an adequate level of performance and reliability. In particular, horizontal replication allows the use of dispatching algorithms that tend to distribute the load uniformly among the nodes [10,3]. Moreover, hardware and software redundancy, provided by horizontal replication, also helps to add a level of fault tolerance to the system.

A more complete fault tolerance requires also *fault detection* and *fail-over* mechanisms. Fault detection mechanisms monitor system components and check whether they are operative or not. When a faulty component is detected, the dispatchers may be instrumented to bypass that node; meanwhile, there are fail-over mechanisms that allow us to substitute the faulty node on-the-fly [12].

6.4 Testing Loop Phase

Once the Web-based service has been designed and deployed, it is necessary to verify services, functional correctness (*functional testing*) and that performance and reliability requirements are satisfied for each workload model included (*performance testing*).

Functional testing aims to verify that a Web application works as expected, without regard to performance. This type of test is carried out by defining and reproducing typical behavioural user patterns for different operations. Each request's output is matched against an expected, desired template. Unexpected behaviours, or failures, imply that the Web system has not been deployed correctly, and that appropriate software corrections are needed. Details of Web system debugging are outside the scope of this chapter. Rather, we focus on performance testing, which allows us to verify whether the Web system guarantees the expected performance. The performance testing of a dynamic resource-oriented Web application is a non-trivial activity that requires the completion of different tasks: *representation of the workload model, traffic generation, data collection and analysis*. Each is detailed in subsequent sections.

6.4.1 Representation of the Workload Model

The first crucial step of testing is the translation of the workload models into a sequence of client requests, to be used by load generation tools to reproduce the appropriate volume of traffic. The choice of a request stream representation depends greatly on the complexity of workload patterns. There are two main approaches, according to the complexity of the workload model.

Simple workload patterns, such as those of static resource-oriented Web applications, are usually well represented through *file lists* (with their access frequencies) and *analytical distributions*. While being fairly straightforward to implement, these two representations present drawbacks that limit their application to more sophisticated workloads. For example, file lists lack flexibility with respect to the workload specification, and do not provide any support for modelling the session-oriented nature of Web traffic.

Analytical distributions allow us to define a wide characterisation, being all features specified through mathematical models. It is an open issue to determine whether an analytical model reflects user behaviour in a realistic way. From our experience, we can say that the large majority of studies has been focused on static content characterisation [8,9,10], while fewer studies consider Web applications with prevalent dynamic and personalised content. Studies related to Web publishing applications can be found in [6,45], and the characterisation of on-line shopping applications has been analysed in [7,45]. In addition, preliminary results for trading and B2B applications can be found in [31] and [45], respectively.

The modelling of more complicated browsing patterns, such as those associated with on-line transactions, may require the creation of ad-hoc workloads, through the use of *file traces* and, in some case, the definition of *finite state automata*.

File traces of a workload model are based on pre-recorded (or synthetically generated) logs, derived from Web server access logs. Traces aim to capture the behaviour of users in the most realistic way. On the other hand, the validity of tests depends strongly on the representativeness of a trace. Some of them may show characteristics peculiar to a specific Web application with no general validity. Furthermore, it may be difficult to adjust the workload described by a trace to emulate future conditions, or varying demands, as well as to reconstruct user sessions.

The workload model may be described through finite state automata, where each state is associated to a Web page. A transition from one state to another occurs with a predefined probability. A user think time is modelled as a variable delay between two consecutive state transitions. The main advantage of finite state automata lies in the possibility of defining complicated browsing patterns, which reflect modern consumer- oriented Web applications. On the other hand, most of these patterns need to be manually specified, which is an error-prone operation.

6.4.2 Traffic Generation

Once the proper representation is chosen, the client request stream has to be replayed through a traffic generator. The main goal of a traffic generator is to reproduce the specified traffic in the most accurate and scalable way. Besides, it also has to reproduce realistically the behaviour of a fully featured Web browser, with support for persistent HTTP connections, cookie management, or secure connections through the HTTPS protocol.

There are four main approaches to generate a stream of Web requests: *trace-based*, *file list-based*, *analytical distribution-driven* and *finite-state automata-based*. Each depends on the workload model that is used as the base for traffic generation.

The imitation of wide area network effects is another important factor that must be taken into consideration during the performance tests. It has been shown that, even in the presence of static resource-oriented Web applications, the performance evaluation is sensibly altered if the network is perturbed by routing delays, packet losses or client bandwidth limitations [34]. If these are not taken into consideration, which typically occurs if the Web application's performance is evaluated using a LAN, then measured performance differs significantly from the reality, thus making the test results almost useless.

6.4.3 Data Collection and Analysis

Data collection is strictly related to the two main goals of the performance testing analysis: to understand if a Web system is performing adequately and, if the expectations are not satisfied, to find the possible causes of performance slowdowns. They are the purpose of *black-box* and *white-box* testing, respectively.

Data collection addresses two main issues of sampling: the choice of representative metrics[2] for a given performance index, and the granularity of samples. The former problem is independent of the black and white-box testing. As Web workload is characterised by heavy-tailed distributions [9], many performance indexes may assume highly variable values with non-negligible probability. Therefore, evaluating the performance only on the basis of mean, minimum and maximum values, may not yield a representative view of a Web system's behaviour. When performance indexes are subject to high variability, the use of higher moments, such as percentiles or cumulative distributions, is highly recommended. This, in turn, typically requires the storage of every sample.

The choice of the sample granularity is related to testing goals. Sampling of performance indexes may occur at different levels of granularity, mainly *system* and *resource*. The former is more related to black-box testing, the latter to white-box testing.

Black-box Testing

The main goal of black-box testing is to check whether the Web system is able to meet performance and reliability requirements, for each workload model, with safe margins. Black-box testing is related to *system performance indexes* that quantify the performance of the entire Web system, as seen from the outside. These are typically coarse-grained samples that aim to verify whether the Web system is performing adequately or not. Many performance indexes may be obtained from the running system, for different purposes. For example, the throughput of a Web system in terms of served pages/hits/bytes per second may be of interest for the administrator, to check if the architecture is able to deliver the requested traffic volume. A Web page response time, i.e. the elapsed time from a user's click until the arrival of the last object composing a Web resource, is of main interest for users for whom system throughput is of no concern, but who wish to check the time they have to wait for the fruition of a given service. Both indexes reflect the performance of the entire Web system, from different points of view. Although we do not consider a QoS-based Web application that has to comply with rigorous Service Level Agreements (SLAs), it is suitable to mention soft constraints, generally accepted in the world of interactive Web-based services. For example, a previous study by IBM [16] provides a ranking of performance parameters (ranging from unacceptable to excellent) in terms of response time for a typical Web page loaded by a dial-up user. The study concludes that a Web page response time higher than 30 seconds is unacceptable, while everything below

[2] Metrics have the same meaning as measures.

20þseconds is considered at least adequate. In [36], the reaction of broadband users to different Web page download times is analysed. One conclusion is that the limit to keep a user's attention focused on the browser window is about 10 seconds. Longer-lasting Web page downloads lead users towards other tasks.

It is important that a Web system works within safe performance margins. The consequences of this claim are twofold: first, the system must follow the performance requirements for any expected workload; second, when the system is subject to the maximum expected workload intensity, it should not show signs of imminent congestion. The former requirement can be verified through a set of independent black-box tests for each representative workload model. The latter requirement is motivated by the observation that a Web system may meet all of its performance requirements, but with critically utilised resources. A similar situation is unacceptable because a burst of client arrivals may easily saturate the resource, thus slowing down the entire Web system. To avoid the risk of drawing false conclusions about a system's performance reliability, we can use a white-box test, or carry out black-box tests to evaluate performance trends. For now we will remain within the context of black-box testing.

Performance trends can be evaluated as a function of different workload mixes, or workload intensities. In the latter case, we can evaluate the page response time as a function of an increasing traffic volume reaching the Web system, possibly even slightly higher than the maximum expected workload intensity.

Figure 6.6 gives an example of performance trend evaluation in a system where the maximum expected workload intensity, and the adequate performance, are clearly defined. Three performance curves (P_1, P_2, P_3) are

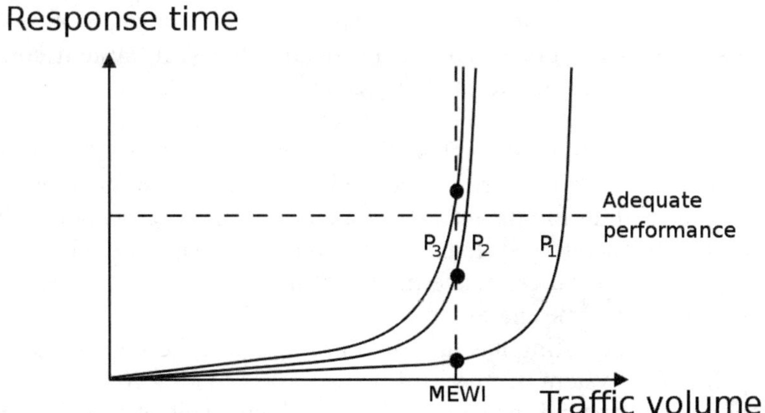

Fig. 6.6. Analysis of performance trends of the Web system

considered, in addition to response times obtained for the maximum expected workload intensity (MEWI). If we limit the black-box analysis to the MEWI point, we can conclude that P_1 and P_2 are acceptable, whereas P_3 does not respect the required service level. However, a trend black-box analysis indicates that even P_2 is not safe enough. Indeed, in association with the maximum expected workload intensity, the P_2 curve already shows an exponential growth. For both the P_2 and P_3 cases, the black-box test should be considered failed, and we should resort to white-box testing to verify the causes of (possible) bottleneck.

White-Box Testing

During black-box testing, it is not necessary to consider the internal parts of a Web system. We can sample performance indexes outside the Web system while it is used with each of the predefined workload models. Conversely, white-box testing aims to evaluate the behaviour of a Web platform's internal system components, for different client request rates (usually, around the maximum expected workload intensity). This task can optionally be performed after a black-box test, to be sure that the utilisation of Web system components is well below critical levels. However, it becomes compulsory in two situations: when the system is violating the performance requirements (e.g., the P_3 curve in Fig. 6.6), and when the trends indicated by black-box testing suggest the presence of possible bottlenecks (e.g. the P_2 curve in Fig. 6.6). To find potential or actual Web system bottlenecks, it is necessary to carry out more detailed analysis, which takes finer-grained performance indexes into account. White-box testing is carried out by applying the expected workload models to the Web-based service, and by monitoring its internals to ensure that system resource utilisation does not exceed critical levels. For this purpose, we use *resource performance indexes* that measure the performance of a Web system's internal resources. They help identify the Web system components most utilised. Examples of resource indexes include component utilisation (CPU, disk, network, central memory), and amount of limited software resources (such as file and socket descriptors, process table entries). These fine-grain resource performance indexes require additional tools that must be executed during the test. Some tools are publicly available within ordinary UNIX operating systems [39,42], but they do not provide samples for every system resource, hence modifications to the source code (when available) are sometimes necessary.

Once white-box testing has indicated the nature of the bottleneck(s) affecting the Web system, it may still be necessary to collect additional information to understand the causes of the problem. This allows us to plan appropriate actions for removing the bottleneck. An insufficient amount of information concerning the problem limits the range of effective and efficient interventions to improve performance and reliability. To deepen the analysis, it is necessary to inspect the Web system at an even finer granularity, that of program functions. This allows us to identify *hot spots:* that is, critical sections of executable code consuming a significant amount of bottleneck resources.

Performance indexes at the function level are associated to the functions of each executable program, including the operating system's kernel. Common examples include the function call frequency and the percentage of time spent by the program in each main function. Function-level analysis requires special tools [30] that collect statistics and provide customisable views for function accesses and service times.

After the bottleneck removal step, a new testing phase follows (involving black-box and white-box testing), in order to verify that performance and reliability targets have been achieved. As outlined in Section 6.1, the entire procedure is a fix-and-test loop that may require several attempts to achieve the desired goals. In the next section, we detail the various categories of possible interventions to remove potential bottlenecks.

6.5 Performance Improvements

Whenever a performance test fails, the Web system is not operating adequately or reliably, and proper intervention is required. As already outlined in Section 6.4, test failures can happen in different cases. First, black-box testing can indicate a performance that is below the expected level. Second, even if the goals for "adequate performance" are met, performance can still be compromised by high utilisation of system resources that can lead to a bottleneck, if the client request traffic further increases. Finally, it is often interesting to carry out capacity planning studies that test the system under expected *future* workload models. These studies tend to put more stress on the resources of the Web system, which may cause saturation and introduce new bottlenecks that need to be removed. In this section, we discuss three main interventions for improving the performance and reliability of a Web system: *system tuning*, *scale-up* and *scale-out.*

6.5.1 System Tuning

System tuning aims to improve system performance by appropriately choosing operating system and application parameters. There are two major ways: first, to increase available software resources related to the operating system and critical applications; second, to reduce hardware resource utilisation. The typical intervention, to improve the capacity of a software resource, tends to raise the number of available file descriptors, sockets and process descriptors. Alternatively, sophisticated mechanisms, such as *caching* and *pooling*, are adopted to limit the utilisation of critical system hardware or software resources. Caching avoids information re-computation by preserving it in memory. Examples of commonly cached entities include database queries and Web pages. In resource pooling, multiple software resources are generated and grouped into a set (called *pool*), previous to being used, so they become immediately available upon request. They are not destroyed on release, but returned to the pool. The main advantage of pooling is the reduced overhead of resource creation and destruction, saving system resources. The TCP connections (especially, persistent TCP connections to a DBMS) are typical resources handled through a pool, because they are expensive to setup and destroy.

The size of caches and resource pools is a typical parameter to be tuned. Increasing the size tends to avoid re-computation (as in the case of caches) and to reduce set-up/destruction overheads (as in the case of pooling). In both cases, the utilisation of critical system resources is reduced. However, restrictions in the available amount of memory (both main and secondary) and operating system resources (e.g. socket and file descriptors) limit the maximum size of caches and pools.

6.5.2 System Scale-up

Scale-up consists of an upgrade of one or more hardware resources, without adding new nodes to the underlying architecture. This intervention is necessary whenever white-box testing shows (the risk of) a saturated hardware resource (e.g. disk bandwidth or CPU power). Usually, a hardware upgrade is straightforward and does not require extensive system analysis. However, two points are important when performing scale-up. First, hardware upgrades are useless if an operating system resource (such as file descriptors) is exhausted. In such a scenario, adding hardware does not increase the capacity of the blocked resource. Second, performance improvements may often be obtained at lower costs through parameter tuning, previously discussed.

6.5.3 System Scale-out

System scale-out interventions aim at adding nodes to the platform. This can be achieved through vertical or horizontal replications. A vertical replication deploys the logical layers over more nodes (e.g. it may pass from a two-node to a three-node architecture); a horizontal replication adds nodes to one or more layers. Both interventions improve system performance. However, horizontal replication can also be used to improve the Web system's reliability. As the redesign of the platform implies non-negligible costs, in terms of time and money, scale-out should be used only when no performance improvement, based on scale-up, can be achieved. Furthermore, not all software technologies are well suited for scale-out. For example, Section 6.3 discusses that scripting technologies do not provide any native support for service distribution. Hence, system scale-out would imply a massive redesign of the applications supporting the Web-based service.

An even greater scale-out intervention may be necessary when performance degradation is caused by the network connecting the Web system to the Internet (the so-called *first mile*). Indeed, locally distributed Web server systems may suffer from bottlenecks that affect the capacity of outbound connections [4]. Performance and scalability improvements can be achieved through a geographically distributed architecture that is managed by the content provider, or by recurring to outsourcing solutions. The deployment of a geographically distributed Web system is expensive and requires uncommon skills. As a consequence, only a few large organisations can afford to handle geographical scale-out by themselves. An alternative is to employ Content Delivery Networks (CDNs) [2], which, by handling Web content and service delivery, thus relieve the content provider from the design and management of a complex, and geographically distributed, architecture. There are many aspects that cannot be exhaustively described in this chapter. For more details on geographically distributed Web applications the reader can refer to [40].

6.6 Case Study

We present a case study that illustrates the main steps introduced in Section 6.1, and detailed in the subsequent sections. After the characterisation of a Web-based service and workload models, we show a possible design and deployment of a Web system. We then carry out white-box and black-box performance testing, aimed at finding and removing system bottlenecks.

6.6.1 Service Characterisation and Design

Web Resources Characterisation

The application used as a case study is an on-line shop Web application that allows users to browse a product catalogue and to purchase goods. These two main user interactions with the Web system illustrate the type of Web resources that will be used. In particular, the workload mix of the Web-based service is characterised by a few static Web resources mainly related to product images. In addition, most HTML documents are generated dynamically. Within the context of this case study, we assume that an external payment gateway system is used; as a consequence, the Web system does not serve secure Web resources. The Web-based service characteristics correspond to those of a predominantly dynamic Web application (see Section 6.2.2).

Workload Model Characterisation

The set of expected workload models for a Web application captures the most common user interactions with the Web-based service. We consider two workload models, namely *browsing* and *buying*, which have their workload mix shown in Table 6.1. The *browsing* workload model is represented predominantly by product browsing actions, which use static and dynamic resources. The presence of static content is motivated by the high amount of images shown during browsing. The *buying* workload model is represented by purchase transactions involving a high amount of dynamic resources. Table 6.1 also shows that no secure, volatile and multimedia resources are present in either workload model.

The amount of clients accessing the application can change at different temporal scales (daily, weekly, season). However, we assume that the maximum expected workload intensity does not exceed 400 concurrent users. Whenever this threshold is reached, the Web system rejects requests for connection. We will allude to this maximum workload intensity when defining the Web system's performance requirements.

Table 6.1. Composition of the workload models

Workload model	Static resource requests (%)	Dynamic resource requests (%)
Browsing	60	40
Buying	05	95

Performance Requirements

Once the workload models have been defined, performance requirements for each workload mix need to be set. The page response time was chosen as the main system parameter. The first performance requirement to be defined is related to user-perceived performance. A previous study [17] showed that a Web page download time exceeding 25 seconds is perceived as slow by ordinary dial-up users. However, due to the growing number of x-DSL and cable modem connections, we chose to use as the basis for performance evaluation page response times that represent faster connections (e.g. ADSL links). Nielsen [36] suggests that an acceptable response time threshold for page downloads, using high-bandwidth Internet connections, is 10 seconds.

Due to a tailed distribution of page response time, we rather represent response time's 90th percentile, i.e. performance requirements are only met if page response time is below the threshold set to 10 seconds. For a system-oriented view, we also evaluate system throughput using served pages per second.

System Design

To design a Web system, software technologies for each of its three logical layers must be chosen. Due to its critical nature, we find it convenient to focus on the middle layer. Since the Web application is of medium size, no extreme scalability requirements are to be met. Hence, we can assume that this system will not use a highly distributed architecture. In addition, many pages are represented by a fixed template, with a significant amount of static HTML code. The application's size and the presence of large HTML page templates suggest that the application's middle layer can be deployed using a scripting technology.

We chose PHP [37] as the scripting language because of its efficiency and for being open source, thus reducing deployment costs. PHP is easily integrated in the Apache Web server [5], which is our choice for the front-end layer. Finally, we chose MySQL [33] as the DBMS for the back-end layer. Our choice is motivated by the fact that MySQL is also open source, and widely adopted. Furthermore, it offers adequate performance, considering the size of our application, and it is well supported by the PHP interpreter.

Next, we need to map the three logical layers onto physical nodes. Scripting technologies typically lead to a two-node vertical architecture. Indeed, separation of the middle and the back-end layers on different nodes is a common choice in most medium-sized Web applications. Due to the application's performance requirements, we can dismiss horizontally replicated architectures, which would introduce significant complexity to the middle layer software.

We can summarise the design choices for the deployment of the Web application as follows. One node runs both the Apache Web server (version 2.0) and the PHP4 engine, used for the front-end and middle layers, respectively. The back-end layer is on a separate node running MySQL database server (version 4.0). All computers are based on the Linux operating system with kernel version 2.6.8. Each node is equipped with a 2.4 GHz hyperthreaded Xeon, 1GB of main memory, 80GB ATA disks (7200 rpm, transfer rate 55MB/s) and a Fast Ethernet 100Mbps adapter.

6.6.2 Testing Loop Phase

Initial black-box testing was carried out to verify if the Web system satisfies the performance requirements for all the workload models considered. The test-bed architecture is rather simple, as shown in Fig. 6.7: a node hosts the *client emulator*; the other two nodes comprise the platform that hosts the Web application.

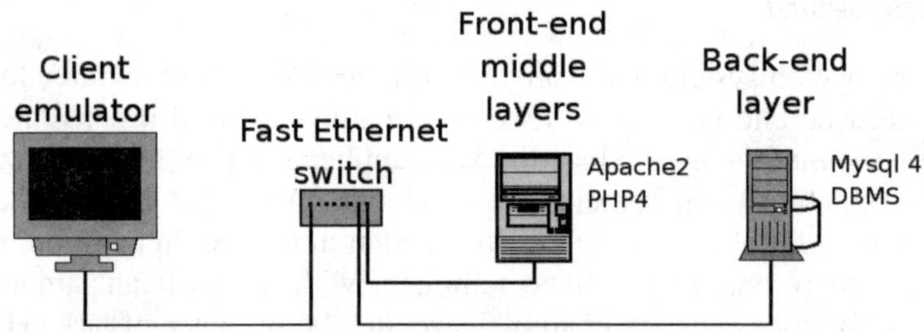

Fig. 6.7. Architecture of the test-bed for the experiments

The client emulator creates a fixed number of client processes, which instantiate sessions made up of multiple requests to the e-commerce system. For each customer session, the client emulator opens a persistent HTTP connection to the Web server, which lasts until the end of the session. Session length has a mean value of 15 minutes. Before initiating the next request, each emulated client waits for a specified time, with an average of 7 seconds. The sequence of requests is emulated by a finite state machine that specifies the probability to pass from one Web page request to another.

To take into account the wide area network effects, we use a network emulator, based on the *netem* packet scheduler [27], that creates a virtual link between the clients and the e-commerce system with the following characteristics: the packet delay is normally distributed with $\upsilon = 200\ ms$ and $\sigma = 10\ ms$, the packet drop probability is set to 1%. Bandwidth limitation in the *last mile* (i.e. the client–Internet connection) is provided directly by the client emulator.

Black-Box Testing

Initially, we consider system-level measures to determine the capacity of the Web system. We carry out tests with browsing and buying workload models, and measure the system's throughput and the Web page response time for different values of the client population.

Figure 6.8 shows the system's throughput (measured as Web pages served per second, including embedded objects) as a function of four client populations for both browsing and buying workload models. The browsing workload model shows a close-to-linear throughput increase with the user population, while the histogram of the buying workload model shows a clear throughput saturation occurring between 300 and 400 clients. Further increases of user population beyond 300 units does not improve the system throughput, which remains close to 40 pages per second.

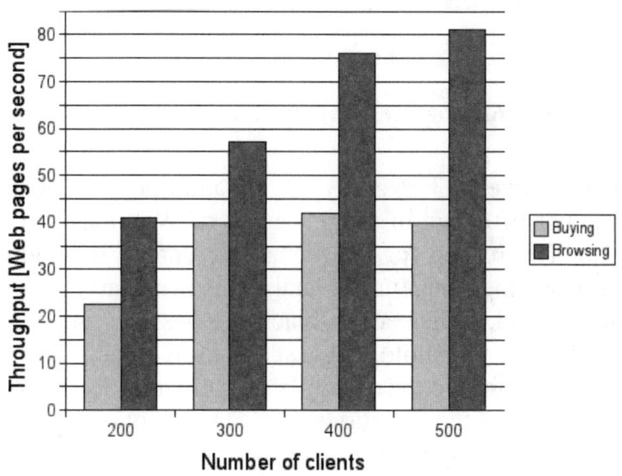

Fig. 6.8. Web system's throughput

In addition, we also assessed the system response time's 90th percentile for both workload models, for different client populations (see Fig. 6.9). The *browsing* model shows response times well below the 10 second threshold. On the other hand, the *buying* workload model shows an increase of nearly one order of magnitude (from 0.9 to 8.8 seconds) in page response time, especially when the population increases from 300 to 400 clients. The expected performance requirement is met: a response time of 8.8 seconds is still below the threshold.

However, the sudden growth in the response time, in association with a critical throughput, is an indication that a bottleneck occurs in the system when the number of clients is between 300 and 400. We also check if the response time's exponential growth trend is also present in association with a higher number of clients. For this reason we continue our black-box testing, increasing the number of clients up to 500; 500 clients corresponds to an increase in relatively small response time, when compared to that for

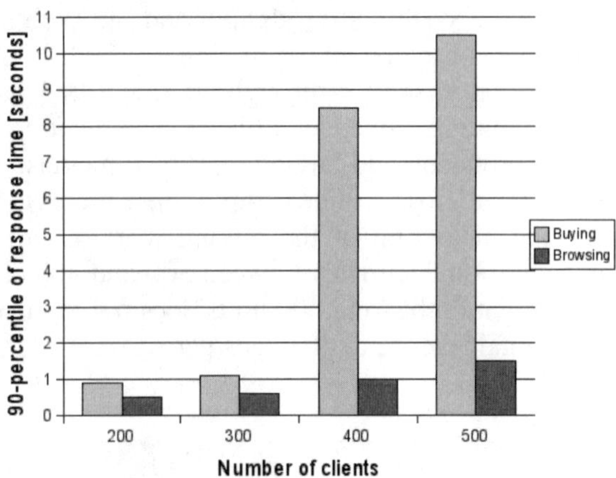

Fig. 6.9. Page response time's 90th percentile

client numbers between 300 and 400. In addition, we observe a non-negligible number of errors in the provision of Web pages and refusal of client requests. The reason for this behaviour cannot be solely explained using black-box testing, thus further analysis is necessary.

The negative trend, indicated by black-box testing, and a performance value close to the set threshold, suggest the need to plan and undertake a countermeasure to improve the system's performance, as described in Section 6.4. To understand the directions that must be followed, it is necessary to carry out white-box testing.

White-Box Testing

We now present the results of white-box testing, in which we investigate the utilisation of the Web system's internal resources. The main goal is to investigate the causes of performance degradation, indicated by black-box testing, when the system is subjected to the buying workload model for a client population between 300 and 400. Furthermore, white-box testing can also help us to understand the reasons for errors in the client request service that was observed for a client population of 500 users. We chose to initiate the white-box analysis using a client population of 400 clients, as it is close to the point where the system's performance declined.

Finer-grained performance evaluations take into account resource performance indexes, such as CPU, disk and network utilisation. Table 6.2 shows the results for white-box testing, for different resources. Utilisation values are reported as the sample averages throughout the entire test's duration. Table 6.2 suggests that the system's bottleneck is caused by the CPU of the node hosting the back-end layer.

This is confirmed by the curve in Fig. 6.10, which displays the CPU utilisation of the back-end node during the experiments (the horizontal dashed line represents the mean value). A CPU utilisation of 0.9 is a clear sign of resource over-utilisation, which may be at the basis of a system bottleneck. The 80%–20% ratio between the time spent in the user and kernel mode, respectively, suggests that the application-level computations on the DBMS are much more intensive than the overhead imposed by the management of the operating system calls.

White-box tests also show an unexpected result: even if the bottleneck is related to the DBMS, the disk utilisation is quite low (0.015). The motivation for this result must be found in the size of the database, which nearly fits completely within the 1Gigabyte main memory. We conclude that, for this case study, the disk activity does not represent a potential bottleneck for the back-end node hosting the database server. Instead, the bottleneck's cause must be found from the back-end node's CPU. Our experiments confirm that due to hardware improvements, even at the entry level, it is becoming common for medium-size e-commerce databases to fit almost completely in main memory.

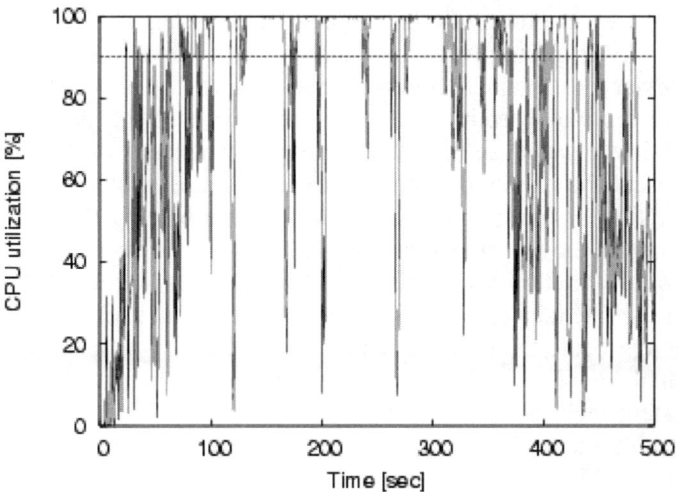

Fig. 6.10. CPU utilisation of the back-end layer node

White-box testing can also help explain errors occurring when the system is subject to heavier load, as in the case of a population of 500 clients. In this case, the finite queue of pending connection requests gets saturated. As a consequence, future client connection attempts are refused, and the actual amount of requests served by the system is only slightly higher than the amount served using 400 clients. The ultimate consequence is that the

Web system tends asymptotically to saturation, as shown by the black-box analysis. However, since the saturation of the pending connections queue only occurs after the back-end node's bottleneck, we will look into this issue in more detail, since it has a significant impact on performance.

Table 6.2. Resource utilisation (white-box testing)

Performance index	Front-end and Middle-layer	Back-end layer
• CPU utilisation	0.31	0.90
– user mode	0.21	0.76
– kernel mode	0.10	0.14
• Disk utilisation	0.003	0.015
• Network interface utilisation	0.012	0.002

The next step aims to eliminate the system's bottleneck. To this end, it is necessary to use operating system monitors to help identify what is causing the bottleneck. Monitors allow us to detect the software component that is utilising a large part of the CPU in user mode. As there is only one major application running on the back-end layer node, we can deduce that the MySQL server process is the source of the bottleneck. However, if we limit the analysis at the process granularity level, we do not have any hint. It is necessary to evaluate finer-grained indexes, at the function level. These indexes will permit us identify the source of the problem and to fully explain the causes of the inadequate performance.

We present the results of the same experiment, executed under an efficient operating system profiler [30], on the node hosting the DBMS. The profiler output shows more than 800 DBMS functions; hence a detailed analysis of all function access times and frequencies is quite difficult, and even useless. The idea is to focus on the functions that use more CPU time, while we aggregate the other functions that are not significant for the bottleneck analysis. The evaluation shows that most CPU time is consumed by consistency checks on stored data, so we can conclude that the real cause of the bottleneck is represented by the asynchronous I/O subsystem adopted in the MySQL process.

6.6.3 System Consolidation and Performance Improvement

The results of the white-box test show that the asynchronous I/O operations on the DBMS require more CPU power than what is currently available. We have three possible interventions to address this issue: system scale-out, system scale-up and system tuning. The goal now is to understand the most appropriate solution.

Scaling out the system is not the best approach to solve the problem. Vertical replication is not effective in reducing the load on the back-end node because it does not allow us to distribute the DBMS over multiple nodes. The only viable solution would be a horizontal replication of the DBMS, but MySQL has no native support to manage consistency in a database distributed over multiple nodes. Furthermore, a similar intervention would require a mechanism to distribute queries over the multiple back-end nodes. This means a complete redesign of the back-end layer and also of significant portions of the middle layer. For these reasons, we avoid interventions based on a system's scale-out.

Scale-up is a viable solution: upgrading the existing hardware is a straightforward approach, in particular if we increase the CPU speed for the back-end node. However, it is also worthwhile to investigate if tuning the DBMS's parameters can be the solution. As the problem is in the asynchronous I/O subsystem, we can try to reduce the asynchronous I/O activity by decreasing the number of buffer accesses. For example, this can be accomplished by increasing the query cache's size.

After this intervention, we re-evaluate the system performance with a second test phase. We find that the CPU utilisation on the back-end node diminishes from 0.9 to 0.6. As expected, reducing the CPU bottleneck on the back-end node improves the performance of the overall system. Figure 6.11 shows the cumulative distributions for the system's response time before and after reconfiguring the system's parameters. It confirms the validity of the intervention, as the 90th percentile for response time drops from 8.8 to 3.1 seconds after the database tuning.

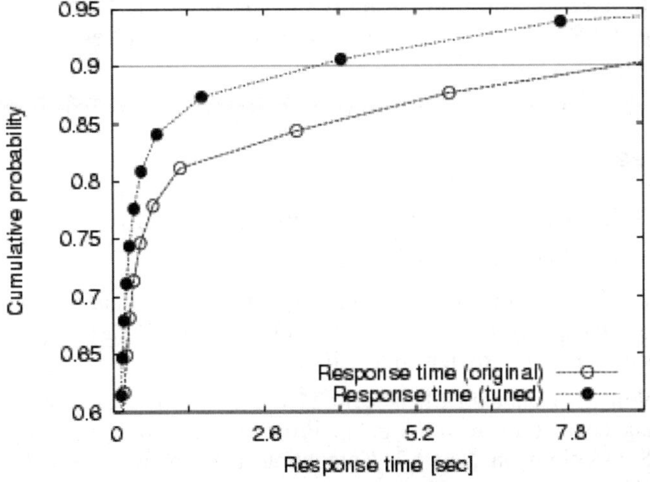

Fig. 6.11. Cumulative distribution functions for system's response time

6.7 Conclusions

Web applications are becoming a critical component of the information society. Modern Web-based services handle a wide, heterogeneous range of data, including news, personal and multimedia data. Due to their growing popularity and interactive nature, Web applications are vulnerable to increases in volume of client requests, which can hinder both performance and reliability. Thus, it is fundamental to design Web systems that can guarantee adequate levels of service at least within the expected traffic conditions.

Throughout this chapter we presented a methodology to design mission-critical Web systems that take into account performance and reliability requirements. The proposed approach is conceptually valid for every Web application, although we focus mainly on systems represented by prevalent dynamic content, since this category presents, in our view, interesting design and implementation challenges.

Besides the design process, we describe the issues related to performance testing by showing the main steps and the goals of black-box and white-box performance tests. We finally consider some interventions that can be carried out whenever performance tests are not satisfactory. After the identification of causes of violation, we present the main interventions to improve performance: system tuning, system scale-up and system scale-out. The chapter concludes with a case study in which we apply the proposed methodology to a medium-size e-commerce application.

Acknowledgements

The authors acknowledge the support of MIUR in the framework of the FIRB project "Performance evaluation of complex systems: techniques, methodologies and tools" (PERF).

References

1 Active Server Pages (2004) http://msdn.microsoft.com/asp

2 Akamai Technologies (2005) http://www.akamai.com

3 Andreolini M, Colajanni M, Morselli R (2002) Performance study of dispatching algorithms in multi-tier web architectures. ACM Sigmetrics Performance Evaluation Review, 30(2):10–20

4 Andreolini M, Colajanni M, Nuccio M (2003) Kernel-based Web switches providing content-aware routing. In: Proceedings of the 2nd IEEE International Symposium on Network Computing and Applications (NCA), Cambridge, MA

5 Apache Web server (2005) http://httpd.apache.org

6 Arlitt MF, Jin T (2000) A workload characterization study of the 1998 World Cup Web site. IEEE Network, 14(3):30–37

7 Arlitt MF, Krishnamurthy D, Rolia J (2001) Characterizing the scalability of a large scale Web-based shopping system. ACM Transaction on Internet Technology, 1(1):44–69

8 Arlitt MF, Williamson CL (1997) Internet Web servers: Workload characterization and performance implications. IEEE/ACM Transactions on Networking, 5(5):631–645

9 Barford P, Crovella M (1998) An architecture for a WWW workload generator. In: Proceedings of SIGMETRICS, Madison, WI

10 Barford P, Crovella M (1998) Generating representative Web workloads for network and server performance evaluation. In Proceedings of SIGMETRICS 1998, Madison, WI, pp 151–160

11 Cardellini V, Casalicchio E, Colajanni M, Yu PS (2002) The state of the art in locally distributed Web-server systems. ACM Computing Surveys, 34(2):263–311

12 Cardellini V, Colajanni M, Yu PS (1999) Dynamic load balancing on Web server systems, IEEE Internet Computing, 3(3):28–39

13 Cardellini V, Colajanni M, Yu PS (2003) Request redirection algorithms for distributed Web systems. IEEE Transactions on Parallel and Distributed Systems, 14(4):355–368

14 Cecchet E, Chanda A, Elnikety S, Marguerite J, Zwaenepoel W (2003) Performance comparison of middleware architectures for generating dynamic Web content. In: Proceedings of the ACM/IFIP/USENIX International Middleware Conference, Rio de Janeiro, Brazil

15 Chen H, Mohapatra P (2002) Session-based overload control in QoS-aware Web servers. In: Proceedings of IEEE Infocom, New York, NY

16 Chiu W (2000) Design pages for performance. IBM High Volume Web Site white papers

17 Chiu W (2001) Design for scalability: an update. IBM High Volume Web Site white papers

18 Coarfa C, Druschel P, Wallach D (2002) Performance analysis of TLS Web servers. In: Proceedings of the Network and Distributed System Security Symposium (NDSS), San Diego, CA

19 Cocoon. The Apache Cocoon Project (2005) http://cocoon.apache.org

20 Cold Fusion (2004) http://www.coldfusion.com

21 Darwin Streaming Server; http://developer.apple.com/darwin/projects/streaming/

22 Edge Side Includes, ESI (2004) http://www.esi.org

23 Elnikety S, Nahum E, Tracey J, Zwaenepoel W (2004) A method for transparent admission control and request scheduling in e-commerce Web sites. In: Proceedings of the 13th International Conference on World Wide Web, New York, NY

24 Fraternali P (1999) Tools and approaches for developing data-intensive Web applications: a survey. ACM Computing Surveys, 31(3):227–263

25 Goldberg A, Buff R, Schmitt A (1998) Secure Web server performance dramatically improved by caching SSL session keys. In: Proceedings of SIGMETRICS, Madison, WI

26 Gray J, Helland P, O'Neil PE, Shasha D (1996) The dangers of replication and a solution. In: Proceedings of the ACM SIGMOD International Conference on Management of Data, Montreal, Canada

27 Hemminger S. (2004) Netem home page: http://developer.osdl.org/shemminger/netem

28 iTunes (2005) http://www.apple.com/itunes

29 Java 2 Platform Enterprise Edition, J2EE (2004) http://java.sun.com/j2ee

30 Levon J (2004) Oprofile: a system profiler for Linux. http://oprofile.sourceforge.net

31 Menascè DA, Almeida VAF, Riedi R, Pelegrinelli F, Fonseca R, Meira V (2000) In search of invariants for e-business workloads. In Proceedings of 2nd ACM Conference on Electronic Commerce, Minneapolis, MN

32 Menascé DA, Barbarà D, Dodge R (2001) Preserving QoS of e-commerce sites through self-tuning: a performance model approach. In: Proceedings of the 3rd ACM Conference on Electronic Commerce, Tampa, FL

33 MySQL database server (2005) http://www.mysql.com

34 Nahum E, Rosu MC, Seshan S, Almeida J (2001) The effects of wide-area conditions on WWW server performance. In: Proceedings of the ACM SIGMETRICS International Conference on Measurement and Modeling of Computer Systems, Cambridge, MA

35 Netcraft (2005) http://www.netcraft.com/survey/archive.html

36 Nielsen J (1994) Usability Engineering. Morgan Kaufmann, San Francisco, CA

37 PHP scripting language (2005) http://www.php.net

38 PostgreSQL database server (2005) http://www.postgresql.org

39 Procps: the /proc file system utilities (2005) http://procps.sourceforge.net

40 Rabinovic M, Spatscheck O (2002) Web caching and replication. Addison-Wesley

41 Rabinovich M, Xiao Z, Douglis F, Kalmanek C (2003) Moving edge side includes to the Real Edge – the clients. In: Proceedings of the 4th USENIX Symposium on Internet Technologies and Systems

42 Sar: the system activity report (2005) http://perso.wanadoo.fr/sebastien.godard

43 Sculzrinne H, Fokus GMD, Casner S, Frederick R, Jacobson V (1996) RTP: A transport protocol for real-time applications, RFC 1889

44 The Tomcat servlet engine (2005) http://jakarta.apache.org/tomcat

45 Vallamsetty U, Kant K, Mohapatra P (2003) Characterization of e-commerce traffic. Electronic Commerce Research, 3(1–2):167–192

Authors' Biographies

Mauro Andreolini is currently a researcher in the Department of Information Engineering at the University of Modena, Italy. He received his masters degree (summa cum laude) at the Univeristy of Roma, "Tor Vergata", in January 2001. In 2003, he spent eight months at the IBM T.J. Watson Research Center as a visiting research student.

His research focuses on the design, implementation and evaluation of locally distributed Web server systems, based on a best-effort service or on guaranteed levels of performance. He is a Standard Performance Evaluation Corporation (SPEC) technician responsible for the University of Modena and Reggio Emilia. He has served in the organization committee of the IFIP WG7.3 International Symposium on Computer Performance Modelling, Measurement and Evaluation (Performance2002).

For additional details, see: http://weblab.ing.unimo.it/people/andreoli.

Michele Colajanni is a Full Professor of Computer Engineering at the Department of Information Engineering of the University of Modena. He was formerly an Associate Professor at the same University in the period 1998–2000, and a Researcher at the University of Roma Tor Vergata. He received the Laurea degree in computer science from the University of Pisa in 1987, and the PhD degree in computer engineering from the University of Roma "Tor Vergata" in 1991. He has held computer science research appointments with the National Research Council (CNR), visiting scientist appointments with the IBM T.J. Watson Research Center, Yorktown Heights, New York. In 1997 he received an award by the National Research Council for the results of his research activities on high- performance Web systems during his sabbatical year spent at the IBM T.J. Watson Research Center.

His research interests include scalable Web systems and infrastructures, parallel and distributed systems, performance analysis, benchmarking and simulation. In these fields he has published more than 100 papers in international journals, book chapters and conference proceedings, in addition to several national conferences. He has lectured at national and international seminars and conferences.

Michele Colajanni has served as a member of organising or programme committees of national and international conferences on system modelling, performance analysis, parallel computing and Web-based systems. He is the general chair of the first edition of the AAA-IDEA Workshop. He is a member of the IEEE Computer Society and the ACM.

For additional details, see: http://weblab.ing.unimo.it/people/colajanni.

Riccardo Lancellotti received the Laurea and the PhD degrees in computer engineering from the University of Modena and from the University of Roma "Tor Vergata", respectively. He is currently a researcher in the Department of Information Engineering at the University of Modena, Italy. In 2003, he spent eight months at the IBM T.J. Watson Research Center as a visiting research student.

His research interests include scalable architectures for Web content delivery and adaptation, peer-to-peer systems, distributed systems and performance evaluation. Dr. Lancellotti is a member of the IEEE Computer Society.

For additional details, see: http://weblab.ing.unimo.it/people/riccardo.

7 Web Application Testing

Giuseppe A. Di Lucca, Anna Rita Fasolino

Abstract: Web applications are characterised by peculiarities that differentiate them from any other software application. These peculiarities affect their testing in several ways, which may result in harder than traditional application testing. Suitable methods and techniques have to be defined and used to test Web applications effectively. This chapter will present the main differences between Web applications and traditional ones, and how these differences impact the testing of Web applications. It also discusses relevant contributions in the field of Web application testing, proposed recently. The focus of the chapter is mainly on testing the functionality of a Web application, although discussions about the testing of non-functional requirements are provided too. Readers are required to have a general knowledge of software testing and Web technologies.

Keywords: Web engineering, Web application testing, Software testing.

7.1 Introduction

In the last decade, with the wide diffusion of the Internet, a growing market request for Web sites and applications has been recorded. As more and more organisations exploit the World Wide Web (WWW) to offer their services and to be reached by larger numbers of customers and users, the request for high-quality Web applications satisfying security, scalability, reliability, and accessibility requirements has grown steadily. In such a scenario, testing Web applications to verify their quality became a crucial problem.

Unfortunately, due to market pressure and very short time-to-market, the testing of Web applications is often neglected by developers, as it is considered to be time-consuming and lack a significant payoff [11]. An inversion of this trend may be obtained if testing models, methods, techniques, and tools that allow testing processes to be carried out effectively and in a cost-effective manner are available.

Although Web application testing shares similar objectives to those of "traditional" application testing, there are some key differences between testing a traditional software system and testing a Web application: the specific features exhibited by Web applications, and not included in other software systems, must be considered to comprehend these differences.

A Web application can be considered as a distributed system, with a client–server or multi-tier architecture, including the following characteristics:

- It can be accessed concurrently by a *wide number of users* distributed all over in the world.
- It runs on complex, *heterogeneous execution environments*, composed of different hardware, network connections, operating systems, Web servers, and Web browsers.
- It has an extremely *heterogeneous* nature that depends on the large variety of software components that it usually includes. These components can be built by different technologies (i.e. different programming languages and models), and can be of a different nature (i.e. new components generated from scratch, legacy ones, hypermedia components, COTS, etc.).
- It is able to generate *software components at run time* according to user inputs and server status.

Each aspect described in the previous list produces new testing challenges and perspectives. As an example, effective solutions need to be identified for executing performance and availability testing to verify a Web application's behaviour when accessed concurrently by a large number of users. Moreover, as users may utilise browsers with different Web content rendering capabilities, Web applications must be tested to make sure that the expected application's behaviour using different Web browsers, operating systems, and middleware is the one expected. Another critical feature of a Web application to be specifically tested is its security and ability to be protected from unauthorised access. The different technologies used to implement Web application components influence the complexity and cost of setting up a testing environment required to test each component. In addition, the different mechanisms used to integrate distributed components produce various levels of coupling and inter-component data flow, impacting the cost for being tested effectively. As for the existence of dynamically generated software components, the issue here is to cope with the difficulty of generating and rerunning the same conditions that produced each component.

Finally, Web application testing also needs to take into account failures in the application's required services/functionality, to verify the conformance of the application's behaviour to specified functional requirements. Considering that the components of a Web application are usually accessed by navigation mechanisms implemented by hyper-textual links, a specific verification activity also needs to be devised to check link integrity, to assure that no unreachable components or pending/broken links are included in the application.

Problems and questions regarding Web applications' testing are, therefore, numerous and complex. In this chapter we discuss these problems and questions and present possible solutions, proposed by researchers, from both academic and industrial settings.

We use two separate perspectives to analyse Web application testing: the first considers aspects related to testing the non-functional requirements of a Web application; the second considers the issue of testing the functionality offered by Web applications.

Section 7.2 introduces several types of non-functional requirements of Web applications and how they should be tested. From Section 7.3 onwards this chapter focuses on testing the functional requirements of Web applications. Section 7.3 presents different categories of models used to obtain suitable representations of the application to be tested. Section 7.4 presents different types of testing scopes for Web applications. In Section 7.5 several test strategies for designing test cases are discussed, while in Section 7.6 the characteristic features of tools for Web application testing are analysed. Section 7.7 shows a practical example of testing a Web application. Finally, Section 7.8 presents our conclusions and future trends.

7.2 Web Application Testing: Challenges and Perspectives

Since the Web's inception the goals and functionality offered by Web applications, as well as the technologies used to implement them, have changed considerably. Early Web applications comprised a simple set of static HTML pages. However, more recent applications offer their users a variety of functions for manipulating data, accessing databases, and carrying out a number of productive processes. These functions are usually performed by means of software components implemented by different technologies such as Java Server Pages (JSP), Java Servlets, PHP, CGI, XML, ODBC, JDBC, or proprietary technologies such as Microsoft's Active Server Pages (ASP). These components exploit a complex, heterogeneous execution environment including hardware, software, and middleware components.

The remainder of this chapter uses the term *Web application* (or simply application) to indicate the set of software components implementing the functionality and services the application provides to its users, while the term *running environment* will indicate the whole infrastructure (composed of hardware, software and middleware components) needed to execute a Web application.

The main goal of testing a Web application is to run the application using combinations of input and state to discover failures. A failure is the manifested inability of a system or component to perform a required function within specified performance requirements [13]. Failures can be attributed to faults in the application's implementation. Generally, there will be failures due mainly to faults in the application itself and failures that will be mainly caused by faults in the running environment or in the interface between the application and the environment on which it runs. Since a Web application is strictly interwoven to its running environment, it is not possible to test it separately to find out exactly what component is responsible for each exhibited failure. Therefore, different types of testing have to be executed to uncover these diverse types of failures [17].

The running environment mainly affects the non-functional requirements of a Web application (e.g. performance, stability, compatibility), while the application is responsible for the functional requirements. Thus, Web application testing has to be considered from two distinct perspectives. One perspective identifies the different types of testing that need to be executed to verify the conformance of a Web application with specified *non-functional* requirements. The other perspective considers the problem of testing the *functional* requirements of an application. It is necessary that an application be tested from both perspectives, since they are complementary and not mutually exclusive.

Questions and challenges that characterise both testing perspectives will be analysed in the next sub-sections.

7.2.1 Testing the Non-functional Requirements of a Web Application

There are different non-functional requirements that a Web application, either explicitly or implicitly, is usually required to satisfy. For each non-functional requirement, testing activities with specific aims will have to be designed. A description of the verification activities that can be executed to test the main non-functional requirements of a Web application are presented below.

Performance Testing

Performance testing is carried out to verify specified system performance (e.g. response time, service availability). Usually, performance testing is executed by simulating hundreds, or even more, simultaneous user accesses over a defined time interval. Information about accesses is recorded and then analysed to estimate the load levels exhausting the system resources.

In the case of Web applications, system performance is a critical issue because Web users do not want to wait too long for a response to their requests; as well, they also expect that services will always be available.

Effective performance testing of Web applications is a critical task because it is not possible to know beforehand how many users will actually be connected to a real-world running application. Thus, performance testing should be considered as an everlasting activity to be carried out by analysing data from access log files, in order to tune the system adequately.

Failures that can be uncovered by performance testing are mainly due to running environment faults (e.g. scarce resources, poorly deployed resources), even if any software component of the application level may contribute to inefficiency, i.e. components implementing any business rule by algorithms that are not optimised.

Load Testing

Load testing is often used as a synonym for performance testing but it differs from the latter because it requires that system performance be evaluated with a predefined load level. It aims to measure the time needed to perform several tasks and functions under predefined conditions. These predefined conditions include the minimum configuration and the maximum activity levels of the running application. Also, in this case, numerous simultaneous user accesses are simulated. Information is recorded and, when the tasks are not executed within predefined time limits, failure reports are generated.

As for the difficulties of executing load testing of Web applications, considerations similar to the ones made for performance testing can also be taken into account. Failures found by load testing are mainly due to faults in the running environment.

Stress Testing

Stress testing is conducted to evaluate a system or component at or beyond the limits of its specified requirements. It is used to evaluate the system's response at activity peaks that can exceed system limitations, and to verify if the system crashes or is able to recover from such conditions. Stress testing differs from performance and load testing because the system is executed on or beyond its breaking point, while performance and load testing simulate regular user activity.

In the case of Web applications, stress testing difficulties are similar to those that can be met in performance and load testing. Failures found by stress testing are mainly due to faults in the running environment.

Compatibility Testing

Compatibility testing is carried out to determine if an application runs as expected on a running environment that has various combinations of hardware, software, and middleware.

In the case of Web applications, compatibility testing will have to uncover failures due to the usage of different Web server platforms or client browsers, and corresponding releases or configurations.

The large variety of possible combinations of all the components involved in the execution of a Web application does not make it feasible to test them all; thus usually only the most common combinations are considered. As a consequence, just a subset of possible compatibility failures might be uncovered.

Both the application and the running environment can be responsible for compatibility failures. A general rule for avoiding compatibility failures is to provide Web application users with appropriate information about the expected configuration of the running environment and with appropriate diagnostic messages to deal with any incompatibilities found.

Usability Testing

Usability testing aims to verify to what extent an application is easy to use. Usually, design and implementation of the user interface both affect usability. Thus, usability testing is mainly centred around testing the user interface: issues concerning the correct content rendering (e.g. graphics, text editing format) as well as the clarity of messages, prompts, and commands that are to be considered and verified.

Usability is a critical issue for a Web application. Indeed, it may determine the success of the application. As a consequence, an application's front-end and the way users interact with it often are aspects that are given greater care and attention during the application's development process.

When Web application usability testing is carried out, issues related to an application's navigation completeness, correctness, and conciseness are also considered and verified. This type of testing should be an everlasting activity carried out to improve the usability of a Web application; techniques of user profiling are usually used to reach this aim.

The application is mainly responsible for usability failures.

Accessibility Testing

Accessibility testing can be considered a particular type of usability testing whose aim is to verify that the access to an application's content is allowed even in the presence of reduced hardware and software configurations on the client side (e.g. browser configurations disabling graphical visualisation, or scripting execution), or in the presence of users with disabilities, such as visual impairment.

In the case of Web applications, accessibility rules such as the one provided by the Web Content Accessibility Guidelines [24] have been established, so that accessibility testing represents verification the compliance of an application with such rules. The application itself is generally the main cause of accessibility problems, even when accessibility failures may be due to the configuration of the running environment (e.g. browsers where the execution of scripts is disabled).

Security Testing

Security testing aims to verify the effectiveness of the overall Web application's defences against undesired access of unauthorised users, its capability to preserve system resources from improper use, and granting authorised users access to authorised services and resources. Application defences have to provide protection mechanisms able to avoid or reduce damage due to intrusions, with costs that should be significantly less than damages caused by a security break.

Application vulnerabilities affecting security may be contained in the application code, or in any of the different hardware, software, and middleware components. Both the running environment and the application can be responsible for security failures.

In the case of Web applications, heterogeneous implementations and execution technologies, together with the very large number of possible users and the possibility of accessing them from anywhere, can make Web applications more vulnerable than traditional applications and security testing more difficult to accomplish.

7.2.2 Testing the Functional Requirements of a Web Application

Testing the functional requirements of an application aims at verifying that an application's features and operational behaviour correspond to their specifications. In other words, this type of testing is responsible for uncovering application failures due to faults in the functional requirements' implementation, rather than failures due to the application's running environment. To achieve this aim, any failures due to the running environment should be avoided, or reduced to a minimum. Preliminary assumptions about the running environment will have to be made before test design and execution.

Most methods and approaches used to test the functional requirements of "traditional" software can also be used for Web applications. Similarly to traditional software testing, a Web application's functionality testing has to rely on the following basic aspects:

- *Testing levels*, which specify the different scope of the tests to be carried out, i.e. the collections of components to be tested.
- *Test strategies*, which define heuristics or algorithms to create test cases from software representation models, implementation models, or test models.
- *Test models*, which represent the relationships between a representation's elements or a component's implementation [3].
- *Testing processes*, which define the flow of testing activities, and other decisions such as when to start testing, who is to perform the testing, how much effort should be used, etc.

However, despite their similarity to conventional applications, Web applications also have distinguishing features that cause specific problems for each aspect described in the previous list. For example, the definition of *testing levels* for a Web application requires greater attention than that applied to traditional software. At the *unit testing* level, the scope of a unit test cannot be defined uniquely, since it depends on the existence of different types of components (e.g. Web pages, script functions, embedded objects) residing on both the client and server side of an application. In relation to *integration testing*, the numerous different mechanisms used to integrate an application's heterogeneous and distributed components can generate several coupling levels and data flow between the components, which have to be considered to establish a correct integration strategy.

As for the *strategies for test design*, the classical approaches of black box, white box, or grey box testing may be taken into account for designing test cases, provided that preliminary considerations are defined. In general, Web applications' *black box testing* will not be different from software applications' black box testing. In both cases, using a predetermined coverage criterion, an adequate set of test cases is defined based upon the specified functionality of the item to be tested. However, a Web application's specific features can affect test design and execution. For example, testing of components dynamically generated by the running application can be very expensive, due to the difficulty of identifying and regenerating the same conditions that produced each component. Therefore, traditional testing models used to represent the behaviour of an application may have to be adapted to these characteristics and to the Web applications' running environment.

White box testing, irrespective of an application's nature, is usually based on coverage criteria that take into account structural features of the application or its components. Adequate models representing an application or component's structure are used, and coverage criteria and test cases are appropriately specified. The aim of white box testing is to cover the structural elements considered. Since the architecture and components of a Web application are largely different from those of a traditional application, appropriate models representing structural information at different levels of granularity and abstraction are needed, and coverage criteria have to be defined accordingly. For example, models representing navigation as well as traditional structural aspects of an application need to be taken into account. Coverage criteria must focus both on hyperlinks, which allow user navigation in the application, and on inner items of an application's component (e.g. its code statements).

Besides black and white box testing, *grey box* testing can also be considered for Web applications. Grey box testing is a mixture of black and white box testing, and considers both the application's behaviour, from the end user's viewpoint (same as black box testing), and the application's inner structure and technology (same as white box testing). According to [17], grey box testing is suitable for testing Web applications because it factors in high-level design, environment, and interoperability conditions. It is expected that this type of testing will reveal problems that are not easily identified by black box or white box analysis, in particular problems related to end-to-end information flow and distributed hardware/software system configuration and compatibility. Context-specific failures relevant to Web applications are commonly uncovered using grey-box testing.

Finally, for the *testing processes*, the classical approach for testing execution that starts from unit test and proceeds with integration, system testing, and acceptance testing can also be taken into account for Web applications. For each phase, however, differences with respect to testing traditional software have to be detected and specific solutions have to be designed. An important testing process issue is, for instance, to set up an *environment* to execute tests at each phase: driver or stub modules are usually required to run tests at the unit or integration phase. Solutions for testing a Web application have to explicitly consider the application's distributed running environment, and to adopt the necessary communication mechanisms for executing the components being tested.

7.3 Web Application Representation Models

In software testing the need for models that represent essential concepts and relationships between items being tested has been documented [3]. Models are able to support the selection of effective test cases, since they can be used to express required behaviour or to focus on aspects of an application's structure believed to have defects.

With regard to Web applications, models for representing their behaviour or structure have been provided by several Web application development methodologies, which have extended traditional software models to explicitly represent Web-related software characteristics. Examples of such models include the *Relationship Management Data Model (RMDM)* used by the Relationship Management Methodology (RMM) [14], which uses entity–relationship-based diagrams to describe objects and navigation mechanisms of Web applications. Other methodologies, such as Object Oriented Hypermedia (OOH) [9], integrate the traditional object-oriented models with a *navigational view* and a *presentation view* of the application. The Object-Oriented Hypermedia Design Model (OOHDM) methodology [22] allows for the construction of customised Web applications by adopting object-oriented primitives to build the application's conceptual, navigational, and interface models. WebML (Web Modelling Language) [2] is, moreover, a specification language that proposes four types of models, *Structural Model*, *Hypertext Model*, *Presentation Model*, and *Personalisation Model*, used to specify different characteristics of complex Web applications, irrespective of their implementation details. Finally, an extension of UML diagrams with new class stereotypes for representing specific Web application components, such as HTML pages, forms, server pages, is proposed in [4].

In addition to these models, other representation models explicitly geared towards Web application testing have been proposed in the literature. Two categories are currently used to classify these models: *behaviour models* and *structural models.* The former are used to describe the functionality of a Web application irrespective of its implementation. The latter are derived from the implementation of the application.

Behaviour models support black box (or responsibility-based) testing. Use case models and decision tables [6], and state machines [1], have been used to design Web application test cases for black-box testing techniques.

Structural models are used for white box testing. Both control flow representation models of a Web application's components [16,18,19], and models describing an application's organisation in terms of Web pages and hyperlinks, have been proposed [6,19]. Further details of these representations are given in Sect. 7.5.

The meta-model of a Web application [7] is now described. This model is presented in Fig. 7.1 using a UML class diagram where various types of classes and associations represent several categories of a Web application's components and their relationships. A Web application can be modelled using a UML class diagram model instantiated from this meta-model.

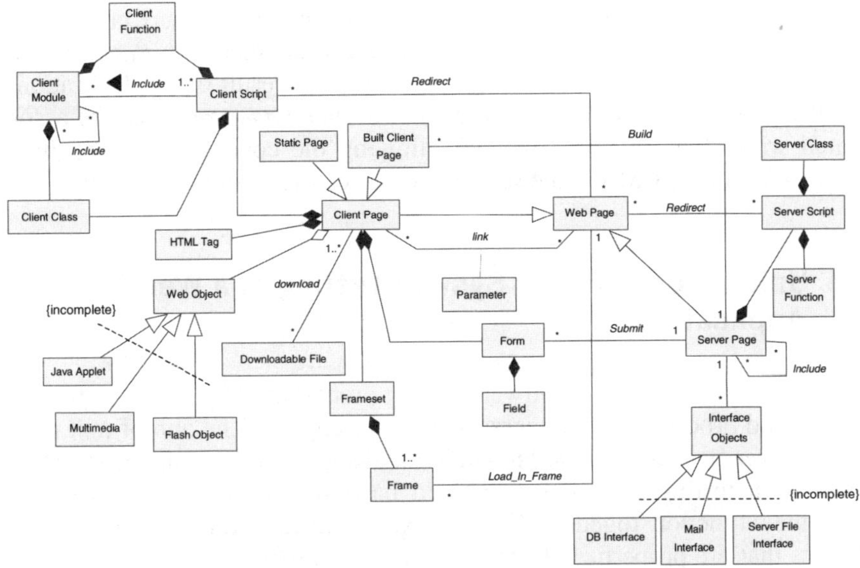

Fig. 7.1. The meta-model of a Web application presented in [7]

The meta-model assumes that a Web application comprises *Web Pages*, which can be grouped as *Server Pages*, i.e. pages that are deployed on the Web server, and *Client Pages*, i.e. pages that a Web server sends back in answer to a client request. As for the *Client Pages*, they can be classified as *Static Pages*, if their content is fixed and stored permanently, or *Client Built Pages*, if their content varies over time and is generated on-the-fly by a *Server Page*. A *Client Page* is composed of *HTML Tags*. A *Client Page* may include a *Frameset*, composed of one or more *Frames*, and in each *Frame* a different *Web Page* can be loaded. *Client Pages* may include finer-grained items implementing processing actions, such as *Client Scripts*. A *Client Page* may also include other *Web Objects* such as *Java Applets*, images and *Multimedia* Objects (e.g. sounds, movies), *Flash Objects* etc. A *Client Script* may include *Client Modules*. Both *Client Scripts* and *Client Modules* can include *Client Functions*, or *Client Classes*. A *Client Script* may redirect the elaboration to another *Web Page*. In addition, a *Client Page* may be linked to another *Web Page*, through a hyperlink to the *Web Page*'s URL: a link between a *Client Page* and a *Web Page* may be characterised by any *Parameter* that the *Client Page* provides to the *Web Page*. A *Client Page* may also be associated with any *Downloadable File*, or it may include any *Form*, composed of different types of *Field* (e.g. select, button, text-area fields). *Forms* are used to collect user input and to *submit* the input to the *Server Page* responsible for its elaboration. A *Server Page* may be composed of any *Server Script*, which can include any *Server Class* or *Server Function*, implementing any processing action, which may either *redirect* the request to another *Web Page*, or dynamically *build* a *Client Built Page* providing the result of an elaboration. Finally, a *Server Page* may include other *Server Pages*, and may be associated with other *Interface Objects* allowing the connection of the *Web application* to a DBMS, a file server, a mail server, or another system.

7.4 Unit Integration and System Testing of a Web Application

The flow of activities of a software testing process usually begins with unit testing and proceeds with integration and system test. The aim of unit testing is to verify each application's individual source code component, while integration testing considers combined parts of an application to verify how they function together. Finally, system testing aims at discovering defects that are properties of the entire system rather than of its individual components.

7.4.1 Unit Testing

To set up Web application unit testing it is important to choose the application components to be tested individually. If we consider the model of a Web application as presented in Fig. 7.1, different types of unit may be identified (e.g. Web pages, scripting modules, forms, applets, servlets). However, the basic unit that can actually be tested is a Web page, if we consider that any page's element should also automatically be considered for testing. As a consequence, *pages* are usually considered at the unit testing level, although there are some differences between testing a client or a server page. We present these differences below.

Testing Client Pages

Client pages constitute the application's user interface. They are responsible for showing textual information and/or hyperlinks to users, for accepting user input, and for allowing user navigation throughout the application. A client page may include scripting code modules that perform simple functions, such as input validation or simple computations. Moreover, client pages may be decomposed into several frames in which other client pages can be visualised.

Testing a client page (including just HTML code) aims to verify:

- Compliance of the content displayed by the page to the one specified and expected by a user (e.g. the rendering in the browser of both textual content and its formatting of forms, images and other Web objects will have to be verified).
- Correctness of target pages pointed to by hyperlinks, i.e. when a link is selected, the right page should be returned.
- Existence of pending links, i.e. links to pages that do not exist.
- Correctness of the actions performed when a button, or any other active object, is selected by a user.
- Correctness of the content visualised in the frames.

If the client page includes scripting code, failures due to scripts will also have to be verified.

Testing dynamically generated client pages (built-in pages) is a particular case of client page testing. The basic problem with this testing is that the availability of built-in pages depends on the ability to identify and repeat the same conditions (in terms of application state and user input) used to build such pages. A second problem is that of having too many pages being generated, since the number of dynamic pages can be considerable, depending on the large number of possible combinations of application state and user input. Equivalence class partitioning criteria (such as those considering exemplar path execution of server pages) should be used to deal with this issue.

Unit testing of client pages can be carried out using white box, black box, or grey box testing techniques. Several implementation-based criteria can be used to evaluate white box test coverage, such as:

- HTML statement coverage.
- Web object coverage, i.e. each image, multimedia component, applet, etc. will have to be tested at least once.
- Script block coverage, i.e. each block of scripting code, such as client side functions, will have to be executed at least once.
- Statement/branch/path coverage for each script module.
- Link coverage.

Testing Server Pages

The main goal of server pages is to implement an application's business logic, thus coordinating the execution of business rules and managing the storing and retrieving of data into/from a database.

Usually, server pages are implemented by a mixture of technologies, such as HTML, script languages (e.g. VBS, JSP), Java servlets, or COTS.

Typical results of server page execution are data storage into a database, or generation of client pages based on user requests.

Testing a server page aims to identify failures of different types, such as:

- Failures in the executions of servlets, or COTS.
- Incorrect executions of data being stored into a database.
- Failures due to the existence of incorrect links between pages.
- Defects in dynamically generated client pages (such as non-compliance of the client page with the output specified for the server page).

Unit testing of server pages can also be carried out using white box, black box, or grey box techniques. White box coverage criteria include:

- Statement/branch/path coverage in script modules.
- HTML statement coverage.
- Servlet, COTS, and other Web object coverage.
- Hyperlink coverage.
- Coverage of dynamically generated pages.

Appropriate driver and stub pages have to be generated to carry out unit page testing effectively (see Sect. 7.6 for a discussion on the generation of such drivers and stubs).

7.4.2 Integration Testing

Integration testing is the testing of a Web application's combined pages to assess how they function together. An integration criterion has to be used to choose the pages to be combined and tested together. Design documentation showing relationships between pages can be used to define an integration strategy.

As an example, the Web application model, obtained by instantiating the meta-model presented in Fig. 7.1, can be used to identify the pages to be combined. Pages chosen will be those linked by direct relationships, such as *hyperlinks*, or by dependency relationships due to *redirect* or *submit* statements (included either in a server or in a client page), or by *build* relationships between a server page and the client page produced.

Another integration criterion may consider a server page and each client page it generates at run time as a unit to be tested. The problem of client page explosion will have to be addressed with equivalence class partitioning criteria.

Page integration can be driven by the use cases implemented by the application, or any other description of the application's functional requirements. For each use case (or functional requirement), Web pages collaborating for its implementation are to be considered for integration purposes. The identification of such Web pages can be made by analysing development documentation or by reverse engineering the application code. Reverse engineering techniques, such as the one described in [5], can be used to analyse the relationships between pages and to identify clusters of interconnected pages that implement a use case.

At the integration testing level, both the behaviour and the structure of the Web application will have to be considered: knowledge of the application structure will be used to define the set of pages to be integrated, while knowledge of the behaviour implemented by these pages will be needed to carry out integration testing with a black box strategy. Therefore, grey box techniques may be more suitable than pure black or white box ones to carry out integration testing.

7.4.3 System Testing

System testing aims to discover defects related to the entire Web application. In traditional software testing, black box approaches are usually exploited to accomplish system testing and to identify failures in the externally visible behaviour of the application. However, grey box techniques that consider the application navigation structure, in addition to its behaviour, for designing test cases may be more effective in revealing Web application failures due to incorrect navigation links among pages (such as links connecting a page to a different one from the specified page, pending links, or links to unreachable pages).

Depending on the testing strategy adopted, coverage criteria for system testing will include:

- User functions/use cases coverage (if a black box approach is used).
- Page (both client and server) coverage (usable for white box or grey box approaches).
- Link coverage (usable for white box or grey box approaches).

7.5 Strategies for Web Application Testing

Testing strategies define the approaches for designing test cases. They can be responsibility based (also known as black box), implementation based (or white box), or hybrid (also known as grey box) [3]. Black box techniques design test cases on the basis of the specified functionality of the item to be tested. White box techniques rely on source code analysis to develop test cases. Grey box testing designs test cases using both responsibility-based and implementation-based approaches.

This section discusses representative contributions presented in the literature for white box, black box, and grey box testing of Web applications.

7.5.1 White Box Strategies

White box strategies design test cases on the basis of a code representation of the component under test (i.e. the *test model*), and of a *coverage model* that specifies the parts of the representation that must be exercised by a test suite. As an example, in the case of traditional software the control flow graph is a typical test model, while statement coverage, branch coverage, or basis-path coverage are possible code coverage models.

As for the code representation models adopted to test Web applications, two main families of structural models are used: the first one focuses on the level of abstraction of single statements of code components of the application, and represents the traditional information about their control flow or data flow. The second family considers the coarser degree of granularity of the pages of the Web application and essentially represents the navigation structure between pages of the application with eventual additional details. As the coverage criteria, traditional ones (such as those involving nodes, edges, or notable paths from the graphical representations of these models) have been applied to both families of models.

Two white box techniques proposed in the literature to test Web applications will be presented in this section. The first technique was proposed by Liu et al. [17] and exploits a test model that belongs to the first family of models, while the second one was proposed by Ricca and Tonella [19, 20] and is based on two different test models, each one belonging to a different family.

The white box technique proposed by Liu et al. [17] is an example of how data-flow testing of Web applications can be carried out. The approach is applicable to Web applications implemented in the HTML and XML languages, including interpreted scripts as well as other kinds of executable components (e.g. Java applets, ActiveX controls, Java beans) at both the client and server side of the application.

The approach is based on a Web application test model, WATM, that includes an object model, and a structure model. The o*bject model* represents the heterogeneous components of a Web application and the ways they are interconnected using an object-based approach. The model includes three types of objects (i.e. client pages, server pages, and components) and seven types of relationships between objects. Each object is associated with attributes corresponding to program variables or other HTML specific document elements (e.g. anchors, headers, or input buttons), and operations corresponding to functions written in scripting or programming languages. Relationships between objects are of seven types: inheritance, aggregation, association, request, response, navigation, and redirect. The first three have the classical object-oriented semantics, while the last four represent specific relationships between client and server pages. A *request* relationship exists between a client and a server page when a server page is requested by a client page; a *response* relationship exists between a client and a server page when a client page is generated by a server page as a response of an elaboration; for two client pages there is a *navigation* relationship if one of them includes a hyperlink to the other page; finally, between two server pages there is a *redirect* relationship if one of them redirects an HTTP request to the other. The *structure model* uses four types of graphs to capture various types of data flow information on a Web application: the *Control Flow Graph* (CFG) of an individual function, the *Interprocedural Control Flow Graph* (ICFG) that involves more than one function and integrates the CFGs of functions that call each other, the *Object Control Flow Graph* (OCFG) that integrates the CFGs of object functions that are involved in sequences of function invocations triggered by GUI events, and, finally, the *Composite Control Flow Graph* (CCFG) that captures the pages where a page passes data to the other one when the user clicks a hyperlink, or submits a form, and is constructed by connecting the CFGs of the interacting Web pages.

The data flow testing approach derives test cases from three different perspectives: intra-object, inter-object, and inter-client. For each perspective, def-use chains of variables are taken into account for defining test paths that exercise the considered def-use chains. Five testing levels specifying different scopes of the tests to be run have been defined, namely: Function, Function Cluster, Object, Object Cluster, and Application level.

For the *intra-object* perspective, test paths are selected for variables that have def-use chains within an object. The def-use chains are computed using the control flow graphs of functions included in the object, and can be defined at three different testing levels: single *function*, *cluster of functions* (i.e. set of functions that interact via function calls within an object), and *object level* (considering different sequences of function invocations within an object).

For the *inter-object* perspective, test paths are selected for variables that have def-use chains across objects. Def-use chains have to be defined at the *object cluster* level, where each cluster is composed by a set of message-passing objects.

Finally, the *inter-client* perspective derives test paths on the basis of def-use chains of variables that span multiple clients, since in a Web application a variable can be shared by multiple clients. This level of testing is called *application* level.

This testing technique is relevant since it represents a first attempt to extend the data flow testing approaches applicable to traditional software to the field of Web applications. However, to make it actually usable in real-world Web application testing, further investigation is required. Indeed, the effectiveness of the technique has not been validated by any experiment involving more than one example Web application: to carry out these experiments, an automated environment for testing execution, including code analysers, data flow analysers, and code instrumentation tools, would be necessary. Moreover, indications about how this data flow testing approach may be integrated in a testing process would also be needed: as an example, the various testing perspectives and levels proposed by the approach might be considered in different phases of a testing process to carry out unit test, as well as integration or system test. However, in this case an experimental validation and tuning would also be required.

A second proposal in the field of structural testing of Web applications has been suggested by Ricca and Tonella [19], who proposed a first approach for white box testing of primarily static Web applications. This approach was based on a test model named the n*avigational model* that focuses on HTML pages and navigational links of the application. Later, the same authors presented an additional lower layer model, the *control flow model*, representing the internal structure of Web pages in terms of the execution flow followed [20]. This latter model has also been used to carry out structural testing.

In the navigational model two types of HTML pages are represented: static pages, whose content is immutable, and dynamic pages, whose content is established at run time by server computation, on the basis of user input and server status. Server programs (such as scripts or other executable objects) running on the server side of the application, and other page components that are relevant for navigational purposes, such as forms and frames, are also part of the model. Hyperlinks between HTML pages and various types of link between pages and other model components are included in this code representation.

As for the control flow model, it takes into account the heterogeneous nature of statements written in different coding languages, and the different mechanisms used to transfer control between statements in a Web application. It is represented by a directed graph whose nodes correspond to statements that are executed either by the Web server or by the Internet browser on the client side, and whose edges represent control transfer. Different types of nodes are shown in this model, according to the programming language of the respective statements.

A *test case* for a Web application is defined as a sequence of pages to be visited, plus the input values to be provided to pages containing forms. Various coverage criteria applicable to both models have been proposed to design test cases: they include p*ath coverage* (requiring that all paths in the Web application model are traversed in some test case), b*ranch coverage* (requiring that all branches in the model are traversed in some test case), and n*ode coverage* (requiring that all nodes in the model are traversed in some test case).

Assuming that the nodes of the representation models can be annotated by definitions or uses of data variables, further data flow coverage criteria have been described too: a*ll def-use* (all definition-clear paths from every definition to every use of all Web application variables are traversed in some test case), a*ll uses* (at least one def-clear path if any exists from every definition to every use of all Web application variables traversed in some test case), a*ll defs* (at least one def-clear path if any exists from every definition to at least one use of all Web application variables is traversed in some test case).

This testing approach is partially supported by a tool, ReWeb, that analyses the pages of the Web application and builds the corresponding navigational model, and another tool, TestWeb, that generates and executes test cases. However, the latter tool is not completely automated, since user intervention is required to generate input and act as an oracle. The main limitation of this testing approach concerns its scalability (consider the problem of path explosion in the presence of cycles on the graphs, or the unfeasibility of the all-do coverage criterion).

A few considerations about the testing levels supported by white box techniques can be made. Some approaches are applicable at the unit level, while others are considered at the integration and system levels. For instance, the first approach proposed by Liu et al. [17] is applicable at various testing levels, ranging from unit level to integration level. As an example, the intra-object perspective can be used to obtain various types of units to be tested, while inter-object and inter-application perspectives can be considered for establishing the items to be tested at the integration level. Conversely, the approaches of Ricca and Tonella are applicable exclusively at the system level. As a consequence, the choice of a testing technique to be applied in a testing process will also depend on the scope of the test to be run.

7.5.2 Black Box Strategies

Black box techniques do not require knowledge of software implementation items under test since test cases are designed on the basis of an item's specified or expected functionality.

One main issue with black box testing of Web applications is the choice of a suitable model for specifying the behaviour of the application to be tested and to derive test cases. Indeed, this behaviour may significantly depend on the state of data managed by the application and on user input, with the consequence of a state explosion problem even in the presence of applications implementing a few simple requirements.

Solutions to this problem have been investigated and presented in the literature. Two examples of proposed solutions are discussed in this subsection. The first example is offered by the black box testing approach proposed by Di Lucca et al. [6] that exploits decision tables as a combinatorial model for representing the behaviour of a Web application and to produce test cases. The second example is provided by Andrews et al. [1] where state machines are proposed to model state-dependent behaviour of Web applications and to design test cases.

Di Lucca et al. [6] suggest a two-stage black box testing approach. The first stage addresses *unit testing* of a Web application, while the second stage considers *integration testing*. The scope of a unit test is a single application page, either a client or server page, while the scope of an integration test is a set of Web pages that collaborate to implement an application's use case.

Unit test is carried out with a responsibility-based approach that uses *decision tables* to represent page requirements, and therefore derive test cases. A decision table can be used to represent the behaviour of software components whose responses are each associated with a specific condition. Usually a decision table has two parts: the *condition section* (listing conditions and combinations of conditions) and the *action section* (listing responses to be produced when corresponding combinations of conditions are true). Each unique combination of conditions and actions is a *variant*, represented as a single row in the table.

As for the *unit testing* of client and server pages, the approach requires that each page under test is preliminarily associated with a decision table describing a set of variants of the page. Each variant represents an alternative behaviour offered by the page and is defined in terms of an Input section and an output section. In the case of client pages, the *input section* describes a condition in terms of *input variables* to the page, *input actions*, and *state before test* where the state is defined by the values assumed, before test execution, by page variables, tag attributes, cookies, and by the state of other Web objects used by page scripts. In the *output section,* the action associated with each condition is described by the *expected results*, *expected output* actions, and *expected state after test* (defined as for the state before test). Table 7.1 shows the template of the decision table for client page testing.

Such specification technique may be affected by the problem of variant explosion. However, criteria for partitioning input section data into equivalence classes may be defined and used to reduce the set of variants to be taken into account.

In the case of server pages, the decision table template is slightly different (see Table 7.2): for each page variant the *input section* includes the *input variables* field that comprises the variables provided to the server page when it is executed, and the *state before test* field that is defined by the values assumed, before test execution, by page session variables and cookies, as well as by the state of the session objects used by the page scripts. In the *output section,* the *expected results* field represents the values of the output variables computed by the server page scripts, the *expected output* field includes the actions performed by the server side scripts (such as composing and sending an e-mail message), and the *expected state after test* field includes the values of variables and cookies, as well as the state of session objects, after execution.

Table 7.1. A decision table template for client page testing

Variant	Input Section			Output Section		
	Input variables	Input actions	State before test	Expected results	Expected output actions	Expected state after test
...	...			...		

Table 7.2. A Decision Table template for server page testing

Variant	Input Section		Output Section		
	Input variables	State before test	Expected results	Expected output actions	Expected state after test
...			...		

As for the definition of the decision tables, the authors propose to compile them by analysing the development documentation (if available) or by reverse engineering the Web application code, and focusing on the page inner components that help to define the conditions and actions of each variant. An object model of a Web application representing each component of the application relevant for testing purposes is specifically presented by the authors to support this type of analysis. This model is actually an extended version of the one reported in Fig. 7.1, including additional relevant details for the aims of testing (such as session variables).

The *test case selection strategy* is based on the decision tables and requires that test cases are defined in order to cover each table variant for both true and false values. Other criteria based on partitioning the input sets into equivalence classes are also suggested for defining test cases.

In this testing approach, decision tables are also used to develop *driver* and *stub* modules which will be needed to execute the client page testing. A driver module will be a Web page that interacts with the client page by populating its input forms and generating the events specified for the test case. The driver page will include script functions, and the Document Object Model (DOM) will allow its interaction with the tested page. Stub modules can be developed as client pages, server pages or Web objects. The complexity of the stub will depend both on the type of interaction between the tested page and the component to be substituted, and on the complexity of the function globally implemented by the pair of components.

As for the *integration testing*, a fundamental question is the one of determining which Web pages have to be integrated and tested. The authors of this approach propose to integrate Web pages that collaborate with the implementation of each use case (or functional requirement) of the application. They propose to analyse the object model of the Web application in order to find client and server pages to be gathered together. A valuable support for the identification of clusters of interconnected pages may be provided by *clustering techniques*, such as the one proposed in [5]. This technique produces clusters of pages on the basis of a measure of coupling of interconnected pages that associates different weights to different types of relationship (*Link*, *Submit*, *Redirect*, *Build*, *Load_in_Frame*, *Include*) between pages. Once clusters have been defined and use cases have been associated to each of them, the set of pages included in each cluster will make up the item to be tested. For each use case a decision table can be defined to drive integration testing. Such a decision table can be derived from the ones defined for the unit testing of the single pages included in the cluster.

The second black box approach for Web application testing considered in this section exploits *Finite State Machines* (FSMs) for modelling software behaviour and deriving test cases from them [1]. This approach explicitly takes into account the state-dependent behaviour of Web applications, and proposes specific solutions for addressing the problem of state explosion.

The process for test generation comprises two phases: in the first phase, the Web application is modelled by a hierarchical collection of FSMs, where the bottom-level FSMs are formed by Web pages and parts of Web pages, while a top-level FSM represents the whole application. In the second phase, test cases are generated from this representation.

The model of the Web application is obtained as follows. First, the application is partitioned into clusters that are collections of Web pages and software modules that implement a logical function. This clustering task is made manually and is thus subjective. Second, Web pages that include more than one HTML form, each of which is connected to a different back-end software module, will be modelled as multiple Logical Web Pages (LWP), in order to facilitate testing of these modules. Third, an FSM will be derived for each cluster, starting from bottom-level clusters containing only modules and Web pages (no clusters), and therefore aggregating lower-level FSMs into a higher level FSM. Ultimately, an Application FSM (AFSM) will define an FSM of the entire Web application. In each FSM, nodes will represent clusters and edges will represent valid navigation among clusters. Moreover, edges of the FSMs will be annotated with inputs and constraints that may be associated with the transitions. Constraints on input, for instance, will indicate if input data are optional and their eventual input order. Information will also be propagated between lower-level FSMs.

Annotated FSMs and aggregate FSMs are thus used to generate tests. Tests are considered as sequences of transitions in an FSM and the associated constraints. Test sequences for lower-level FSMs are combined to form the test sequences for the aggregate FSMs. Standard graph coverage criteria, such as *all nodes* and *all edges,* are used to generate sequences of transitions for clusters and to aggregate FSMs.

While the approach of Di Lucca et al. provides a method for both unit and integration testing, the one by Andrews et al. mainly addresses integration and system testing. Both approaches use clustering to identify groups of related pages to be integrated, even if in the second one the clustering is made manually, and this may limit the applicability of the approach when large-size applications are tested.

The second method can be classified as a grey box rather a than pure black box technique. Indeed, test cases are generated to cover all the transitions among the clusters of LWPs, and therefore knowledge of the internal structure of the application is needed. Grey box testing strategies will be discussed in the next subsection.

7.5.3 Grey Box Testing Strategies

Grey box testing strategies combine black box and white box testing approaches to design test cases: they aim at testing a piece of software against its specification but using some knowledge of its internal workings.

Among the grey box strategies we will consider the ones based on the collection of user session data. These methods can be classified as grey box since they use collected data to test the behaviour of the application in a black box fashion, but they also aim at verifying the coverage of any internal component of the application, such as page or link coverage.

Two approaches based on user session data will be described here.

7.5.4 User Session Based Testing

Approaches based on data captured in user sessions transparently collect user interactions with the Web server and transform them into test cases using a given strategy.

Data to be captured about the user interaction with the Web server include clients' requests expressed in form of URLs and name value pairs. These data can be obtained from the log files stored by the Web servers, or by adding script modules on the requested server pages that capture the name value pairs of exchanged parameters. Captured data about user sessions can be transformed into a set of HTTP requests, each one providing a separate test case.

The main advantage of this approach is the possibility of generating test cases without analysing the internal structure of a Web application, thus reducing the costs of finding inputs. In addition, generating test cases using user session data is less dependent on the heterogeneous and fast-changing technologies used by Web applications, which is one of the major limitations of white box testing techniques. However, it can be argued that the effectiveness of user session techniques depends on the set of user session data collected: the wider this set, the greater the effectiveness of the approach to detect faults; but the wider the user session data set, the greater the cost of collecting, analysing and storing data. Therefore there is a trade-off between test suite size and fault detection capability.

Elbaum et al. [8] propose a user session approach to test a Web application and present the results of an empirical study where the effectiveness of white box and user session techniques was compared. In the study, user session collected data consist of sequences of HTTP requests made by users. Each sequence reports the pages (both client and server ones) the user visited together with the data he/she provided as input, in addition to the data resulting from the elaboration of requests made by the user.

The study considered two implementations of the white box testing approach proposed by Ricca and Tonella [19], and three different implementations of the user session approach. The first implementation transforms each individual user session into a test case; the second implementation combines interactions from different user sessions; and the third implementation inserts user session data into a white box testing technique. The study explored the effectiveness of the techniques in terms of the fault detection they provide, the cost-effectiveness of user-session- based techniques, and the relationship between the number of user sessions and the effectiveness of the test suites generated based on those sessions' interactions. As a general result, the effectiveness of white box and user session techniques was comparable in terms of fault detection capability, even if the techniques showed it was possible to find different types of faults. In particular, user session techniques were not able to discover faults associated with rarely entered data. The experiment also showed that the effectiveness of user session techniques improves as the number of collected user sessions increases. However, as the authors recognised, the growth of this number puts additional challenges on the cost of collecting and managing sessions, such as the problem of finding an oracle to establish the expected output of each user request. The possibility of using reduction techniques, such as the one described in [10], is suggested by the authors as a feasible approach for reducing test suite size, but its applicability needs further investigation. A second empirical study carried out by the same authors and described in [8] essentially confirmed the results of the first experiment.

Sampath et al. [21] have explored the possibility of using *concept analysis* to achieve scalability in user-session based testing of Web applications. Concept analysis is a technique for clustering objects that have common discrete attributes. It is used in [21] to reduce a set of user sessions to a minimal test suite, which still represents actual executed user behaviour. In particular, a user session is considered as a sequence of URLs requested by the user, and represents a separate use case offered by the application. Starting from an original test suite including a number of user sessions, this test suite is reduced by finding the smallest set of user sessions that covers all the URLs of the original test suite. At the same time, it represents the common URL of the different use cases represented by the original test suite. This technique enables an incremental approach that updates the test suite on-the-fly, by incrementally analysing additional user sessions. The experiments carried out showed the actual test suite reduction is achievable by the approach, while preserving the coverage obtained by the original user sessions' suite, and with a minimal loss of fault detection. The authors have developed a framework that automates the entire testing process, from gathering user sessions through the identification of a reduced test suite to the reuse of that test suite for coverage analysis and fault detection. A detailed description of this framework can be found in [21].

7.6 Tools for Web Application Testing

The effectiveness of a testing process may significantly depend on the tools used to support the process. Testing tools usually automate some tasks required by the process (e.g. test case generation, test case execution, evaluation of test case results). Moreover, testing tools may support the production of useful testing documentation and its configuration management.

A variety of tools for Web application testing has been proposed, where the majority was designed to carry out performance and load testing, security testing, or to implement link and accessibility checking and HTML validation. As for the functional testing, existing tools' main contribution is limited to managing test case suites created manually, and to matching the test case results with respect to an oracle created manually. Greater support for automatic test case generation would help enhance the practice of testing Web applications. User session testing can also be useful since it captures details of user interactions with the Web application. Test scripts that automatically repeat such interactions could also be created to assess the behaviour exhibited by the application. A list of more than 200 either commercial or freeware Web testing tools for Web applications is presented in [12].

Web application testing tools can be classified using the following six main categories:

a) Load, performance and stress test tools.
b) Web site security test tools.
c) HTML/XML validators.
d) Link checkers.
e) Usability and accessibility test tools.
f) Web functional/regression test tools.

Tools belonging to categories a), b), e) can be used to support non-functional requirement testing, while tools from categories c) and d) are more oriented to verifying the conformance of a Web application code to syntactical rules, or the navigability of its structure. This functionality is often offered by Web site management tools, used to develop Web sites and applications. Tools from category f) support functionality testing of Web applications and include, in addition to capture and replay tools, other tools supporting different testing strategies such as the one we analysed in Sect. 7.5.

Focusing on tools within category f), their main characteristics are discussed below, where the main differences from tools usable for traditional applications testing are also highlighted.

Services that are generic and aim to aid the functionality testing of a Web application should include:

- *Test model generation*: this is necessary to produce an instance of the desired/ specified test model of the subject application. This model may be either one of the models already produced in the development process, and the tool will have just to import it, or produced by reverse engineering the application code.
- *Test Case Management*: this is needed to support test case design and testing documentation management. Utilities for the automatic generation of the test cases would be desirable.

- *Driver and Stub Generation*: this is required to produce automatically the code of the Web pages implementing the driver and stub modules, needed for test case execution.
- *Code Instrumentation*: this is necessary to instrument automatically the code of the Web pages to be tested, by inserting probes that automatically collect data about test case execution.
- *Test result analysis*: this service will analyse and automatically evaluate test case results.
- *Report generation*: this service will produce adequate reports about analysis results, such as coverage reports about the components exercised during the test.

A generic possible architecture of such a tool is depicted in Fig. 7.2, comprising the following main components:

- *Interface* layer: implements a user interface providing access to the functions offered by the tool.
- *Service* layer: includes the components implementing tool services.
- *Repository* layer: includes the persistent data structures storing the Web application model, test cases and test logs, and the files of the instrumented Web pages, driver Web pages, stub Web pages, as well as the test reports.

Services offered by the tool, such as driver and stub generation, as well as code instrumentation and test model generation, are more reliant on the specific technologies used to implement the Web application, while others will be largely independent of the technologies. As an example, different types of drivers and stubs will have to be generated for testing client and server Web pages as the technology (e.g. the scripting languages used to code the Web pages) affects the way drivers and stubs are developed.

In general, the driver of a client page has the responsibility of loading the client page into a browser, where it is executed, while the driver of a server page requires the execution of the page on the Web server. Stubs of a client page have to simulate the behaviour of pages that are reachable from the page under test by hyperlinks, or whose execution on the Web server is required by the page. Stubs of a server page have to simulate the behaviour of other software components whose execution is required by the server page under test. Specific approaches have to be designed to implement drivers and stubs for Web pages created dynamically at run time.

Depending on the specific technology used to code Web pages, different code instrumentation components also have to be implemented. Code analysers, including different language parsers, have to be used to identify automatically the points where probes are to be inserted in the original page code.

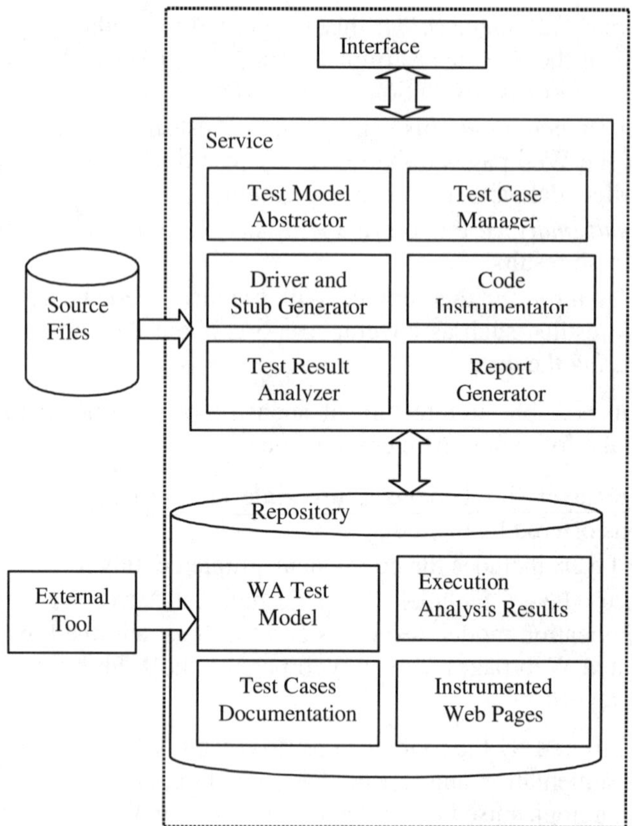

Fig. 7.2. The layered architecture of a tool supporting Web application testing

Analogously, the test model generator component that has to reverse-engineer the application code for generating the test model is largely dependent on the technologies used to implement the application. Code analysers are also required in this case.

The other modules of such a generic tool are less affected by the Web application technologies, and can be developed as in the case of traditional applications.

7.7 A Practical Example of Web Application Testing

In this section we present an example where the functional requirements of an industrial Web application are tested. It addresses the problem of testing an existing Web application using poor development documentation. We also present additional analysis techniques needed to support the application testing in the case of existing and scarcely documented Web applications. Such a problem may also exist within the development process, where the testing of scarcely documented Web applications is often encountered.

The application's unit, integration and system testing will be analysed and testing approaches proposed in the literature are used to accomplish these tasks.

The Web application presented is named "Course Management", and was developed to support the activities of undergraduate courses offered by a Computer Science Department. The application provides students and teachers with several distinct services: a teacher can publish course information, and manage examination sessions and student tutoring agendas, while students can access course information, and register for a course or an examination session. A registered student can also download teaching material.

The technologies used to implement the application are HTML, ASP, VB Script and Javascript. The application includes a Microsoft Access database, and is composed of 106 source files whose total size is close to 500 Kbytes. As for the development documentation, just a textual description of user functions was available.

The first step is to carry out a preliminary *reverse engineering* process to reconstruct design documentation that is essential for a testing activity. Such documentation includes a specification of functional requirements implemented by the application, design documentation providing the application's organisation in terms of pages and their interconnection relationships, as well as traceability information.

To obtain this information, the reverse engineering approach and the WARE tool presented in [7] were used. This tool the allows main components of a Web application and relationships between components to be automatically obtained by source code static analysis. The tool also provides the graphical representation of this information, called WAG (Web Application connection Graph). Table 7.3 lists a count of the items found in the application code for each category of components and relationships identified by the tool, while Fig. 7.3 reports the WAG depicting all the identified components and relationships. In this graph, which is an instantiation of the application's meta-model, different shapes have been used to distinguish different types of components and relationships. As an example, a box is used for drawing a Static Page, a trapezium for a Built Client Page and a diamond for a Server Page.

Using the clustering technique described in [5] and exploiting the available documentation on user functions, the application's use case model was reconstructed, and groups of pages, each implementing a use case, were identified. Figure 7.4 shows this use case model.

The testing process carried out was driven by the application's use case model. For each use case, a unit testing of the Web pages implementing the case was executed, using the black box technique based on the decision tables proposed in [6]. After the unit testing, an integration testing was carried out. In what follows, we will refer to the use case named "Teacher and course management" to show how testing was carried out.

The "Teacher and course management" use case implements the application behaviour permitting a registered teacher to manage his/her personal data and data about courses he/she teaches. This use case allows a teacher to:

- F1: register, update or delete personal data.
- F2: add a new course and associate it to the teacher for the current academic year.
- F3: update/delete the data about a course taught by the teacher.

Figure 7.5 specifies the functional requirements of the function F2. Figure 7.6 shows, using the UML extensions from Conallen [4], an excerpt of the WAG, made up by the pages implementing the function F2..

Figure 7.7 shows the rendering of the client page AddCourse.html (all the labels/prompts in the page are in Italian) including a form that allows the input of data needed to register a new course and to be added to the ones taught by the teacher in the current year.

The unit testing of this page has been carried out using the following approach. We started by analysing the responsibilities of this page. The page is in charge of visualising a form (see Fig. 7.7) that allows the input of required data, checking that all fields have been filled in, checking the validity of the academic year value, and submitting the input data to the server page AddCourse.asp. Moreover, a Reset button in the page allows to be "blanked" all the form fields while a couple of radio buttons labelled by YES/NO in the page are used to ask if the user wants to input data for more than one course.

Finally, this page automatically computes the value of the second year of the academic year field, after the first year value has been provided.

In order to associate the Web page with the decision table required by the testing approach, for each page input item (such as form fields, buttons, selection box, etc.) domain analysis was carried out to identify sets of valid and not valid values. The functional specifications reported in Fig. 7.5 were used to accomplish domain analysis, whose results are reported in Table 7.4. In the table, the input element named "More Courses?" is referred to the pair of radio buttons labelled YES/NO.

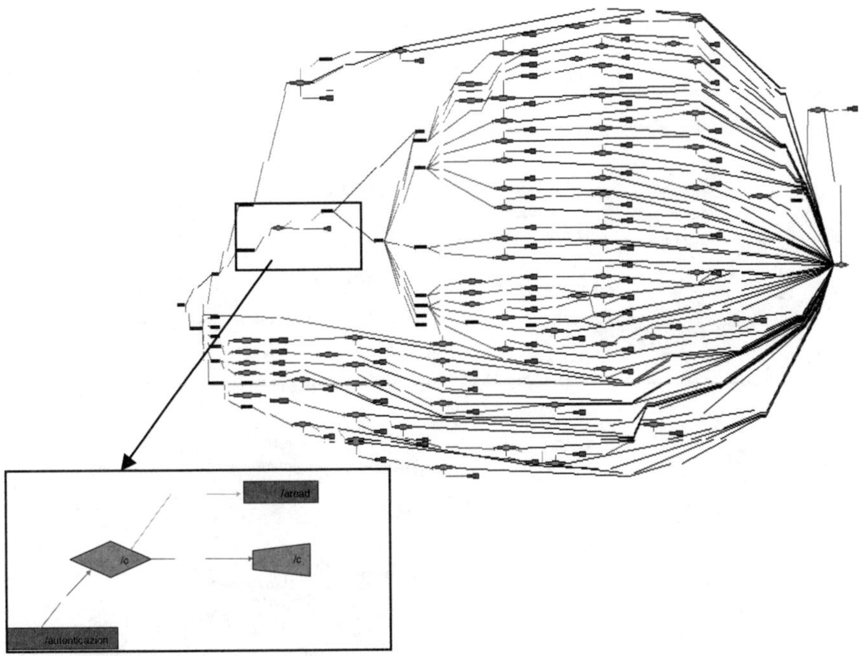

Fig. 7.3. The WAG of the "Course Management" Web application

Table 7.3. Type and count of Web application items identified by static analysis

Item type	Count
Server Page	75
Static Page	23
Built Client Page	74
Client Script	132
Client Function	48
Form	49
Server Script	562
Server Function	0
Redirect (in Server Scripts)	7
Redirect (in Client Scripts)	0
Link	45
Submit	49
Include	57
Load in Frame Operation	4

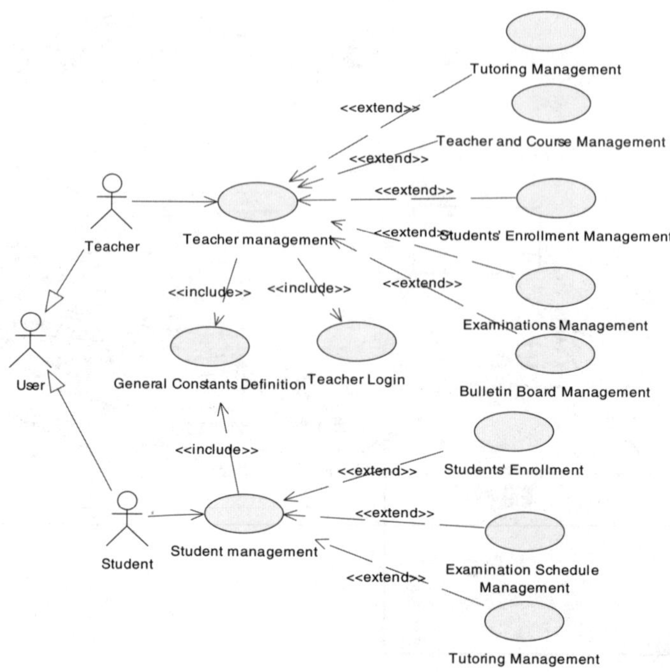

Fig. 7.4. The use case model of the "Course Management" Web application

Function: *F2* Creates a new course and associates it with a registered teacher for the current academic year.
Pre-condition: The teacher has to be already registered at the Web application.

- The teacher inputs Course Code and Name, and the Academic Year. If any datum is missing, an error message is displayed.
- The Course Code must not yet exist in the database; the Course Name may already exist in the database but associated to a different code. If the Course Code already exists, an error message is displayed.
- The Academic Year and the current Academic Year must coincide, otherwise a message error is displayed.
- If all the data are valid, the new course is added into the database and a message is sent to client to notify the success of the operation.

Post-condition: The teacher is associated with the new course for the current academic year.

Fig. 7.5. Functional requirements of function F2

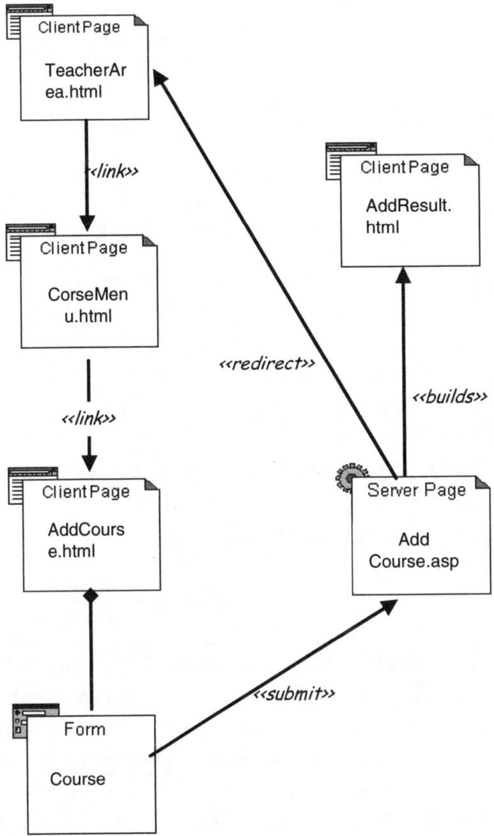

Fig. 7.6. An excerpt of the WAG using Conallen's graphical notation

Based on the specifications in Fig. 7.5 and information in Table 7.4, the decision table reported in Table 7.5 was obtained. This decision table reports all the admissible combinations, deduced by the page implementation, of valid/not valid sets of values of the input elements, together with the expected results and actions.

In Table 7.5, the columns reporting status before and after test have not been shown for the sake of readability. The status before and after the test was specified with respect to the status of the database. For each variant, the state before test is always: "The teacher is registered in the database and is allowed to do this operation". The status after test is "The execution of the test cases does not change the status of the database".

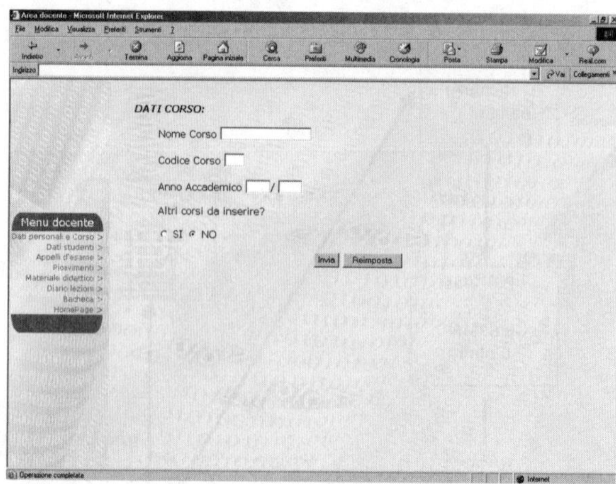

Fig. 7.7. The rendering of the client page `AddCourse.html`

Table 7.4. Valid and not valid sets of values of the input elements in the client page `AddCourse.html`

Input Name	Valid Values	Not Valid Values
Course Code	The course code does not exist in the database	The course code already exists in the database
Course Name	The course name does not exist in the database or it already exists but it is not associated with the same inputted Course Code in the database	The course name already exists in the database and it is associated with the same inputted Course Code
Academic Year	The current academic year	Not Equal to current academic year
More Courses?	{Yes, No}	Not in {Yes, No}
Submit Button	{Clicked, NotClicked}	Not in {Clicked, NotClicked}
Reset Button	{Clicked, NotClicked}	Not in {Clicked, NotClicked}

Page testing was carried out with the aim of verifying that the page was correctly visualised in the browser, and that validated data were sent correctly to the server page AddCourse.asp. To test the page, a driver module allowing the client page to be loaded into a browser, after a registered teacher's login, had to be developed as well as a stub module simulating the execution of the AddCourse.asp server page. This stub module just had to verify that received data coincided with data sent by the client page, and notify the result by a message sent to the client.

Table 7.5. Decision Table for testing the client page `AddCourse.html`

#	Input Section						Output Section	
	Course Name	Course Code	More Courses?	Academic Year First field	Submit	Reset	Expected results	Expected output actions
1	DC	DC	DC	Not Valid	DC	Not Clicked	Academic Year Error Message	Academic year second field filled with the right value.
2	DC	DC	DC	Valid	Clicked	Not Clicked	Data submitted to server page AddCourse.asp Stub notification message about submission correctness	Academic year second field filled with the right value
3	DC	DC	DC	DC	Not Clicked	Click	All the fields in the form have 'blank' values	The page AddCourse.html is Visualized

Note: DC = Don't Care

A set of test cases was defined to exercise all the variants in Table 7.5. These test cases are not reported due to lack of space. The execution of the test cases revealed a failure in the validity check for the AcademicYear values. Indeed, also the value of the Academic Year successive to the current one is accepted (e.g. 2004/2005 is also the valid value of the current Academic Year, and the value 2005/2006 is accepted as valid, while all other successive values, such as 2006/2007, are correctly refused).

This page was also submitted for white box testing. The AddCourse.html page includes HTML code for visualising and managing data input, and two JavaScript functions for validating the Academic Year value. The branch coverage criterion was used to test this page, and all the branches were covered by the set of test cases (the page was instrumented to collect data and verify the coverage). A test model similar to the control flow model proposed by Ricca and Tonella [19] was used to model the structure of the AddCourse.html page and design the test cases.

As an example of server page testing, we consider the AddCourse.asp server page. The responsibility of this page is to register the new course in the database and a course to its teacher, when input values are valid.

To test a server page its code has to be analysed to identify input variables. The input variables found in AddCourse.asp were the ones submitted by the AddCourse.html page (i.e. Course Code, Course Name, More Courses?, Academic Year variables), besides the session variables LoginOK and TeacherCode. Domain analysis was carried out to define valid and invalid sets of values of the input elements. As for the session variable TeacherCode, its valid values were all the ones corresponding to registered teachers and stored in the database. The valid value for the variable LoginOK was the logical value TRUE associated with the condition of an authorized user who made a successful login.

Table 7.6. Decision table for testing the server page `AddCourse.asp`

#	Input section					Output section		
	Course Name	Course Code	More Courses?	Academic Year	LoginOK	Expected results	Expected output actions	Expected state after test
1	Valid	Valid	NO	Valid	True	Data registered into the data base. Success Message	The page TeacherArea.html is visualised	The new course and its association to the teacher has been added to database
2	Valid	Valid	YES	Valid	True	Data registered in the data base	AddCourse.html page is visualised	The new course and its association to the teacher has been added to database
3	DC	Not Valid	DC	DC	True	Error Message	The page CourseMenu.html is visualised	It coincides with the before test state
4	DC	DC	DC	DC	False	Error Message	A new login is required	Coincides with the before test state
5	Not Valid	Valid	DC	DC	True	Error Message	None	Coincides with the before test state
6	DC	DC	Not Valid	DC	True	Error Message	None	Coincides with the before test state

DC – Does not care

To compile the decision table associated with the page, expected results and actions were also looked for. Table 7.6 shows the set of variants we used to test the AddCourse.asp page. The TeacherCode variable was not included in the table because it did not affect the page's behaviour.

As for the testing of the page, a set of test cases was defined in order to exercise each variant for both true and false values. To execute the page test, a driver simulating the HTTP requests by a client, as well as a stub simulating the client pages returned to the client, were developed. No stub was used to simulate the connection to the database, but a test database was used. The execution of this functional testing did not reveal any failure. The same page was submitted for white box testing, using the linearly independent paths coverage criterion. The page included four lincarly independent paths which were all covered by the test cases we designed.

At the integration testing level, these two pages were combined and retested together. Table 7.7 reports the decision table including the set of variants used for integration testing. No more failures were observed during the integration testing.

Unit and integration testing were executed for each group of pages implementing the remaining Web application use cases. Thanks to the unit testing, a few failures in some pages were observed. They were mostly due to defects in the validation of user input data. Moreover, we observed that some client pages included JavaScript functions that were not activated during the execution, because they were dead code left in the page after a maintenance intervention that replaced them with new (correctly activated) functions. A similar datum was observed in a few server pages too. As for the integration testing, no additional failure was observed.

As for the unit testing of dynamically generated Web pages, an additional effort was required to design test cases of the server pages responsible for building them. These test cases had to be run, so the client pages were generated, and therefore were captured and stored on-the-fly, to be successively tested. In some cases, the user-session-based approach was exploited to identify test cases able to generate and cover the built client pages.

Table 7.7. Decision table for integration testing of the client page AddCourse.html and server page `AddCourse.asp`

#	Input Section							Output Section	
	Course Name	Course Code	More Courses?	Academic Year	Submit	Reset	Expected results	Expected output actions	Expected state after test
1	DC	DC	DC	Not Valid	Clicked	Not Clicked	Error Message	The page AddCourse.html is visualised	The same as before test
2	DC	Not Valid	DC	DC	Clicked	Not Clicked	Data submitted to server page AddCourse.asp Error Message	The page CorseMenu.html is Visualised	The same as before test
3	Valid	Valid	NO	Valid	Clicked	Not-Clicked	Data submitted to server page AddCourse.asp. Success Message	The page TeacherArea.html is visualized	The new course and its association to the teacher added to database
4	Valid	Valid	YES	Valid	Clicked	Not-Clicked	Data submitted to server page AddCorse.asp. Success Message	The page AddCourse.html is visualized again	The new course and its association to the teacher added to database
5	DC	DC	DC	DC	Not-Clicked	Clicked	All the fields in the form put to blank	The page AddCourse.html is visualized	

DC – Does not care

We also executed a system test aimed at exercising each use case implemented by the application at least once. This testing did not reveal any other failures. Moreover, the page coverage reached by this testing was evaluated. All static pages were covered, except one server page which was unreachable, since it was an older version of a page replaced in a maintenance operation.

In conclusion, the experience of functional testing of the "Course Management" Web application was successfully accomplished. Indeed, the fact that testing revealed just a few failures in the application (most of which were due to incorrectly executed maintenance interventions) could be attributed to the "maturity" level of the Web application, which had been running for two years.

The testing experience also highlighted that a considerable effort was required to reconstruct the design documentation needed for test design and execution. This effort might have been saved, or reduced, if this documentation had already been available before testing. This datum can be considered as a strong similarity point between functional testing of a Web application and functional testing of a "traditional" system.

7.8 Conclusions

The openness of Web applications to plenty of users and the strategic value of the services they offer oblige us to consider seriously the verification of both non-functional and functional requirements of a Web application. While new and specific approaches must be necessarily used for the verification of non-functional requirements (see the problems of security or accessibility testing that are specific for Web applications), most of the knowledge and expertise in the field of traditional application testing may be reused for testing the functional requirements of a Web application.

In this chapter we have reported the main differences and points of similarity between testing a Web application and testing a traditional software application. We considered testing of the functional requirements with respect to four main aspects, i.e. testing scopes, test models, test strategies and testing tools. The main contributions to these topics presented in the literature have been taken into account to carry out this analysis.

The main conclusion we can draw from this discussion is that all testing aspects that are directly dependent on the implementation technologies (such as test models, testing scopes, white box testing strategies) have to be deeply adapted to the heterogeneous and "dynamic" nature of the Web applications, while other aspects (such as black box strategies, or the objectives of testing tools) may be reused with a reduced adaptation effort. This finding also indicates that further research efforts should be spent to define and assess the effectiveness of testing models, methods, techniques and tools that combine traditional testing approaches with new and specific ones.

A relevant issue for future work may be the definition of methods and techniques for improving the effectiveness and efficiency of a Web application testing process. As an example, the adequacy of mutation testing techniques for the automatic validation of test suites should be investigated, as well as the effectiveness of statistical testing techniques in reducing testing effort by focusing on those parts of a Web application that are most frequently used by massive user populations [15]. Moreover, the possibility of combining genetic algorithms with user session data for reducing the costs of test case generation may be a further research question to be investigated. Finally, in the renewed scenario of Web services, new research challenges are being provided by the necessity to consider testing of Web services too.

References

1 Andrews AA, Offutt J, Alexander RT (2005) Testing Web Applications by Modeling with FSMs. Software Systems and Modeling, 4(2)

2 Bangio A, Ceri S, Fraternali P (2000) Web Modeling Language (WebML): a Modelling Language for Designing Web Sites. In: Proceedings of the 9th International Conference on the WWW (WWW9). Elsevier: Amsterdam, Holland, pp 137–157

3 Binder RV (1999) Testing Object-Oriented Systems. Models, Patterns, and Tools. Addison-Wesley: Reading, MA

4 Conallen J. (1999) Building Web Applications with UML. Addison-Wesley: Reading, MA

5 Di Lucca GA, Fasolino AR, De Carlini U, Pace F, Tramontana P (2002) Comprehending Web Applications by a Clustering Based Approach. In: Proceedings of 10th Workshop on Program Comprehension. IEEE Computer Society Press: Los Alamitos, CA, pp 261–270

6 Di Lucca GA, Fasolino AR, Faralli F, De Carlini U (2002) Testing Web Applications. In: Proceedings of International Conference on Software Maintenance. IEEE Computer Society Press: Los Alamitos, CA, pp 310–319

7 Di Lucca GA, Fasolino AR, Tramontana P (2004) Reverse Engineering Web Applications: the WARE Approach. Software Maintenance and Evolution: Research and Practice. John Wiley and Sons Ltd., 16:71–101

8 Elbaum S, Karre S, Rothermel G (2003) Improving Web Application Testing with User Session Data. In: Proceedings of International Conference on Software Engineering, IEEE Computer Society Press: Los Alamitos, CA, pp 49–59

9 Elbaum S, Rothermel G, Karre S, Fisher M (2005) Leveraging User-Session Data to support Web Application Testing. IEEE Transactions on Software Engineering, 31(3):187–202

10 Gomez J, Canchero C, Pastor O (2001) Conceptual Modeling of Device-Independent Web Applications. IEEE Multimedia, 8(2):26–39

11 Harrold MJ, Gupta R, Soffa ML (1993) A Methodology for Controlling the Size of a Test Suite. ACM Transactions on Software Engineering and Methodology, 2(3):270–285

12 Hieatt E, Mee R (2002) Going Faster: Testing The Web Application. IEEE Software, 19(2):60–65

13 Hower R (2005) Web Site Test Tools and Site Management Tools. Software QA and Testing Resource Center. www.softwareqatest.com/qatWeb1.html (accessed 5 June 2005)

14 IEEE Std. 610.12–1990 (1990). Glossary of Software Engineering Terminology, in Software Engineering Standard Collection, IEEE Computer Society Press, Los. Alamitos, CA

15 Isakowitz T, Kamis A, Koufaris M (1997) Extending the Capabilities of RMM: Russian Dolls and Hypertext. In: Proceedings of 30th Hawaii International Conference on System Science, Maui, HI, (6):177–186

16 Kallepalli C, Tian J (2001) Measuring and Modeling Usage and Reliability for Statistical Web Testing. IEEE Transactions on Software Engineering, 27(11):1023–1036

17 Liu C, Kung DC, Hsia P, Hsu C (2000) Object-based Data Flow Testing of Web Applications. In: Proceedings of First Asia-Pacific Conference on Quality Software. IEEE Computer Society Press, Los Alamitos, CA, pp 7–16

18 Nguyen HQ (2000) Testing Applications on the Web: Test Planning for Internet-Based Systems. John Wiley & Sons, NY

19 Ricca F, Tonella P (2001) Analysis and Testing of Web Applications. In: Proceedings of ICSE 2001 IEEE Computer Society Press, Los Alamitos CA, pp 25–34

20 Ricca F, Tonella P (2004) A 2-Layer Model for the White-Box Testing of Web Applications. In: Proceedings of Sixth IEEE Workshop on Web Site Evolution IEEE Computer Society Press, Los Alamitos, CA, pp 11–19

21 Sampath S, Mihaylov V, Souter A, Pollock L (2004) A Scalable approach to user-session based testing of Web Applications Through Concept Analysis. In: Proceedings of 19th International Conference on Automated Software Engineering, IEEE Computer Society Press: Los Alamitos, CA, pp 132–141

22 Sampath S, Mihaylov V, Souter A, Pollock L (2004) Composing a framework to automate testing of operational Web-based software. In: Proceedings of 20th International Conference on Software Maintenance IEEE Computer Society Press pp 104–113

23 Schwabe D, Guimaraes RM, Rossi G (2002) Cohesive Design of Personalized Web Applications. IEEE Internet Computing. 6(2):34–43

24 Web Content Accessibility Guidelines 2.0 (2005), http://www.w3.org/TR/WCAG20 (accessed 5 June 2005)

Authors' Biographies

Giuseppe A. Di Lucca received the Laurea degree in Electronic Engineering from the University of Naples "Federico II", Italy, in 1987 and the PhD degree in Electronic Engineering and Computer Science from the same university in 1992.

He is currently an Associate Professor of Computer Science at the Department of "Ingegneria" of the University of Sannio. Previously, he was with the Department of 'Informatica e Sistemistica' at the University of Naples "Federico II". Since 1987 he has been a researcher in the field of software engineering and his list of publications contains more than 50 papers published in journals and conference proceedings.

He serves on the programme and organising committees of conferences in the field of software maintenance and program comprehension. His research interests include software engineering, software maintenance, reverse engineering, software reuse, software reengineering, Web engineering and software migration.

Anna Rita Fasolino received the Laurea degree in Electronic Engineering (cum laude) in 1992 and the PhD degree in Electronic Engineering and Computer Science in 1996 from the University of Naples "Federico II", Italy, where she is currently an Associate Professor of Computer Science. From 1998 to 1999 she was at the Computer Science Department of the University of Bari, Italy.

Her research interests include software maintenance and quality, reverse engineering, Web engineering, software testing and reuse, and she has published several papers in journals and conference proceedings on these topics. She is a member of programme committees of conferences in the field of software maintenance and evolution.

8 An Overview of Process Improvement in Small Settings

Khaled El Emam

Abstract: Existing software process improvement approaches can be applied successfully to small projects and small organisations. However, they need to customised and the techniques used have to be adapted for small settings. This chapter provides a pragmatic discussion of issues requires to implement software process improvement in small settings, covering the practical obstacles that are likely to be faced and ways to address them.

Keywords: Software process improvement, IDEAL model, Small organisations.

8.1 Introduction

Software process improvement (SPI) efforts in small settings tend to be, in general, less successful than in large settings [4]. The approaches needed to improve the practices of small projects are somewhat different from those required for larger projects. Web development projects are still typically small with just a handful of developers and possibly additional resources in the form of graphics artists and technical writers.

This chapter will discuss the issues relevant to software process improvement (SPI) in a small project context and present examples of assessment and improvement approaches that have worked in the past. Some of this knowledge is based on the research literature, and some on our own experience working with small organisations over the past ten years, improving their software engineering practices. Some of our examples include our experience of process improvement at TrialStat Corporation, where we were responsible for continuous process improvement over a four-year period.

Small projects may occur in large or small organisations. If the former, it is possible for small projects to take advantage of some of the resources of the parent company, e.g. their training programs, internal consultants and corporately licensed tools. However, if the latter, projects do not have these advantages, and the organisation will be limited to one or two projects at most. In this chapter we will not differentiate between the two cases explicitly, unless it is material to the discussion. We therefore refer to *small settings* in the general case.

To start we need to be more precise about what constitutes a small setting. There have been numerous definitions used in the literature and governments, where they all tend to be vague. European Union projects used to classify organisations as *small* if they had up to 50 IT staff [15], also supported by [6,7]. Varkoi et al. [17] considered a company *small* if it had less than 100 employees, Cater-Steel [2] as one with less than 20 employees [2], and Dyba [4] as one with up to 35 employees. The US census considers companies with up to 50 employees as small [10]. Therefore we will define a small setting as one with up to 50 employees.

8.1.1 Why Do Organisations Initiate SPI Efforts?

It is important to understand what motivates organisations to start an SPI effort. Motivations will have an influence on the amount of resources they will make available on and the management's commitment.

Anecdotally, our experience suggests that the three main drivers are:

- A crisis has hit the organisation or a particular project. For example, shipping a product extremely late or delivering a release with a large number of defects, with the result that important clients have complained or abandoned the product. The crisis initiates a search for solutions. In some organisations the crisis will result in some key people taking the blame and being fired. In others, the search for solutions may result in an SPI initiative.
- An important client demands that suppliers have an SPI initiative in place. In such case, SPI is driven by the client, and the organisation or project is obliged to respond.
- In some cases it is a business requirement to demonstrate that good practices are followed, e.g. in regulated domains. For the clinical trials sector, Title 21 Code of Federal Regulations (21 CFR Part 11) is the Food and Drug Administration regulation that governs software development and operations. The interpretations of this regulation stipulate a set of software development practices to be in place. Passing an audit is a requirement for being a part of this business, and therefore management is obliged to have an SPI effort in place to ensure compliance.

However, in addition to our anecdotal evidence, previous research also indicates that there are additional reasons for initiating SPI efforts. An analysis performed by the Software Engineering Institute, based on feedback data collected from assessment sponsors, showed that over half of the sponsors stated that the primary goals of their assessments were either to monitor the progress of their existing software process improvement programs, or to initiate new programs [3]. Furthermore, over a third of the sponsors said that validating an organisation's maturity level was a primary goal of their assessment.

In another study [9], assessment sponsors were asked the reasons for performing a software process assessment in their organisations. The question asked was "To what extent did the following represent important reasons for performing a software process assessment?". The responses were measured using a 5-point scale of importance, structured as follows:

- 1 corresponds to "Very Important".
- 2 corresponds to "Important".
- 3 corresponds to "Somewhat Important".
- 4 corresponds to "Not Very Important".
- 5 corresponds to "Not At All Important".

Table 8.1 summarises the average calculated for each response, and sponsors' answers.

Table 8.1. Reasons for performing a software process assessment

No.	Reason	Variable Name
1	Gain market advantage	ADVANTAGE
2	Customer demand to improve process capability	DEMAND
3	Improve efficiency	EFFICIENCY
4	Improve customer service	CUSTOMER
5	Improve reliability of products	PRODREL
6	Improve reliability of services in supporting products	SERVREL
7	Competitive/marketing pressure to demonstrate process capability	COMPETITIVE
8	Generate management support and buy-in for software process improvement	MANAGEMEN T
9	Generate technical staff support and buy-in for software process improvement	TECHSTAFF
10	Establish best practices to guide organisational process improvement	BESTPRACT
11	Establish project baseline and/or track projects' process improvement	TRACKPROJ
12	Establish project baseline and/or track organisation's process improvement	TRACKORG

Figure 8.1 presents a range plot that shows square points representing the response mean (average) for each reason asked. The mean is based on scores obtained from a single study, i.e. from a single sample of the population of interest. If we were to repeat this study with a different sample it is very likely that the means of all responses would differ from those in Fig. 8.1. For this reason we have also included a 95% confidence interval,

represented by upper and lower whiskers. A confidence interval delimits the range of values where the true mean is likely to lie, and 95% represents the probability of that occurring.

Assuming that a sponsor is indifferent to a given *reason* if the score given is 3, we can use the confidence intervals provided in the range plot to find the reasons sponsors are indifferent to. Whenever whiskers cross the value of three, then there is evidence, with a 95% confidence, that the mean response for that *reason* is not significantly different from 3. Only the two reasons SERVREL and ADVANTAGE are indifferent to sponsors. This means that sponsors exhibited indifference on "gaining market advantage" and "improving the reliability of services in supporting products" as reasons for performing an assessment.

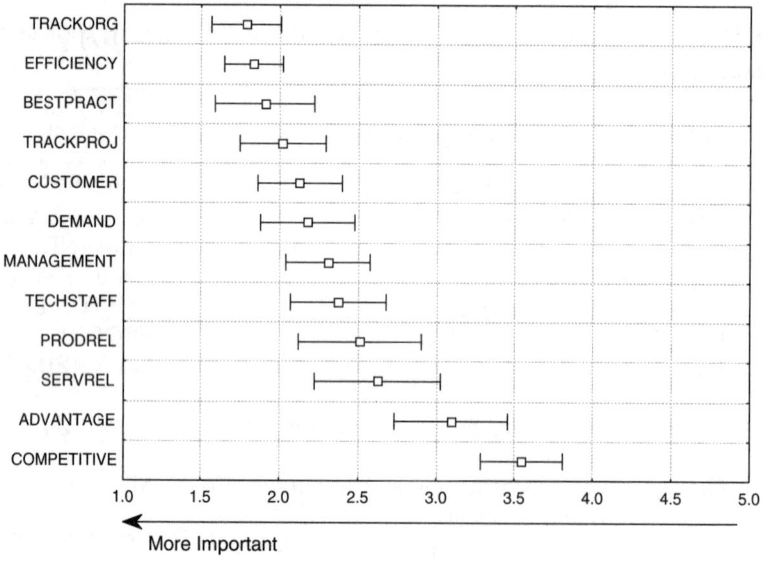

Fig. 8.1. Mean of importance scores with 95% confidence interval

In addition, "competitive/marketing pressure to demonstrate process capability" (COMPETITIVE) was clearly not a reason for performing assessments.

The five most important reasons sponsors chose for conducting their process assessments were: to establish process capability baselines and/or track progress with project and organisational process improvement (TRACKORG, TRACKPROJ); to improve efficiency and customer service (EFFICIENCY, CUSTOMER); and to establish best practices to guide process improvement (BESTPRACT). The importance which the sponsors assigned to "establishing capability baselines" clearly indicates that they tend to recognise that assessments are an important measurement procedure. To choose "Improving efficiency and customer service" indicates these sponsors believe that SPI based on the assessment would provide tangible benefits to their projects. The choice of "Establish best practices to guide organisational process improvement" suggests that sponsors expected that existing good practices embodied in the models would be transferred to their organisations.

The three reasons scored in the middle range were: the need to generate support and buy-in for process improvement among the technical staff and management (MANAGEMENT, TECHSTAFF); customer demand to improve process capability (DEMAND). Again, these are consistent with the two basic reasons for performing assessments, namely to build support for process improvement as well as to accurately measure organisational capability.

No differences were found in these responses between small and large organisations.

8.1.2 Process Improvement Cycle

The IDEAL[SM] model [14] (see Fig. 8.2) provides the overall framework for SPI. This model has been used in the past for successful improvements in small projects [13]. It consists of five phases:

- I Initiating: to initiate the improvement program
- D Diagnosing; to diagnose the current state of practice
- E Establishing: to establish the plans for the improvement program
- A Acting: to act on the plans and recommended improvements
- L Leveraging: to leverage the lessons learned and the business results of the improvement effort

The *Initiating* phase establishes the business reasons for undertaking a software process improvement effort. It identifies high-level concerns in the organisation that can be the stimulus for addressing various aspects of quality improvement. Communication of these concerns and business perspectives is required during the *Initiating* phase to gain visible executive buy-in and sponsorship at this early stage of the improvement effort.

The *Diagnosing* phase is used to build a common understanding of the current processes of the organisation, most especially the strengths and weaknesses of the processes currently employed. It will also help identify priorities for improving software processes. This diagnosis is based on a software process assessment (see below).

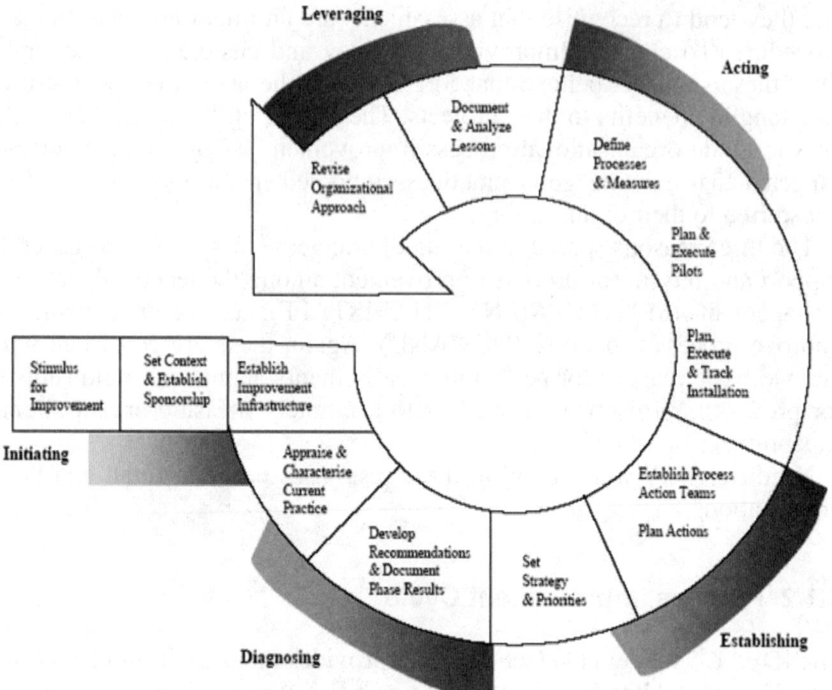

Fig. 8.2. The SEI's IDEAL Model for SPI (source [14]).

The *Establishing* phase finalises the strategy and supporting plans for the software process improvement program. It sets the direction and guidance for the next three to five years, including strategic and tactical plans for software process improvement.

The *Acting* phase takes action to effect changes in organisational systems that result in improvements to these systems. Improvements are made in an orderly manner and in ways that will cause them to be sustained over time. Techniques used to support and institutionalise change include defining software processes and measurements, pilot testing, and installing new processes and measurements throughout the organisation.

The *Leveraging* phase completes the process improvement cycle. Lessons learned from the pilot projects and improvement efforts are documented and analysed to improve the process improvement program for the future. The business needs determined at the beginning of the cycle are revisited to see if they have been met. Sponsorship for the program is revisited and renewed for the next cycle of software process improvement.

8.1.3 Process Assessments

SPI efforts should begin with some form of software process assessment. A process assessment identifies the strengths and weaknesses for the overall practices of the target project(s). This is achieved through a series of interviews and document inspections (e.g. looking at project plans and test execution results) to determine how software is currently developed and maintained. Most process assessments rely on a model of best practices to drive the interviews and document inspections, such as the CMM for Software [16], the CMMI [1], and ISO/IEC 15504 [8].

Figure 8.3 depicts the context of process assessment, showing that process assessment provides the means of characterising the current process capabilities of an organisation or project. Analysis of the assessment results is used to identify process strengths and weaknesses. For SPI, this would ultimately lead to an improvement initiative, which identifies changes to the processes to improve their capabilities. For capability determination, the assessment results identify whether or not the assessed processes meet a target capability. If the processes do not match up to the target capability, this may initiate an improvement effort. Our focus in this chapter is on process assessment for improvement.

The performance of an assessment requires three different types of inputs:

- An assessment definition, which includes the identification of the assessment sponsor, the purpose and scope of the assessment, any relevant constraints, and the assessment responsibilities (e.g. who will be on the assessment team, and who will be interviewed).
- An assessment method that describes the activities that need to be performed during an assessment.
- An underlying best practice model is required. This model consists of the definitions of the processes that will be assessed, the assessment criteria, and a scheme to produce quantitative ratings at the end of the assessment.[1]

[1] The quantitative ratings are good for communicating the status of the process internally or externally. However, they are not necessary for a successful improvement program.

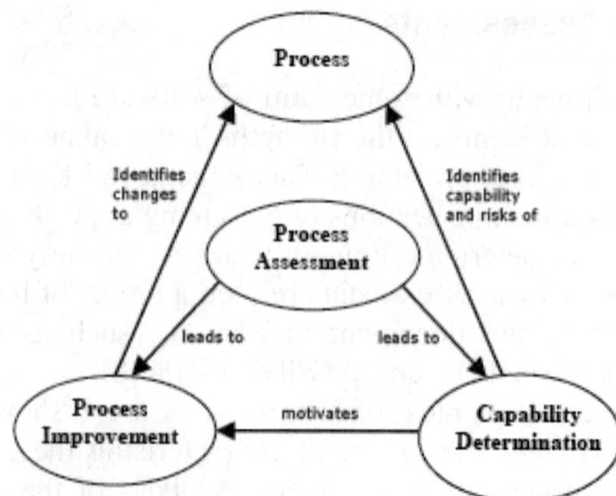

Fig. 8.3. The context of process assessment [9]

In most projects the development team knows where the large problems are. However, they may not have management support to do something about it; they may not know where to start because there are so many problems; they may not know the best practices to implement to improve their current situation. Process assessments address these three issues directly. This is the recommended way to get started with SPI, with some exceptions mentioned below.

The assessment can be formal and conducted by a third-party according to a well defined method; it can be informal and performed internally within the organisation; it can be a mixture of the two.

Formal assessments have the advantage of being credible and are more likely to have repeatable results. However, they also tend to be more expensive.

Internal assessments work well only if the internal assessor has extensive experience with SPI (e.g. from a job in a previous organisation and/or extensive training and coaching). Then (s)he can act as a surrogate for external assessors and would have sufficient background knowledge and access to resources to perform a meaningful assessment.

In some cases management or other staff will not believe an internal assessment and hence will not act on recommendations. This will be partially driven by the credibility of the internal assessor(s) and the existence of conflicts between different groups. In such a case it would be better to hire external consultants.

There are a number of process assessment methods that have been developed specifically for small projects and small organisations [2,12,18]. These reduce the scope of assessments to the processes that are believed to be most relevant in small settings, and rely more upon interviews and less on document inspections.

8.2 Implementation in Small Settings

8.2.1 Availability of Funds

Projects in small organisations are often characterised as lacking funds. The same is true for small projects in large organisations where the project is an independent cost centre. This makes it difficult to sanction heavy investment in process improvement. For example, there are cases where a large company invests $1m on SPI and obtains a seven-fold return on investment (ROI). Getting such returns is often contingent in making such a large investment. For a small project that can only invest say $10,000, the question is, would they too get the same level of ROI? The most likely answer is *no*. Small projects and small organisations need to get credible returns with small investments.

The most realistic approach for SPI in small settings is incremental improvement, with each increment requiring a small investment. Each small investment must show a value to the project otherwise it will be difficult to sustain such an investment over time.

Many of the SPI challenges in small settings result from the availability of limited funds.

8.2.2 Resources For Process Improvement

A typical starting point in an SPI effort is to setup a Software Engineering Process Group (SEPG) [11]. While there have been some examples in small projects where this has worked, for most projects there are insufficient resources to create a dedicated SEPG.

In practice, one or two developers or managers are assigned, on a part-time basis, to be responsible for process improvement. This may be difficult because their primary priority is to deliver the software. Therefore, unless the regular development workload is reduced to accommodate the additional responsibility, this approach may not work effectively.

Another model that has been used requires that individuals responsible for much of the work to implement SPI are consultants external to the organisation. These consultants are hired for an extended period of time and assist the project in their SPI effort. This model raises two challenges. The first is that external consultants tend to be quite expensive. Second, unless the consultants are well integrated with the project and have management's strong support, they may not be able to affect meaningful change within the projects.

Government support has frequently alleviated the former challenge. This reduces the financial burden on projects and makes the successful implementation of SPI more likely.

8.2.3 Process Model

The ability to handle changing requirements is critical for software projects. Requirements change because the business processes that are being automated change, and because users develop a better understanding of their needs over time. An effective process model for these kinds of projects is an iterative one. This breaks up the delivery of functions into several small iterations. At the beginning of each iteration, the software requirements are prioritised and allocated to the subsequent iterations. The users (or customers) are key participants in this prioritisation exercise.

The more successful iterative projects develop a system architecture at the very beginning of the project. This requires an understanding of the total functionality of the system that will be developed, and which parts of the system need to be flexible to accommodate change.

In an iterative environment SPI should allocate improvements to each iteration. E.g. a small change to the process to improve testing practices is introduced in an iteration. After the iteration the team evaluates the changes. If the evaluation was positive then the change is kept. If the experience was negative then additional changes are made for the next iteration step. With such a mechanism it is possible to introduce incremental process improvements at a cost that the project can sustain. This is a very effective way to introduce change in small settings.

8.2.4 Training

Small projects often implement SPI without any formal training because of limited funding. A study of the implementation of agile practices in small projects found that none of the projects' team members had received any training or mentoring on agile methods [5]. Most of the information was obtained from conferences, books and the Web.

The consequence of this approach is that it is fraught with trial and error. Most good practices need to be tailored to the specifics of the organisation. If the project team has a lot of patience for error, then this may work. But the reality is that it takes time to converge to a solution that works.

This is where government funding, technology transfer institutes and universities can help. Such organisations can provide access to low cost training for teams working on small projects, therefore reducing some of the risks involved in an SPI effort.

8.2.5 Relevance of Practices in Assessment Models

Some of the practices in contemporary process assessment (best practice) models would be hard to follow for small projects. E.g. it is frequently required that an independent quality assurance (QA) group exist, and part of the function of that group would be to ensure process compliance.

It is not always possible to have an independent group because of the additional costs of the extra layers of management. A common approach is to have the QA and development groups report to the same project manager. This is especially true in small settings.

Another requirement is for documentation. Because small projects have small teams, informal communication can be very effective for exchanging information. However, over reliance on informal communication causes problems when key members of the team leave. This results in key domain and technical knowledge leaving the company. Therefore, a certain amount of documentation is necessary, especially technical documentation about the system (e.g. architecture documentation).

A good assessor with background in software engineering would be able to modulate the requirements of the assessment model with the realities of a small setting. This makes the selection of assessors a critical task for small projects and small organisations.

8.2.6 Changing Behaviour

Some people work for small companies because such environments have fewer standards and procedures to follow. These staff may resist SPI efforts since SPI is mainly about standardisation of practices to ensure repeatability.

There are two general approaches for dealing with such staff:

- To give staff key roles in the SPI initiative. This will help them get a better understanding of what the objectives are, and will help gain their support.
- To have senior management provide strong signals that the SPI effort is important for the organisation and for the projects. This will dilute attempts to derail or sabotage the SPI efforts (since it would be clear that the consequences of such actions would be much more severe).

8.2.7 Piloting Practices

It is important to pilot the necessary practices before their implementation. This is particularly important for two reasons:

- Most practices need to be customised and it is not always possible to get the customisation correct the first time round. Having an experienced person (either internal or as a consultant) does help ensure that practices are properly customised. One can never be sure until it is used.
- Sometimes there are implicit dependencies between different practices and this may cause problems if not all of the practices are implemented at the same time or in an appropriate order.[2]

It is often a good idea to document the practices that work to ensure that there is an organisational memory. Documentation of practices should follow a successful pilot to avoid having to continuously update the documentation and to ensure that the documented practices reflect what the projects are actually doing. It is frequent that process documentation is prescriptive and does not match reality, which results in documentation with little added value. A stipulation that process documentation should be descriptive would avoid this.

8.2.8 Where To Start

One advantage of staged assessment models, such as the CMM for Software, is that they provide clear guidance as to the order in which practices should be implemented. For small projects that are attempting to improve their practices, there are typically many problems that need to be addressed and it is not possible to tackle all of them at once. This is particularly true when there are fiscal constraints. A staged model helps the SPI effort to focus on a few key practices.

Some argue that every organisation is different and therefore one implementation order does not fit all. In practice organisations tend to follow patterns of bad behaviour and there is a limited set of ways to remedy the situation. E.g. low maturity organisations need first to manage the change process, have basic project management in place, repeatable releases, and to obtain control on the way they make commitments to clients. Without this, it will be difficult to implement any other practices that would be

[2] Many practices in agile methodologies will not work well if refactoring is not performed regularly. Therefore, not having refactoring in place at the same time can cause problems.

lasting. This set of practices is the first step in most staged software engineering assessment models.

Even with staged models, the number of practices that an organisation needs to focus on at any one time, even though it is a limited set, may still seem overwhelming. Therefore, the number of practices employed may need to be reduced further, taking into account the business objectives of the organisation.

Recent research has identified specific practices that small projects and small organisations find valuable. The eight practices that are the focus of the RAPID assessment process are [2]:

- Requirements gathering
- Software development
- Project management
- Configuration management
- Quality assurance
- Problem resolution
- Risk management
- Process establishment

Another study tried to identify the CMMI (specific) practices that are valued the most by small organisations [18]:

- Obtain an understanding of requirements (requirements management)
- Obtain commitment to requirements (requirements management)
- Identify configuration items (configuration management)
- Create or release baselines (configuration management)
- Estimate the scope of the project (project planning)
- Establish budget and schedule (project planning)
- Establish the project plan (project planning)
- Obtain plan commitment (project planning)
- Conduct progress reviews (project monitoring and control)
- Conduct milestone reviews (project monitoring and control)
- Analyze issues (project monitoring and control)
- Take corrective action (project monitoring and control)

One can also focus process improvement activities on these initial set of practices. It should be noticed that the two lists converge in many of their practices and are consistent with the recommendations of the staged models in terms of what to focus on first.

8.3 Conclusions

In general, small projects in both small and large organisations pursue process improvement for the same reasons. However, the models and methods employed need to be customised to the organisations' context, which, for small settings, include reduced funds for investment on improvement and a rapidly changing business environment. In this chapter we reviewed some of the main issues specific to small settings, and provided a pragmatic guidance for dealing with those issues, based on the literature and experience working in small settings.

References

1 Ahern D, Clouse A, Turner R (2003) CMMI Distilled: A Practical Introduction to Integrated Process Improvement. Addison-Wesley

2 Cater-Steel A (2004) Low-rigour, rapid software process assessments for small software development firms. In: Proceedings of the 2004 Australian Software Engineering Conference, Melbourne, pp 368–377

3 Dunnaway D, Goldenson D, Monarch I, White D (1998) How well is CBA IPI working? User feedback. In: Proceedings of the 1998 Software Engineering Process Group Conference

4 Dyba T (2003) Factors of software process improvement success in small and large organisations: An empirical study in the Scandinavian context. In: Proceedings of the European Software Engineering Conference

5 El Emam K (2003) Finding Success in Small Software Projects. Cutter Consortium 4(11)

6 El Emam K, Birk A (2000) Validating the ISO/IEC 15504 Measures of Software Development Process Capability. Journal of Systems and Software, 51:119–149

7 El Emam K, Birk A (2000) Validating the ISO/IEC 15504 Measures of Software Requirements Analysis Process Capability. IEEE Transactions on Software Engineering, 26:541–566

8 El Emam K, Drouin J -N, Melo W (1998) SPICE: The Theory and Practice of Software Process Improvement and Capability Determination, IEEE Computer Society Press

9 El Emam K, Goldenson D (2000) An Empirical Review of Software Process Assessments. J Advances in Computers, 53:319–423

10 M. Fayad, M. Laitinen, and R. Ward, "Software engineering in the small," Communications of the ACM, vol. 43, pp. 115–118, 2000.

11 Fowler P, Rifkin S (1990) Software Engineering Process Group Guide. Software Engineering Institute CMU/SEI-90-TR-24

12 Grunbacher P (1997) A software assessment process for small software enterprises. In: Proceedings of 23rd EUROMICRO Conference'97, New Frontiers of Information Technology

13 Kautz K, Hansen H, Thaysen H (2000) Applying and adjusting a software process improvement model in practice: The use of IDEAL model in a small software Enterprise. In: Proceedings of the International Conference on Software Engineering, June, pp 626–633

14 McFeeley B (1996) IDEAL: A User's Guide for Software Process Improvement. Software Engineering Institute CMU/SEI-96-HB-001

15 Sanders M (1998) The SPIRE Handbook: Better, Faster, Cheaper Software Development in Small Organisations. European Comission

16 Software Engineering Institute (1995) The Capability Maturity Model: Guidelines for Improving the Software Process: Addison Wesley

17 Varkoi T, Mäkinen T, Jaakkola H (1999) Process improvement priorities in small software companies. In: Proceedings of the PICMET´99

18 Wilkie FG, McFall D, McCaffery F (2005) An evaluation of CMMI process areas for small to medium-size software development organisations. Software Process: Improvement and Practice, April/June, 10:189–201

Author's Biography

Dr. El Emam is an Associate Professor at the University of Ottawa, Faculty of Medicine, Canada Research Chair in Electronic Health Information at the University of Ottawa, and a Senior Scientist at the Children's Hospital of Eastern Ontario Research Institute, where he is leading the eHealth research program. In addition, Khaled is the Chief Scientist at TrialStat Corporation and a Senior Consultant with Cutter Consortium's Agile Software Development & Project Management Practice. Previously Khaled was a senior research officer at the National Research Council of Canada, where he was the technical lead of the Software Quality Laboratory, and prior to that he was head of the Quantitative Methods Group at the Fraunhofer Institute for Experimental Software Engineering in Kaiserslautern, Germany. In 2003 and 2004, Khaled was ranked as the top systems and software engineering scholar worldwide by the Journal of Systems and Software based on his research on measurement and quality evaluation and improvement, and ranked second in 2002 and 2005. Currently, he is a visiting professor at the Center for Global eHealth Innovation at the University of Toronto (University Health Network) and at the School of Business at Korea University in Seoul. He holds a Ph.D. from the Department of Electrical and Electronics Engineering, King's College, at the University of London (UK).

9 Conceptual Modelling of Web Applications: The OOWS Approach

Oscar Pastor, Joan Fons, Vicente Pelechano, Silvia Abrahão

Abstract: This chapter introduces a method that integrates navigational and presentational designs to object-oriented conceptual modelling, and also provides systematic code generation. The essential expressiveness is provided using graphical schemas that specify navigation and presentation features, and use high-level abstraction primitives. Using conceptual schemas as input, a methodology is defined to systematically take a problem space to the solution space by defining a set of correspondences between conceptual modelling abstractions and the final software components. We also provide a case study that details the application of the proposed methodology.

Keywords: Web development, Conceptual model, Object-oriented model, OOWS.

9.1 Introduction

The development of quality and reliable software applications based on their conceptual schema seems a never ending challenge for the software engineering community. Nowadays, with the wide extension of the Model Driven Architectures (MDA), it is more than ever accepted that the right strategy is to start with a sound, precise and unambiguous description of an information system in the form of a Conceptual Schema (CS). This CS must be properly transformed into its corresponding software product by defining the mappings between conceptual primitives and software representations. The implementation of such mappings has driven the development of model compilers, and there are already interesting academic and industrial proposals for that [1,2].

The emerging Web engineering discipline [3] is making this challenge even bigger. Conventional applications have done an acceptable job in specifying static and dynamic aspects, structure and behaviour. But a Web application requires consideration of some other particular aspects, not properly addressed with all those conventional, basically UML-based methods. Navigation and presentation become first-order citizens, and the conceptual modelling step must consider them accordingly. Conceptual modelling of Web applications has become a strong area of research trying to provide methods and tools to overcome the problem, and an interesting set of proposals is starting to exist.

Basically, these approaches introduce new models and abstraction mechanisms to capture the essentials of Web applications and to give support for the full development of a Web solution. Some representative efforts to introduce Web features into classical conceptual modelling approaches are OOHDM [4], WebML [5], UWE [6] and WSDM [7].

Our proposal provides a concrete contribution in this context. We introduce a conceptual-modelling-centred method that integrates navigational and presentational design with a classical object-oriented (OO) conceptual modelling that provides systematic code generation. The essential expressiveness is introduced in graphical schemas in order to properly specify navigation and presentation features, using high-level abstraction primitives. Taking CS as an input, a precise methodological guide is defined for going systematically from the problem space to the solution space by defining a set of correspondences between the conceptual modelling abstractions and the final software components.

The work introduced in this chapter focuses on the required extensions needed to enhance "classical" OO software production methods (in particular the OO-Method [1]) in order to define a systematic Web modelling method. It also discusses the high-level abstraction primitives to capture Web applications' features by extending CS.

Last but not least, the Web CS can be used as the basic artefact to measure functional size of the future Web application. Doing so, size measurement can be done at the earliest stages of the software production process. Considering that the CS is converted into a final application, this measurement provides the functional size of the final product from the CS.

The structure of this work is the following. Section 9.2 presents the methodological approach to model Web applications. The conventional models of the OO-Method are introduced, together with the extension where two new models are defined: the navigational model, which captures the navigation semantics of a Web application, and the presentational model, which specifies aspects related to user interfaces' layout with a set of basic patterns. In Sect. 9.3 the model transformation strategy to go from the CS to the software product is briefly discussed. Section 9.4 puts all the ideas into practice using a case of study, dealing with the Web application for a Spanish soccer club.

9.2 A Method to Model Web Applications

OOWS (Object-Oriented Web Solutions) is the extension of the object-oriented software production method OO-Method [1] that introduces the required expressiveness to capture the navigational and presentational requirements of Web applications.

OOWS provides a full software development method for Web applications that defines a set of activities to be fulfilled to properly specify the functional, navigational and presentational dimensions of Web applications' requirements.

The proposed software production method comprises two major steps: *system specification* and *solution development*. A full specification of a system's functional requirements is built in the *system specification* step. A strategy oriented towards generating the software components of the solution (the final software product) is defined in the second step. This model transformation strategy, from the system specification to the software solution, is graphically depicted in Fig. 9.1.

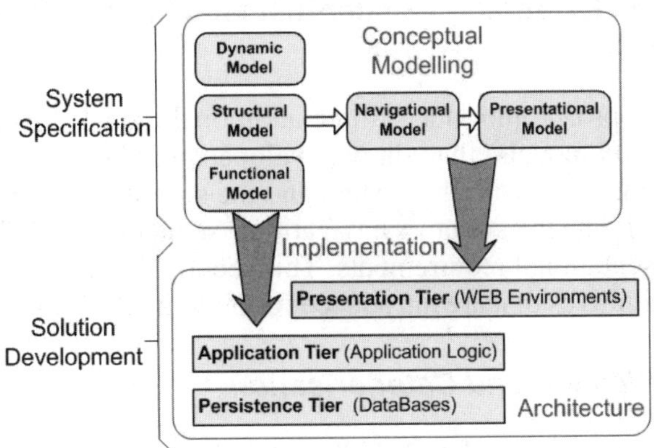

Fig. 9.1. Methodological approach

9.2.1 OO-Method Conceptual Modelling

OO-Method [1] is an OO software production method that provides the model-based code generation capabilities and integrates formal specification techniques with conventional OO modelling notations.

In the "System Specification" step, a conceptual schema is built to represent an application's requirements. The modelling tools that are used by the method allow the specification of structural and functional requirements of dynamic applications by means of a set of models. Those models are the following:

- A *structural model* that defines the system structure (its classes, operations and attributes) and relationships between classes (specialisation, association and aggregation) by means of a *class diagram*.

- A *dynamic model* that describes the different valid object-life sequences for each system class using *State Transition Diagrams*. Also in this model object interactions (communications between objects) are represented by *sequence diagrams*.
- A *functional model* that captures the semantics of state changes to define service effects using a textual formal specification [1].

As stated in [3], Web applications have additional properties that should be modelled. We want to extend the OO-Method to deal with navigation specification, user interface definition, and user categorisation and personalisation, in order to properly capture Web application requirements. The following sections explain these extensions.

9.2.2 OOWS: Extending Conceptual Modelling to Web Environments

The OOWS approach introduces three additional models (*user*, *navigation* and *presentation* models) that allow developers to: (1) express the types of users that can interact with the system and the sort of system visibility they can have; (2) define the system's navigational semantics; and (3) specify the system's presentational requirements. This section discusses the conceptual modelling primitives that are introduced for building these three models.

User Identification and Categorisation

Before modelling the system's navigation, the method provides a *user diagram* (see Fig. 9.2) to express which kind of users can interact with the system and what visibility they should have over class attributes and operations. This diagram provides mechanisms to properly cope with additional user management capabilities, such as the *user specialisation*, which allows for the definition of user taxonomies to improve navigational specification reuse [8].

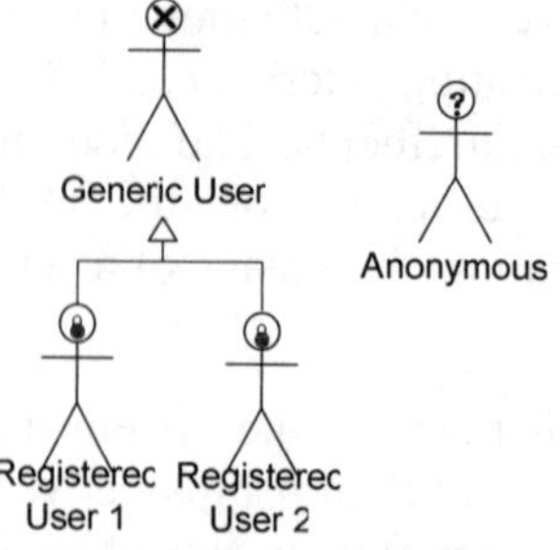

Fig. 9.2. User diagram

There are three types of users, determined by how they connect to the system:

- *Anonymous users* (depicted with a '?' in the head) users who do not need to provide information about their identity.
- *Registered users* (depicted with a lock in the head) users who need to be identified to connect to the system. They must provide their user type.
- *Generic users* (depicted with a cross in the head) users who cannot connect to the system.

Representing Navigation

Once users have been identified, a structured and organised system view, for each user type, must be specified. These views are defined over the class diagram (structure), in terms of the visibility of class attributes, operations and relationships. Navigation specifications are captured in two steps: the "Authoring-in-the-large" (global view) and the "Authoring-in-the-small" (detailed view).

The "Authoring-in-the-large" step refers to the specification and design of global and structural aspects of the Web application. It is achieved by defining a set of system user abstract interaction units and how the user can navigate from one to another. These requirements are specified in a n*avigational map* that provides the system view and accessibility that each kind of user will have. It is represented using a directed graph whose nodes are navigational contexts or navigational subsystems (forward defined) and arcs denote navigational links or valid navigational paths (see Fig. 9.3).

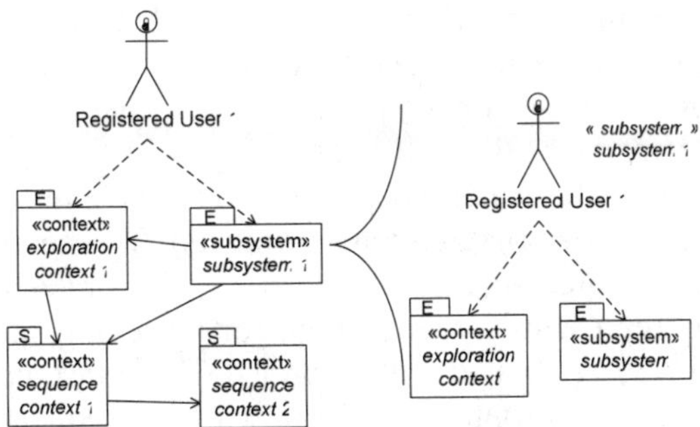

Fig. 9.3. Navigational map and navigational subsystem

Navigational contexts (graphically represented as UML packages stereotyped with the *«context»* keyword) represent the user interaction units that provide a set of cohesive data and operations to perform certain activities. Depending on the context reachability, there are contexts of two types:

- *Exploration navigational contexts* (depicted with the "*E*" label) represent reachable nodes from any node.[1] These contexts define implicit navigational links starting from any node and ending at themselves. These links, named exploration links, use dashed arrows, and are explicitly represented from the root of the map represented by the user (see Fig. 9.3) to the exploration context. One exploration context can be marked as *default* or *home* by adding an "*H*" label to its exploration link. This *home* context will be accessed automatically when the user connects to the system.
- *Sequence navigational contexts* (depicted with the "*S*" label) can only be accessed via a predefined navigational path by selecting a sequence link (forward defined).

The *navigational links* (navigational map arcs) represent context reachabilities or *navigational paths*. There are two types of navigational links:

- *Sequence links* or *contextual links* (represented with solid arrows) define a *semantic* navigation between contexts. Selecting a sequence link implies carrying contextual information to the target context (the object that has been selected, the source navigational context etc.).
- *Exploration links* or *non-contextual links* (represented with dashed arrows) represent a user intentional change of task. When an exploration link is crossed, no contextual information is carried to the target context.

In order to cope with complex navigational models, the navigational map is structured using navigational subsystems. A navigational subsystem is a primitive that allows us to define a sub-graph within the full graph (hyper graph). Recursively, the content of a subsystem is a graph defined by a navigational map (see the right-side of Fig. 9.3).

The "Authoring-in-the-small" step refers to the detailed specification of the contents of the nodes (navigational contexts). To specify this content, each navigational context comprises a set of *abstract information units* (AIUs). An AIU represents a requirement for retrieving specific information. Contextual AIUs (labelled with a circled C) are instantiated when the system arrives at that context by following a sequence link. Non-contextual AIUs (labelled with a circled NC) do not depend on sequence links.

AIUs comprise *navigational classes* that represent *class views* (stereotyped with the *«view»* keyword) over class diagram classes. These classes

[1] Similar to the *Landmark* pattern in the hypermedia community.

contain the visible attributes and executable operations that will be available for the user in this context.

Each AIU has one *mandatory* navigational class, called *manager class*, and *optional* navigational classes, called *complementary classes*, to provide complementary information about the manager class.

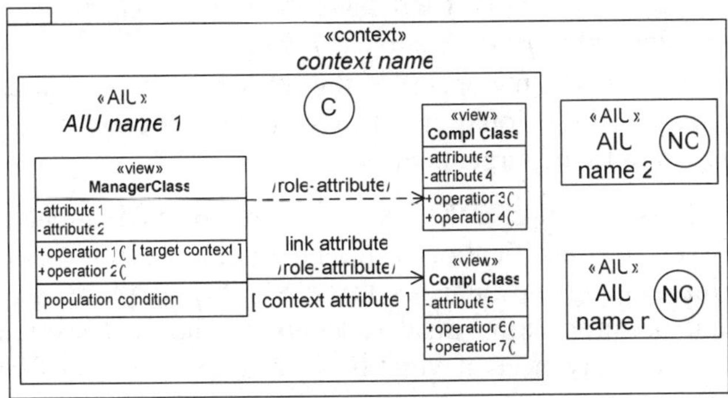

Fig. 9.4. Navigational context

Service links can also be attached to a service. A service link represents the target navigational context that the user will reach after that service execution. Figure 9.4 shows a service link related to the *operation1()* of the *ManagerClass*. This specifies that after the execution of the *operation1()* operation, the system must automatically navigate to the navigational context specified in *[target context]*.

In addition, a *population condition filter* can be specified to any navigational class. This condition defines an object retrieval condition that must be satisfied. It is described by means of an Object Constraint Language (OCL) formula.

All navigational classes must be related by unidirectional binary relationships, called *navigational relationships*. They are defined over existing aggregation–association–composition or specialization–generalisation relationships, and represent the retrieval of related instances. When more than one structural relationship exists between two classes, the role name of the relationship must be specified (depicted as */role-attribute/*) to avoid ambiguities. Two types of navigational relationships can be defined, depending on whether or not they define a navigation capability:

1. A *context dependency relationship* (graphically represented using dashed arrows) represents basic information recovery by crossing a structural relationship between classes. When a context dependency relationship is defined, all the related object instances to the origin class object are retrieved.

2. A *context relationship* (graphically represented using solid arrows) represents the same information recovery as the context dependency relationship, in addition to navigation capability to a target navigational context, creating a sequence link in the navigational map. Context relationships have the following properties:
   - A *context attribute* that indicates the target context of the navigation (depicted as *[target context]*).
   - A *link attribute* that specifies the attribute (usually an attribute of the target navigational class) used as the "anchor" to activate the navigation to the target context.

These primitives comprise the core elements for navigational specifications. However, the specification of the navigational semantics can be enriched by introducing mechanisms to help a user explore and filter the large amount of information inside a context. The next section presents how to introduce advanced navigational features to the OOWS navigational model.

Advanced Navigational Features

Navigational contexts retrieve the classes' population of the CS. We define the cardinality of a navigational context as the number of instances it should retrieve. Sometimes the retrieved information is difficult to manage. To help users browsing that amount of information, it is necessary to define mechanisms for browsing and filtering that information in a navigational context. There are two main search mechanisms: indexes and filters. Both are described at the bottom of each abstract information unit, under a dashed line.

An *index* is a structure that provides an *indexed access* to the manager class population. Indexes create a list of summarised information by using an attribute or a set of attributes. If the indexed property belongs to the manager class, it should be defined as an attribute index. If the indexed property belongs to any complementary class, the index should be defined as a relationship index, and the relationship must be specified. When an index is activated, a list of all possible values for the indexed attribute(s) is/are created. By choosing one of these values, all objects that present the same value will be shown in a search view. This search view describes the information that will be available to the users to aid them select an instance, which will be active in the navigational context.

A *filter* defines a *population condition* that can restrict the object instances to be retrieved. They are applied to attributes of the manager class (attribute filters) or to attributes of complementary classes (relationship filter). There are three types of filters:

- *Exact* filters, which take one attribute value and return all matching instances,
- *Approximate* filters, which take one attribute value and return all the instances whose attribute values include this value as a sub-string.
- *Range* filters, which take two values (a maximum and a minimum) and return all the instances whose attribute values fit within the range. If we specify only one value, it is only bounded on one side.

Optionally, it is possible to define a *static population condition* to specify predefined filtering conditions (for instance, "retrieving all books that are best-sellers"). When a filter is activated, the instances that fulfil the condition become visible within the search view. This search view behaves as an index.

Presentational Modelling

Once the navigational model is built, we must specify presentational requirements of Web applications using a *presentation model* (see Fig. 9.1). This model is strongly based on the navigational model and it uses its navigational contexts (system–user interaction units) to define the presentation properties.

Presentation requirements are specified by means of patterns that are associated to the primitives of the navigational context (navigational classes, navigational links, searching mechanisms, etc.). The basic presentation patterns are as follows:

Information paging. This pattern allows us to define information "scrolling". All the instances are "broken" into "logical blocks", so that only one block is visible at a time. Mechanisms to move forwards or backwards are provided. This pattern can be applied to *the manager class*, *navigational relationship*, *index or filter*. The required information is:

- *Cardinality*, which represents the number of instances that form a block.
- *Access mode*. *Sequential* access provides mechanisms to go to the next, previous, first and last logical blocks. *Random* access mode allows the user to go directly to a desired block.
- *Circularity*. When this property is active, the set of blocks behaves as a circular buffer.

Ordering criteria. This pattern defines a class population order (*ASC*endant or *DESC*endant) according to the value of one or more attributes. It can be applied to navigational classes, to specify how retrieved instances will be sorted, or to access structures and search mechanisms, to sort the results.

Information layout. Four basic layout patterns are provided: *register*, *tabular*, *master-detail* (with a presentation pattern for the detail) and *tree*. They can be applied to the *manager class* or to a *navigation relationship.*

These presentation patterns, in addition to the specified navigation features, capture the essential requirements for the construction of Web interfaces. More specialised presentation patterns can be introduced at the modelling stage to "beautify" the final Web user interface.

9.3 A Strategy To Develop the Web Solution

OOWS follows the OO-Method strategy for systematically moving from the problem space to the solution space (Fig. 9.1). Although this chapter is not focused on exploiting this, we introduce the main ideas that will guide the reification of OOWS conceptual schemas into a software product.

A three-tier architectural style has been selected to generate final applications: a *presentation tier*, an *application tier* and a *persistence tier*.

The information (persistence tier) and functionality (application tier) of the Web application are generated by the OlivaNova Model Transformation Engines [2] taking as basis the OO-Method structural and behavioural models. This tool provides an operational, MDA-compliant framework, where a model compiler transforms a CS into its corresponding software product.

Taking into account the new features introduced in the OOWS enhanced Web schema, the generation process is enriched by providing a new translation process to systematically generate the *presentation tier* for Web applications. A brief overview of this process is presented below.

Starting from the navigational and presentational models, a group of connected Web pages, for each type of user, can be obtained in a systematic way. These Web pages define the Web application's user interface (presentation tier) for navigating, visualising the data and accessing the application's functionality.

A Web page, created for each navigational context in the navigational map, is responsible for retrieving the specified information in its AIUs. This strategy divides Web pages into two logical areas:

- The *information* area, which presents the specific system view defined by a context. The presentation model specification is applied to obtain the layout of this area in the following way. All AIUs are placed as a part of the Web page. The instances of the manager class are shown as their layout pattern determines, applying (if defined) the ordering criteria and the information paging. The instances of navigational classes related by a navigational relationship follow the same strategy.

- The *navigation* area, which provides navigation meta-information to the user, in order to improve quality (usability) aspects of the final application. The meta-information is as follows:
  - *Where the user is*. States what Web page (context) is being currently shown to the user.
  - *How the user reached here*. Shows the navigational path that has been followed to reach that page.
  - Where the user can go to. Shows a link to any exploration context.
  - Which filters and index mechanisms can be used by the user.
  - *Applicational links*. Provides additional links to navigate to the home page, to log into the system, etc. (e.g. *login*, *logout*, *home*).

Detailed information on how to implement a Web interface using the navigational and presentation models is described in [9].

9.4 Case Study: *Valencia CF Web Application*

The Valencia CF Web Application[2] was developed to publicise information about the competitions in which the Valencia CF Football Team takes part, its matches, opponent teams, players, line-ups, members and supporters, partnerships, etc. The main functionality comprises a shopping area, tickets and season bonus tickets selling, and betting for a particular football match.

This section describes the conceptual model that led to this implementation, based on the OO-Method approach and focusing on the OOWS navigational properties.

Due to the application's size, it is not possible to present the entire modelling in detail. Thus, we have selected a subset, which is detailed in this section. The subset represents the functionality related to making a bet for matches where the Valencia CF team is going to play. A registered user should be able to bet in any match of any competition where the Valencia CF Football Team plays. To aid in making bets, the system must provide registered users with statistics on each team, previous results etc. Using this information, a registered user can make a bet by predicting the final score. At any time, users should be able to see the results of previous bets, their betting cash, and to modify their proposed final score for forthcoming matches.

---

[2] http://www.valenciacf.com.

9.4.1 Valencia CF Web Conceptual Model

Following the OO-Method/OOWS approach, the first step is to describe the structural and behavioural aspects of the Web application. These are to be gathered by means of a class diagram, state transition diagrams and a functional model (see Sect. 9.4.1.1).

Section 9.4.1.2 describes the navigational properties of the Valencia CF Web Application, by means of a User Diagram, describing the different user types and corresponding Navigational Models describing the accessibility through the system.

Finally, Sect. 9.4.1.3 introduces abstract presentation requirements related to the specified navigational model.

Valencia CF OO-Method Conceptual Model

The first step to build an OO-Method conceptual model is to describe its structural model (by means of a class diagram), and its behavioural model (using a dynamic and functional model). According to the main objectives of the Valencia CF Web application, the structural model must capture information about competitions where the Valencia CF Football Team plays, its matches, teams, players, tickets, partnerships, etc. The main functionality involves a shopping area, tickets and season bonus tickets selling, and betting for a particular match. Figure 9.5 presents the class diagram, containing close to 50 classes and 60 relationships.

This figure emphasises the portion related to the betting information. A *RegisteredUser* can make a *Bet* for a *Match* between two *Teams* by specifying her/his predicted *localScore* and *visitorScore*. The betting amount must always be less than the betting *cash*. To fulfil this requirement, a *do_a_bet()* operation is created at the *Bet* class, and also an agent relationship between the *RegisteredUser* and the *do_a_bet()* constructor operation is established to specify that this type of user is able to execute this operation. This operation needs a precondition to avoid invalid bets:

```
do_a_bet(p_localScore, p_visitorScore, p_amount) if
  p_localScore ≥ 0 AND p_visitorScore ≥ 0 AND Match. closedForBetting =
  FALSE AND p_amount ≤ RegisteredUser.cash
```

Following the same criteria, the *change_a_bet()* operation at the *Bet* class has a similar precondition.

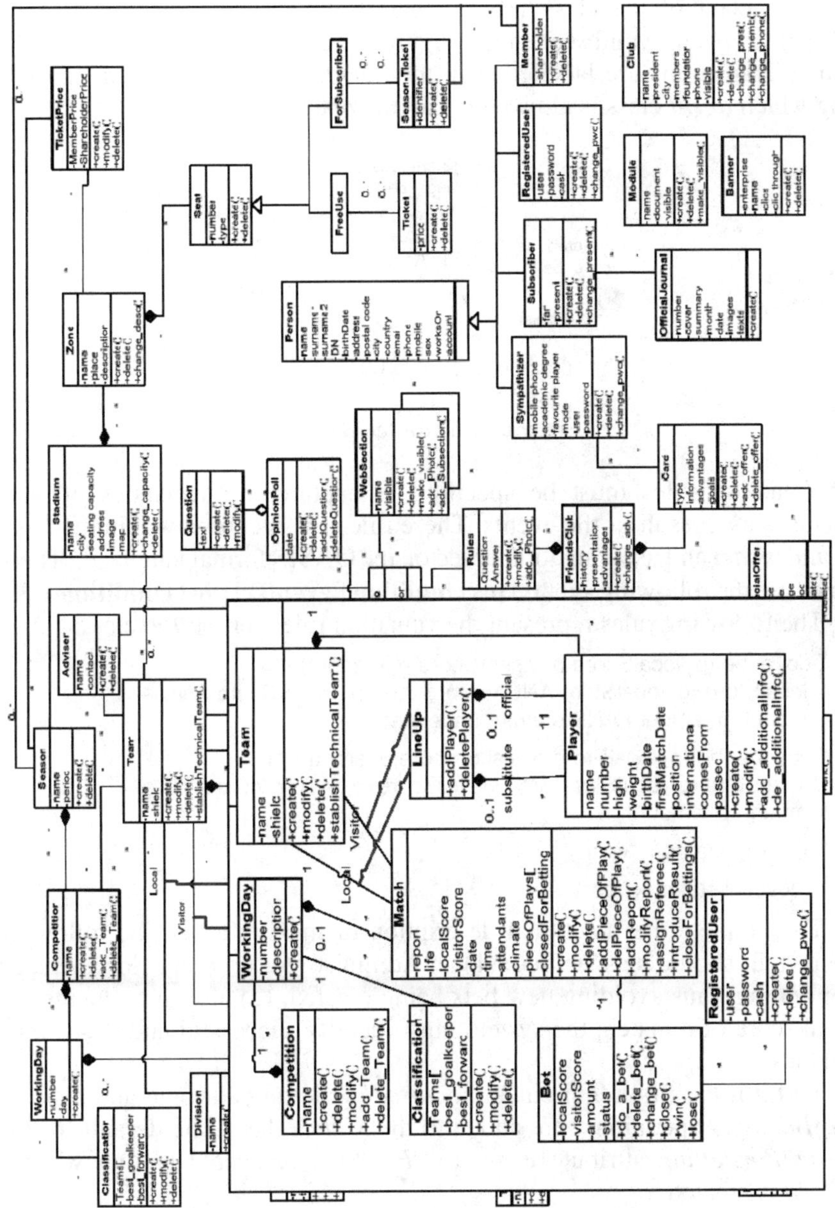

Fig. 9.5. Class diagram of the Valencia CF Web application

Each class of the class diagram has its own state transition diagram (STD) to specify valid sequences. Figure 9.6 describes the STD for the Bet class. Transitions are labelled with the *agent:operation* notation, specifying which *agent* class is allowed to call the *operation*.

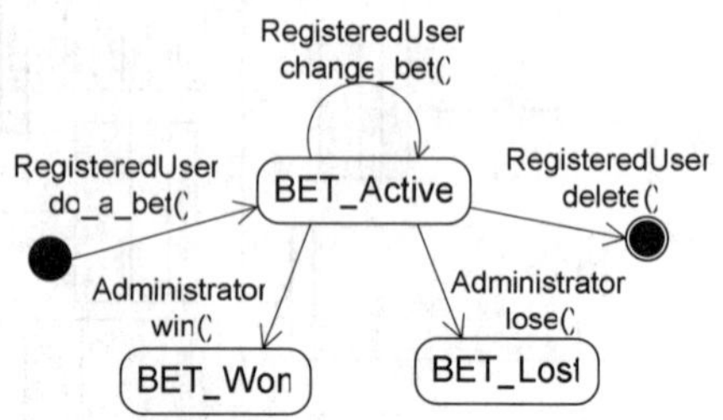

Fig. 9.6. STD for the *Bet* class

Valuation rules must be specified to capture the semantics of state changes as a result of the events. These rules are specified within the *functional model* and use a notation based on the OASIS formal language.[3] These rules use the following syntax: **precondition [event()] post condition.**

The following rules represent the valuation rules for the *Bet* class:

[do_a_bet(p_localScore,p_visitorScore,p_amount)]
localStore=p_localStore AND visitorScore=p_visitorScore AND amount=p_amount AND status="undefined"

[change_bet(p_localStore,p_visitorScore,p_amount)]
localStore=p_localStore AND visitorScore=p_visitorScore AND amount=p_amount

[win()] status = "won"

[lose()] status = "lost"

To complete the functional description of making a bet, the following behaviour should be specified: (1) an Administrator user can close a match for betting, thus avoiding new bets being created; (2) after introducing the final score of a match, the system must identify successful and unsuccessful bets.

To fulfil the first requirement, a *closedForBetting* attribute and a *closeForBetting()* operation were added to the *Match* class. The default for the *closedForBetting* attribute is set to "*FALSE*", to enable betting when a *Match* is created.

3 http://www.oasis-open.org/specs/index.php.

The *Match.closeForBetting()* operation must change the value of the *closedForBetting* attribute. This requirement is described by means of a valuation formula in the *Match* class:

```
[ closeForBetting() ] closedForBetting = TRUE
```

Finally, we need an operation to set a *Match*'s final score, and obtain successful and unsuccessful bets. This is not an atomic operation. So, we must define a *transaction* within the *Match* class, as follows:

```
introduceResult(p_localScore, p_visitorScore) {
  FOR ALL <Bet[4]>
  WHERE Bet.localScore = p_localScore AND Bet.visitorScore =
  p_visitorScore
  DO Bet.win()
  .
  FOR ALL <Bet[2]>
  WHERE Bet.localScore <> p_localScore OR Bet.visitorsScore <>
  p_visitorScore
  DO Bet.lose()
  }
```

To complete the functional description of this event, a valuation rule must be specified to this operation within the *Match* class, to establish the value for the final scores:

```
[ introduceResults(p_localScore, p_visitorScore) ]
  localScore = p_localScore AND visitorScore = p_visitorScore
```

Valencia CF Navigational Model

Once the structural and functional requirements have been determined, the next step is to specify the navigational capabilities through the system. Following the OOWS approach, the following diagrams must be specified:
(1) a user diagram, describing the different types of users able to use the application; (2) a navigational map for each user, describing her/his accessibility and visibility while navigating the system; and (3) a presentation model, describing presentation requirements for the final Web interfaces.

There are different user types that can interact with the system. *Anonymous* users can explore public information, such as matches, competitions, last results and teams. *RegisteredUsers* can use the shopping area, make a bet on the Valencia CF matches, and buy tickets via the Internet. *Sympathizer* users have bonus season tickets, discounts at the shopping area and special prices for the matches. Finally, the *Administrator* user manages the

[4] Those *Bets* refer to bets that belong to the *Match* in which the transaction is being executed.

system. Figure 9.7 shows the user diagram for the system, specifying the four user types. The *Anonymous* user type is labelled with a "?" because it does not need identification to access the system. The other three user types are specialised from the *Anonymous* to inherit the navigational map [8]. They are labelled with a "lock" as they need to be identified to enter the system. Each one of these user types is directly related with its corresponding class in the class diagram.

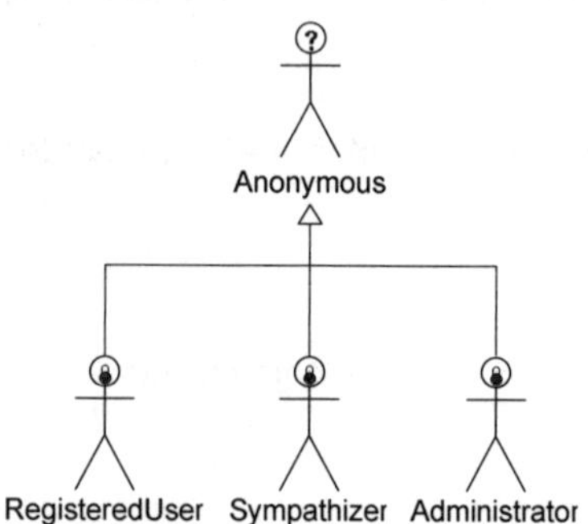

Fig. 9.7. Valencia CF user diagram

A *navigational map* is defined for each user type. This navigational map defines the user accessibility within the system. Figure 9.8 presents the navigational map for the *RegisteredUser* user type. Due to the large number of navigational contexts that belong to this user type, its navigational map was organised as seven first-level (exploration) navigational subsystems, and nine first-level (exploration) navigational contexts. "*The Club*" navigational subsystem provides several navigational contexts to show different types of information on the Valencia CF Football Team (e.g. history, managers, best players); the "*Competitions*" navigational subsystem provides information on the matches within the competitions where the team participates. This subsystem also allows *RegisteredUsers* to make a bet for specific matches; All navigational nodes are exploration nodes, i.e. always accessible for this user type.

The "*Last News*" navigational context presents the latest and important news about the team and special events (see Fig. 9.9). It was tagged with an "H" to show that it is the default (*home*) context used when the user logs into the system. This navigational context has ten AIUs. Nine of those AIUs refer to advertising (e.g. *Web Services, The Team 2004–2005,... , The Shop*), and appear in every navigational context for this user. The main AIUs are: *Last Hour* AIU, which provides the latest news about the team, and *Last News* AIU, which provides the most recent news. Both AIUs comprise one *News* navigational class that presents a view over the class diagram's *News* class. The *Last Hour* AIU retrieves the news

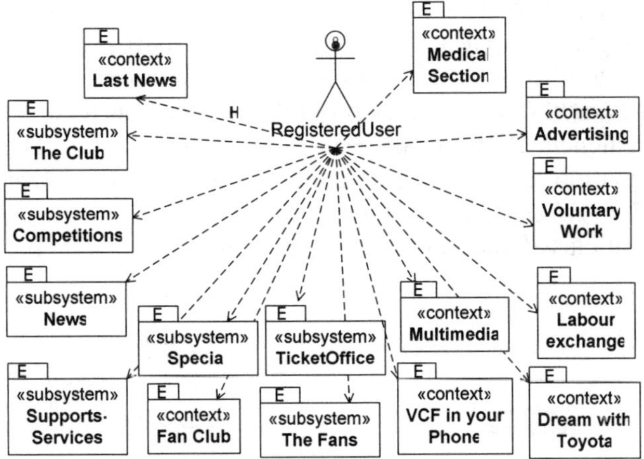

Fig. 9.8. *RegisteredUser* navigational map

date_time, *headline* and *content*. This AIU also has a population filter, within the *News* navigational class, to describe that only the news with attribute *last_hour* set to *TRUE* must be shown. The *Last News* AIU provides the news *date_time* and *headline*.

Each AIU has a contextual navigational relationship that uses the *content* or the *headline* attribute as the anchor to the *News Details* context inside the *News* subsystem. Figure 9.13 below presents the actual Web page that implements this context, where it is possible to observe all AIUs. The context relationship appears implemented as links for each of the news, pointing to the *News Details* Web page.

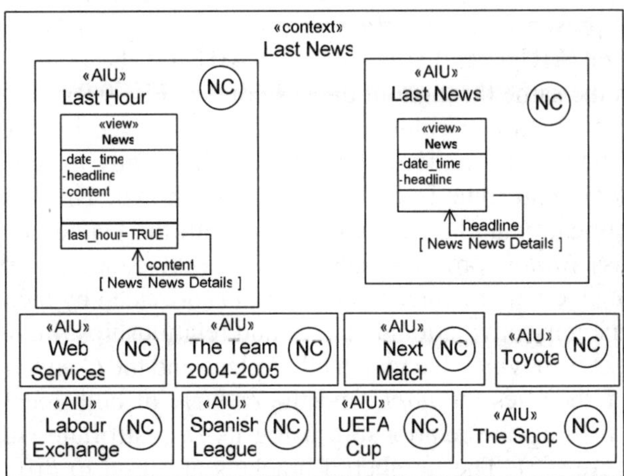

Fig. 9.9. *Last News* navigational context

To make a bet, a *RegisteredUser* must go to the *Competitions* subsystem (see the navigational map). Figure 9.10 shows the *Competitions* navigational subsystem specification comprising two other subsystems: *Next Match* and *Matches*. The former provides information related to the next match the Valencia CF Football Team is scheduled to play. The latter provides information about future (*Calendar*), present (*Live Match Report*) and past (*Live Match Historic*) matches, and also statistics, results (*Results*), current classification (*Classification*) and active bets (*Bets* and *Your Bets*).

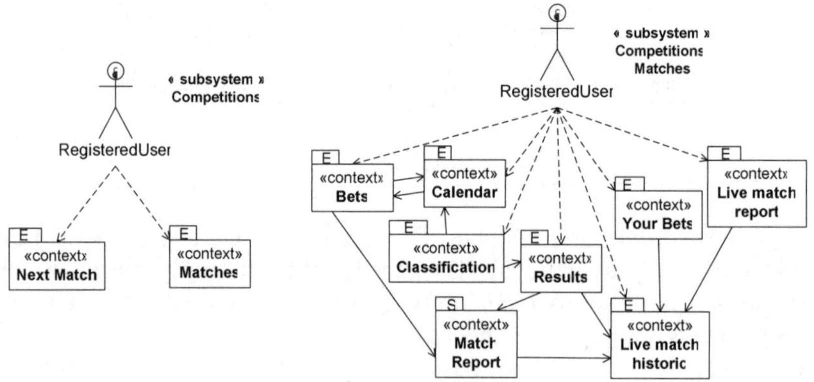

Fig. 9.10. *Competitions* and *Competitions.Matches* subsystems

Once inside the *Competitions* subsystem, a user must reach the *Matches* subsystem. From there, the user can navigate to the *Bets* navigational context to make a bet for a specific game. This context must provide the user with facilities to explore matches, teams and competitions' working days. Figure 9.10 presents the specification of this navigational context, comprising several AIUs. Marketing-oriented AIUs (at the bottom of the context) remain the same throughout the system (see Fig. 9.9).

The *Bets* navigational context has a main AIU (see Fig. 9.11), named *Bet*, which shows information related to matches. Only matches where the *closedForBetting* attribute is set to FALSE are shown. The *Bets* AIU comprises six navigational classes (stereotyped with the *«view»* keyword): the manager class, *Match*, provides date and time (navigational attributes).

From Match, complementary information is provided by means of different complementary navigational classes and relationships. First, it specifies the *WorkingDay* in which the match takes place and the *Competition name*.

Second, it specifies the *name* and the *emblem* of both local and visitor *Teams* by labelling the relationship using its *role* attribute (see class diagram in Figure 9.5). The numbered brackets are used to differentiate between navigational classes. Finally, the *do_a_bet()* operation is provided to the *RegisteredUser*, within the *Bet* complementary class, to activate the *do_a_bet()* operation, defined in the behavioural models.

Two context relationships (solid arrows) have been defined within this context. They allow users to navigate from this context to another by selecting a piece of information, from a source context, that is further detailed in the destination context. Within the *Match–Bet* context relationship, selecting the *number* (link attribute) of a *WorkingDay*, takes a user to the *Calendar* (context attribute) navigational context, which shows the matches within this selected *WorkingDay*. As no link attribute is specified as a *Match–Match* context relationship, a text "Match Report" and a link are used to allow the *RegisteredUser* to navigate to the *Match Report* navigational context for the selected *Match*, and to to get the report details for that selected match.

The *Bets* navigational context has been defined as a contextual AIU (labelled with a circled C) because it is possible to navigate from the *Calendar* navigational context to this context by selecting a *Match* (see the navigational map related to this *Competitions.Matches* subsystem in Fig. 9.10). In this case, the *Bet* AIU will be instantiated to the selected match and will only provide information about that selected match.

The specification of advanced navigational features to improve navigability inside this navigational context is presented below the dashed lines. They allow searching for a specific match. It has one index and two filters. All three search mechanisms share the same *Search view* structure, which is composed of information to aid the user search for a desired match. The search view shows the Match date, the WorkingDay number, the Competition's name, and the name of both teams that will play.

The index is defined as a "Relationship Index" because the indexing property belongs to a complementary class (*WorkingDay*), not to the manager class (*Match*). When this index is activated, a list of *WorkingDay numbers* and *Competitions' name* is shown. When the user selects a *WorkingDay number* (link attribute), all the information about the matches belonging to this *WorkingDay number*, specified in the search view, will be shown. Finally, by selecting a *Match date*, all the information specified in the *Bet* AIU will be visible, allowing for a bet to be made (see Fig. 9.14 below).

The other two filters let a user search for a team on which (s)he wants to make a bet. A user can search for a team that plays as "local" in the match, or a team that plays as "visitor". In this case, we want the user to introduce the (partial) name of the required team. As *Team name* belongs to a class that is not the manager class in this context, these filters have been defined as "Relationship Filters".

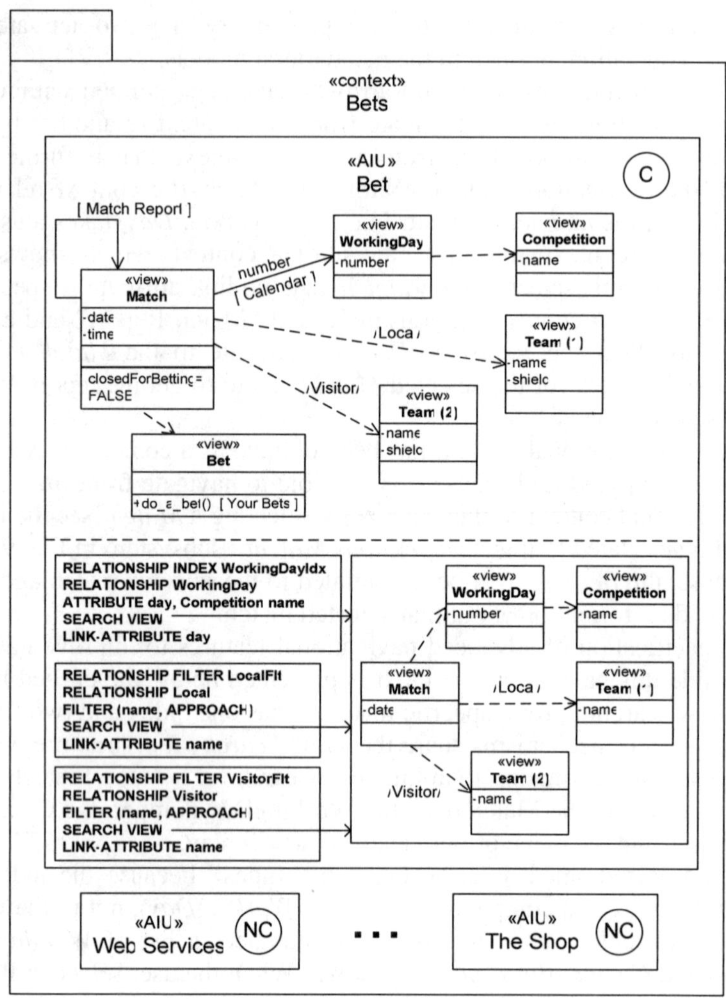

Fig. 9.11. *Bets* navigational context

The *LocalFlt* Filter has been defined over the *Match–Team* relationship (see class diagram), navigating through the *Local* role. Using *Team name* as the filter attribute and filter type being "approximated" (see filter definition in Fig. 9.11), this filter allows the *RegisteredUser* to search for local teams with a name similar to the one (s)he provided. This filter retrieves all the information specified by the search view and behaves as described for previous indexes. The other filter will do the same, but using the *Visitor* role of the *Match–Team* relationship.

Valencia CF Presentation Model

Once the navigational model has been built, we specify specific presentational requirements using the *presentation model.*

The *Last News* navigational context is responsible for retrieving the last hour's news and the latest news. The presentation requirements for this context are the following: each last hour must be shown according to the "Register" pattern; *Last News* must be presented in a table, in groups of six elements, sorted by decreasing date–time, and showing only the six most recent news items.

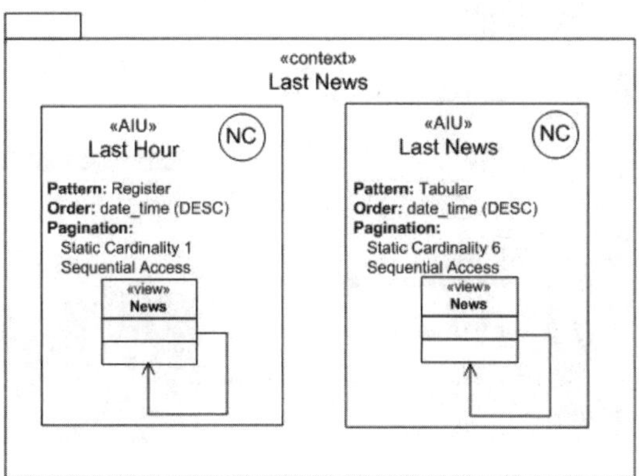

Fig. 9.12. *Last News* presentation context

Figure 9.12 shows the presentation context specified for the *Last News* navigational context. Presentation requirements have been implemented, as shown in Fig. 9.13.

9.4.2 Implemented Valencia CF Web Application

This section presents the implemented Valencia CF Web application graphical interface and the direct relationship with its conceptual model, described in the previous sections. Each navigational context described in the navigational map will be converted into a Web page. Links between pages are defined by the context relationships defined within each navigational context.

Within a Web page, an important issue is how to distribute the different AUIs. This layout distribution can be easily included in the presentation modelling stage.

When a *RegisteredUser* connects to the CF Web application using the login functionality in the upper right of the Web page (see Fig. 9.13), (s)he will automatically navigate to the *Last News* Web page. This Web page is

Fig. 9.13. Implemented Web page of *Last News* (home) navigational context

obtained from the *Last News* navigational context, placed in the navigational map (Fig. 9.8) as the *H*ome context, and described in Fig. 9.9.

This Web page comprises a navigational area (including a navigational menu with all the exploration contexts of the navigational map) and an information area in which all the AIUs specified in the navigational context are placed. The *Last Hour* AIU provide the date, time, headline and content about the news that has the *last_hour* attribute set to true, presented according to the "Register" pattern. The *Last News* AIU provides the date, time and headline for the six latest news items. The pagination cardinality is set to six and ordering criteria by *date_time* descending (see Fig. 9.12).

If the *RegisteredUser* wants to make a bet, (s)he must follow the *Competitions* link (placed at the left of the Web page, in the navigational menu), and then the *Matches* link. Those links come from the navigational structure induced by the *Competitions* and *Matches* subsystems. The navigational menu of Fig. 9.14 shows the implementation of this subsystem's concept.

Fig. 9.14. Implemented Web page of *Bets* navigational context

Once inside this *Competitions.Matches* subsystem, the RegisteredUser can get to the *Bets* Web page by clicking on the *Bets* link in the navigational menu. When the user selects a match using the index, or one of the filters, the selected match is displayed. For instance, if we select the match between Vilareal FC (as local) and Valencia CF (as visitor) within the 39th working day of the Spanish Football League, the *Bets* Web page will provide the information shown in Fig. 9.14, according to the navigational specification in Fig. 9.11.

When the user tries to make a bet (specifying a local and a visitor score), assuming that it is possible to achieve this functionality according to the behaviour specification of the dynamic model (see Sect. 9.4.1.1), the system will update its state and then navigate to the *Your Bets* Web page, as specified in the service link attached to the *do_a_bet()* operation, within the *Bet* AIU of the *Bets* context.

As can also be seen in Fig. 9.11, two navigational links appear within this Web page: a link that allows the user to navigate to the *Calendar* by selecting a WorkingDay (see the 39th Working Day link), and a link that allows the user to navigate to the *Match Report* Web page, by clicking on the arrow beside the Match Report text. Both links were specified in the *Bets* context as context relationships.

9.5 Conclusions

Model-driven architectures are, in our view, the right approach for building Web applications. This is the main conclusion of this work. We have shown that a conventional[5] conceptual modelling approach can be extended with navigational and presentation modelling views, thus properly integrating all the involved models.

The required conceptual primitives have been presented, their graphical representation has been introduced, and how to go from the CS to the corresponding final Web application has been studied. The approach has been explained by introducing a case study, where all the relevant aspects of the method have been considered.

This way of working opens the door to the implementation of real Web model compilers. Having identified the set of mapping between conceptual primitives and their corresponding software representations, the implementation of those mappings will be the core of such a model compiler. This is one of the major contributions of the OOWS approach, when compared to others. Its close link with the MDA-based tool OlivaNova Model Executions [1], allows us to provide a conceptual modelling-based environment, where the model becomes the program. Thus, how to go from the specification (model) to the implementation is fully detailed, and can be automated.

Further work is mainly required for defining presentation aspects that should be included in the presentation model to allow for the creation of a complete Web Application, from an aesthetical point of view, and to enrich the model expressiveness whenever needed. The implementation of fully operative Web model compilers is the subject of future work, especially for covering different software architectures and Web technologies.

References

1 Pastor O, Gomez J, Insfran E, Pelechano V (2001) The OO-Method Approach for Information Systems Modelling: From Object-Oriented Conceptual Modeling to Automated Programming. Information Systems, 26:507–534

2 CARE Technologies. OlivaNova Model Transformation Engines. http://www.care-t.com

3 Muruguesan S, Desphande Y (2001) Web Engineering, Software Engineering and Web Application Development. Lecture Notes in Computer Science - Hot Topics. Springer, Berlin

[5] Conventional here means a method specifying system structure and behaviour.

4 Rossi G, Schwabe D (2001) Object-Oriented Web Applications Modeling. Information Modeling in the New Millennium, 463–484

5 Ceri S, Fraternali P, Matera M (2002) Conceptual Modeling of Data-Intensive Web Applications. IEEE Internet Computing, 6(4): 20–30

6 Knapp A, Koch N, Zhang G, Hassler HM (2004) Modeling Business Processes in Web Applications with ArgoUWE. In: Proceedings of UML 2004, LNCS 3273, Springer, Berlin, pp 69–83

7 De Troyer O (2001) Audience-driven Web Design. Information Modeling in the New Millennium, 442–462

8 Fons J, Valderas P, Pastor O (2002) Specialization in Navigational Models. In: Proceedings of the Argentine Conference on Computer Science and Operational Research, 31:16–31

9 Fons J, Pelechano V, Albert M, Pastor O (2003) Development of Web Applications from Web Enhanced Conceptual Schemas. In: Proceedings of the ER'2003, LNCS 2813, Springer, Berlin. pp 232–245

Authors' Biographies

Professor **Oscar Pastor** is the head of the Computation and Information Systems Department at Valencia University of Technology (Spain). PhD in 1992. Former researcher in HP Labs, Bristol, UK. Author of over 100 research papers in conference proceedings, journals and books. Received numerous research grants from public institutions and private industry. Research activities focus on Web engineering, object-oriented conceptual modelling, requirements engineering, information systems and model-based software production. Leader of the project, undertaken since 1996 by the Valencia University of Technology and CONSOFT S.A., that has originated the OlivaNova Model Execution, an advanced MDA-based tool that produces a final software product starting from a Conceptual Schema where the system requirements are captured. Within this tool scope, he is responsible of the research team working from the university on the improvement of the underlying framework, focusing on business process modelling, Web technologies and how to use software and architectural patterns properly to go from the problem space to the solution space in an automated way.

He is also a member of over 50 scientific committees of well-known international conferences and workshops such as CAiSE, ER, WWW, DSV/IS, RE, ADBIS, ICWE, CADUI, DEXA, EC-WEB, ICEIS. Member of several editorial boards of journals and book series, a participant researcher in national and international research projects, and has been invited to give over 30 talks and presentations in different universities and research centres.

Joan Fons is Assistant Professor in the Department of Information Systems and Computation (DSIC) at the Valencia University of Technology, Spain. His research involves Web engineering, adaptive systems, conceptual modelling, model-driven development and pervasive systems. He is a member of the OO-Method Research group, and he has published several contributions to well-known international conferences (ER, WWW, CAiSE, ICWE, AH, etc.). His PhD is on OOWS, a Web engineering method to automatically develop a Web solution from a conceptual model.

Vicente Pelechano is Associate Professor in the Department of Information Systems and Computation (DISC) at the Valencia University of Technology, Spain. His research interests are Web engineering, conceptual modelling, requirements engineering, software patterns, Web services, pervasive systems and model-driven development. He received his PhD degree from the Valencia University of Technology in 2001. He is currently teaching software engineering, design and implementation of Web services, component-based software development and design patterns in the Valencia University of Technology. He is a member of the OO-Method Research Group at DISC. He has published in several well-known scientific journals (Information Systems, Data & Knowledge Engineering, Information and Software Technology, etc.) and at international conferences (ER, CAiSE, WWW, ICWE, DEXA, etc.). He is a member of scientific commitees of well-known international conferences and workshops as CAiSE, ICWE and IADIS.

Silvia Abrahão is Assistant Professor in the Department of Information Systems and Computation (DSIC) at the Valencia University of Technology, Spain. She woks mainly in the domain of software metrics, functional size measurement, empirical software engineering and Web engineering. She has published over 45 papers in these fields. She gained a PhD in Computer Science from Valencia University of Technology in 2004. Currently, she is a member of the OO-Method Research Group at DISC and a board member of the Spanish Association of Software Metrics. She takes a keen interest in industry activities and has been representing Spain in the 2004 meeting of the International Software Benchmarking Standard Group (ISBSG) in Bangalore. She also has been an editorial board member of the Spanish Journal on Process and Metrics for Information Technologies and a program committee member of the following venues: 3rd Latin American Web Congress (LA-Web 2005), IADIS Ibero-American Conference on WWW/Internet 2005, Interact'2005 Workshop on User Interface Quality Models, the Spanish Software Metrics Association Conference series, and the 2nd Software Measurement European Forum (SEMF 2005).

10 Model-Based Web Application Development

Gustavo Rossi, Daniel Schwabe

Abstract: In this chapter we present our experience with the Object-Oriented Hypermedia Design Method (OOHDM), a model-based approach for developing Web applications. We first describe the main activities in OOHDM and then we illustrate the application of the method with a simple example, a CD store.

Keywords: OOHDM, Web development, conceptual model, navigation model, hypermedia development.

10.1 The OOHDM approach – An Overview

The Object-Oriented Hypermedia Design Method (OOHDM) is a model-based approach to the development of Web applications. OOHDM uses different abstraction and composition mechanisms in an object oriented framework to, on one hand, allow a concise description of complex information items, and on the other hand, allow the specification of complex navigation patterns and interface transformations. OOHDM provides a clear roadmap that allows answering the following key questions, generally asked when building Web applications:

- What constitutes an "information unit" with respect to navigation?
- How does one establish what are the meaningful links between information units?
- How does one organise the navigation space, i.e., establish the possible sequences of information units the user may navigate through?
- How will navigation operations be distinguished from interface operations and from "data processing" (i.e., application operations)?

In OOHDM, a hypermedia application is built in a five-step process supporting an incremental or prototype process model. Each step focuses on a particular design concern, and an object-oriented model is built. Classification, aggregation and generalisation/specialisation are used throughout the process to enhance abstraction power and reuse opportunities. Table 10.1 summarises the steps, products, mechanisms and design concerns in OOHDM.

Table 10.1. Activities and formalisms in OOHDM

Activities	Products	Formalisms	Mechanisms	Design Concerns
Requirements gathering	Use cases, Annotations	Scenarios; user interaction diagrams; design patterns	Scenario and use case Analysis, Interviews, UID mapping to conceptual model	Capture the stakeholder requirements for the application.
Conceptual design	Classes, subsystems, relationships, attribute perspectives	Object-oriented modelling constructs; design patterns	Classification, aggregation, generalisation and specialisation	Model the semantics of the application domain
Navigational design	Nodes, links, access structures, navigational contexts, navigational transformations	Object-oriented views; object-oriented State charts; context classes; design patterns; user-centred scenarios	Classification, aggregation, generalisation and specialisation.	Takes into account user profile and task. emphasis on cognitive aspects. build the navigational structure of the application
Abstract interface design	Abstract interface objects, responses to external events, interface transformations	Abstract interface widgets; concrete widgets; ontologies; design patterns	Mapping between navigation and perceptible objects	Model perceptible objects, implementing chosen metaphors. Describe interface for navigational objects. Define layout of interface objects
Implementation	Running application	Those supported by the target environment	Those provided by the target environment	Performance, completeness

We next summarise the different OOHDM activities; detailed syntax and semantics can be found in [3,6]. Further information about OOHDM can be found online at the OOHDM Wiki (http://www.ooohdm.inf.puc-rio.br:8668).

10.1.1 Requirements Gathering

The first step during requirements gathering is to gather stakeholders' requirements. To achieve this, it is necessary to first identify the actors (stakeholders) and the tasks they must perform. Next, scenarios are collected (or drafted), for each task and type of actor. The scenarios are then used to form use cases, which are represented using User Interaction Diagrams (UIDs). These diagrams provide a concise graphical representation of the interaction between the user and the system during the execution of a task. UIDs are validated with the actors, and redesigned if necessary. In sequence, a set of guidelines are applied to the UIDs to extract a conceptual model. Details about UIDs can be found in [9].

10.1.2 Conceptual Design

During the conceptual design, an application domain's conceptual model is built using object-oriented modelling principles, augmented with primitives, such as attribute perspectives (multiple valued attributes, similar to HDM perspectives). Conceptual classes may be built using aggregation and generalisation/specialisation hierarchies. There is no concern for the types of users and tasks, only for the application domain semantics. A conceptual schema is built out of sub-systems, classes and relationships. OOHDM uses UML (with slight extensions) for expressing the conceptual design.

10.1.3 Navigational Design

In OOHDM, an application is seen as a navigational view over the conceptual model. This reflects a major innovation of OOHDM, which recognises that the objects (items) the user navigates are *not* the conceptual objects, but objects that are "built" from one or more conceptual objects.

For each user profile we can define a different navigational structure, which will reflect objects and relationships in the conceptual schema according to the tasks a user must perform. The navigational class structure of a Web application is defined by a schema containing navigational classes. In OOHDM, there is a set of pre-defined types of navigational classes: nodes, links, anchors and access structures. The semantics of nodes, links and anchors are as usual in hypermedia applications. Nodes in OOHDM represent logical "windows" (or views) on conceptual classes, defined during conceptual design. Links are the hypermedia realisation of conceptual relationships, as well as task-related links. Access structures, such as indexes, represent possible ways to start a navigation.

Different applications (in the same domain) may contain different linking topologies according to a user's profile. For example, in an academic Web application we may have a view to be used by students and researchers, and another view for use by administrators. In the second view, a professor's node may contain salary information, which would not be visible in the student's view.

The main difference between our approach and others', in relation to object viewing mechanisms, is that while others consider Web pages mainly as user interfaces built by "observing" conceptual objects, we favour the explicit representation of navigational objects (nodes and links) during design.

The navigational structure of a Web application is described in terms of navigational contexts, which are generated from navigation classes, such as nodes, links, indices and guided tours. Navigational contexts are sets of related nodes that possess similar navigation alternatives (options), and that are meaningful for a certain step in a task pursued by a user. For example, we can model the set of courses in a semester, the paintings of a painter, the products in a shopping cart, etc.

10.1.4 Abstract Interface Design

The abstract interface design defines perceptible objects (e.g. a picture, a city map) in terms of interface classes. Interface classes are aggregations of primitive classes (e.g. text fields, buttons) and, recursively, of other interface classes. Interface objects are mapped to navigational objects in order to have a perceptible appearance. An interface behaviour is defined by specifying how to handle external and user-generated events, and how the communication between interface and navigational objects is to take place.

10.1.5 Implementation

Implementation maps interface and navigation objects to implementation objects, and may involve elaborated architectures (e.g. client–server), in which applications are clients to a shared database server containing conceptual objects. A number of CD-ROM-based applications, as well as Web applications, have been developed using OOHDM, and employing numerous technologies, such as Java (J2EE), .NET (aspx), Windows (asp), Lua (CGILua), ColdFusion and Ruby (RubyOnRails).

An open source environment for OOHDM, based on a variation of Ruby on Rails, is available at:

http://server2.tecweb.inf.puc-rio.br:8000/projects/hyperde/trac.cgi/wiki.

10.2 Building an Online CD Store with OOHDM

We next illustrate our method using as a case study the design of a simple CD store. To keep it simple, we focus mainly on the process of finding products in the store catalogue, with less emphasis on the check-out process (see [5]). This example is somewhat archetypical, as different Web applications can be modelled using similar ideas to those we show next. We emphasise the process of mapping requirements into conceptual and navigational structures, and ignore user interface and implementation issues (see [1,2,8] for discussions about interfaces and implementation).

In OOHDM we build a different navigational model for each user profile. In this application we have at least two orthogonal profiles: the client (who is looking for CDs to buy) and the administrator (who maintains the CD store); we will illustrate the application focusing on the client profile.

10.2.1 Requirements Gathering

The first step is to identify the actors in the application; in the example, our only actor is the client who buys CDs in the online store. Next, for each actor, we have to identify the tasks that will evolve into potential use scenarios, and later into use cases. The most important tasks identified are the following:

- To buy a CD given its title
- To buy a CD given the name of a song
- To buy a CD given the name of the performer
- To find information about a performer
- To find CDs given a musical genre
- To find best-selling CDs
- To find CDs on offer

Scenario Construction

The next activity consists of describing usage scenarios. Scenarios represent the set of tasks a user has to perform to complete a task. Scenarios in OOHDM are specified textually, from the point of view of the end users. In this instance, the role of an end user (client) can also be performed either by different members of the design team, or by the CD store employees. For the sake of conciseness, we describe two of the eighteen scenarios we elicit from three different users.

Scenario 1: To buy a specific CD.
"I enter the CD title. For each CD matching that title I obtain the CD's cover, availability and price. It is possible to obtain detailed information, such as track names, duration, details of performing artists, and to listen to CD tracks. It is also possible to obtain additional data on artists. After reading the information I decide to buy the CD or to quit"

Scenario 2: To buy a CD given its title.
"I enter the CD title and I obtain the list of matching titles. I choose one and add it to the shopping cart. Whenever the CD information is shown, I should see information on its availability"

Use Case Specification

Next, we define use cases, based on the set of scenarios and tasks previously defined; we use the following heuristics:

1. Identify those scenarios related to the task at hand. We will use the two previous scenarios.
2. For each scenario, identify information items that are exchanged between the user and the application during their interaction.
3. For each scenario, identify data items that are inter-related. In general, they appear together in a use case text.
4. For each scenario, identify data items organised as sets. In general, they appear as sets in a use case text.
5. The sequences of actions presented in scenarios should also be present in a use case.
6. For each scenario, the operations on data items should be included in a use case.

Once the data involved in the interaction, the sequence of actions and the operations have been defined, we next specify a use case. A use case is constructed from the sequence of actions, enriched with data items and operations. Use cases can also be complemented with information from other use cases, or from the designer.

The resulting use case for the previous scenario is the following:

Use Case: To buy a CD from its title

1. A user enters the CD title (or part of it).
2. The application returns a list of matching CDs. If only one CD matches, see step 4. For each CD, its title, artist, price, cover and availability are shown.

3. If the user wants to buy one or more CDs from the list, (s)he adds them to the shopping cart. The sale is dealt with using another use case – *Use Case: Buy*. Further CD information is available by selecting it.
4. If a single CD is selected, the application provides further information: title, cover, availability, price, track names and durations, performers, description, year, genre and country of origin. If the user wants to buy this CD, (s)he can either add it to the shopping cart, or leave and buy it later (*Use Case: Buy*). The user can listen to a track segment if willing to.
5. Further information about any artists who participated in the CD can be obtained by selecting the artist's name. Once selected, the application returns the artist's name, date of birth, a photograph and a short biography.

The specification of the remaining use cases follows a similar process. Thus, only those use cases that are clearly different from the one described above will be described next.

Use Case: Verify Shopping Cart

1. The shopping cart displays information on all the CDs selected by a user. For each CD the following information is provided: title, quantity, artist's name and price. Total price and the estimated delivery date are also shown.
2. The quantity relative to each CD can be edited, if necessary, by selecting the CD.

Use Case: Buy CD

1. To buy CD(s) a user must provide a name and, optionally, a password.
2. If a user does not have a password, the following information must then be provided: name, address, telephone, e-mail address and birth date.
3. Once the necessary information is given, a user is able to further supply the necessary payment data: payment options (cash or deferred), payment type (cheque or credit card), delivery options (surface or air) and optionally delivery address.[1] The operation is completed only after being confirmed by the user.
4. After the operation is confirmed, the user receives an order number.

[1] The delivery address only needs to be provided if it differs from the user's contact address.

Specifying User Interaction Diagrams

For each previously defined use case, a User Interaction Diagram (UID) must be specified. The specification of UIDs from use cases can be done following the guidelines described below. As an example, we detail below the process of building the UID for the use case: *To buy a CD given its title.*

1. Initially the use case is analysed to identify the information exchange between the user and the application. Information provided by the user and information returned by the application are tagged. Next, the same information is identified and made evident in the use case.
2. Items that are exchanged during the interaction are shown as the UID's states. Information provided by the user and by the system are always in separate states. Information produced from computations and information used as input to the computations should be in separate states. The ordering of states depends on the dependencies between the data provided by the user, and those returned by the application. In Fig. 10.1, we show the first draft of a UID where parts of the use case are transcribed.

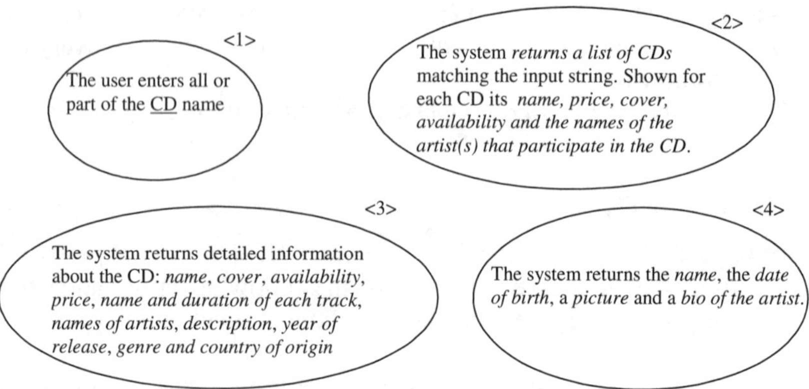

Fig. 10.1. Defining a UID

The exchange data items, once identified, must be clearly indicated in the UID. Data entered by the user (e.g. a CD title) is specified using a rectangle: if it is mandatory, the border is a full line; if it is optional, the border is a dashed line (see Fig. 10.2). An ellipsis (…) in front of a label indicates a list (e.g. …CD indicates a list of CDs). The notation Artist(name, date of birth, bio, photo) is called a *structure*.

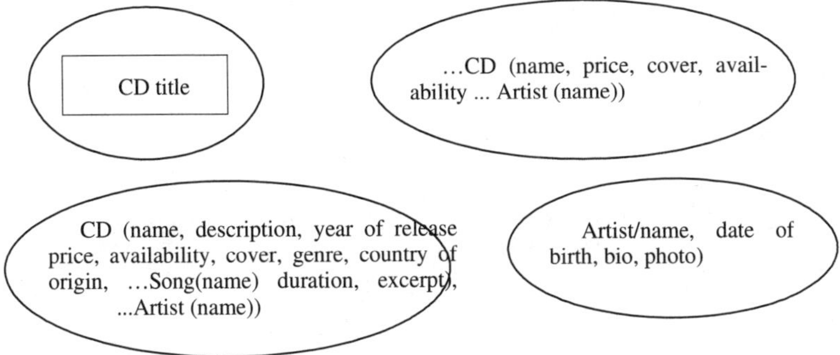

Fig. 10.2. Refining interaction states

Transitions between interaction states must be indicated using arrows. Multiple paths, as indicated in the use cases, might arise (see Fig. 10.3). Labels between brackets indicate conditions (e.g. [2..N] indicates more than one result); a label indicating cardinality represents a choice (in the example, "1" indicates that only one may be chosen).

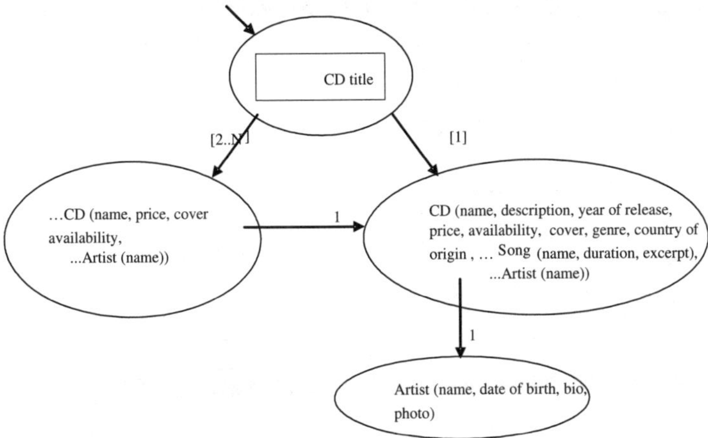

Fig. 10.3. Transitions between interaction states

Finally, operations executed by the user are represented using a line with a bullet connected to the specific information item to which it is applied, as shown in Fig. 10.4. The name of the operation appears in parentheses.

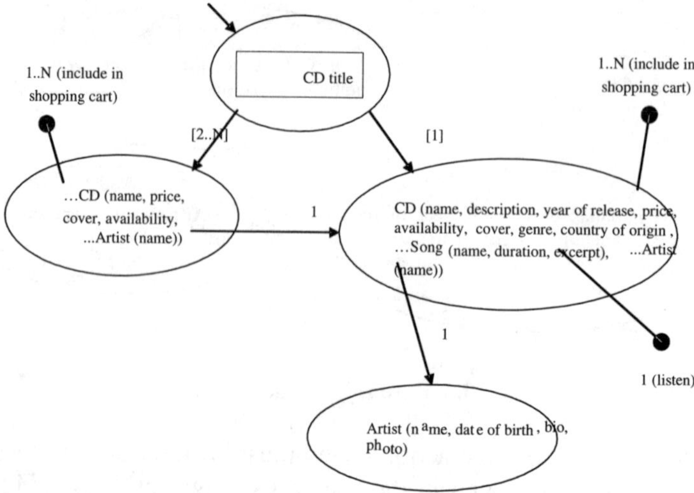

Fig. 10.4. Complete specification of the UID for use case *To buy CD given its title*

Figure 10.5 and Fig. 10.6 present UIDs corresponding to the use cases *To verify Shopping Cart* and *to buy CD*, respectively. Once we finish the specification of UIDs for all use cases, we can then design the application's conceptual model.

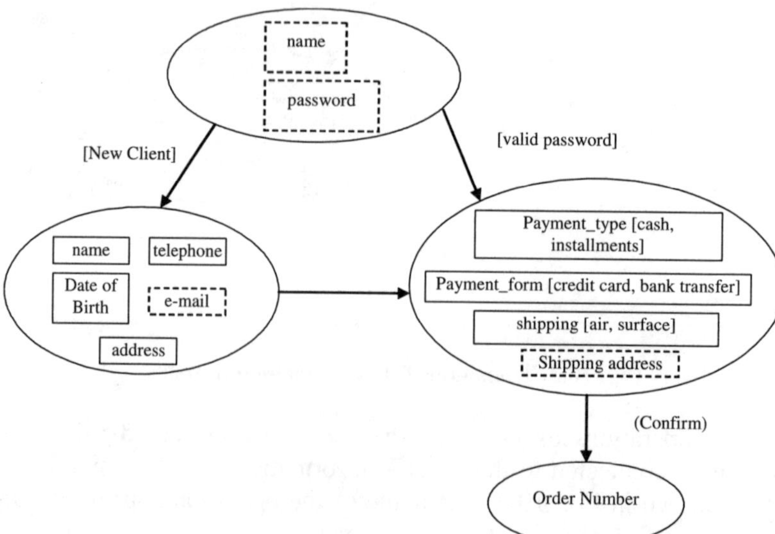

Fig. 10.5. UID for use case *To buy CD*

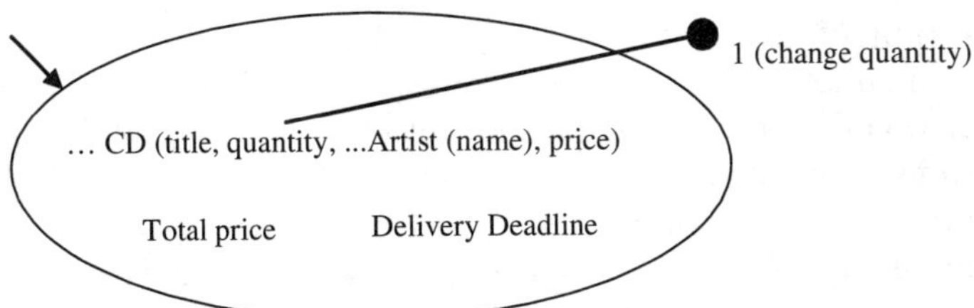

Fig. 10.6. UID for use case *To verify Shopping Cart*

10.2.2 Conceptual Modelling

To define classes, their attributes, operations and relationships is not an easy task. However, the information gathered from use cases and UIDs can help identify core information classes that can be later refined. Next, we describe a set of guidelines to derive classes from UIDs, exemplified using the UID in Fig. 10.4 (To buy CD).

1. **Class definition.** For each data structure in the UID we define a class. In the example, classes are: CD, Artist, Song.
2. **Attribute definition.** For each information item appearing in the UID, either provided by the user or returned by the application, an attribute is defined according to the following validations:
   a. If, given an instance of class *X*, it is possible to obtain the value for attribute *A*, then *A* can be an attribute of *X* (provided *X* is the only class fulfilling this condition).
   b. If, given classes *X* and *Y*, it is possible to obtain the value of attribute *A*, then *A* will be an attribute of an association between *X* and *Y*.
   c. If the attribute corresponding to a data item does not depend on any existing class, or combination of classes, we need to create a new one.

The following attributes were identified from the information returned by the application, as shown in the UID in Fig. 10.4:

- CD: title, description, year, price, cover, availability, genre, country of origin.
- Artist: name, birth date, description, photograph
- Song: name
- CD-Song: track, duration.

3. **Definition of associations.** For each UID, for attributes contained within a structure that does not correspond to their class, include the association if there is a relationship between its class and the class representing the structure.
4. **Definition of associations.** For each UID, for each structure *s1*, containing another structure *s2*, create an association between the classes corresponding to structures *s1* and *s2*.
5. **Definition of associations.** For each transition of interaction states in each UID, if there are different classes representing the source interaction state and the target interaction state, define an association between corresponding classes.

The following associations were identified by applying 3, 4 and 5 to the UID in Fig. 10.4:

- CD-Artist
- CD-Song

6. **Operations definition.** For each option attached to a state transition in each UID, verify if there is an operation that must be created for any of the classes that correspond to the interaction states.

The following operations were identified from this last guideline:

- CD: includeInShoppingCart
- CD-Music: listenTrack

In Fig. 10.7 we show an initial conceptual model derived from the UID: *To buy CD from title*.

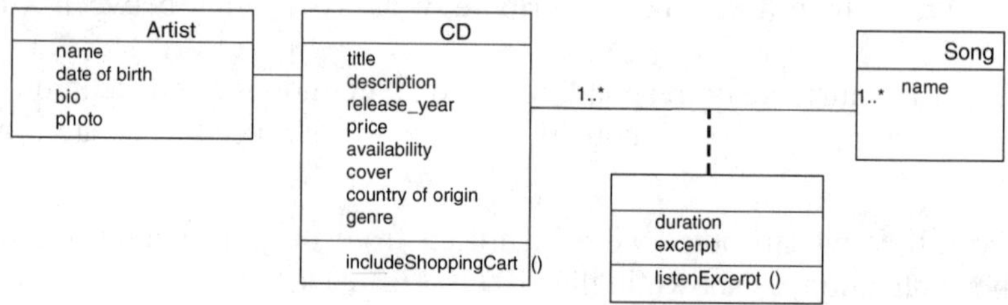

Fig. 10.7. Initial conceptual model

After analysing the complete set of UIDs and performing the required adjustments we obtain the conceptual model shown in Fig. 10.8.

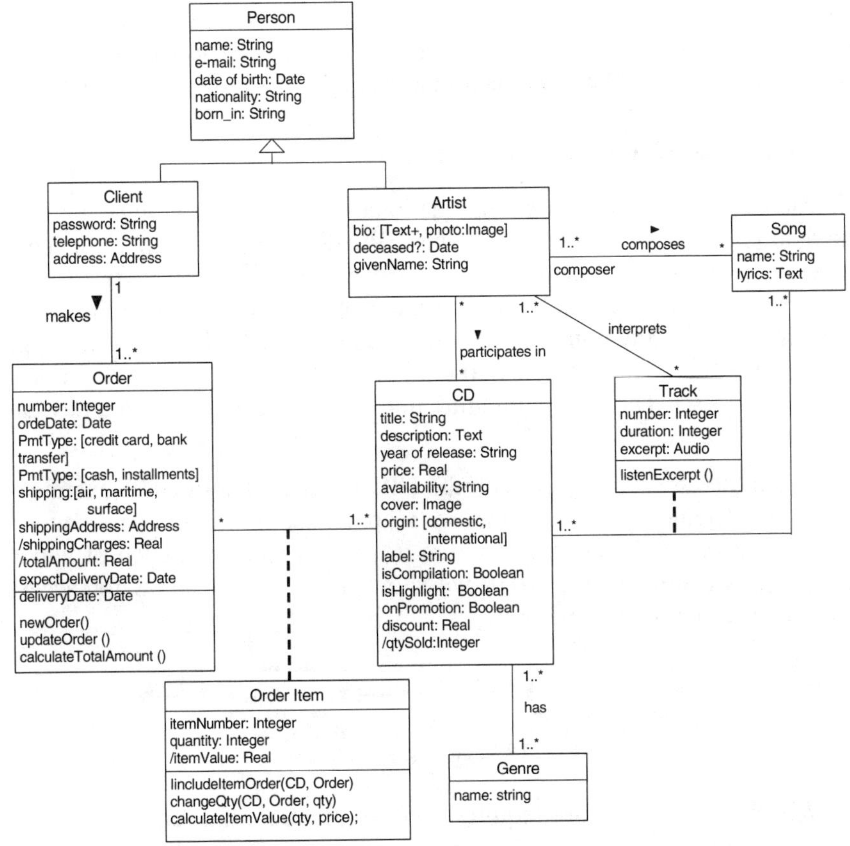

Fig. 10.8. Conceptual model for the CD store

Note that this conceptual model might need further improvements as the application evolves, since these classes are simply the ones we derive from the requirement's gathering activity. However, this evolution belongs more to the general field of object-oriented design and is not important in the context of this chapter.

10.2.3 Navigation Design

During the navigation design activity we generate two schemas: the navigational contexts and the navigational class schemas. The former indicate possible navigation sequences to help users complete their tasks; the latter specify the navigation objects being processed. Designers create both schemas from different sources. UIDs and scenarios are important to obtain a sound navigational model. The conceptual model that has also been obtained from requirements is also an important source of information. Finally, designers use previous experience, e.g. using navigation patterns, as described in [4,7]. Next we detail the creation of navigational contexts.

Derivation of Navigational Contexts

For each task we define a partial navigational context representing a possible navigational structure to support the task. We detail the creation of the navigational contexts corresponding to the use case: *To buy CD given its title.*

First, each structure that has been represented in the UID (and the corresponding class in the conceptual model) is analysed to determine the type of primitive that it will give rise to (e.g. an access structure, a navigational context or a list). The following guidelines can be used to obtain a navigational context:

1. When the task associated with the UID requires that the user examines a set of elements to select one, we map the set of structures into an access structure. An access structure is a set of elements, each of which contains a link. In Fig. 10.9, we show the partial diagram for access structures CDs and Artists.

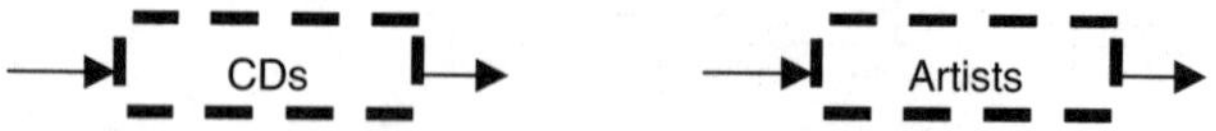

Fig. 10.9. Access structures

2. When the task does not require such examination, but requires the elements to be accessed simultaneously, map the set into a list, e.g. the list of songs in a CD (see Fig. 10.10).

CD ?

title, description, year of release, price,
cover, availability, genre, country of origin,
songs: list of <s: Song, t:Track, s.name,
t.duration, t.excerpt where Track(t, c, s)>

Fig. 10.10. List for CD

3. After mapping the different sets of structures we analyse singular structures in the UID using the following guideline. When the task requires that an element's information be accessed by the user, we map the structure into a navigational context. In Fig. 10.11 we show the partial context diagram from this example.

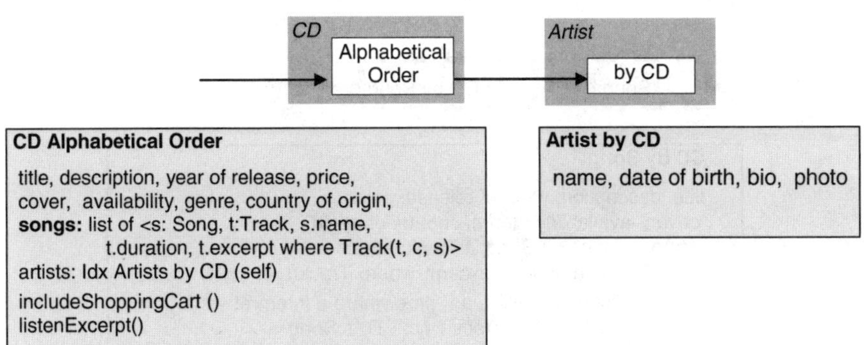

Fig. 10.11. Partial context for UID: *Buy CD given its title*

In the example, both "CD Alphabetical Order" and "Artist by CD" are contexts, which correspond to sets of elements. The elements that constitute each set are described in the grey boxes.

In Fig. 10.12 and Fig. 10.13 we show other partial contexts obtained from previously mentioned UIDs. Other UIDs, such as "CD by Genre", "CD on Promotion", would have similar definitions.

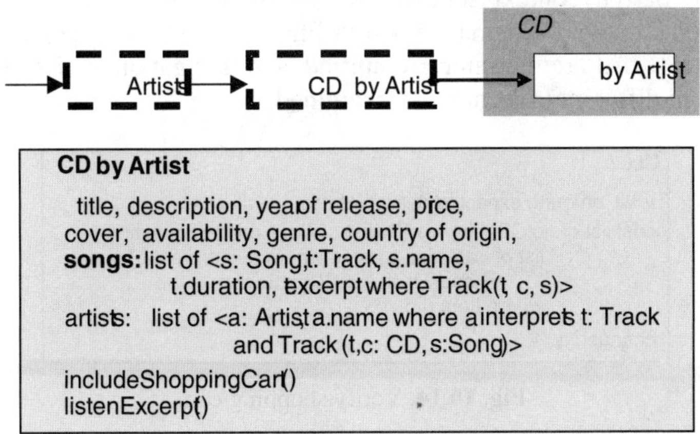

Fig. 10.12. Partial context for UID: *To buy CD given an artist's name*

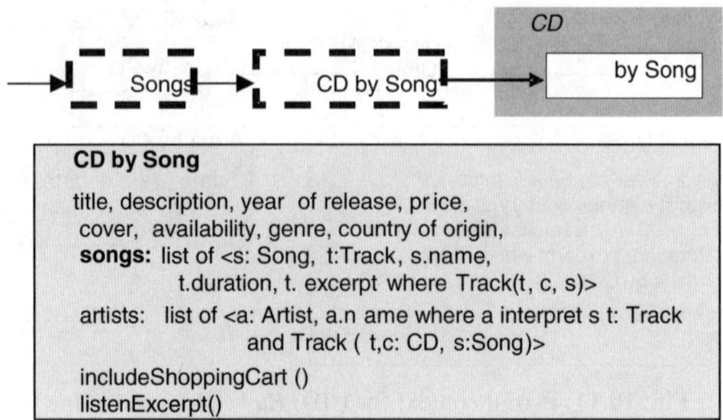

Fig. 10.13. Partial context for UID: *To buy CD given a song's name*

Fig. 10.14 and Fig. 10.15 show other kinds of contexts and their element definitions.

After obtaining the context diagram for each individual task, we integrate the partial context schemas to obtain the application's complete navigational context schema, shown in Fig. 10.16. In the integration process, contexts that are the same are unified, and navigation choices between contexts in different tasks are also examined.

Fig. 10.14. Verify shopping cart

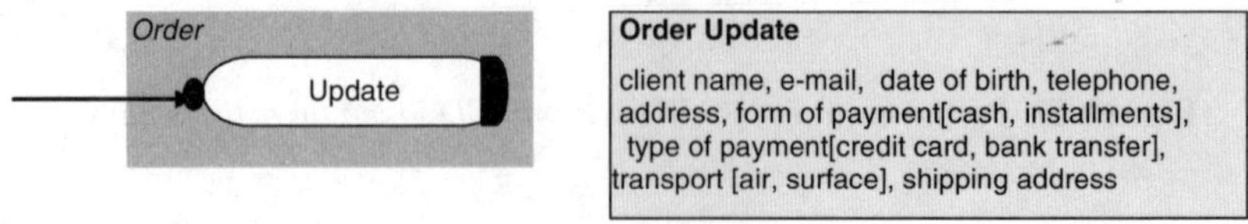

Fig. 10.15. To buy CD

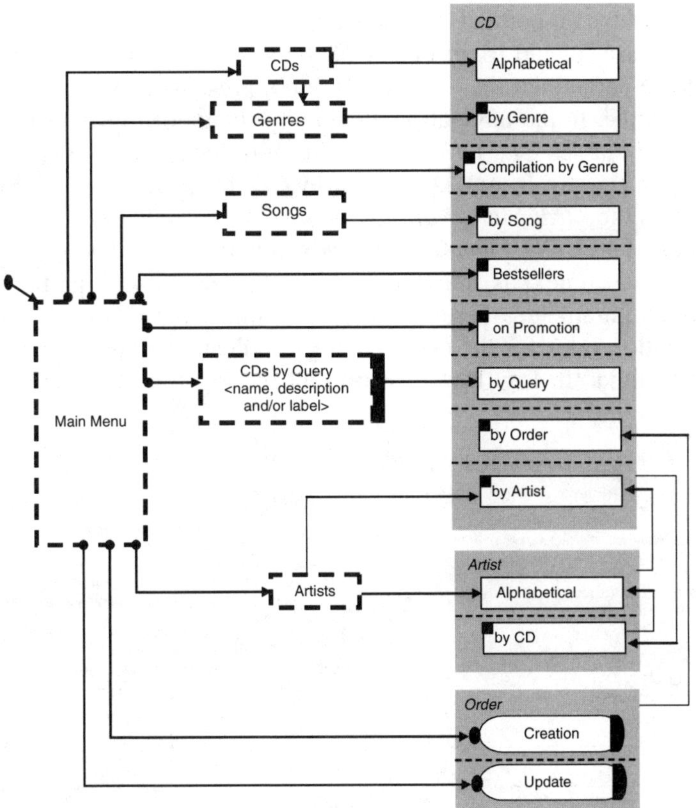

Fig. 10.16. Navigation context schema

We can see that from the main menu, the user can access different access structures (for CDs, Musical Genres, Songs, CDs by Query, and Artists). Each one of them provides access to sets of nodes that support the achievement of the different tasks identified at the outset.

Specification of the Navigational Class Schema

During the specification of the navigational class schema the designer derives the navigational schema using both the conceptual model and the navigational contexts schema. Navigational classes, such as nodes, represent views over conceptual classes: a navigational class can present information from one or more conceptual classes. All classes from the navigational contexts schema are node classes. Meanwhile links are derived from navigation relationships between classes in the navigational contexts schema. Note that not all navigation in this schema represents a link. The rule for selecting the target context is analysed (especially when it involves navigation between contexts of the same class). If the elements of the target context are related to an object of the same original class, and if this object is the parameter, then the navigation represents a link.

For example, in the navigational context schema of Fig. 10.16, we have navigational classes *CD*, *Order* and *Artist*. We have the following navigations among classes: from *CD* to *Artist by CD*, from *Order* to *CD by Order* and from *CD* to *Order in Creation/Update*. The selection rule for *Artist by CD* (Parameter: *c:CD-Elements: a: Artist* where *a participates in c*) indicates that the context is integrated by artists related to a particular CD, which is its parameter; therefore there is a link from *CD* to *Artist*. Similarly, selection rules for the other contexts indicate which navigations correspond to links. In Fig. 10.17 we present the resulting navigational class schema.

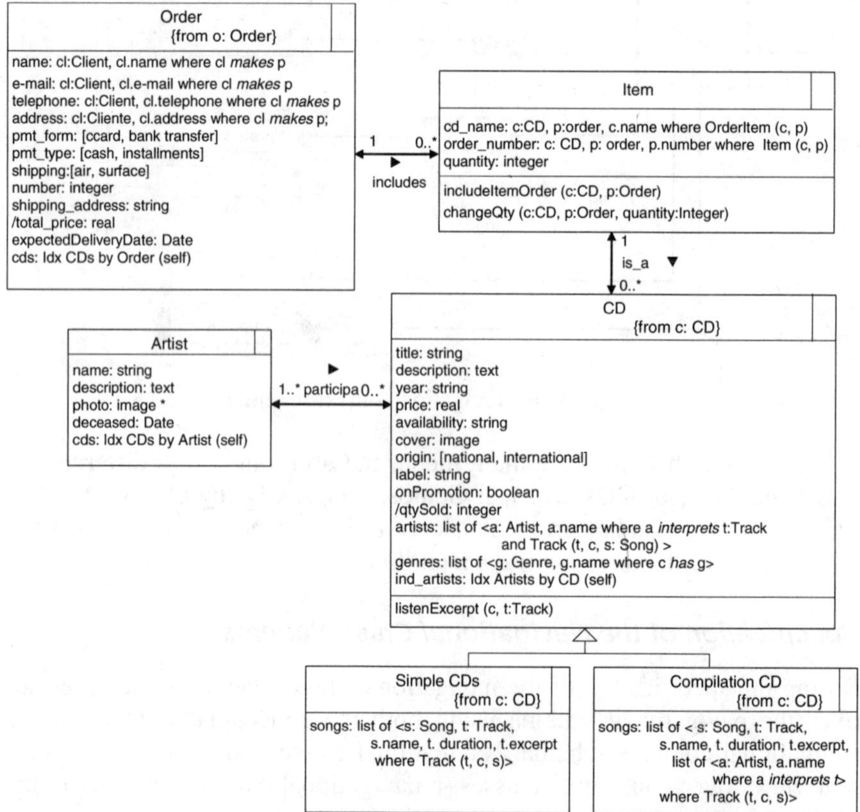

Fig. 10.17. Navigational schema

10.2.4 Abstract Interface Design

The abstract interface design focuses on making navigation objects and application functionality perceptible to the user, which must be done at the application interface level. At the most abstract level, the interface functionality can be regarded as supporting information exchange between the application and the user, including activation of functionalities. In fact, from this standpoint, navigation is just another (albeit distinguished) application functionality.

Since the tasks being supported drive this information exchange, it is reasonable to expect that this exchange in itself will be less sensitive to runtime environment aspects, such as particular standards and devices being used. The design of this interface aspect can be carried out by interaction designers or software engineers.

For the actual running application, it is necessary to define the concrete look and feel of the application, including layout, font, colour and graphical appearance, which is typically carried out by graphics designers. This part of the design is almost totally dependent on the particular hardware and software runtime environment.

Such separation allows shielding a significant part of the interaction design from inevitable technological platform evolution, as well as from the need to support users in a multitude of hardware and software runtime environments.

The entire interface is specified by several ontologies, currently described using RDFS (RDFS W3C) and OWL (OWL W3C) as a formalism.

Abstract Widget Ontology

The type of functionality offered by interface elements is called the abstract interface. It is specified using the Abstract Widget Ontology, which establishes the interface vocabulary, as shown in Fig. 10.18. This ontology can be thought of as a set of classes whose instances will comprise a given interface.

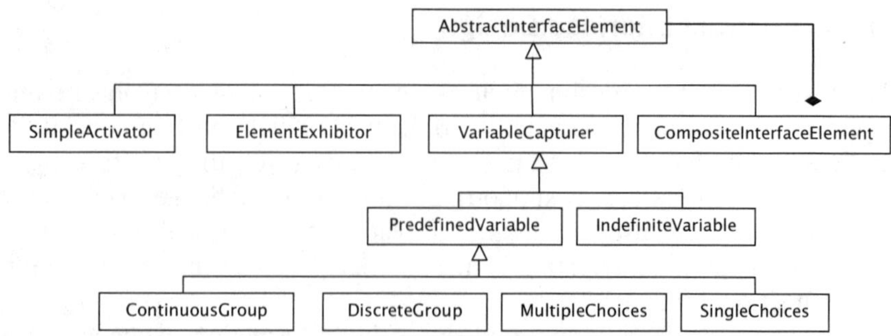

Fig. 10.18. Abstract Widget Ontology

An abstract interface widget can be any of the following:

- *SimpleActivator,* which is capable of reacting to external events, such as mouse clicks.
- *ElementExhibitor,* which is able to exhibit a type of content, such as text or images.
- *VariableCapturer,* which is able to receive (capture) the value of one or more variables. This includes input text fields, selection widgets such as pull-down menus and checkboxes, etc. It generalises two distinct (sub) concepts.
- *IndefiniteVariable,* which allows entering previously unknown values, such as text strings typed by the user.
- *PredefinedVariable,* which abstracts widgets that allow the selection of a subset from a set of pre-defined values; often this selection must be a singleton. Specialisations of this concept are *ContinuousGroup*, *DiscreetGroup*, *MultipleChoices* and *SingleChoice*. The first allows selecting a single value from an infinite range of values; the second is analogous, but for a finite set; the remainder are self-evident.
- *CompositeInterfaceElement,* which is a composition of any of the above.

It can be seen that this ontology captures the essential roles that interface elements play with respect to the interaction – they exhibit information, react to external events, or accept information. As customary, composite elements allow building more complex interfaces out of simpler building blocks.

The software designer, who understands the application logic and the types of information exchange that must be supported, should carry out the abstract interface design. The software designer does not need to take usability issues or the “look and feel” into account, as they will be dealt with during the concrete interface design, normally carried out by a graphics (or “experience”) designer.

Once the abstract interface has been defined, each element must be mapped onto both a navigation element, which will provide its contents, and a concrete interface widget, which will actually implement the element in a given runtime environment. Fig. 10.19 provides an example of an interface for a page describing an artist, and Fig. 10.20 shows an abstract representation of this interface.

Concrete widgets correspond to widgets usually available in most runtime environments, such as labels, text boxes, combo boxes, pulldown menus, radio buttons, etc.

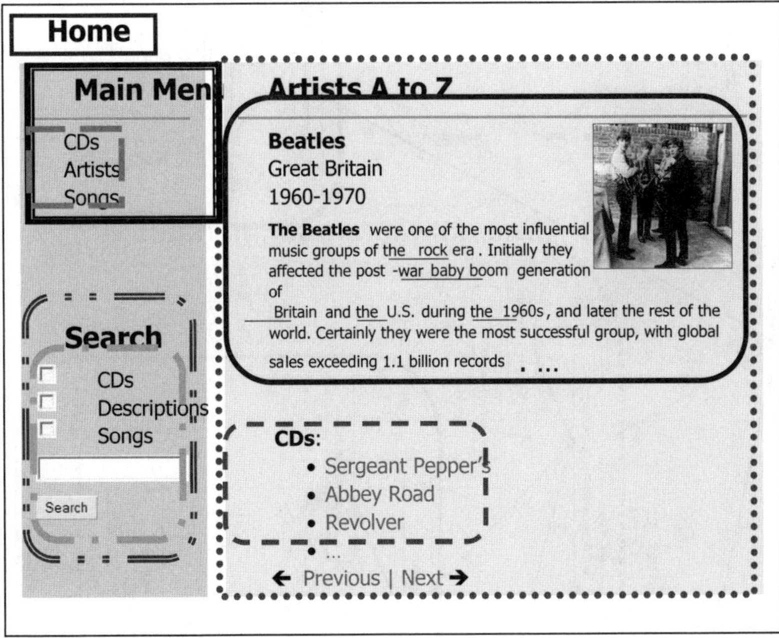

Fig. 10.19. An example of a concrete interface

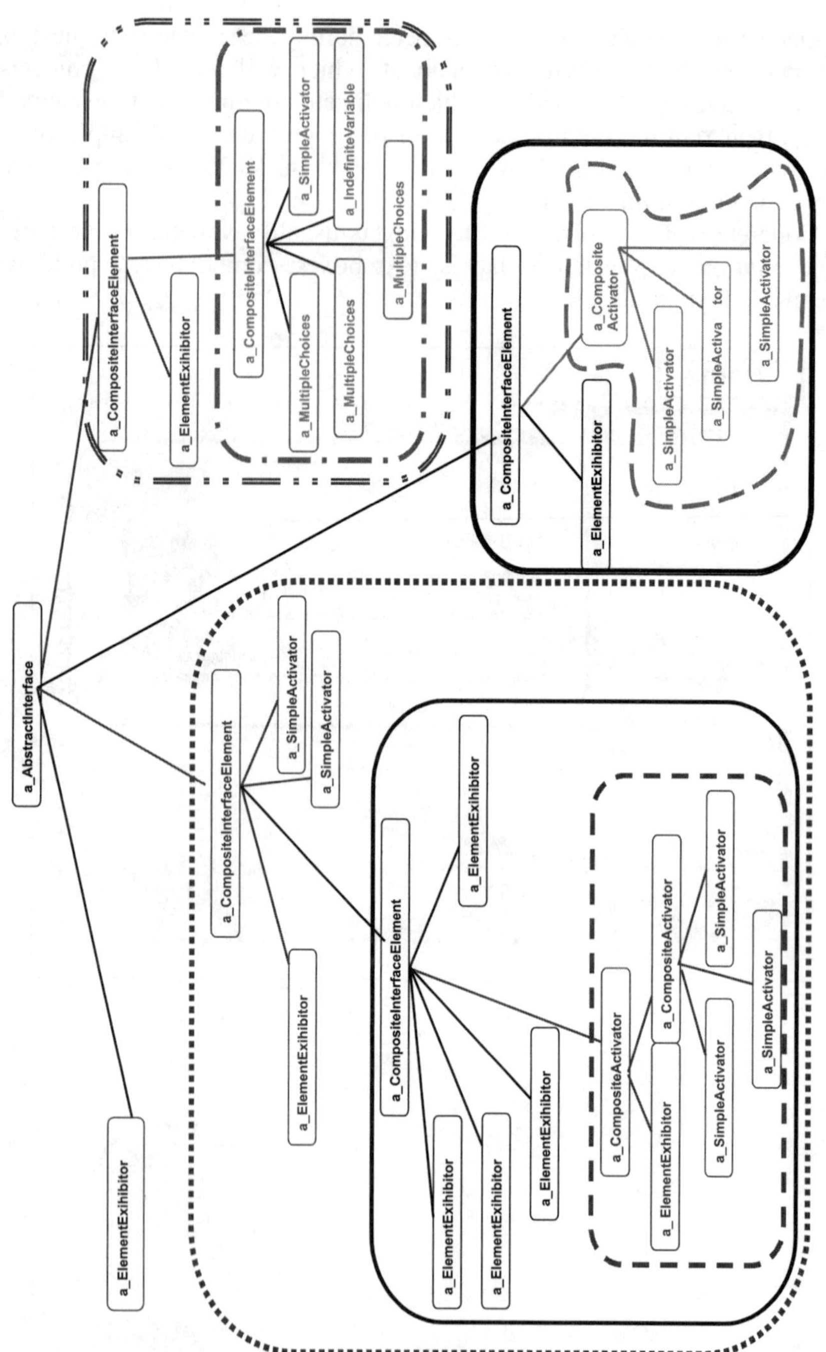

Fig. 10.20. Abstract Widget Ontology instance for the example in Fig. 10.19

Mappings

The Abstract Interface Ontology contains, for each abstract interface widget, the mapping both to navigation elements, which are application specific, and to a concrete interface element.

There is additional information in the ontology that restricts each abstract interface widget to compatible concrete interface widgets. For example, a "SimpleActivator" abstract interface widget can only be mapped into the "Link" or "Button" concrete interface widgets.

Actual abstract interface widget instances are mapped onto specific navigation elements (in the navigation ontology) and onto concrete interface widgets (in the Concrete Interface Widget Ontology). Fig. 10.21 shows the specification of the "Previous Artist" abstract interface widget (class "SimpleActivator"), shown in Fig. 10.20, which is mapped onto a "Link" concrete interface element.

```
...
<awo:SimpleActivator rdf:ID="ArtistAlphaPrevious">
        <awo:mapsTo rdf:resource= "http://www.inf.puc-rio.br/~sabrina/ontology/CW/cwo#Link" />
        <awo:fromElement>ctxArtistAlpha</awo:fromElement>
        <awo:fromAttribute>_Prev</fromAttribute>
        <awo:AbstractInterface>ArtistAlpha</AbstractInterface>
</awo:SimpleActivator>
```

Fig. 10.21. Mapping between abstract interface widget and navigation element

Fig. 10.22 shows an example illustrating how an application's functionality is integrated, by providing the OWL specification of the "Search" abstract interface element. It is composed of two abstract widgets, "ElementExhibitor" (lines 9–12), and "CompositeInterfaceElement" (lines 14–46). The first shows the "Search" string, using a "Label" concrete widget. The second aggregates the four elements used to specify the field in which the search may be performed, namely, three "MultipleChoices" – SearchProfessors (lines 25–29), SearchStudents (31–35) and SearchPapers (37–41) and one "IndefiniteVariable" – "SearchField" (lines 43–46).

The *CompositeInterfaceElement* element, in this case, has the properties: *fromIndex*, *isRepeated*, *mapsTo*, *abstractInterface* and *hasInterfaceElement*. The *fromIndex* property in line 2 indicates which navigational index this element belongs to. This property is mandatory if no previous element of type *compositeInterfaceElement* has been declared. The association with the "idxSearch" navigation element in line 2 enables the generation of the link to the actual code that will run the search. Even though this example shows an association with a navigation element, it could just as well be associated with a call to application functionality such as "buy".

```
...
<awo:CompositeInterfaceElement rdf:ID="Search">
    <awo:fromIndex>idxSearch</awo:fromIndex>
    <awo:mapsTo rdf:resource="&cwo;Composition"/>
    <awo:isRepeated>false</awo:isRepeated>
    <awo:hasInterfaceElement rdf:resource="#TitleSearch"/>
    <awo:hasInterfaceElement rdf:resource="#SearchElements"/>
</awo:CompositeInterfaceElement>

<awo:ElementExihibitor rdf:ID="TitleSearch">
    <awo:visualizationText>Search</awo:visualizationText>
    <awo:mapsTo rdf:resource="&cwo;Label"/>
</awo:ElementExihibitor>

<awo:CompositeInterfaceElement rdf:ID="SearchElements">
    <awo:fromIndex>idxSearch</awo:fromIndex>
    <awo:abstractInterface>SearchResult</awo:abstractInterface>
    <awo:mapsTo rdf:resource="&cwo;Form"/>
    <awo:isRepeated>false</awo:isRepeated>
    <awo:hasInterfaceElement rdf:resource="#SearchCDs"/>
    <awo:hasInterfaceElement rdf:resource="#SearchDescriptions"/>
    <awo:hasInterfaceElement rdf:resource="#SearchSongs"/>
    <awo:hasInterfaceElement rdf:resource="#SearchField"/>
</awo:CompositeInterfaceElement>

<awo:MultipleChoices rdf:ID="SearchCDs">
    <awo:fromElement>SearchCDs</awo:fromElement>
    <awo:fromAttribute>name</awo:fromAttribute>
    <awo:mapsTo rdf:resource="&cwo;CheckBox"/>
</awo:MultipleChoices>

<awo:MultipleChoices rdf:ID="SearchDescriptions">
    <awo:fromElement>SearchCDs</awo:fromElement>
    <awo:fromAttribute>description</awo:fromAttribute>
    <awo:mapsTo rdf:resource="&cwo;CheckBox"/>
</awo:MultipleChoices>

<awo:MultipleChoices rdf:ID="SearchSongs">
    <awo:fromElement>SearchSongs</awo:fromElement>
    <awo:fromAttribute>name</awo:fromAttribute>
    <awo:mapsTo rdf:resource="&cwo;CheckBox"/>
</awo:MultipleChoices>

<awo:IndefiniteVariable rdf:ID="SearchField">
    <awo:mapsTo rdf:resource="&cwo;TextBox"/>
</awo:IndefiniteVariable>
...
```

Fig. 10.22. Example of the OWL specification of the "Search" part of Fig. 10.19

The *isRepeated* property indicates if the components of this element are repetitions of a single type (false in this case). The *mapsTo* property indicates which concrete element corresponds to this abstract interface element. The *abstractInterface* property specifies the abstract interface that will be activated when this element is triggered. The *hasInterfaceElement* indicates which elements belong to this element.

The *ElementExhibitor* element has the *visualizationText* and *mapsTo* properties. The former represents the concrete object to be exhibited, in this case the string "Search".

The *MultipleChoices* element has the *fromElement*, *fromAttribute* and *mapsTo* properties. The *fromElement* and *fromAttribute* properties indicate the corresponding element and navigational attribute in the navigational ontology, respectively. The *IndefiniteVariable* element has the *mapsTo* property.

10.3 From Design to Implementation

Mapping design documents into implementation artefacts is usually time-consuming and, in spite of the importance of software engineering approaches be generally accepted, implementers tend to overlook the advantages of good modelling practices. The relationship between design models and implementation components is lost, making the traceability of design decisions, which is a fundamental aspect for supporting evolution, a nightmare. We claim that this problem is not only caused by the relative youth of Web implementation tools but mainly due to:

- Lack of understanding that navigation (hypertext) design is a defining characteristic of Web applications.
- The fact that languages and tools are targeted more to support fine-grained programming than architectural design.
- The inability of methodologists to provide non-proprietary solutions to the aforementioned "mapping" dilemma.

For example, we can use the Model View Controller (MVC) architecture to map design constructs onto implementation components. The MVC architecture has been extensively used for decoupling the user interface from application data, and from its functionality. Different programming environments provide large class libraries that allow the programmer to reuse standard widgets and interaction styles by plugging corresponding classes into her/his "model".

The model contains application data and behaviours, and also provides an interface for the view and the controller. For each user interface, a view object is defined, containing information about presentation formats, and is kept synchronised with the model's state. Finally, the controller processes the user input and translates it into requests for specific application's functionality. This separation reflects well the fact that Web applications may have different views, in the sense that it can be accessed through different clients (e.g. browsers, WAP clients, Web service clients), with application data separated from its presentation. The existence of a separate module (the controller) to handle user interaction, or, more generally, interaction with other systems or users, provides better decoupling between application behaviour and the way in which this behaviour is triggered.

However, while the MVC provides a set of structuring principles for building modular interactive applications, it does not completely fulfil the requirements of Web applications to provide rich hypermedia structures, as it is based on a purely transactional view of software. In addition, it does not take into account the navigation aspects that, as we have previously argued, should be appropriately supported.

The view component includes structure and presentation of data, while contents are kept in the model. Specifically, a simple use of the MVC is for nodes and their interfaces to be handled by the same software component (typically a JSP object).

In addition, the MVC does not take into account that navigation should always occur within a context and that context-related information should be provided to the user. For example, if we want the same node to have a slightly different structure, depending on the context in which it is accessed (e.g. CD in a thematic set or in the shopping cart), we have to use the context as a parameter for the JSP page, and write conditional statements to insert context-sensitive information as appropriate. The JSP becomes overloaded, difficult to manage and evolution becomes practically unmanageable. The same problem occurs if we use different JSPs for different contexts, thus duplicating code.

An alternative approach is to use a single JSP that generates the information common to all contexts (basic node), and one JSP for each node in context, which dynamically inserts that common JSP, adding the context-sensitive information. This is still unsatisfactory, since in this case, the basic node layout becomes fixed and we have lost flexibility.

To overcome these limitations we have developed a software architecture, OOHDM-Java2, which extends the idea of the MVC by clearly separating nodes from their interfaces, thus introducing navigation objects; it also recognises the fact that navigation may be context-dependent. Details on the architecture are presented in [1].

In Fig. 10.23 the higher-level components of the OOHDM-Java2 architecture are presented, in addition to the most important interactions between components, while handling a request.

The main components of OOHDM-Java2 are summarised in Table 10.2.

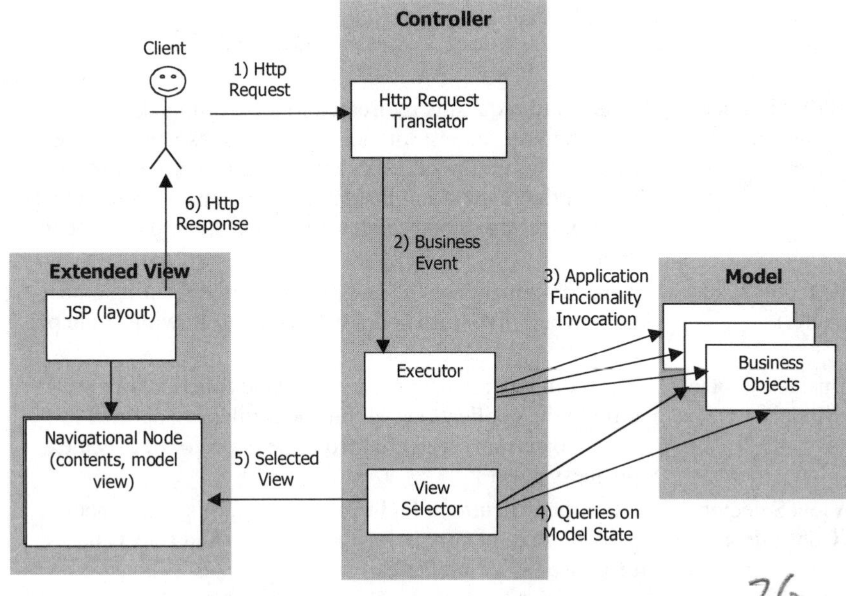

Fig. 10.23. Main components of OOHDM-Java2

Fig. 10.24 outlines the implementation architecture for the interface [2]. Starting with the navigation and abstract interface designs, the corresponding ontology instances are used as input into a JSP generator, which instantiates the interface as a JSP file using TagLibs. The interpreter uses the Jena library to manipulate the ontology information.

The actual TagLib code used is determined by the concrete widget definition that has been mapped onto the corresponding abstract widget. The abstract interface determines the nesting structure of elements in the resulting page. It is expected that the designer will group together functionally-related elements.

It is possible to use different instances of the TagLib implementation by changing its declaration. Thus, for each possible concrete widget, a different implementation of the TagLib code will generate the desired HTML (or any other language) version for that widget.

Table 10.2. Main components of OOHDM-Java2

Component	Description
HTTP Request Translator (Controller)	Every http request is redirected to this component. It translates the user request into an action to be executed by the model. This component extracts the information (parameters) of the request and instantiates a business event, which is an object that encapsulates all data needed to execute the event.
Executor (Controller)	This component has the responsibility of executing a business event, invoking model behaviours following some predefined logic.
Business Object (Model)	This component encapsulates data and functionality specific to the application. All business rules are defined in these objects and triggered from the executor to execute a business event.
View Selector (Controller)	After the execution of a business event, this component gets the state of certain business objects and selects the response view (interface).
Navigational Node (Extended View)	This component represents the product of the navigational logic of the application; it encapsulates attributes that have been obtained from some business objects and other navigational sub-components such as indexes, anchors, etc. This component has the contents to be shown by the response interface (JSP).
JSP (Extended View)	This component generates the look-and-feel that the client component receives as a response to its request. To achieve this, it instantiates the corresponding navigational node component and adds the layout to the node's contents. Notice that the JSP component does not interact directly with model objects. In this way we can have different layouts for the same navigational node.

The actual values of navigation elements manipulated in the page are stored in Java Beans, which correspond to the navigation nodes described earlier. The *element* property, generated in the JSP file, contains calls to the bean that the Tag Library uses to generate the HTML code seen.

Our current implementation of the TagLib code simply wraps each element that has the "DIV" CSS tag with its own ID, and its CSS class is defined according to its abstract widget type. In this way, we can attach CSS style sheets to the generated HTML to produce the final page rendering.

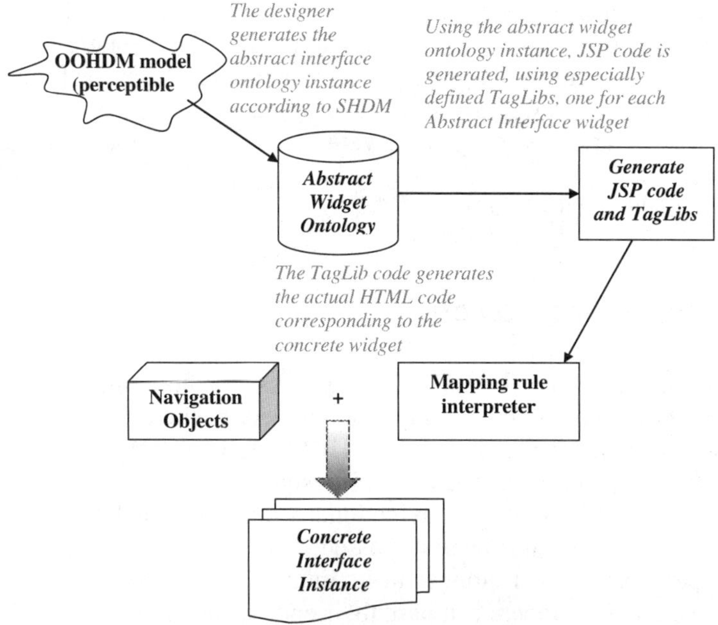

Fig. 10.24. Outline of the implementation architecture

Given the expressive power of CSS, the concrete page definition format allows a large degree of flexibility for the graphic designer, both in terms of layout itself and in terms of formatting aspects. Nevertheless, if a more elaborate page layout is desired, it is possible to edit the generated JSP manually, altering the relative order of generated elements. For a more automated approach, it might be necessary to apply XSLT transformations to the JSP.

10.4 Discussion and Lessons Learned

One of the main advantages of using a model-based approach for Web applications' design is the construction of a set of technology-independent models that can evolve together with application requirements, and that are largely neutral with respect to other types of changes in the application (e.g. runtime settings change).

While working with the OOHDM approach we have found that stakeholders feel comfortable with our notation for requirements acquisition (UID diagrams). In addition, we have used this notation several times to discuss requirements and requirements evolution.

The transition from requirements to design can be managed in a seamless way (perhaps simpler than the transition to implementation). Regarding the implementation, we have found that the instability of frameworks for Web applications deployment usually hinders the use of model-based approaches, as developers tend to devote much time to implementation and to neglect design aspects. In this sense, we have tried to keep our notation simple to make it easy to use.

10.5 Concluding Remarks

This chapter presented the OOHDM approach for building Web applications. We have shown with a simple but archetypical example how to deal with the different activities in the OOHDM life cycle. We have also presented several guidelines that allow a designer to systematically map requirements to conceptual and navigational structures. Finally, implementation alternatives have also been discussed.

Web engineering is no longer in its infancy; many mature methods already exist and developers can base their endeavours on solid model-based approaches like OOHDM and others in this book. The underlying principles behind OOHDM, essentially the clear separation of concerns (e.g. conceptual from navigational and navigational from interfaces), allow not only "just in time" development but also seamless evolution and maintenance of complex Web applications.

Acknowledgements

The authors wish to thank the invaluable help of Adriana Pereira de Medeiros in preparing the example used in this chapter. Gustavo Rossi has been partially funded by Secyt's project PICT No 13623, and Daniel Schwabe has been partially supported by a grant from CNPq - Brazil.

References

1 Jacyntho MD, Schwabe D, Rossi G (2002) A software Architecture for Structuring Complex Web Applications. Web Engineering, 1(1)

2 Moura SS, Schwabe D (2004) Interface Development for Hypermedia Applications in the Semantic Web. In: Proceedings of LA Web 2004, Ribeirão Preto, Brazil, IEEE CS Press, pp 106–113, Los Alamitos, CA

3 Rossi G, Schwabe D (1999) Web application models are more than conceptual models. In: Proceedings of the World Wild Web and Conceptual Modeling'99 Workshop, LNCS 1727, Springer, Paris, pp 239–252

4 Rossi G, Schwabe D, Lyardet F (1999) Integrating Patterns into the Hypermedia Development Process. New Review of Hypermedia and Multimedia, December

5 Schmid H, Rossi G (2004) Modeling and Designing Processes in E-commerce Applications. IEEE Internet Computing, January/February: 19–27

6 Schwabe D, Rossi G (1998) An Object Oriented Approach to Web-Based Application Design. Theory and Practice of Object Systems, 4(4):207–225

7 Schwabe D, Rossi G, Lyardet F (1999) Improving Web Information Systems with navigational patterns. Computer Networks and Applications, May

8 Schwabe D, Szundy G, de Moura SS, Lima F (2004) Design and Implementation of Semantic Web Applications. In: Proceedings of the Workshop on Application Design, Development and Implementation Issues in the Semantic Web (WWW 2004), CEUR Workshop Proceedings, http://ceur-ws.org/Vol-105/, May

9 Vilain P, Schwabe D, Souza CS (2000) A Diagrammatic Tool for Representing User Interaction in UML. In: Proceedings UML'2000, LNCS 1939, Springer Berlin, pp 133–147

Authors' Biography

Gustavo Rossi is full Professor at Facultad de Informática of La Plata National University, Argentina, and heads LIFIA, a computer science research lab. His research interests include Web design patterns and frameworks. He coauthored the Object-Oriented Hypermedia Design Method (OOHDM) and is currently working on separation of design concerns in context-aware Web applications. He has a PhD in Computer Science from Catholic University of Rio de Janeiro (PUC-Rio), Brazil. He is an ACM member and IEEE member.

Daniel Schwabe is an Associate Professor in the Department of Informatics at Catholic University in Rio de Janeiro (PUC), Brazil. He has been working on hypermedia design methods for the last 15 years. He is one of the authors of HDM, the first authoring method for hypermedia, and of OOHDM, one of the mature methods in use by academia and industry for Web applications design. He earned a PhD in Computer Science in 1981 at the University of California, Los Angeles.

11 W2000: A Modelling Notation for Complex Web Applications

Luciano Baresi, Sebastiano Colazzo, Luca Mainetti, Sandro Morasca

Abstract: This chapter presents W2000, a complete notation for modelling complex Web applications. All W2000 concepts are based on a precise meta-model that characterises the different notation elements and identifies the relationships between them. After introducing the modelling concepts and the hierarchical organisation of W2000 models, the chapter exemplifies the main modelling features through a case study and clarifies some design alternatives. The chapter also describes the tool support offered by W2000.

Keywords: W2000, Web development, Complex Web applications, Application modelling.

11.1 Introduction

Web applications are complex software systems with Web-based user interfaces. They can be more data- or process-oriented, but in either case they integrate the user experience provided by the Web with the capability of executing distributed processes; the Internet glues together the two aspects [15].

The Web is an easy and simple way to allow users to access remote services without forcing them to install special-purpose software on their computers. The browser renders the interface and lets the user interact with the business logic. Such a complexity must be suitably addressed from the very beginning of the development process. Even though we can distinguish between navigation capabilities and business logic, the user must perceive an integrated solution, where the two components are carefully blended in a homogeneous product.

Pages must be functional to the services offered by the application, but, at the same time, services must be structured such that they can be accessed through the pages. Even though the Web still privileges a user-centred approach to the design of Web applications, the *page-first* approach is not always the right choice.

The design of a complex Web application is, in our view, a software engineering problem. Many traditional methodologies and notations can be used. However, the user interface plays a key role in the overall quality of the application, the architecture is heavily constrained by technology, and the lifetime –at least of the Web interface– is limited.

W2000 [2] is a complete notation for modelling complex Web applications. It borrows concepts from different domains, which are integrated as a homogeneous solution. W2000 originates from HDM (Hypertext Design Model [7]), i.e. from hypermedia and data-centric Web applications, but also borrows principles from UML (Unified Modeling Language [6]) to support the conception of business processes. W2000 allows the designer to model all the aspects of Web applications, from Web pages to business transactions, in a coherent and integrated way. It also adopts a model-driven approach [8] to allow designers to refine their models incrementally and move smoothly from specification to design.

This chapter introduces the main concepts of W2000 through its meta-model. According to the Object Management Group (OMG)[1] definition, the meta-model defines the modelling elements of a notation without concentrating on their concrete syntax. Thus, the meta-model covers both the hierarchical organisation of user specifications and the actual elements that describe Web applications. The explicit availability of the meta-model is important to help designers assess the *consistency* of their models and define automatic transformations between them. All defined models must comply with the constraints set by the meta-model; transformations among models are specified by means of special-purpose rules that work on the meta-objects to create, modify, and delete them. Their purpose is the automated creation of models as well as the derivation of new models from existing ones. These rules, along with the meta-model that enforces consistency, are of key importance in the context of a *family* of applications, where the same core functionality is embedded in a set of similar applications. For example, we can imagine that the adoption of a new device –say, a PDA instead of a traditional PC– requires that the application be reorganised to cope with the specialties of the new channel (i.e. the small screen, in this case).

All these concepts are available through the tool support offered by W2000. Our prototype framework is implemented as a set of add-ons to the Eclipse integrated development environment [4].

The chapter also describes a simple Web-based conference manager to exemplify the main modelling features and discuss the rationale behind them.

The chapter is organised as follows. Section 11.2 introduces the main concepts behind W2000 through its meta-model, discusses the idea of consistent models, and introduces *transformation rules* as a means to support evolution and adaptability. Section 11.3 clarifies the rationale behind

[1] http://www.omg.org/.

W2000, sketches a high-level modelling process, and describes the supporting tools. Section 11.4 exemplifies the modelling features on the models of a simple Web-based conference manager. Section 11.5 concludes the chapter.

11.2 Modelling Elements

The OMG organises models and meta-models around a four-level hierarchy [13]: *objects* (level 0) are instances of elements specified in a *model* (level 1). *Meta-models* (level 2) define the languages used to render the *models* and the *meta-meta-model* (level 3) defines the unique language that must be used to define *meta-models*. OMG proposes MOF (Meta Object Facility [13]) as the unique meta-meta-model and UML classes and objects to render the modelling elements. MOF concepts can be seen as suitable UML classes, objects as UML objects, but the elements that belong to models and meta-models can be seen as both objects and classes. They are objects when we consider them as instances of their higher level concepts, but they become classes when we consider the modelling features they offer. For example, a level 2 element is an object (instance) of a level 3 element, but it is also the class –something that can be instantiated– of level 1 elements; that is, of the models that originate from the meta-model.

In this section, we describe W2000 as a meta-model, and later we demonstrate W2000 level 1 models in Sect. 11.4. Fig. 11.1 shows the hierarchical organisation of W2000 models[2]. All concepts are fully specified with attributes and methods: interested readers can refer to [10] for a detailed description of all W2000 elements; here we only introduce concepts informally.

A *W2000 Model* comprises some *Models*. Each *Model* has a predefined *Package*, which acts as a root for the hierarchy of other *Packages* and *W2000 Elements* that belong to the *Model*. This is implemented through the abstract class *Element* with *Package* and all the *W2000 Elements* as sub-classes. *Elements* belong to the *Package* in which they are defined, but are rendered in *Diagrams*, which could also belong to different *Packages*.

[2] For the sake of simplicity, the meta-models we present slightly simplify some relations and only assume multiplicities 1..*n*.

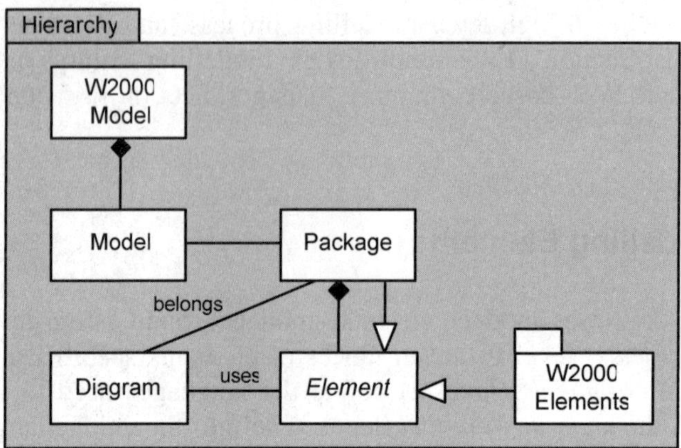

Fig. 11.1. W2000 hierarchy

Figure 11.2 shows the meta-model of package *W2000 Elements* and all the concepts that come from it. Conceptually, the starting point is the package *Information*, whose goals are the identification and organisation of all the data that the application should deal with. The former goal belongs to the package *Hyperbase*, while the latter belongs to the package *Access Structures*.

The package *Hyperbase* identifies the *Entities* that characterise the application. They define conceptual "data" that are of interest for the user. *Components* are then used to structure the *Entities* into meaningful fragments. They can be further decomposed into sub-components, but the actual contents can be associated with leaf nodes only. Since a *Component* is also a *Generalisable Element*, from the package *Common Elements*, it is further decomposed into *Slots* and *Segments*.

Slots identify primitive information elements and are the typed attributes that specify the contents of leaf components. *Segments* define "macros", i.e. sets of slots that can be reused in different elements. Both *Slots* and *Segments* belong to package *Common Elements*.

Semantic Associations identify navigational paths between related concepts. Their sources and targets are *Connectible Elements*, i.e. *Entities*, other *Semantic Associations*, or *Collections*, which are explained later in this section.

An *Association Centre* –subclass of the abstract class *Centre* of the package *Common Elements*– describes the set of "target" elements identified by a *Semantic Association*. In a 1 to *n* association, it defines how to identify either the entire set of targets as a whole or each individual element in the set.

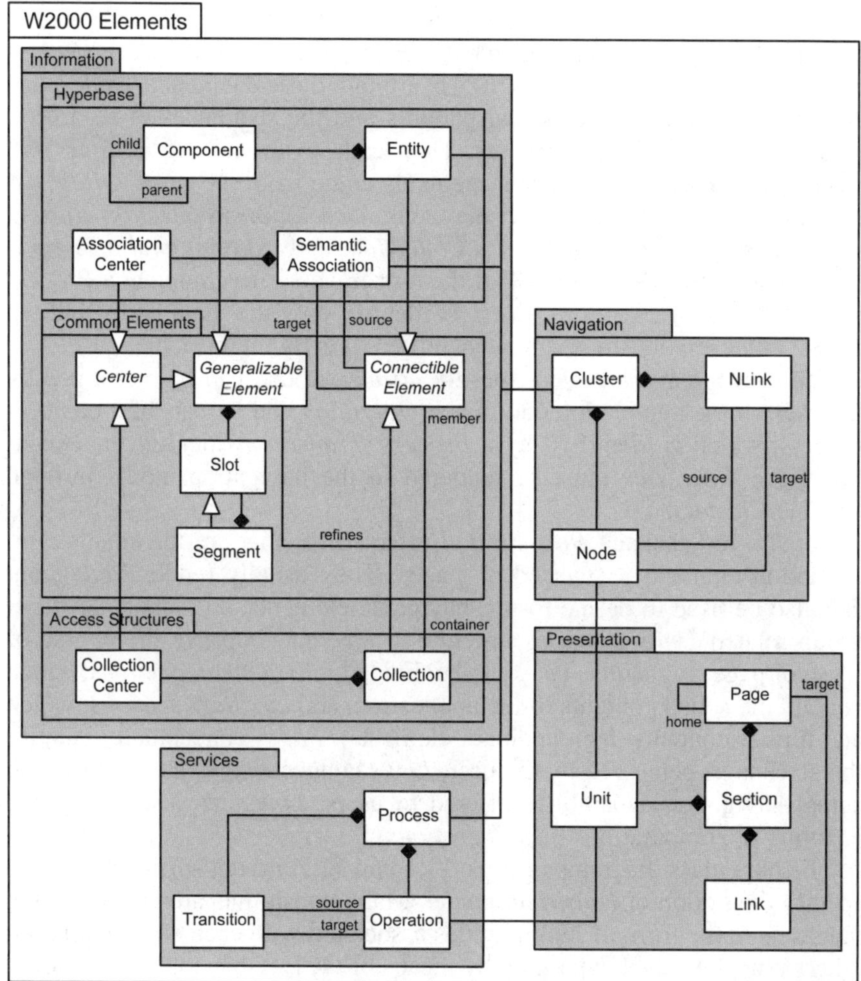

Fig. 11.2. W2000 elements

The package *Access Structures* organises the information defined so far. It specifies the main access points to the application and only comprises *Collections*, which define groups of elements that should be perceived as related by the user. *Collections* organise data in a way that complies with the mental processes of the application domain. Also *Collections* can have special-purpose centres called *Collection Centres*.

When we move to the package *Navigation*, we define how the user can browse through the application. It reshapes the elements in the previous packages to specify the *actual* information elements that can be controlled. *Nodes* are the main modelling elements and define atomic consumption units. Usually, they do not define new contents, but render information already defined by *Generalisable Elements*. *Clusters* link sets of *Nodes* and define how the user can move around these elements. *Nodes* and *NLinks* identify the navigational patterns and the sequences of data traversed while executing *Processes*. This leads to organising *Clusters* in[3]: *structural clusters* if all of their elements come from the same *Entity*; *association clusters* if they render *Semantic Associations*; *collection clusters* if they describe the topology of a *Collection*; and *transactional clusters* if they relate to the set of nodes that the user traverses to complete a *Process* (i.e. a business transaction). *Clusters* identify only the main paths through nodes; other relationships can be identified directly on the actual pages.

The package *Services* describes the *Processes* that can be performed by the user on the application data. Each *Operation* can be part of a business process, which is identified by a *Process*. *Transitions* identify the execution flow. *Processes* must be rendered in the navigation model through suitable *Clusters*.

Finally, the package *Presentation* offers *Units* that are the smallest information elements visualised on pages. They usually render *Nodes*, but can also be used to define forms, navigable elements, and labels. *Sections* group related *Units* to better structure a page and improve the degree of reuse of page fragments. They can be divided into *contents sections*, which contain the actual contents of the application, and *auxiliary sections*, which add further contents (e.g. landmark elements). *Pages* conceptually identify the screens as perceived by the user. *Links* connect *Pages* and identify the actual navigation capabilities offered to users. *Links* can also "hide" the enabling of computations (i.e. *Operations*).

The pure class diagrams of Figs. 11.1 and 11.2 are not sufficient to fully specify the notion of *consistent model*. Many constraints are already in the diagrams in the form of multiplicities associated with each association, but others must be stated externally by means of OCL (Object Constraint Language [6]) assertions. Among these, we can identify *topological constraints*, which must always hold true and complement those already embedded in the class diagram, and *special-purpose constraints*, which impose specific restrictions on the notation and identify a new dialect.

If we consider the first set, one of the obvious constraints is that each element must be unique in its scope. For example, the following OCL invariant:

```
Context Entity
   inv: allInstances -> forAll(e1, e2 |
            e1.Name = e2.Name implies e1 = e2)
```

---

[3] This specialisation is not rendered with sub-classes, but is specified using a simple flag associated with class *Cluster*.

requires that *Entity* names be unique in a model. If two *Entities* have the same name, they are the same *Entity*. An invariant is defined using *inv*, a property that must always be satisfied for all the objects of the class (*Entity*, in this case). Similarly, we have defined invariants for all other W2000 elements.

Special-purpose constraints characterise particular instantiations of W2000. For example, in a simplified version of W2000 for small devices, we could impose that each *Page* renders exactly one *Section*. This condition can be easily stated as an invariant associated with class *Page*:

```
Context Page
   inv: sections->size = 1
```

In this case, we use the name *sections* to refer to the aggregation between *Page* and *Section* of Fig. 11.2.

The distinction between topology and special-purpose constraints allows us to better tune the *consistency* of models. Several dialects can share the same meta-model in terms of the topology of the class diagram, and also some other OCL constraints, but they are characterised by special-purpose restrictions.

The meta-model, along with its constraints, supplies the means to assess the consistency of designed models. We can cross-check every model against its definition (the meta-model) and see if the first is a proper instance of the second. The meta-model is necessary to pave the way to *coherence* and *adaptability*.

11.3 Models

W2000 fosters *separation of concerns* and adopts a *model–view–control* approach. A complete W2000 model is organised in four models: information, navigation, services, and presentation. *Information* defines the data used by the application and perceived by the user. *Navigation* and *Services* specify the control; that is, how the user can navigate through information chunks and modify them through suitable business processes. *Presentation* states how data and services are presented to the user; that is, it specifies pages and activation points for business services.

The same language can be used to specify each model at two different abstraction levels. We use the term *in-the-large* when we refer to general aspects, which are only sketched and in many cases are placeholders to structure the whole application. We use the term *in-the-small* when we fully specify all designed concepts.

Conceptually, a number of models can be designed in parallel, and –as often happens– designers are required to rework the same artefacts several times to accommodate the design decisions made while developing the application to enforce consistency between the different parts. We propose an iterative approach organised around the following steps:

- *Requirements analysis*, which is not addressed in this chapter, extends "conventional" requirements analysis to Web-based applications. It must cover the analysis of both navigational and functional requirements, which are complementary and intertwined. The analysis of navigational requirements has the goal of highlighting the main information and navigation structures needed by the different users of the application. The analysis of the functional requirements concentrates on the identification of the business processes, as perceived by the different classes of users.
- *Hypermedia design* starts with drafting the information, navigation, and presentation models. These *in-the-large* models embed a preliminary design of the Web application that is very close to the requirements and is mainly intended to focus on the essential properties of the Web application. Following a conventional *model-driven* approach [8], hypermedia models are refined to introduce all the details that must be set before implementing the application. This step produces the *in-the-small* version of addressed models and requires more precision and completeness.
- *Service design* runs in parallel with *Hypermedia design* and specifies the main business transactions supported by the application. It extends the standard specification of the procedural capabilities of a given application by adopting a user-oriented view and by blending the business logic with the user experience offered by the hypermedia parts of the application.
- *Customisation activities*, if needed, define those features that need to be specialised, their special-purpose contexts, and also the strategies to move from the initial models to their customised versions.

Not all of the steps must be necessarily executed for all applications. For instance, if we think of simple Web applications, we can easily concentrate on the presentation model and skip all the others. The set of design activities only define a homogeneous framework that must be suitably adapted to the different situations.

Customisation activities, which are orthogonal to the main modelling activities, let the designer define which application features –content, navigation, presentation, and services– need to be specialised with respect to the context. *Context* here comprises all the aspects that concern the situation of use: device characteristics (i.e., traditional browser, PDA, or mobile phone), user preferences, etc. This activity results in special-purpose models, which can be generated automatically by means of transformation rules or can be defined manually according to particular design decisions.

The problem of customising the design to the requirements of a particular context can be addressed in different ways:

- If customisation starts while designing the information model, the designer produces an information model for each context, that is, for specifying the content structures that are specific to each context. Thus special-purpose navigation and presentation models can be derived incrementally.
- If customisation is postponed to navigation, the designer specifies a single information model, which defines all possible content structures. It is while working on navigation aspects that this information is filtered and restructured according to the need of every specific context. The result is a set of context-specific navigation models coupled with the corresponding presentation models.
- If customisation only addresses presentation, the designer produces a single information model and a single navigation model, but multiple presentation models. The specification of context-specific contents and links is only constrained in the presentation structures.

Customisation also affects the design of services. Different contexts– and thus different navigation and presentation models– may impose particular services and specific ways to interact with the user.

11.3.1 Adaptability

Given the organisation of W2000 models, where *Navigation* and *Services* are built on top of *Information*, and *Presentation* exploits the two previous models, we can identify two kinds of relationships between models:

- *Horizontal relationships* support customisation and relate different versions of the same model. For example, the *Presentation* for a PC-based application and that for a PDA-based system define a horizontal relationship.
- *Vertical relationships* relate two models in the hierarchy. For example, the *Information* and *Navigation* for a PC-based application define a vertical relationship.

Both relationships can be implemented by means of *transformation rules* that work on instances of the meta-model. They add model elements automatically. More generally, all modelling activities that are intrinsically automatic can be rendered through rules. They help the designer save time and produce correct models. For example, rules could add a component to each entity, a node for each component, and a cluster for each entity, association, and collection in the model.

Transformation rules help customise and adapt (parts of) models. Adaptation can be required by new requirements or the need for delivering a new member of the family by modifying some model elements with well-known patterns. For example, we can support a new device by reshaping navigation and presentation models. Transformation rules also enforce the use of modelling patterns. Instead of relying on the ability of designers to embed significant patterns in their models, rules offer a ready-to-use means to exploit them.

Finally, transformation rules can convert models, specified using a given W2000 dialect, into models that comply with another dialect. This is important because we want to stress the *interchangeability* among W2000 dialects and the fact that special-purpose applications (e.g. for particular devices or with specific restrictions on accessibility) could motivate ad-hoc dialects.

Even if users exploit these rules, they are free to modify their artefacts by hand to change and complete them. As already stated, we want to make the modelling phase easier and not completely substitute design intuitions with machine-based rules. This is also supported by the idea that the approach can be adopted in different ways. At one end, it can be used to define a first framework for the application and leave plenty of room to the designer to complete it. At the other end, it could offer a complete library of rules to produce the application almost automatically. In either case, the meta-model oversees the correctness of produced models.

Given the meta-model presented in Fig. 11.2, we can design several different rules. A rule is a standard graph transformation production rendered here by using a pair of UML object diagrams: The left-hand side describes the configuration (sub-graph) that must exist to apply the rule; the right-hand side describes how the sub-graph is modified by applying the rule. In other words, the former is the pre-condition and the latter is the post-condition associated with the rule. The meta-model supplies the *type graph* on which rules can predicate.

Here, we introduce rules informally and with the aid of an example. For the sake of understandability, they do not deal with the structure (*Models* and *Packages*), but we assume a simple flat organisation. If we added hierarchy, concepts would be the same, but the rule would become more complex and less readable.

The rule[4] of Fig. 11.3 is a typical example of a vertical relationship. It helps define the *Navigation model* by “refining” the components of the *Information model*. It adds a new *Node* element that corresponds to a leaf *Component* and the new *Node* inherits all the *Slots* that define the *Component*. Notice that since the cardinality of the set of *Slots* that belong to the *Component* can vary, we use the UML *multiobject* to identify a variable collection of objects.

```
1.leaf == true
```

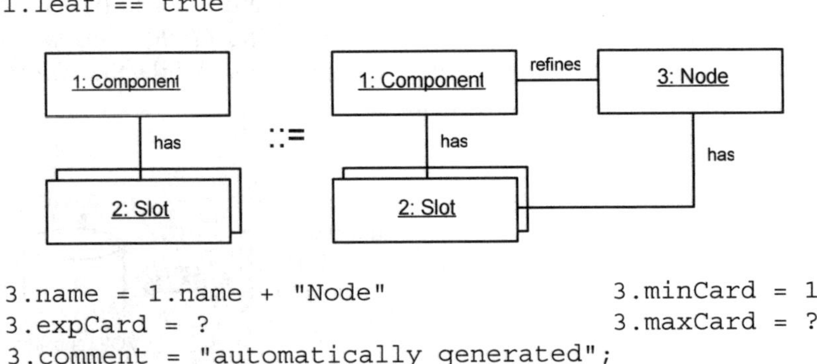

Fig. 11.3. Rule to create a new *Node* in the *Navigation* model given a leaf *Component* in the *Information* model (vertical refinement)

The rule comprises two object diagrams and two text blocks. The expression before the diagrams defines constraints on the attribute values of the left-hand side elements to enable the rule. The block after the diagrams defines how to set the attributes of the right-hand side elements. In this case, the rule imposes that the *Component* be a leaf one and shows that the *name* of the new *Node* is the name of the *Component* augmented with suffix *Node*. *minCard* is equal to one, *expCard* and *maxCard* are left unspecified, and *comment* says that the *Node* is *generated automatically*.

This rule allows designers to apply it to as many leaf *Components* as they want. A slightly more complex rule could enforce the iteration on all leaf *Components* that belong to the model. This modification implies the capability of programming the application of a rule a number of times that cannot be fixed statically. This is beyond the scope of this section, but interested readers can refer to [1] for a more detailed presentation of *transformation rules* and their applicability.

---

[4] As general solution, compositions (black diamonds) of Fig. 11.2 are rendered with *has* labels in the rules.

11.3.2 Tool Support

W2000 is supported by an innovative modelling toolset. According to the architecture in Fig. 11.4, the user interacts with the toolset using the *Editor*, which is a W2000-specific graphical editor, implemented as an add-in to *Eclipse* [4]. A first prototype of this component is available.

Designed models are stored in an *MOF repository*, implemented with *MDR/netbeans* [12]. Topological constraints are embedded directly in the meta-model, while special-purpose constraints are checked by an external *Constraints validator* based on *xlinkit* [11]. The *MOF repository* is released and works in conjunction with the *Editor*, while the *Constraints validator* is still under development.

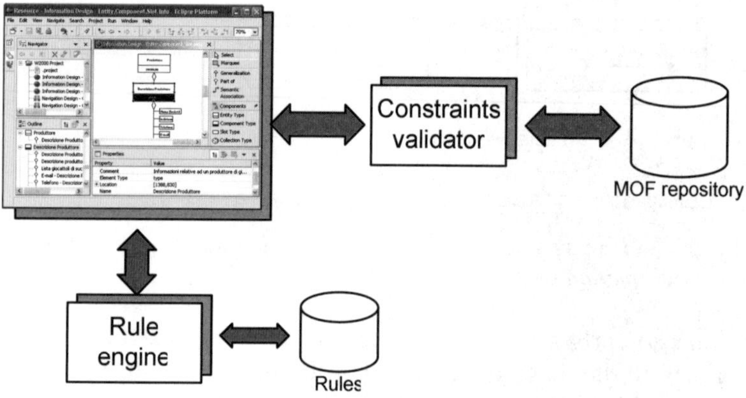

Fig. 11.4. High-level architecture of the tool support

Both the *Editor* and the *MOF repository* support XMI (XML Metadata Interchange [13]) as XML-based neutral format for exchanging artefacts and fostering the integration with other components (for example, automatic generators of code and documentation).

The *Rule Engine* is based on *AGG* (Attributed Graph Grammar System [5]). It applies transformation rules on the instances of the meta-model. This is not yet fully integrated with the *Editor*, but we have already conducted experiments with some rules.

11.4 Example Application

This section explains and exemplifies the main modelling features of W2000 through a simple *Web conference manager*, an application that helps chairs run the organisation and bureaucracy associated with running a conference.

Briefly, a Web-based conference management system guides the different classes of users involved in a conference to accomplish their tasks. This means that it must support authors while submitting papers, guide programme committee members while reviewing papers, and help the general (programme) chair select papers and set up a programme. Involved roles impose constraints on the way they can use the application. Generic users should only be allowed to browse through the public pages that advertise the conference and contain the "usual" information associated with a conference. These users should not be allowed to browse submitted papers and reviews. Authors should be able to access the information about their papers, but not that of other papers nor the information about the reviewing process. Programme Committee members (PC members) should see all papers and optionally reviews, except those for which they have declared conflicts of interest. The chair must be able to have full access to the application. After accepting papers, the application should notify all the authors, asking authors of accepted papers for the camera-ready version of their submissions.

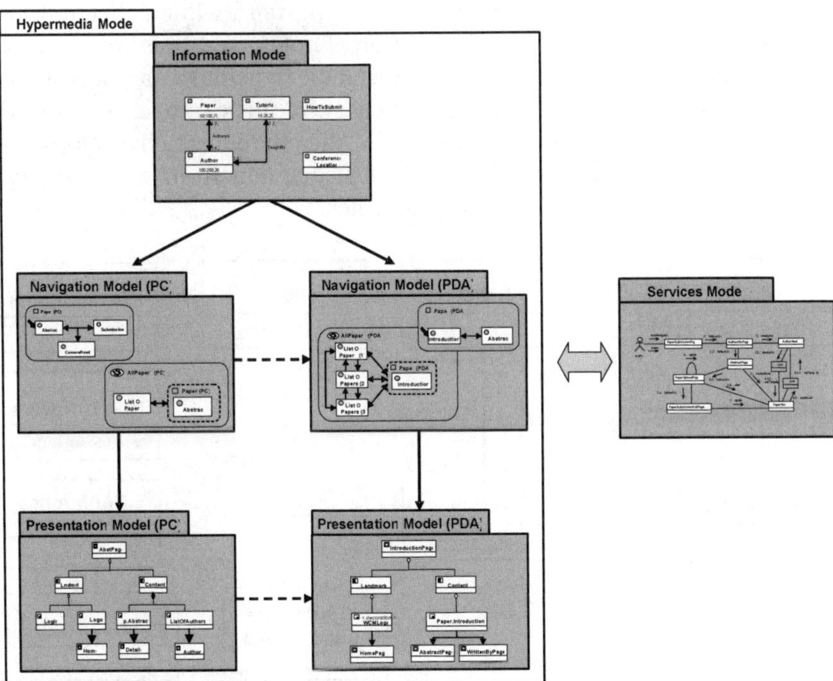

Fig. 11.5. Hierarchical organisation of the application models (generic user)

Another important requirement is that users can access the application through different devices: for example, they can use conventional PCs or more advanced PDAs. Devices and user profiles add interesting modelling dimensions: this means special-purpose models in W2000. For example, Fig. 11.5 shows the organisation of the models of the Web conference system for the generic user. In this case, we assume a single information model, and we distinguish between navigation and presentation models for PCs and those for PDAs. We do not detail the service model to keep the figure simple; we will discuss it in Sect. 11.4.4.

11.4.1 Information Model

The information model comprises the identification of the contents of the application and its high-level structures. It describes the macro-categories of information objects (*entities* according to the W2000 jargon) needed by the different users, the relationships between them (*semantic associations*), and the main ways they can be grouped (*collections*). Entities and semantic associations are described using *hyperbase diagrams*, while collections are described in *access diagrams*. The different roles, and thus the need for adapting the design artefacts, impose different hyperbase and access diagrams for each context (i.e. role in this case). In this example, we start by concentrating on the hyperbase diagram of the conference chair (shown in Fig. 11.6). This diagram is also the global diagram from which we can derive the diagrams specific to the other roles.

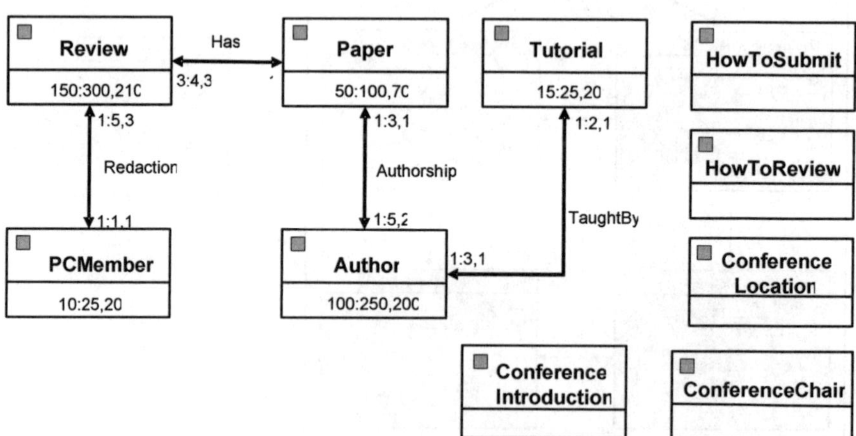

Fig. 11.6. Global hyperbase diagram (*in-the-large* view)

Paper, *Author*, *Tutorial*, *PCMember*, and *Review* are the entities for which we assume the existence of several instances. This is why each name is followed by the minimum, maximum, and average number of instances. These figures can only be estimated at this stage, but it is important to start thinking of the expected number of elements both to design the database and to work on the navigation and presentation.

In contrast, *ConferenceIntroduction*, *ConferenceLocation*, *HowToSubmit*, *HowToReview*, and *ConferenceChair* are entities for which we imagine a single instance; that is, they are singletons in the information space and thus do not need any cardinality. The diagram is completed by the semantic associations that link the different entities. The absence of connections among these entities means that we do not foresee any semantic relation between them. They will be related to the other elements by means of suitable links while modelling navigation and presentation.

The common hyperbase diagram is the starting point to define the customised versions of the particular roles. The generic user, for example, can only browse the public information about the conference, i.e. entities *ConferenceLocation*, *ConferenceIntroduction*, *ConferenceChair*, and *HowToSubmit*, and also the instances of the entities *Paper*, *Tutorial*, and *Author* as soon as they become available (i.e. the review process is over and final decisions are taken). Information about *PCMembers* and *Reviews* will never be available to this class of users.

Figure 11.7 presents the hyperbase diagram from the viewpoint of the generic user: the entities and semantic associations that cannot be "seen" by these users are deleted from the diagram.

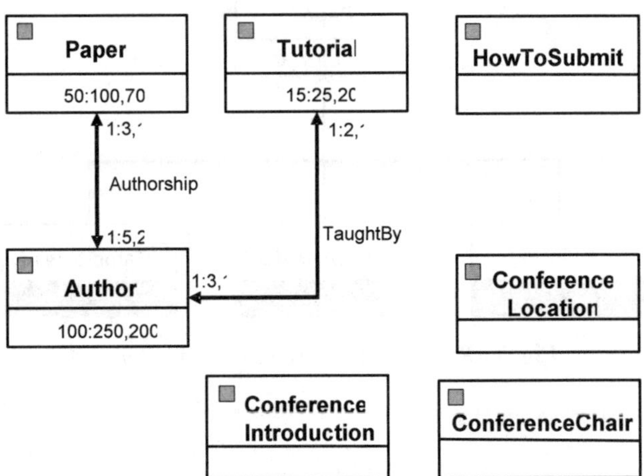

Fig. 11.7. Hyperbase diagram (in-the-large) for generic users

This is a case of simple derivation, where the hyperbase diagram of Fig. 11.6 acts as a starting point for all the other specialisations. In other cases, the starting point can be a particular view of the system and thus the other views do not only filter the contents of the starting diagram, but add special-purpose elements.

Each entity, represented in the hyperbase diagrams, needs to be structured in terms of components to organise its content into meaningful parts. For example, Fig. 11.8 the presents entity *Paper* and its three components: *Abstract*, *Submission*, and *CameraReady*. Cardinalities prescribe the minimum, maximum, and average number of components of the same type associated with a single instance of the root entity. This does not mean that the three components must be defined simultaneously and are available to all users, but Fig. 11.8 only specifies the structure of all *Paper* entities. Cardinalities say that all papers must have an *Abstract* and a first *Submission*, but only accepted papers have also a *CameraReady* (this is why its minimum cardinality is equal to zero).

The definition of collections leads to *access diagrams*. A collection represents a container of entities or other collections. These elements, called *collection members*, can be selected and organised according to different criteria. Given the roles of our conference manager, we need special-purpose collections for each role. For example, generic users might be interested in skimming through all accepted papers, or all the papers by a given author, while PC members may be interested in navigating through the papers they are supposed to review.

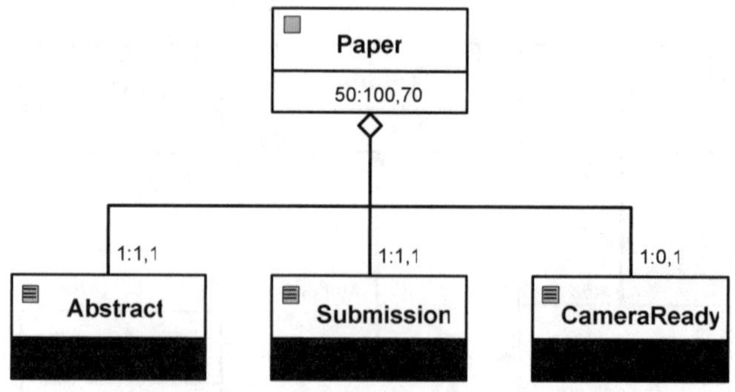

Fig. 11.8. Component tree for entity *Paper*

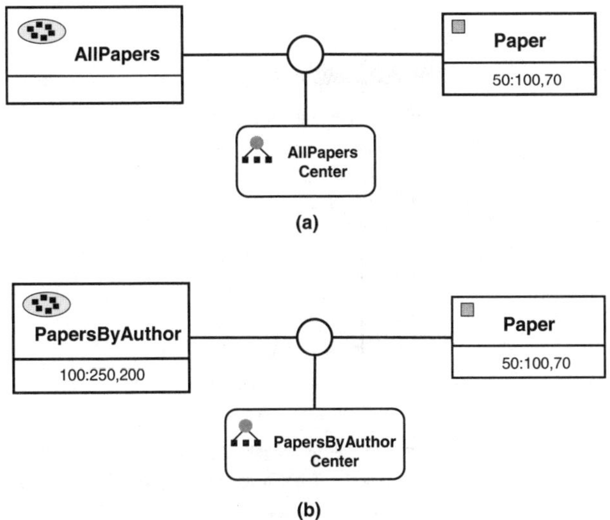

Fig. 11.9. Collections *AllPapers* (a) and *PapersByAuthor* (b)

Collections can be shared among roles: for example, all users perceive the same collection *AllPapers* (Fig. 11.9(a)). Given the *user perspective* adopted by W2000, we can foresee collections like *AllPapers*, which are instanced once for the whole application, collections like *PapersToReview*, which are instantiated once for each PC member (or, more generally, for each user), and collections like *PapersByAuthor* (Fig. 11.9(b)), which can be instantiated several times for the same user since he/she can ask for the papers of different authors, and thus create new instances of the same collection.

Hyperbase and *access diagrams* can be refined to specify the slots associated with the various information structures. This *in-the-small* activity completes the definition of the elements identified so far. Slots can be either atomic or structured, but W2000 does not provide any built-in library of slot types. Designers are free to define their own sets of types. As an example, Fig. 11.10 shows the slots of *Abstract* components. Types are defined only informally, but we need to distinguish among: slots like *number* or *title* whose type is primitive; slots like *mainTopic* or *submissionCategory*, which are strings of a given length; and slot *author*, which is compound and whose structure is represented by the sub-tree drawn below the slot name. Cardinalities have the usual meaning of setting the minimum, maximum, and expected number of elements. In this case, each *Paper* must have at least one *author*, no more than five authors, and we estimate an average number of three authors.

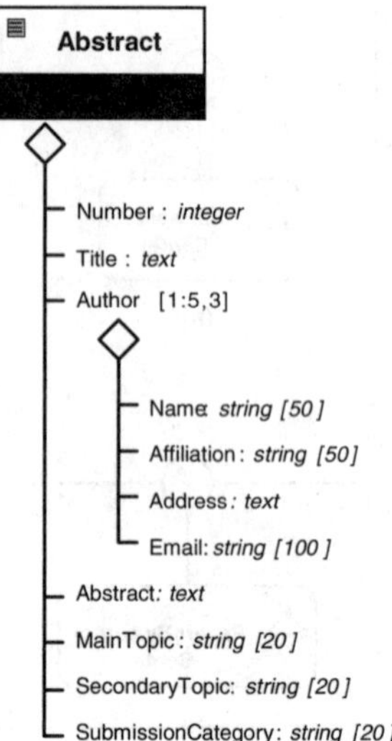

Fig. 11.10. Slots for component *Abstract*

Slots and operations define the actual structure of components and entities, but also specify the centres of semantic associations and collections. Centres are information structures that users exploit for navigating the associations or collections of interest. They contain the slots that describe the members of the association (or collection). These slots are partially borrowed from the members and can also be introduced explicitly to characterise the container (either an association or a collection). The centres of semantic associations also identify the directions through which the associations can be navigated: bi-directional associations imply two different centres. If we consider association *Authorship* of Fig. 11.6, which is fully detailed in Fig. 11.11, we can use centres *HasWritten* and *WrittenBy* to allow the information flow from *Author* to *Paper* and the other way around.

The last elements that the designer must specify are the segments. They are introduced to make the design more efficient and maintainable, by improving the reuse of definitions. A segment groups a set of related slots and makes them become a single element that can be reused as such in different parts of the model. Using a segment corresponds to using the entire group of slots associated with it. For example, we can define the segment *PaperShortIdentification* as the union of the slots *Title*, *Author.Name*,[5] and *MainTopic* of entity *Paper*. This segment can then be used to characterise centre *HasWritten*, but also collections *AllPapers*, *PapersByAuthor*, or *PapersToReview*: they all need a short description of the papers they contain.

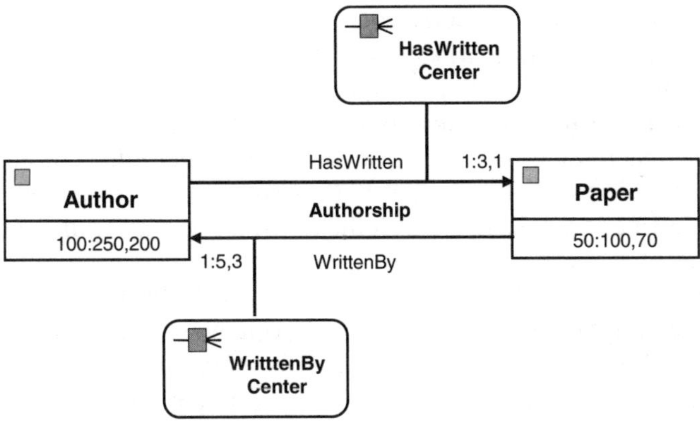

Fig. 11.11. Semantic association *Authorship*

11.4.2 Navigation Model

After the information model, we need to define how the contents are organised for fruition. By means of a navigation model, designers specify the navigation structures that describe how the user navigates the contents by exploiting the relevant relationships defined in the information model. Semantic associations and collections are the starting points to implement the hypertext that specifies how the user can navigate the application. W2000 introduces the concepts of node and navigation cluster. A node corresponds to the elementary granule of information from/to which the user can navigate. It is an aggregate of contents meaningful to the user in a given situation and that cannot be broken into smaller pieces. Instead, a cluster represents a cognitively well-defined interaction context; it is a container that groups a set of closely related nodes. A cluster aggregates the nodes that come from an entity (structural cluster), a semantic association (association cluster), a collection (collection cluster), or a process (process cluster). The overall navigation across the application is determined by shared nodes that belong to different clusters.

Navigation in-the-large means identifying which clusters are derived from the information structures and which nodes belong to each cluster. Structural clusters require that the designers identify the first node, i.e the node to which users should be moved if they are interested in the entity rendered by the cluster. Designers must also define the connections among nodes, to state how users can move from one node to the others, and the content of each node as a list of slots or segments. The navigation among nodes can be expressed by using navigation patterns (e.g. index or guided tour). This in-the-small activity completes the navigation model.

Clusters,[5] and nodes are derived from the information model through a set of rules and design heuristics. For example, in the simplest case, we could imagine that each entity motivates a structural cluster, whose nodes correspond to the leaf components of the entity (Fig. 11.12(a)). We also assume that each node is reachable from all the other nodes in the cluster. However, this hypothesis does not hold if we need to reorganise the contents with a finer granularity. Given the information model of Sect. 11.4.1, we can say that the rule that associates a cluster with each entity works well if the user uses a PC-based Web browser. If the user moves to a PDA, the designer might prefer to split the information about papers into two nodes (Fig. 11.12(b)): node *Introduction* contains information about the author and the main topics of the paper and node *Abstract* contains the abstract of the paper.

To derive association clusters from semantic associations, we can say that the user can navigate from each node of the source structural cluster (i.e. the source entity of the association) to a centre node, derived from the association centre, and then, after selecting an item, to the default node of the target structural cluster. Figure 11.13 exemplifies this solution on the semantic association *WrittenBy*: the user can navigate from each node of cluster *Paper* to node *ListOfAuthors* and, after selecting an author, to node *ShortDescription* of cluster *Author*. The dashed rectangles correspond to already defined clusters with which cluster *WrittenBy* is linked.

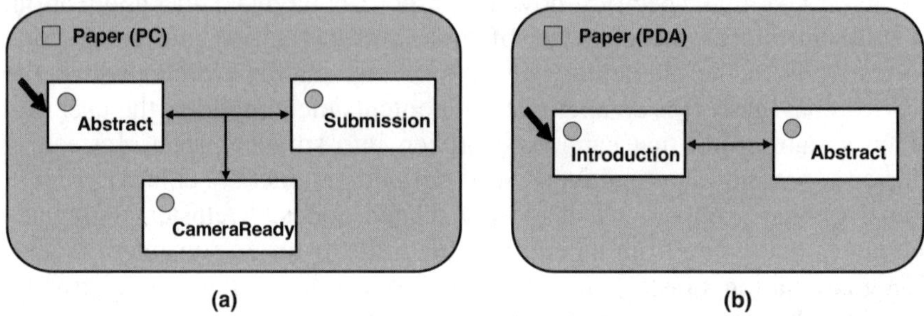

Fig. 11.12. Structural cluster *Paper*

We need also to specify how the user can navigate the nodes of collection clusters. For example, Fig. 11.14 shows the case of collection *AllPapers*. Figure 11.14(a) shows the collection cluster designed with the hypothesis that the user accesses the application through a PC-based Web browser, while Fig. 11.14(b) shows the same collection cluster modelled for PDAs. In the first case, users can navigate from node *ListOfPapers*,

[5] Notice that the different cluster types use special-purpose symbols in the upper left corner of the rectangle.

derived from the collection centre, to node *Abstract* of the selected paper and back. In the second case, the collection centre is rendered with three nodes (i.e. the list of papers is split in the three nodes) and users can navigate from each node to the next/previous node or they can navigate to node *Introduction* of the selected paper.

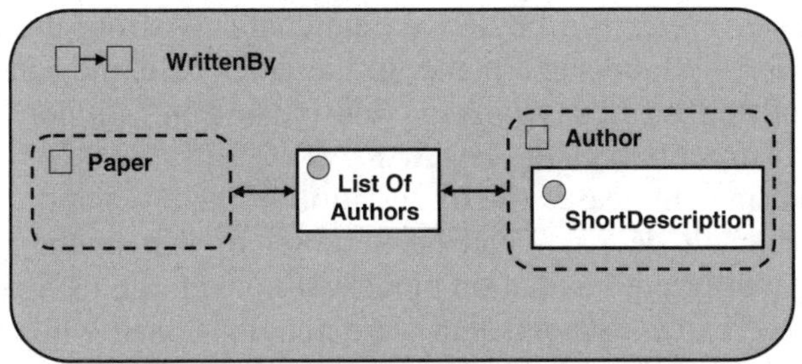

Fig. 11.13. Association cluster *WrittenBy*

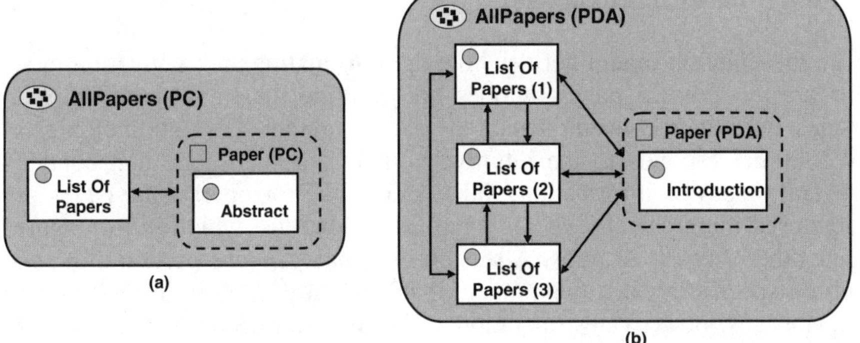

Fig. 11.14. Collection cluster *AllPapers*

Finally, to define the navigation steps implied by business processes, we need to introduce process clusters, which are the bridge between the hypertext and operations and organise the nodes involved in the execution of a process. Nodes can come from the information model, and be already used in other clusters (since they are part of the hypertext behind the application), or they can be added explicitly to define information units that are needed to complete the process (i.e. forms that collect the actual parameters of a computation before sending them to the system).

Process clusters describe the information units touched by the user during the execution of a process, along with the navigation steps. In this case, navigation links must also consider anomalous or error conditions: for example, what happens if the user wants to log into the application, but the username is wrong, or what happens if one of the actual parameters supplied to the operation is incorrect?

To complete the *in-the-small* view of the navigation model, the designer must specify the slots associated with each node. We can imagine a straightforward derivation from the information model, but also something more articulated. In the former case, for example, the slots of node *Abstract* of cluster *Paper* can be derived automatically from the component of entity *Paper* with the same name. In the latter case, the same slots can be accommodated on nodes *Introduction* (slots *Title*, *Author*, and *MainTopic*) and *Abstract* (slots *Title* and *Abstract*).

Notice that in some cases the information in the navigation model –for example, for small devices– can be a subset of that in the information model, or in a different navigation model. Moreover, the navigation model may introduce "extra" contents that were not envisioned while conceiving the information model.

11.4.3 Presentation Model

The presentation model defines how the information and navigation models are rendered in pages. It does not describe the final layout of Web pages, but it only concentrates on the pages' content. The notion of page in W2000 corresponds to the intuitive notion of a Web page that contains several pieces of information, links, and hooks for operations. Pages are organised hierarchically as aggregations of sections, which in turn aggregate other sections or units. A section is a *homogeneous* portion of a page with a specific goal: it contains a set of related data, coordinates links to other pages, or activates operations. The different sections of a page are often completely unrelated.

The units are the smallest elements that we identify in a page. *Content units* deliver the application contents and are basically nodes of the navigation model. The content units of a section correspond to nodes of the same cluster. *Decorator units* deliver new contents: they embed layout content defined for pure aesthetic/communication reasons. *Interaction units* are pure interaction placeholders: they are graphical elements that embed links to other pages or the capabilities of triggering operations.

The presentation model contains the set of pages that constitute the user experience supplied by the application. Pages usually come from the structures defined in the navigation model. The *in-the-large* design ends with the identification of the sections that belong to each page. The *in-the-small* refinement adds the publishing units to the sections previously identified. The designer must also include those pages that support the execution flow of operations and processes. Usually, the designer is not able to identify all these pages without concentrating on the single business processes. This is why the actual process can be summarised as follows:

- The designer specifies the interaction units to interact with operations and processes while conceiving the presentation model.
- The designer defines the details of operations and processes in the service model, where he/she specifies the execution flow of each process and intertwines operations and pages. These pages can be defined in the presentation model, but can also be new since the are not foreseen. If these pages only contain the interaction units that govern operations, the designer must rework just the presentation model.
- The designer can also rework the navigation model, to add new nodes or process clusters, if the design of the different processes highlights holes in the blending between navigation and operations. These changes must then be transferred to the presentation model.

Moving to the example application, the structural cluster *Paper* could motivate three pages if we consider a conventional browser (*AbstractPage*, *CameraReadyPage*, and *SubmissionPage*) and two pages for a PDA version (*IntroductionPage* and *AbstractPage*). The designer should also decide to structure each page in two sections: section *Landmark*, which allows the user to trigger operations and contains some links to other relevant sections of the application; and section *Content*, which conveys the actual information about the paper. Figure 11.15 shows the *in-the-small* definition of page *AbstractPage*: section *Landmark* contains an interaction unit, which allows users to log into the application, and a decorator unit, which contains the

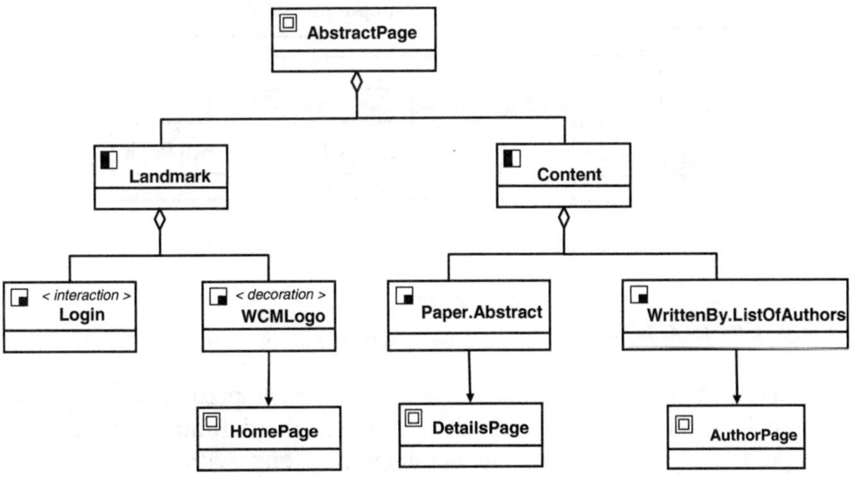

Fig. 11.15. Page *Abstract* (PC version)

conference logo and allows users to navigate to the *HomePage*. Section *Content*, on the other hand, embeds the content unit *Paper.Abstract* (derived from node *Abstract* of cluster *Paper*) and the content *WrittenBy.ListOfAuthors* (derived from node *ListOfAuthors* of association centre *WrittenBy*).

In contrast, Fig. 11.16 represents the *in-the-small* specification of the *IntroductionPage* of the presentation model for the PDA version of the application. Although it contains the two sections *Landmark* and *Content*, the first section only embeds a decorator unit with the conference logo, while the content section only has the content unit *Paper.Introduction* (derived from node *Introduction* of cluster *Paper*). This is the starting point to let the user navigate to page *AbstractPage* or to page *WrittenByPage* with the list of the authors of the paper. The restricted display dimensions require that the list of authors be displayed in another page: this is different from the PC-based version.

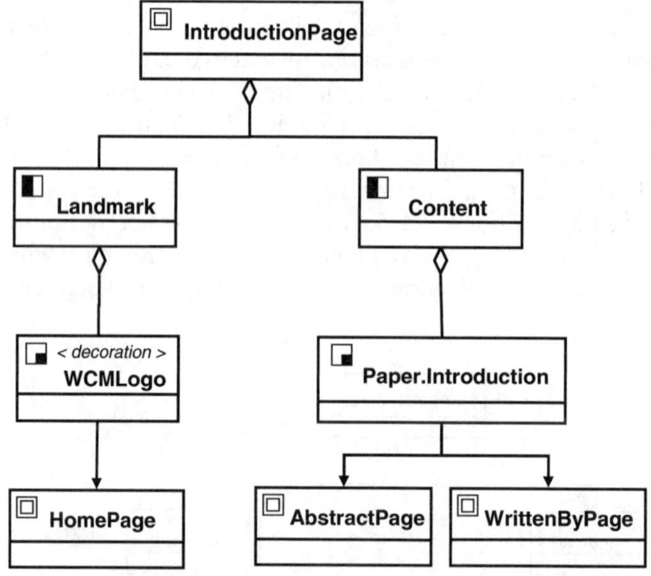

Fig. 11.16. Page *Introduction* (PDA version)

11.4.4 Service Model

The service model complements and extends the hypermedia part of the Web application. The service model comprises the definition of the business processes supplied by the application, along with the operations needed to implement them.

W2000 identifies a preliminary taxonomy for Web operations [2] and the requirements that they induce. Web operations can allow users to:

- *Select the actual parameters to complete an operation.* In many cases, while users browse the information repository, they also collect the data that will become the actual parameters of their operations. For example, when they select a book they want to buy, they identify it as the parameter of the *buy* operation. Even if users perceive they are navigating, they change the way the available information is organised (according to the W2000 jargon, they change the collections defined for the application). This may also lead to changing the state of the pointed element (e.g. the application immediately decrements the number of available copies of the selected book) and the way users can navigate through the application (e.g. the application forbids users from navigating through the pages of unavailable books).
- *Change the way users can navigate through pages.* Even if operations do not change the application contents, they can guide the user while navigating through the pages. Specific choices could allow some links, but disallow others. For example, the operation could change the order used to present the elements of a collection: books could be presented by title or by author. In this case, we would not change the elements in the collection, but simply the links among them.
- *Enter new data in the system.* For example, all pages that embed forms implicitly provide these operations. However, this means that if we have forms, the application data are augmented and changed. It could be the case also that not all the inserted data become "navigable", i.e. they are not rendered in Web pages. In many cases, when we supply a system with our personal data to register ourselves, we cannot browse them.
- *Perform complex state-aware computations.* For example, consider applications that log their users and adjust what they can do with respect to what they have already done. Otherwise, we can mention those applications that embed a high degree of computation, such as billing or special-purpose applications. These operations must store the state of the computation for the particular user, but they can also compute complex algorithmic tasks that could hardly be carried out on a DBMS.

Besides these services, we can also think of other operations that we do not want to consider now. The first group can be seen as fake navigation: for example, when users graphically reshape the elements they are browsing. The second group comprises all those operations that we could term as *advanced*; that is, those that deal with customising the application with respect to specific contexts [9]: devices, user profiles, quality of service, etc. Finally, we should model the fact that sets of operations should be considered *logical transactions*.

W2000 supports Web operations with two different types of services: *simple operations*, which are atomic (with respect to their execution) computational steps that can be invoked by the user; and *processes*, which are not atomic, and can be seen as business transactions. Simple operations are triggered by the user through the interactive units added to pages. The designer can only control a page's output and use it to decide upon the next steps in terms of presentation and navigation flows. Processes require a finer-grained interaction: they are usually composed of simple operations, but their workflow must be suitably supported by navigation and pages. We use pre- and post-conditions, to specify simple operations, and collaboration and activity diagrams, to model processes.

The complete presentation of the extensions to UML diagrams and of the language we use for pre- and post-conditions is beyond the scope of this chapter. Here we concentrate on the example application to describe the main concepts. The conference manager supplies, among others, the following services:

- *registration* is an operation that allows generic users to register to the conference. After registering, users become authors and can submit papers.
- *login* is a single operation that allows generic users to log into the application. The actual pages and services that they can access depend on their roles and the devices they use.
- *submitPaper* is an operation that allows authors to submit their papers.
- *reviewPaper* is a process that allows PC members to submit their paper reviews.
- *assignPaper* is an operation that allows the conference chair to assign papers to PC members.
- *defineFinalProgram* is a process that allows the conference chair to define the final programme of the conference.

Operations are specified using an OCL-like assertion language, extended with special-purpose keywords. Figure 11.17 presents a possible definition for operation *submitPaper*, as if it were a single operation.

```
context: submitPaper(a: Author, p: Paper)
pre:     registeredAuthors->exists(ra | ra = a) AND
         currentPage = "PaperSubmissionPage";
post:    submittedPapers += p AND
         p.links->exists(l | l.target = a) AND
         a.links->exists(l | l.target = p)
```

Fig. 11.17. Operation *submitPaper*

This contract states that the operation can be invoked if the author is registered and is browsing page *PaperSubmissionPage*. The post-condition states that the paper p is added to the collection of *submittedPapers* and suitable links are added to connect the newly added paper with the author that submitted it. Notice that the capability of adding the paper to the proper collection also means the creation of the new components that characterise the entity.

Processes are suitable aggregations of operations and must be described either through activity diagrams or through collaboration diagrams. In the former case, the designer wants to concentrate on the execution flow of the process and does not consider the right sequence of clusters and pages. There must be a consistent process cluster that specifies how the execution flow described by the activity diagram is supported in terms of nodes (and thus pages). In the latter case, the designer uses a collaboration diagram to show the execution flow in terms of the single operations that are triggered on the particular interaction units, the way the user can navigate the different pages to reach the units of interest, and the elements that are created while executing the operations.

For example, if we consider process *reviewPaper* (see Fig. 11.18), we can describe it as a sequence of three operations: *selectPaper*, *downloadPaper*, and *submitReview*, but we allow the PC member to leave the process after downloading the paper, or to submit the review directly after identifying the paper. This description must be suitably paired with a process cluster that describes the navigation behind the process.

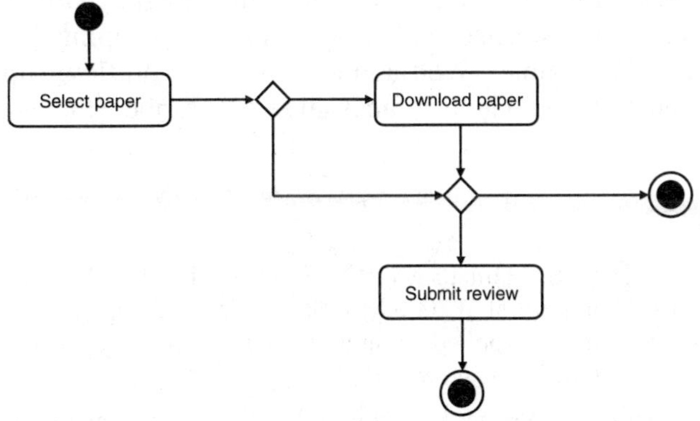

Fig. 11.18. Process *reviewPaper*

The activity diagram in Fig. 11.18 shows how single operations can be organised in more complex computations. The same operations can be used as building blocks in different processes: for example, operation *selectPaper* can be the starting point of all the processes that manage papers.

The composition, i.e., the actual process, can change because of the different roles or, in general, because of the context in which the process is executed. For example, we can imagine that processes executed on PDAs must be simpler than those on PCs. The simplification can only benefit the process, or require that smaller operations be conceived. This is the case, for example, of all those operations that let the user provide inputs to the application: the smaller the screen is, the simpler the operation must be. We cannot foresee that we get the same amount of data with a single PC-based page and with a PDA-based page.

11.5 Conclusions and Future Work

The chapter presents W2000, along with its main modelling features. Although space limitations do not allow us to deeply explain some key features, like the support to application families and transformation rules, the chapter presents a wide introduction to W2000. Its precise meta-model and significant excerpts of the models and diagrams of an example application help the reader understand the key elements.

The actual use of W2000 in some industrial projects is giving encouraging results and is paving the way to our future work. In some cases, industrial partners have highlighted the complexity of the modelling notation as a possible negative aspect and these comments are motivating the development of a lighter version of W2000 that, coupled with a heavy use of transformation rules, should better help and assist the designer while conceiving new applications. We are also exploiting the idea of swapping the viewpoint and thinking of a complex Web application as a workflow supported by Web pages, but this is still in its infancy and needs further studies.

References

1 Baresi L, Colazzo S, Mainetti L (2005) Beyond Modeling Notations: Consistency and Adaptability of W2000 Models. In: Proceedings of the 20th Annual ACM Symposium on Applied Computing -- Track on Web Technologies and Applications, ACM Press, New York (to appear)

2 Baresi L, Denaro G, Mainetti L, Paolini P (2002) Assertions to Better Specify the Amazon Bug. In: Proceedings of the 14th International Conference on Software Engineering and Knowledge Engineering, ACM Press, New York pp 585–592

3 Baresi L, Garzotto F, Maritati M (2002) W2000 as a MOF Metamodel. In: Proceedings of the 2002 World Multiconference on Systemics, Cybernetics and Informatics, 1

4 Eclipse consortium (2005) Eclipse - Home page. www.eclipse.org/

5 Ermel C, Rudolf M, Taentzer G (1999) The AGG Approach: Language and Tool Environment. In: Ehrig H, Engels G, Kreowski H-J, Rozenberg G (eds) Handbook of Graph Grammars and Computing by Graph Transformation, 2: Applications, Languages, and Tools, World Scientific, Singapore, pp 551–601

6 Fowler M (2004) UML Distilled. Addison-Wesley, Reading MA

7 Garzotto F, Paolini P, Schwabe D (1993) HDM- A Model-Based Approach to Hypertext Application Design. ACM Transactions on Information Systems, 11(1):1–26

8 Gerber A, Lawley MJ, Raymond K, Steel J, Wood A (2002) Transformation: The Missing Link of MDA. In: Proceedings of the 1st International Conference on Graph Transformation (ICGT 2002), LNCS 2505, Springer Verlag, Berlin pp 90–105

9 Kappel G, Proll B, Retschitzegger W, Schwinger W, Hofer T (2001) Modeling Ubiquitous Web Applications - A Comparison of Approaches. In: Proceedings of the Third International Conference on Information Integration and Web-based Applications and Services, pp 163–174

10 Maritati M (2001) Il Modello Logico per W2000. MSc. thesis, Università degli Studi di Lecce - Politecnico di Milano

11 Nentwich C, Capra L, Emmerich W, Finkelstein A (2002) xLinkIt: A Consistency Checking and Smart Link Generation Service. ACM Transactions on Internet Technology, 2(2):151–185

12 netBeans.org (2005) Metadata Repository MDR home. mdr.netbeans.org/

13 Object Management Group (2002) Meta Object Facility MOF Specification - v.1.4. Technical report, OMG, March

14 Object Management Group (2002) XML Metadata Interchange (XMI) Specification. Technical report, OMG

15 Powell TA (1998) Web Site Engineering: Beyond Web Page Design. Prentice Hall, Upper Saddle River, NJ

Authors' Biographies

Luciano Baresi is an Associate Professor at Dipartimento di Elettronica e Informazione at Politecnico di Milano, where he earned both his Laurea degree and PhD in Computer Science. He was also junior researcher at Cefriel (a research consortium among technical universities and industry in the Milan area) and Visiting Professor at University of Oregon at Eugene (USA), University of Paderborn (Germany), and University of Buenos Aires (Argentina). He has published and presented some 50 papers in the most important national and international journals and conferences. He served as programme co-chair of ICECCS 2002 (International Conference on Engineering Complex Computer Systems), GTVMT 2001 (International Workshop on Graph Transformation and Visual Modeling

Techniques, co-located with ICALP), UMICS 2003 and 2004 (the CAiSE Workshop on Ubiquitous Information and Communication Systems), the WISE Workshop on Mobile and Multichannel Information Systems and the ICWE Workshop on Web Quality. He has been a PC member for several conferences: among them, WWW, ICWE, SAC, and GT-VMT. His research interests are on Web engineering, with special emphasis on modeling complex applications, validation, and quality estimation.

Sebastiano Colazzo is a PhD student in Computer Science at the Polytechnic of Milan. He graduated in Computer Science at the University of Lecce (Italy), with a thesis on databases. He works for HOC (Hypermedia Open Center) Multimedia Lab at the Polytechnic of Milan as a consultant and researcher on various projects (both research and industrial) in the Web application fields. His interests span Web technology and ubiquitous Web applications design, tools for design and prototyping of Web application, application usability, and conceptual and logical design.

Luca Mainetti is an Associate Professor in the Department of Innovation Engineering at the University of Lecce (Italy). His research interests include Web design methodologies, notations and tools, Web and services-oriented architectures and applications, and collaborative computer graphics. He received a PhD in computer science from Politecnico di Milano (Italy). He is a member of the IEEE and ACM. Contact him at luca.mainetti@unile.it

Sandro Morasca is a Professor of Computer Science at the Dipartimento di Scienze della Cultura, Politiche e dell'Informazione of Università degli Studi dell'Insubria in Como, Italy. In the past, he was with the Dipartimento di Elettronica e Informazione of Politecnico di Milano in Milan, Italy. He was a Faculty Research Assistant and later a Visiting Scientist at the Department of Computer Science of the University of Maryland at College Park, and a Visiting Professor at the University of Buenos Aires, Argentina. He has published around 20 papers in international journals (eight of which are in IEEE or ACM Transactions) and around 40 papers in international conferences. In his research and professional activities, he has investigated the theoretical and practical aspects of measurement in several software engineering areas and in Web engineering, and has been involved in several projects with software companies and the public administration. He has served on the Programme Committee of a number of software engineering conferences, including ICWE and METRICS, the International Workshop on Software Metrics. He was the General Chair for METRICS 2005, which was held in Como, Italy, in mid-September 2005. Sandro Morasca serves on the Editorial Board of "Empirical Software Engineering: An International Journal," published by Kluwer. He organised, with Luciano Baresi, a workshop on Web quality at ICWE 2004, held in Munich, Germany.

12 What You Need To Know About Statistics[1]

Katrina D. Maxwell

Abstract: How do you measure the value of data? Not by the amount you have, but by what you can learn from it. Statistics provides a way to extract valuable information from your data. It is a science concerned with the collection, classification, and interpretation of data according to well-defined procedures. For a manager, however, statistics is simply one of many diverse techniques that may improve decision-making.

The purpose of this chapter is to develop a deeper understanding of the statistical methods used to analyse software project data. The methods used to analyse software project data come from the branch of statistics known as multivariate statistical analysis. These methods investigate relationships between two or more variables. However, before we delve into detailed explanations of chi-square tests, correlation analysis, regression analysis, and analysis of variance, you need to understand some basic concepts.

Keywords: Statistical concepts, Regression, Correlation, Distribution, sampling.

12.1 Describing Individual Variables

In this section, you will learn how to categorise and meaningfully summarise data concerning individual variables.

12.1.1 Types of Variables

All data is not created equal. Information can be collected using different scales. This has an impact on what method you can use to analyse the data. There are four main types of scales: nominal, ordinal, interval, and ratio.

Nominal scales – Variables such as business sector, application type, and application language are nominal-scale variables. These variables differ in kind only. They have no numerical sense. There is no meaningful order. For example, let's say that a business sector has four categories: bank,

---

[1] Maxwell, Katrina D., Applied Statistics for Software Managers, 1st Edition, ©2002. Adapted by permission of Pearson Education, Inc., Upper Saddle River, NJ. The original chapter has been adapted to this book by Emilia Mendes

insurance, retail, and manufacturing. Even if we label these with numbers instead of names in our database (say 101, 102, 103, and 104), the values of the numbers are meaningless. Manufacturing will never be "higher" than bank, just different.

Ordinal scales – The values of an ordinal-scale variable can be ranked in order. The 10 risk factors discussed in Chapter 5 of my book "Applied Statistics for Software Managers" are ordinal-scale variables. It is correct to say that Level 5 is riskier than Level 4, and Level 4 is riskier than Level 3, and so on; however, equal differences between ordinal values do not necessarily have equal quantitative meaning. For example, even though there is an equal one-level difference between 3 and 4, and 4 and 5, Level 4 may be 50% more risky than Level 3, and Level 5 may be 100% more risky than Level 4.

Interval scales – The values of an interval-scale variable can be ranked in order. In addition, equal distances between scale values have equal meaning. However, the ratios of interval-scale values have no meaning. This is because an interval scale has an arbitrary zero point. A start date variable is an example of an interval-scale variable. The year 1993 compared to the year 1992 only has meaning with respect to the arbitrary origin of 0 based on the supposed year of the birth of Christ. We know that 1993 is one year more than 1992, and that 1991 is one year less than 1992. Dividing 1993 by 1992 makes no sense. For example, we could decide to make 1900 year zero and count from there. In this case, 1993 would simply become 93 and 1992 would become 92 in our new scale. Although in both cases there is a one-year difference, the ratio 1993/1992 does not equal the ratio 93/92.

Another example of an interval scale is a Likert-type scale. Factors are rated on a scale of equal-appearing intervals, such as very low, low, average, high, and very high, and are assigned numerical values of 1, 2, 3, 4, and 5, respectively. However, in real life, it is virtually impossible to construct verbal scales of exactly equal intervals. It is more realistic to recognise that these scales are approximately of equal intervals. Thus, a Likert scale is really somewhere between an ordinal scale and a true interval scale.

Ratio scales – Variables such as effort, application size, and duration are measured using a ratio scale. Ratio-scale variables can be ranked in order, equal distances between scale values have equal meaning, and the ratios of ratio-scale values make sense. For example, it is correct to say that an application that required 10 months to develop took twice as long as an application that took 5 months. Another ratio scale is a percentage scale. For example, the percentage of COBOL used in an application is also a ratio-type variable.

A summary of variable type definitions is presented in Table 12.1.

Table 12.1. Summary of Variable type definitions

Variable type	Is there a meaningful order?	Do equal distances between scale values gave equal meaning?	Does the calculation of ratio make sense?
Nominal	No	No	No
Ordinal	Yes	No	No
Quasi-interval	Yes	Approximately	No
Interval	Yes	Yes	No
Ratio	Yes	Yes	Yes

I often refer to variables as being either numerical or categorical. What do I mean by a numerical variable? I mean a variable that has numerical sense. It can be ordered in a meaningful way. Variables measured using the ordinal, interval, or ratio scales are numerical-type variables. What do I mean by a categorical variable? A categorical variable cannot be interpreted in a quantitative sense. We know there are different levels, but we cannot answer the question "How much of a difference exists between two levels?" Variables measured using the nominal or ordinal scales are categorical variables. Categorical variables are also referred to as qualitative or non-metric variables. Non-categorical variables are often described as quantitative or metric variables.

12.1.2 Descriptive Statistics

The purpose of descriptive statistics is to meaningfully summarise large quantities of data with a few relatively simple terms. It is important to fully understand these terms because they are used in many statistical methods. In addition, descriptive statistics can be used to present easily understandable summary results to decision-makers. They provide answers to questions such as: What was the percentage of projects developed using XYZ? This corresponds to how many projects? What is a typical project? What was the smallest or largest project we ever developed? Are our projects fairly similar in size or do they vary a lot? You can learn an enormous amount about your data just from descriptive statistics.

Describing the Average

Three measures, the mode, the median, and the mean, can be used to describe a typical project. These measures are often referred to as measures of central tendency.

Mean – Here, we are referring to the arithmetic mean, which is the most common measure. It is what we usually consider to be the "average" in our daily lives. It is computed by adding together the observed values and dividing by the number of observations. For example, consider the ages of five software developers: 20, 25, 25, 30, and 45. The mean is calculated by adding all the ages together and dividing by 5 (see Eq. 12.1):

$$\frac{20+25+25+30+45}{5} = 29 \tag{12.1}$$

The mean is 29 years.[2] The mean is expressed mathematically by the following formula:

$$\bar{x} = \frac{\Sigma x_i}{n} \tag{12.2}$$

The mean is represented by $\bar{x}$. The age of each software developer is considered to be an observation value (x_i): 20 is x_1, 25 is x_2, and so on. The summation sign, Σ, means that we should add (sum) the observation values. Finally, we divide by the number of observations (n). There were five software developers in this example, so we have five observations.

Median – This is the middle value when the data is ordered from smallest to largest value; it is also referred to as the 50th percentile. In the previous example, the median value is 25. If we have an even number of observations, we determine the median by averaging the two middle observation values. For example, the median of 20, 25, 30, and 45 is (25 + 30) / 2 = 27.5 years.

Mode – This is the most frequent value. In our example of five software developers, the most frequent age is 25, so 25 years is the mode. Sometimes there is no mode, and sometimes there is more than one mode. For example, if the ages were 20, 24, 25, 29, and 45, there would be no mode. If the ages were 20, 20, 25, 35 and 35, there would be two modes: 20 years and 35 years.

Describing the Variation

The variation of individual variables in our sample can be described by three commonly used variability measures: the range, the sample variance, and the sample standard deviation. "Sample" refers to the set of projects for which we have data.

---

[2] It is important when dealing with numbers to identify the measurement units. Age is measured in years.

Range – Technically, the range is the difference between the largest and smallest values. However, as the range is most useful for providing information about the values beyond which no observations fall, I describe a data set's range as "the smallest value to the largest value". If the ages of three software developers are 20, 25, and 30, the range is from 20 to 30 years.

Sample variance (s^2) – This measures the average distance between each value and the mean. It is the sum of the squared differences between each observation (x_i) and the mean value ($\bar{x}$) divided by the number of observations (n) minus one.[3] This is expressed mathematically by the following formula:

$$s^2 = \frac{\Sigma(x_i - \bar{x})^2}{n-1} \tag{12.3}$$

For example, let's consider the ages of three software developers: 23, 25, and 27. The mean of their ages is 25 years. The sample variance is calculated as follows:

$$s^2 = \frac{\left[(23-25)^2 + (25-25)^2 + (27-25)^2\right]}{2} = 4 \tag{12.4}$$

Thus, the sample variance is 4 years squared. Unfortunately, most people find it hard to relate to the variance because the measurement units are squared. What does "years squared" really mean?

Sample standard deviation (s) – The standard deviation is an easier-to-understand measure of the average distance between each value and the mean. It is the square root of the sample variance.

$$s = \sqrt{s^2} \tag{12.5}$$

Thus, the sample standard deviation of our previous example is 2 years. The larger the variance and standard deviation, the more the projects differ from one another.

Perhaps you are wondering why we go through the bother of squaring the differences and then taking their square root. Why not just use the actual differences in the calculation? Well, the reason why the differences are squared is so that the positive and negative differences do not cancel each other out. However, it is true that this could also be achieved by taking the absolute value of the differences. So why don't we do that? The

[3] One is subtracted as a corrective measure. Statisticians have found that the variance is underestimated for small samples if we just divide by n.

reason is because certain mathematical operations necessary for the development of advanced statistical techniques cannot be carried out on absolute values. What is an absolute value? It is the positive value of a number. For example, 3 is the absolute value of both positive 3 and negative 3. This is expressed mathematically as $|3| = 3$ and $|-3| = 3$.

Unfortunately, we cannot calculate these six measures for all variable types. Table 12.2 shows which measures are authorised for each variable type.

Table 12.2. Authorised operations by variable type

Variable type	Nominal	Ordinal	Interval	Ratio
Mean			X	X
Median		X	X	X
Mode	X	X	X	X
Range		X	X	X
Variance			X	X
Standard deviation			X	X

Now, let's look at an example of how to determine these measures for a hypothetical sample of seven projects in which all variables are already ordered from lowest to highest (Table 12.3). In this example, application type is a nominal-scale variable. There are two values for application type: customer service and MIS. Risk level is an ordinal-scale variable measured using a scale of *1–5*. We know that some applications are riskier than others, but that is all. Quality requirements, a quasi-interval scale variable, are carefully measured using a Likert scale with 1, 2, 3, 4, and 5 representing very low, low, average, high, and very high. Effort is a ratio-scale variable; it is measured in hours.

First, let's describe a typical project using the mean, median, and mode. In Table 12.3, we can see that the most frequent application type is customer service. The mode is the only central tendency measure authorised for nominal variables. For ordinal variables, we can calculate the median and mode. Project 4 is the middle observation. There are three observations above it and three observations below it. Thus, the median risk level is 2. There are two modes: 2 and 4. Therefore, there is no single typical risk level.

Table 12.3. Examples of central tendency and variability measures for each variable type

Variable type	Nominal application type	Ordinal risk level	Interval quality requirements	Ratio effort
Project 1	Customer service	1	1	300
2	Customer service	2	2	400
3	Customer service	2	3	500
4	Customer service	2	3	600
5	MIS	4	3	1000
6	MIS	4	4	5000
7	MIS	4	5	30,000
Mean			3	5400 hours
Median		2	3	600 hours
Mode	Customer service	2 and 4	3	None
Range		1 to 4	1 to 5	300 to 30,000 hours
Sample variance			1.67	120,456,667 hours^2
Sample standard deviation			1.29	10,975.3 hours

For interval and ratio variables, we can also calculate the mean in addition to the median and mode. The mean value of quality requirements is 3. The median value is 3, and 3 is the most frequent value. It looks like we can safely say that a typical project has average quality requirements.

For effort, the mean is 5,400 hours, the median is 600 hours, and there is no mode as no number appears more than once. In this case, we have two different numbers describing a typical project's effort. The advantages and disadvantages of each of these measures are summarized in Table 12.4. For example, one of the disadvantages of the mean is that it is very sensitive to extreme values. As you can see, the one effort of 30,000 hours has a very big impact on the mean value. Most projects actually have efforts below the mean value. The median is insensitive to extreme values. Even if the effort of the last project was 90,000 hours, the median would remain unchanged.

Table 12.4. Relative merits of mean, median, and mode

	Advantages	Disadvantages
Mean	Located by simple process of addition and division Affected by every item in group	Affected by the exceptional and the unusual Calculated value may not actually exist
Median	Not affected by items having extreme deviation from the normal Unlike the mode, not overly affected by small number of items	Not as easy to calculate (by hand) as the mean Not useful when extreme variations should be given weight Insensitive to changes in minimum and maximum values Calculated value may not actually exist (when there is even number of observations)
Mode	Not affected by extreme values Only way to represent nominal variable	No single, well-defined type may exist Difficult to determine accurately Ignores extreme variations May be determined by small number of items

Now, let's consider the three variability measures: range, sample variance, and sample standard deviation. The range can be described for all variable types except nominal. The sample variance and sample standard deviation can only be calculated for interval and ratio variables as they depend on the mean. Like the mean, they are also sensitive to extreme values. The one project with a 30,000 hour effort has a big impact on all three variability measures.

Frequency Distributions

Data can also be described with frequency distributions. A frequency distribution refers to the number or percentage of observations in a group. The group can be either a category or a numerical interval. For example, Table 12.5 shows the frequency distribution of a categorical variable application type (*app*). We can see that we have 20 transaction processing (*TransPro*) applications. This is the number under *Frequency.* This corresponds to approximately 59% of all applications in our sample (*Percent*). The cumulative frequency (*Cumulative*) is more applicable to numerical intervals, for example, if you want to know the total number of projects less than a certain size. Here it just means that 85% of the applications were customer service (*CustServ*), management information system (*MIS*), or transaction processing (*TransPro*) applications. While this table provides valuable information to data analysts, it is a bit boring to show upper management.

Table 12.5. Application type frequency distribution

Application Type	Frequency	Percent	Cumulative
CustServ	6	17.65	17.65
MIS	3	8.82	26.47
TransPro	20	58.82	85.29
InfServ	5	14.71	100.00
Total	34	100.00	

Frequency distribution tables can be used to make attractive graphs for your presentations (see Fig. 12.1). You have probably been making pie charts like this most of your professional life without realising you were calculating frequency distributions.

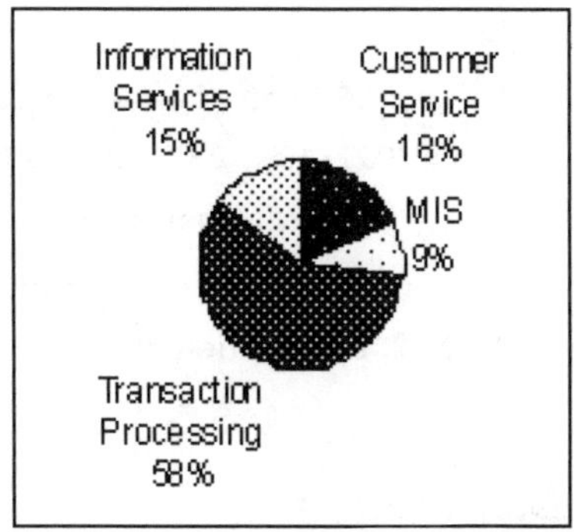

Fig. 12.1. Application-type breakdown

Now let's look at the frequency distribution of a numerical variable. If I wanted to make a frequency distribution for a size variable (*size*) where size is measured, for example, in function points, I would first separate the data into meaningful groups of increasing size, say 0–999 function points, 1000–1999 function points, and so on. Then I would count how many applications fell into each interval (see Table 12.6).

With numerical data, we are usually interested in knowing the shape of the distribution. We can see the shape by making a histogram. A histogram is a chart with a bar for each class. Figure 12.2 shows the histogram of size using the percentage of projects in each class. We can easily see from this graph that most projects have a size of less than 1000 function points. Often we make histograms to determine if the data is normally distributed.

Table 12.6. Size frequency distribution

Size in function points	Frequency	Percent	Cumulative
0-999	29	85.30	85.30
1000–1999	3	8.82	94.12
2000–2999	1	2.94	97.06
3000–3999	1	2.94	100.00
Total	63	100.00	

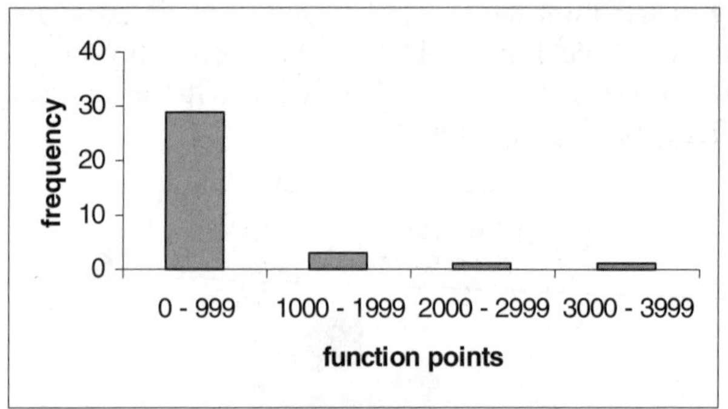

Fig. 12.2. Distribution of size

12.2 The Normal Distribution

One very important frequency distribution is the normal distribution. Figure 12.3 shows the fundamental features of a normal curve. It is bell-shaped, with tails extending indefinitely above and below the centre. A normal distribution is symmetrical about the average. In a normal distribution, the mean, median, and mode all have the same value and thus all describe a typical project.

A normal curve can be described mathematically in terms of just two parameters, the mean and standard deviation. The width of a normal distribution is a function of the standard deviation of the data. The larger the standard deviation, the wider the distribution. If our numerical data follows a normal distribution, we know that about 68% of all observations fall within plus or minus one standard deviation of the mean. About 95.5% of the observations lie within plus or minus two standard deviations of the mean, and 99.7% fall within plus or minus three standard deviations.

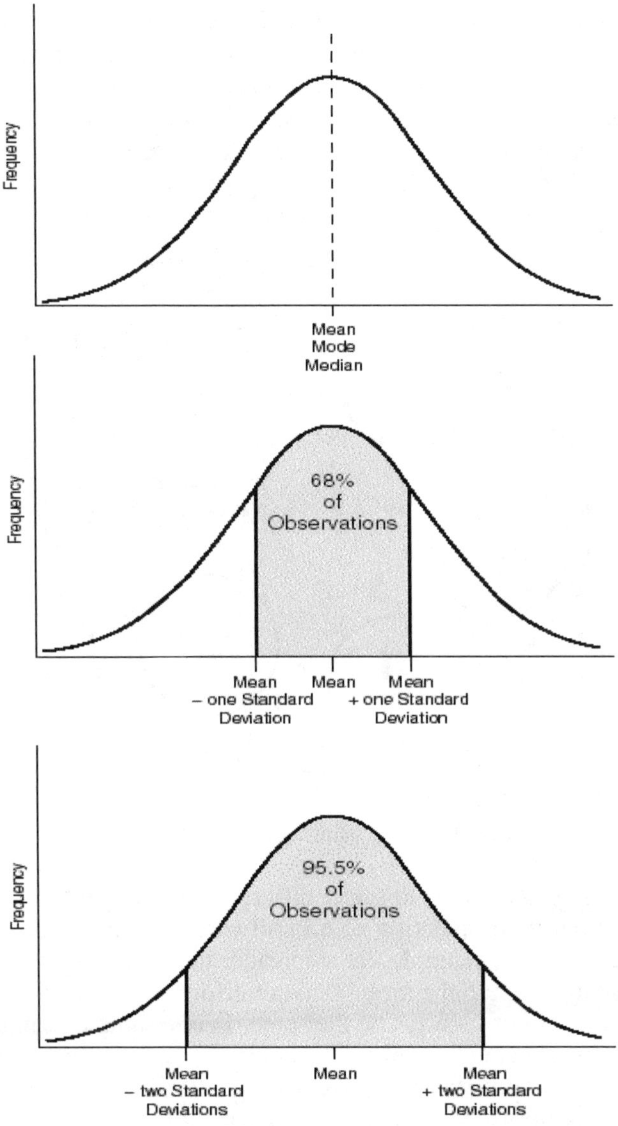

Fig. 12.3. Example of normal distribution

12.3 Overview of Sampling Theory

Now that you know how to describe and summarise individual variables, there is another key concept to understand before we can proceed to identifying relationships in data: the difference between samples and populations.

This is important because you probably haven't been able to collect valid data for every software project your company has ever undertaken. So, if we consider that the population of software project data is data for all projects in your company, what you have is a sample of that data. How, then, can you be sure that what you find in your sample is true for all projects in your company?

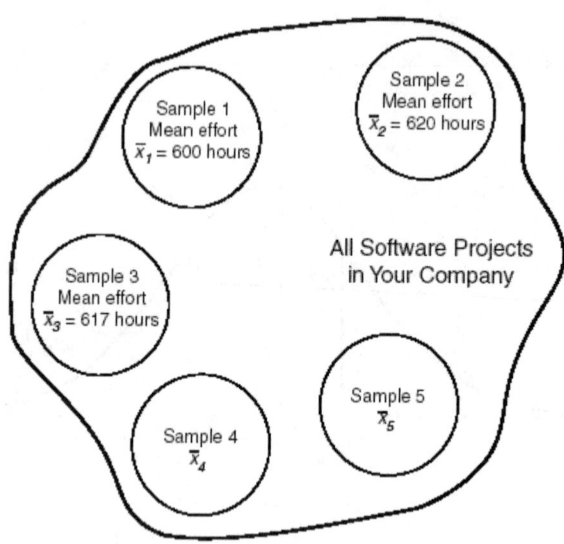

Fig. 12.4. Sampling from a population

Imagine that you are able to select different samples (groups of projects) at random[4] from the population of all software projects in your company (see Fig. 12.4). As an example, let's consider the variable *effort.*[5] For each sample, we can compute the mean value of effort. The mean value of effort in each sample will not always be the same. In one sample, it might be 600 hours ($\bar{x}_1$), in a second sample, 620 hours ($\bar{x}_2$), in a third sample, 617 hours ($\bar{x}_3$), and so on. We can make a frequency distribution of the mean efforts of each sample. This distribution is called the sampling distribution of the sample means. The mean value of an infinite number of sample means is equal to the population mean (see Fig. 12.5).

4 As all inferential (i.e. predictive) techniques assume that you have a random sample, you should not violate that assumption by removing projects just because they do not fit your model!.

5 To simplify this complicated discussion, the effort in my example is normally distributed. In practice, this is not the case.

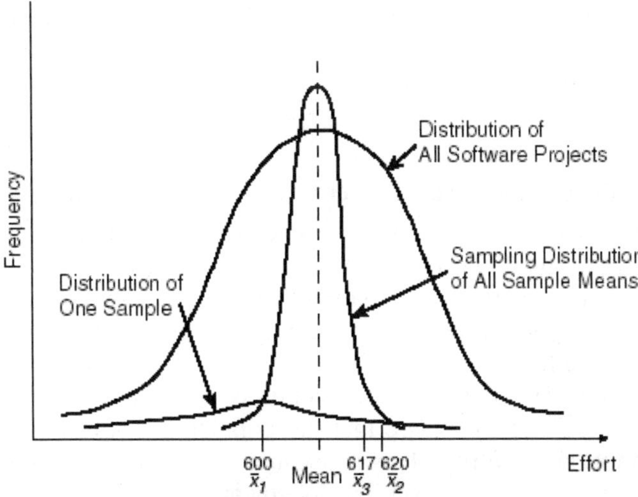

Fig. 12.5. Distributions of one sample, means of all samples, and the population

If the sample size is large (≥30), the sampling distribution of the sample means is approximately a normal distribution. The larger the sample, the better the approximation. This is true even if the *effort* variable in the population is not normally distributed. This tendency to normality of sampling distributions is known as the Central Limit Theorem.[6] This theorem has great practical importance. It means that it doesn't matter that we don't know the distribution of effort in the population. This is handy because, in practice, all we have is one sample. If we have a sample of at least 30 projects, we can use a normal distribution to determine the probability that the mean effort of the population is within a certain distance of the mean effort of our one sample.

As you can see in Fig. 12.5, the sampling distribution of all sample mean efforts is not as wide as the distribution of all software projects' efforts. In fact, one of the most important properties of the sample mean is that it is a very stable measure of central tendency. We can estimate the hypothetical standard deviation of the sampling distribution of sample means from the variation of effort in our one sample. This is known as the standard error of the mean. Note that "error" does not mean "mistake" in this context. It really means deviation. The term "error" is used to distinguish the standard deviation of the sampling distribution (the standard error) from the standard deviation of our sample. Otherwise, it is not clear

---

6 In addition, it has also been shown that if a variable is normally distributed in the population, the sampling distribution of the sample mean is exactly normal no matter what the size of the sample.

just what standard deviation we are talking about. The standard error is expressed mathematically as:

$$s_{\bar{x}} = \frac{s}{\sqrt{n}} \tag{12.6}$$

where $s_{\bar{x}}$ is the estimated standard error of the mean, s is the standard deviation of our one sample, and n is the size of our one sample. You can see that if s is very small and n is very large, the standard error of the mean will be small. That is, the less variation there is in the variable *effort* in our sample, and the more projects we have in our sample, the smaller the standard error of the mean (and the narrower the sampling distribution of the sample means). The narrower the sampling distribution of the sample means, the more certain we are that the population's mean effort is near our one-sample mean effort. This is because in a very narrow distribution, the population mean is near every sample mean.

The standard error of the mean is important because we can use it to calculate the limits around our one-sample mean which probably contain the population mean–probably, because we specify these limits with a certain degree of confidence. Typically, we are interested in 95% confidence intervals. The 95% confidence interval estimate of the mean states that the population mean is equal to the sample mean plus or minus 1.96 multiplied by the standard error of the mean. That is:

$$\textit{population mean} = \bar{x} \pm 1.96 s_{\bar{x}} \tag{12.7}$$

The value 1.96 is related to the normal curve. Recall that approximately 95.5% of the observations lie within plus or minus two standard deviations of the mean (see Fig. 12.3). If 95% confidence intervals were constructed for many samples, about 95% of the intervals would contain the true population mean. Thus, there is still a 5% probability that the true population mean effort lies outside the 95% confidence interval of our one sample. The accuracy of this probability increases with larger sample sizes.

12.4 Other Probability Distributions

Three additional common probability distributions are described in this chapter. You don't need to worry about which distribution to use in which circumstance, what they actually look like, or how to read probabilities from the complicated tables that you find in the appendices of many statistics books. Your statistical analysis package automatically applies the correct distribution. All you need to know is how to read the probability from the statistical output.

- *Student t-distribution*–If the sample size is less than 30 projects, then the t-distribution must be used instead of the normal distribution. The Student t-distribution assumes that the population from which we are drawing our sample is normally distributed. (i.e. the Central Limit Theorem does not apply). The Student t-distribution tends to coincide with the normal distribution for large sample sizes. Because it is appropriate for either large or small samples, the t-distribution is used in place of the normal distribution when inferences must be made from accessible samples to immeasurable populations. Think of it as a modified normal distribution. You will see the t-distribution referred to in correlation and regression analysis output.
- *Chi-square distribution*–If a population is normally distributed, the sample distribution of the sample variance is approximated by the chi-square distribution. This test is explained in detail later in this chapter.
- *Fisher F-distribution*–If samples taken from two different normally distributed populations are independent, the F-distribution can be used to compare two variances. The calculation of the F-ratio is explained in detail in Sect. 12.5.4.

Each of these probability distributions assumes that the underlying data is normally distributed. You can now appreciate why the normal distribution is so important in statistics, and why we must check if the numerical variables in our software project database are normally distributed—it is even more important when we don't have very many projects in our sample.

12.5 Identifying Relationships in the Data

Now that you have learned the basics, you are ready to identify relationships between variables. Table 12.7 shows which statistical methods can be used in which circumstances. It is important to know what types of variables you have to apply the correct method. Choosing the correct statistical method is extremely important. Your statistical analysis package does not automatically decide what method to use– *you do.*

The concept of dependent and independent variables does not apply to the chi-square test for independence, nor does it apply to Spearman's and Pearson's correlation coefficients. However, to use the analysis of variance (ANOVA) method, you need to pay attention to which variable is the dependent variable. The dependent variable is the variable you want to predict. For example, if you have a ratio-type variable (effort) and an ordinal-type variable (risk level) as in Table 12.3, you can calculate Spearman's correlation coefficient between these two variables. You can also run an ANOVA procedure to determine how much of the variation in effort (dependent variable) is explained by the variation in the risk level (independent variable). However, you cannot run an ANOVA procedure with risk level as the dependent variable.

Table 12.7. Mappings of statistical methods in this chapter to variable types

Variable type	Independent variable			
Dependent variable	Nominal	Ordinal	Interval	Ratio
Nominal	Chi-square test for independence	Chi-square test for independence		
Ordinal	Chi-square test for independence	Spearman's correlation, chi-square test for independence	Spearman's correlation	Spearman's correlation
Interval	ANOVA	Spearman's correlation, ANOVA	Spearman's correlation, Pearson's correlation, regression	Spearman's correlation, Pearson's correlation, regression
Ratio	ANOVA	Spearman's correlation, ANOVA	Spearman's correlation, Pearson's correlation, regression	Spearman's correlation, Pearson's correlation, regression

12.5.1 Chi-Square Test for Independence

Two events are independent whenever the probability of one happening is unaffected by the occurrence of the other. This concept can be extended to categorical variables. The chi-square test for independence compares the actual and expected frequencies of occurrence to determine whether or not two categorical variables are independent. For example, let's consider two nominal variables, Telon[7] use (*telonuse*) and application type (*subapp*). Telon use can be "yes" or "no", and application type can be customer service, management information system, transaction processing, or information/online service. We want to know if Telon use is independent of application type. We will base our conclusion on data from 62 software projects. This is our sample size. Table 12.8 summarises the actual frequencies found in our sample. This table is called a contingency table because it shows the frequency for every combination of attributes (i.e. every possible contingency).

[7] Telon is a tool that generates code.

If two variables are independent, the proportion of observations in any category should be the same regardless of what attribute applies to the other variable. So, if Telon use and application type are independent, we would expect the percentage of Telon use to be the same for all four application types. It is easy to see in Table 12.9 that the percentages are not exactly the same.

Table 12.8. Contingency table–actual frequencies

Application type	Telon use		
	No	Yes	Total
CustServ	12	6	18
MIS	4	0	4
TransPro	24	5	29
InfServ	8	3	11
Total	48	14	62

The frequencies we would expect if the percentages were the same are computed in the following way: the overall proportion of projects in our sample that did not use Telon is approximately 0.77 (= 48/62); the proportion that used Telon is approximately 0.23 (= 14/62). This proportion can be used to compute the expected number of Telon projects for each application type. There were 18 customer service (*CustServ*) applications. If approximately 23% used Telon this makes 4.1 expected Telon/customer service projects.[8] Out of a total of four *MIS* applications, we would expect 4*(14/62) = 0.9 to use Telon. For transaction processing (*TransPro*) applications, 29*(14/62) = 6.5 is the expected number of Telon projects. For information service (*InfServ*) applications, 11*(14/62) = 2.5 is the expected number of Telon projects. Then for each application type, the expected number of projects that did not use Telon is simply the total number for each application type minus the number that did use Telon. The expected frequencies are presented in Table 12.10.

Table 12.9. Percentage of applications that did/did not use Telon

Application type	Telon use		
	No	Yes	Total
CustServ	66.67	33.33	100.00
MIS	100.00	0.00	100.00
TransPro	82.76	17.24	100.00
InfServ	72.73	27.27	100.00
Total	77.42	22.58	100.00

8 Obviously, a fraction of a project does not exist; however, it is necessary to keep the decimal places for the calculations.

Table 12.10. Contingency table – expected frequencies

Application type	Telon use		
	No	Yes	Total
CustServ	13.9	4.1	18
MIS	3.1	0.9	4
TransPro	22.5	6.5	29
InfServ	8.5	2.5	11
Total	48	14	62

Our null hypothesis is that there is no relationship between Telon use and application type. If we demonstrate that:

- the actual frequencies differ from the frequencies expected if there was no relationship, and
- the difference is larger than we would be likely to get through sampling error,

then we can reject the null hypothesis and conclude that there is a relationship between Telon use and application type. So far in our example, we have seen that the actual and expected frequencies are not exactly the same (Condition 1). Now we need to see if the difference is significant (Condition 2). We compare the difference between the actual and expected frequencies with the chi-square statistic.

The chi-square statistic is calculated with the following expression:

$$\chi^2 = \Sigma \frac{(actual_{ij} - expected_{ij})^2}{expected_{ij}} \tag{12.8}$$

where $actual_{ij}$ is the actual frequency for the combination at the ith row and j^{th} column, and $expected_{ij}$ is the expected frequency for the combination at the ith row and j^{th} column (Table 12.10). For example, $actual_{11}$ refers to the actual frequency of customer service (*CustServ*) applications that did not use Telon; $expected_{42}$ refers to the expected frequency of information service (*InfServ*) applications that used Telon.

Table 12.11 shows the calculation of the chi-square statistic for our example. First we subtract the expected value (*exp*) from the actual value (*act*) for each attribute combination. The farther the expected value is from the actual value, the bigger the difference. Then we square this value. This allows negative differences to increase rather than reduce the total. Next, we divide by the expected value. Finally, we sum (Σ) the values in the last column to arrive at the chi-square statistic.

Table 12.11. Example of chi-square statistic calculation

(i,j)	act	exp	act–exp	$(\text{act–exp})^2$	$(\text{act–exp})^2/\text{exp}$
(1,1)	12	13.9	–1.9	3.61	0.260
(1,2)	6	4.1	1.9	3.61	0.880
(2,1)	4	3.1	0.9	0.81	0.261
(2,2)	0	0.9	–0.9	0.81	0.900
(3,1)	24	22.5	1.5	2.25	0.100
(3,2)	5	6.5	–1.5	2.25	0.346
(4,1)	8	8.5	–0.5	0.25	0.029
(4,2)	3	2.5	0.5	0.25	0.100
Sum	62	62	0		Chi-square = 2.877

The chi-square distribution provides probabilities for different values of χ^2. There is a separate distribution for each number of degrees of freedom. The number of degrees of freedom refers to the number of independent comparisons. In our example, the number of degrees of freedom is 3 because once we have calculated frequencies for Telon use for three application types in Table 12.10, the remaining five cells can be filled in without any further calculation of frequencies. For example, the expected frequency for information service (*InfServ*) applications that used Telon is the total number of applications that used Telon minus the expected frequencies of the three other application types that used Telon (14 – 4.1 – 0.9 – 6.5 = 2.5). We don't need to calculate its frequency because we can derive it from the information we already have. The number of degrees of freedom for the chi-square test is always the number of rows minus one multiplied by the number of columns minus one. Here, (4 – 1) (2 – 1) = 3.

Once we have our chi-square value and the number of degrees of freedom, we can see if the difference between actual and expected frequencies is significant using a chi-square distribution table (see example below). However, in practice, you will not be undertaking these calculations yourself and you do not need to learn how to use the chi-square distribution tables. A computer will calculate everything for you.

Example

My statistical analysis package informs me that the chi-square statistic (*Pearson chi2*) associated with the table above has 3 degrees of freedom and a value of 2.9686. There is a small difference between the computer's value and my value because of rounding errors. The computer's value is more precise. The significance level is 0.396 (approximately 40%). The significance level states the probability (*Pr*) that we are making an error when we reject the null hypothesis. Only if the *Pr* is less than or equal to 0.05 can we reject the hypothesis that application type and Telon use are independent at the 5% significance level. Thus, our null hypothesis that there is no relationship between Telon use and application type cannot be rejected.

```
. tabulate app telonuse, chi2

Application| Telon Use
Type       |          No          Yes |      Total
-----------+-----------------------+----------
  CustServ |          12            6 |         18
       MIS |           4            0 |          4
  TransPro |          24            5 |         29
   InfServ |           8            3 |         11
-----------+-----------------------+----------
     Total |          48           14 |         62

   Pearson chi2(3) =   2.9686   Pr = 0.396
```

12.5.2 Correlation Analysis

A correlation coefficient measures the strength and direction of the relationship between two numerical variables. The correlation coefficient can have any value between –1 and +1 (see Fig. 12.6).

If the correlation coefficient is –1, this means that the two variables are perfectly negatively correlated. High values of one are associated with low values of the other, and vice versa.

If the correlation coefficient is +1, this means that the two variables are perfectly positively correlated. High values of one are associated with high values of the other, and vice versa.þ If the correlation coefficient is 0, this means that the two variables are not correlated at all. In practice, we rarely see perfect correlation or complete non-correlation. Figure 12.7 shows a more typical relationship.

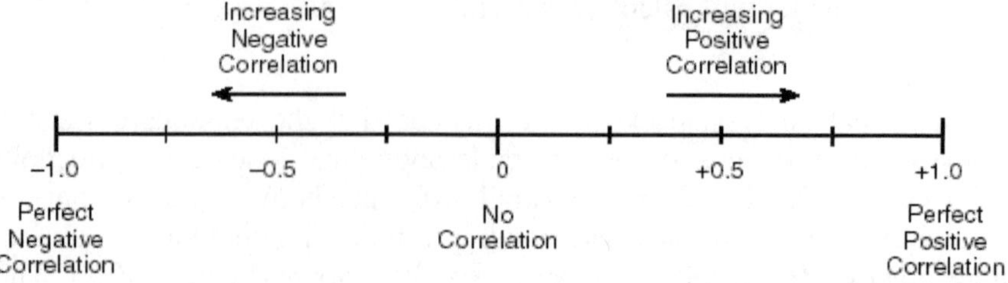

Fig. 12.6. Interpreting the correlation coefficient

We can see that development effort and software size are positively correlated because the relationship looks linear and the slope of the line is increasing. But how strong is the relationship? How can we measure the correlation?

Two measures of correlation are commonly used when analysing software project data. Spearman's rank correlation coefficient must be used when the data is ordinal,[9] or when the data is far from normally distributed. Pearson's correlation coefficient can be used when the data is of an interval or ratio type. Pearson's correlation coefficient is based on two key assumptions: (1) the data is normally distributed, and (2) the relationship is linear.

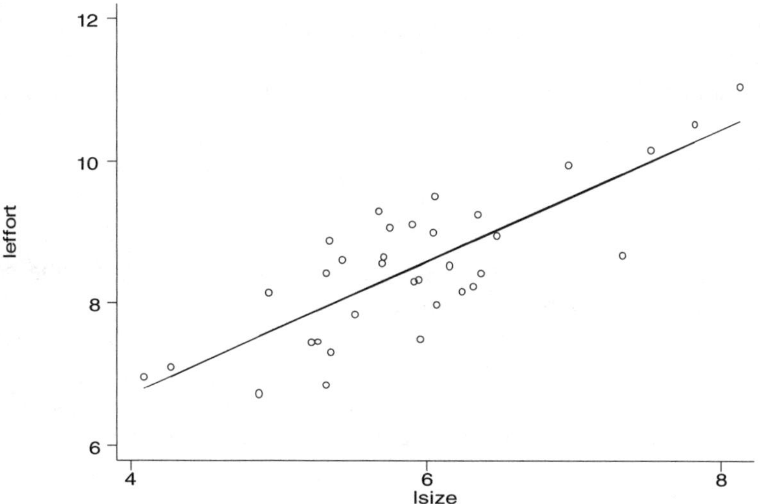

Fig. 12.7. Typical relationship between ln(*effort*) and ln(*size*).

Spearman's Rank Correlation

Spearman's rank correlation coefficient compares the differences in two variables' rank for the same observation. A variable's rank refers to its placement in an ordered list. For example, consider the following five software development projects, which are shown in Table 12.12.

---

9 I also prefer Spearman's rank correlation coefficient for quasi-interval variables.

Table 12.12. Data for five software development projects

Id	size	sizerank	effort	effrank
2	647	4	7871	4
3	130	1	845	1
5	1056	5	21272	5
6	383	3	4224	3
15	249	2	2565	2

We are interested in the relationship between size and effort. First we have to rank the projects' size. There are five projects, so the rank of each project will be a number between 1 and 5. The smallest size project is given rank 1, the second smallest 2, and so on. We do the same thing for project effort. We now have two new variables, *sizerank* and *effrank*, which are the respective ranks of the variables *size* and *effort*.

We can easily calculate Spearman's rank correlation coefficient, ρ, using the following equation:

$$\rho = 1 - \frac{6\sum D^2}{n(n^2 - 1)} \tag{12.9}$$

where D is the difference between the two variables' rank for the same project, and n is the number of projects.

How strong is the relationship between effort and size? Some calculation steps are shown in Table 12.13.

The sum of the squared differences is 0. This results in a Spearman's rank correlation coefficient of 1. This is an example of perfect positive correlation.

$$\rho = 1 - \frac{6(0)}{5(5^2 - 1)} = 1 \tag{12.10}$$

Table 12.13. Calculation of Sum of Squared Differences

Project id	Rank of size	Rank of effort	Difference between ranks, D	Square of difference, D^2
2	4	4	4 – 4 = 0	0
3	1	1	1 – 1 = 0	0
5	5	5	5 – 5 = 0	0
6	3	3	3 – 3 = 0	0
15	2	2	2 – 2 = 0	0
n = 5				$\Sigma D^2 = 0$

The second example compares the quality requirements and development time constraints of five hypothetical projects. Quality requirements and development time constraints are quasi-interval variables measured using a Likert scale from 1 (very low) to 5 (very high). We see that very low quality requirements are associated with very high development time constraints, low quality requirements are associated with high development time constraints, and so on. Table 12.14 shows how the sum of the squared differences was calculated for this example.

The sum of the squared differences is 40. Plugging this into Spearman's equation results in a correlation coefficient of –1. This is an example of perfect negative correlation.

Table 12.14. Calculation of sum of squared differences

Project id	Rank of quality requirements	Rank of development time constraints	Difference between ranks, D	Square of difference, D^2
P01	1 (very low)	5 (very high)	1 – 5 = -4	16
P22	2 (low)	4 (high)	2 – 4 = -2	4
P33	3 (average)	3 (average)	3 – 3 = 0	0
P54	4 (high)	2 (low)	4 – 2 = 2	4
P65	5 (very high)	1 (very low)	5 – 1 = 4	16
n = 5				$\Sigma D^2 = 40$

$$\rho = 1 - \frac{6(40)}{5\left(5^2 - 1\right)} = -1 \tag{12.11}$$

These calculations are slightly more complicated when there are ties in the ranks. However, as your statistical analysis package will automatically calculate the correlation coefficient, you do not need to be concerned about this.

Pearson's Correlation

Pearson's correlation coefficient uses the actual values of the variables instead of the ranks. So, it takes into account not only the fact that one value is higher than another, but also the size of the quantitative difference between two values. It can be calculated with the following formula:

$$r = \frac{\Sigma(x_i - \bar{x})(y_i - \bar{y})}{(n-1)s_x s_y} \tag{12.12}$$

where $x_i - \bar{x}$ is the difference between a project's value on the x variable from the mean of that variable, $y_i - \bar{y}$ is the difference between a project's value on the y variable from the mean of that variable, s_x and s_y are the sample standard deviations of the x and y variables, respectively, and n is the number of observation pairs.

There is no better way to understand an equation than to try out the calculation with some real data. So let's return to our software project data in Table 12.12. In the example below, we have the mean and standard deviation of effort and size for the five projects in our sample.

Example

```
. summarize effort size

Variable |      Obs        Mean    Std. Dev.        Min        Max
---------+--------------------------------------------------------
  effort |        5      7355.4    8201.776         845      21272
    size |        5         493    368.8123         130       1056
```

For our sample of five projects, the mean of the effort is 7355.4 hours and its standard deviation is 8201.776 hours. The mean of the size is 493 function points and its standard deviation is 368.8123 function points. Table 12.15 demonstrates some steps for the calculation of Pearson's correlation coefficient between effort and size for these projects.

Plugging these numbers into our formula gives us the following result:

$$r = \frac{11791035}{(5-1)\times 368.8123\times 8201.776} = 0.9745 \tag{12.13}$$

Table 12.15. Calculation of Pearson's Correlation Coefficient Numerator

Project id	x, size	y, effort	$(x_i-\bar{x})$	$(y_i-\bar{y})$	$(x_i-\bar{x})(y_i-\bar{y})$
2	647	7871	154	515.6	79,402.4
3	130	845	–363	–6510.4	2,363,275.2
5	1056	21,272	563	13,916.6	7,835,045.8
6	383	4224	–110	–3131.4	344,454.0
15	249	2565	–244	–4790.4	1,168,857.6
					Σ= 11,791,035

Pearson's correlation coefficient is 0.9745. Recall that we calculated a Spearman's rank correlation coefficient of 1 for this data in the previous section. Pearson's correlation coefficient is a more accurate measurement of the association between interval- or ratio-scale variables than Spearman's coefficient, as long as its underlying assumptions have been met. This is because some information is lost when we convert interval- or ratio-scale variables into rank orders. One of the assumptions underlying Pearson's correlation coefficient is that the relationship between the two variables is linear. Let's look at the data and see if this is the case. We can

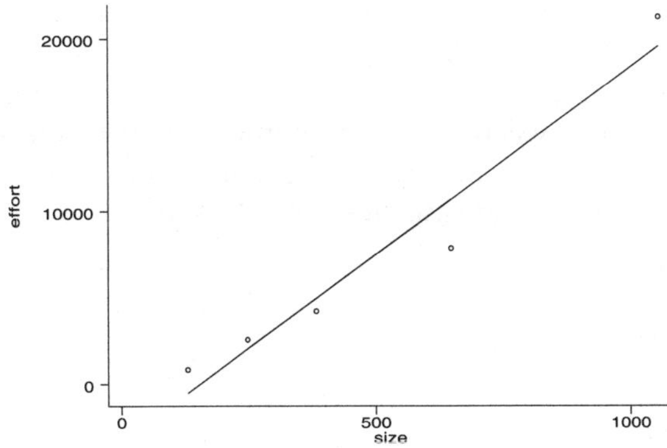

Fig. 12.8. *effort* vs. *size* for correlation example

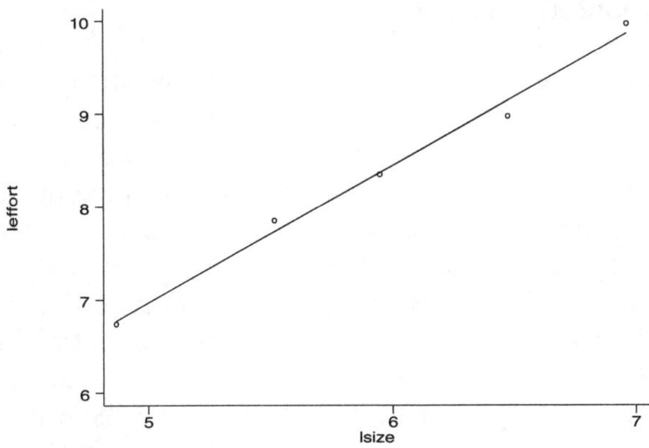

Fig. 12.9. ln(effort) vs. ln(size) for correlation example

see in Fig. 12.8 that although it is possible to fit a straight line close to the five data points, the relationship is really a bit curved.

Taking the natural log of the variables *effort* and *size* results in a more linear relationship (Fig. 12.9).

Pearson's correlation coefficient between ln(*size*) and ln(*effort*) is shown in the example below.

Example

```
. corr lsize leffort
(obs=5)

        |    lsize  leffort
--------+------------------
   lsize|   1.0000
 leffort|   0.9953   1.0000
```

Thus, the linear association is stronger between the natural log of size and the natural log of effort (0.9953) than it is between size and effort (0.9745). As you can see in the next example, the natural log transformation has no effect on Spearman's rank correlation coefficient because although the actual values of the variables change, their relative positions do not. Thus, the ranking of the variables stays the same.

Example

```
. spearman lsize leffort

 Number of obs =        5
Spearman's rho =        1.0000
```

12.5.3 Regression Analysis

Whereas a correlation coefficient measures only the strength and direction of the relationship between two variables, regression analysis provides us with an equation describing the nature of their relationship. Furthermore, regression analysis allows us to assess the accuracy of our model.

In simple regression analysis, we are interested in predicting the dependent variable's value based on the value of only one independent variable. For example, we would like to predict the effort needed to complete a software project based only on knowledge of its size. In this case, effort is the dependent variable and size is the independent variable. In multiple regression analysis, we are interested in predicting the value of the dependent variable based on several independent variables. For example, we would like to predict the effort needed to complete a software project based on knowledge about its size, required reliability, duration, team size, and other factors. Because it is easier to grasp multiple regression analysis if you understand simple regression analysis, we'll start with that.

Simple Regression

The least-squares method fits a straight line through the data that minimises the sum of the squared errors. The errors are the differences between the actual values and the predicted (i.e. estimated) values. These errors are also often referred to as the residuals.

In Fig. 12.10, the three points, (x_1,y_1), (x_2,y_2), and (x_3,y_3), represent the actual values. The predicted values, $(x_1, \hat{y}_1), (x_2, \hat{y}_2)$, and $(x_3, \hat{y}_3)$, are on the line. The errors are the differences between y and $\hat{y}$ for each observation. We want to find the straight line that minimizes $error_1^2 + error_2^2 + error_3^2$.

You may recall from algebra that the equation for a straight line is of the form:

$$\hat{y} = a + bx \tag{12.14}$$

where $\hat{y}$ is the predicted value of the dependent variable, y, given the value of the independent variable, x. The constant a represents the value of $\hat{y}$ when x is zero. This is also known as the y-intercept. The constant b represents the slope of the line. It will be positive when there is a positive relationship and negative when there is a negative relationship.

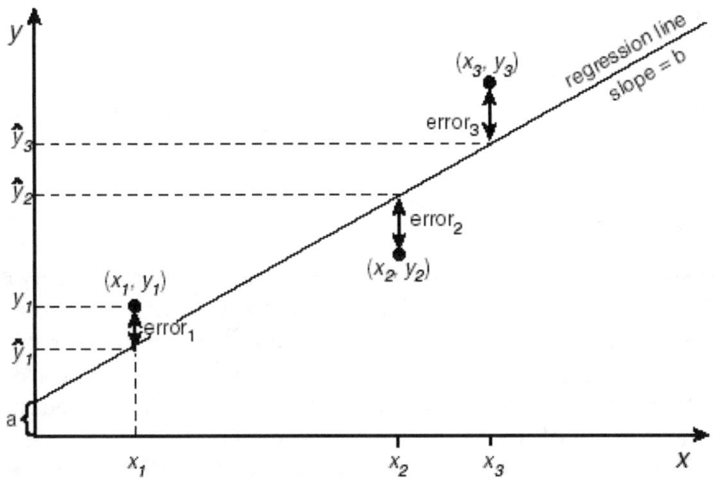

Fig. 12.10. Illustration of regression errors

To find the a and b values of a straight line fitted by the least-squares method, the following two equations must be solved simultaneously:

$$\begin{aligned} \sum y &= na + b\sum x \\ \sum xy &= a\sum x + b\sum x^2 \end{aligned} \tag{12.15}$$

where n is the number of observations. By plugging in the known values of x and y, a and b can be calculated. Table 12.16 demonstrates some steps in the calculation of the regression line for the five projects from our correlation example.

Table 12.16. Calculation of sums needed to solve regression equations

Project id	x, size	y, effort	x^2	xy
2	647	7871	418,609	5092537
3	130	845	16,900	109850
5	1056	21,272	1,115,136	22,463,232
6	383	4224	146,689	1,617,792

15	249	2565	62,001	638,685
n = 5	Σx = 2465	Σy = 36,777	Σx^2 = 1,759,335	Σxy =29922096

We can now solve these two equations for *a* and *b*:

$$\begin{aligned} 36{,}777 &= 5a + 2465b \\ 29{,}922{,}096 &= 2465a + 1{,}759{,}335b \end{aligned} \tag{12.16}$$

This results in the following regression line:

$$\textit{predicted effort} = -3328.46 + 21.67 \times \textit{size} \tag{12.17}$$

This is what your statistical analysis package is doing when you ask it to regress two variables.

Regression Accuracy

A regression line is only a measure of the average relationship between the dependent and independent variable. Unless there is perfect correlation, in which all the observations lie on a straight line, there will be errors in the estimates. The farther the actual values are from the regression line, the greater the estimation error. How can we translate this into a measure that will tell us if the fit of the regression line is any good?

Imagine that you join a company and you need to estimate a project's effort. The only data available is the effort of past projects. You don't even know if there were any similar projects in the past or what the projects' sizes were. How can you use this data? Well, the simplest thing to do would be to use the average effort of past projects as an estimate for the new project. You are not happy with the result and convince your company that you could improve future effort estimation if you also knew the sizes of past projects. Obviously, if you then collected and used this size data to develop a regression model to estimate effort, you would expect your model to perform better than just taking the average of past efforts. Otherwise, you would have wasted a great deal of your company's time and money counting function points. Similarly, comparing the results obtained by the regression equation with the results of using averages is how the accuracy of the regression model is determined.

Figure 12.11 shows an example using three projects. Let's pretend that y is the project effort and x is the size. We can see that for Project 1, the mean value of effort, $\bar{y}$, overestimates the actual value of effort, y_1. The predicted value of effort, $\hat{y}_1$, underestimates the actual effort. For Project 2, both the mean value of effort and the predicted value of effort, $\hat{y}_2$, overestimate the actual effort, y_2. For Project 3, both the mean value of effort and the predicted value of effort, $\hat{y}_3$, underestimate the actual effort, y_3. We need to compare the differences between the actual values, the predicted values, and the mean for each project to calculate the overall accuracy of our model.

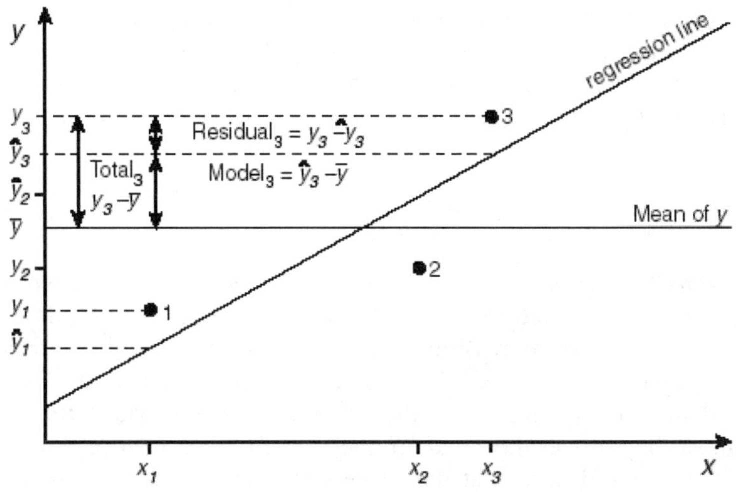

Fig. 12.11. Illustration of regression accuracy

The total squared error between the actual value of effort and the mean value of effort for each project is:

$$Total\ SS = \Sigma(y_i - \bar{y})^2 \tag{12.18}$$

This is the total variation of the data.[10] If effort really does depend on size, then the errors (residuals) should be small compared to the total variation of the data. The error (*Residual SS*) is the sum of the squared differences between the actual value of effort and the predicted value of effort for each project.

$$Residual\ SS = \Sigma(y_i - \hat{y}_i)^2 \tag{12.19}$$

This can also be thought of as the total variation in the data not explained by our model. The total variation of the data equals the variation explained by the model plus the variation not explained by the model, that

[10] The statistical term "variance" is defined as the sum of squared deviations divided by the number of observations minus one. It is a measure of the average variation of the data. Here I am referring to the total variation of the data (i.e. we don't divide by the number of observations).

is, *Total SS* = *Model SS* + *Residual SS*. The variation in the data explained by our model is:

$$Model\ SS = \Sigma(\hat{y}_i - \overline{y})^2 \tag{12.20}$$

Thus, if effort really does depend on size, the *Residual SS* will be small and the differences between the predicted values of effort and the mean value of effort (*Model SS*) will be close to the *Total SS*.

This is the logic that underlies the accuracy measure of the regression model, r^2:

$$r^2 = \frac{Model\ SS}{Total\ SS} \tag{12.21}$$

This is the R-squared (r^2) value. It is the fraction of the variation in the data that can be explained by the model. It can vary between 0 and 1 and measures the fit of the regression equation. If the model is no better than just taking averages, the *Model SS* will be small compared to the *Total SS* and r^2 will approach 0. This means that the linear model is bad. If the *Model SS* is almost the same as the *Total SS*, then r^2 will be very close to 1. An r^2 value close to 1 indicates that the regression line fits the data well. Our effort example has an r^2 value of 0.95. This means that 95% of the variation in effort is explained by variations in size. In simple regression, r^2 is also the square of Pearson's correlation coefficient, r, between two variables.

You may wonder how high of an r^2 value is needed for a regression model to be useful? The answer is that it depends. If I didn't know anything about the relationship between quality requirements and productivity, I would find any r^2 to be useful. Before I knew nothing, but now I know something. If the r^2 is very small, then I know there is no linear relationship. If the r^2 of productivity as a function of quality requirements is 0.25, I would find it useful to know that quality requirements explain 25% of the variation in productivity. This is quite a high percentage of productivity for one variable to explain. However, 0.25 is too small for a good predictive model. In this case, an r^2 over 0.90 would be great. But, I would also need to check for influential observations and consider the 95% confidence intervals before I got too excited. A very high r^2 is sometimes due to an extreme value.

Multiple Regression

Multiple regression is basically the same as simple regression except that instead of the model being a simple straight line, it is an equation with more than one independent variable. As a result, the calculations are more complex. In addition, once we get beyond three dimensions (two independent variables), we can no longer visualize the relationship. For example, at the most, we can draw a three-dimensional graph of effort as a function of application size and team size. The three-dimensional model is the plane that minimizes the sum of the squared deviations between each project and the plane. However, it is impossible to draw a four-dimensional diagram of effort as a function of application size, team size, and reliability requirements. In multiple regression, the r^2 is capitalized, R^2, and is called the coefficient of multiple determination.

Significance of Results

In both simple and multiple regression, the final step is to determine if our result is significant. Is our model significant? Are the coefficients of each variable and the constant significant? What does "significant" mean? Significance is best explained as follows. The lower the probability that our results are due to chance, the higher their significance. The probability is related to our sample size (i.e. the number of projects) and the number of variables we used to model the dependent variable. Different distributions, namely the F-distribution and the t-distribution, are used to determine these probabilities. Our statistical analysis package knows which distributions to use and will calculate the probability of our results being due to chance. We usually consider significant a probability value lower than or equal to 0.05. In research papers, it is common to read that results are significant at the 5% level (for a probability value lower than or equal to 0.05) or the 1% level (for a probability value lower than or equal to 0.01).

How To Interpret Regression Output

Now that you know some basics of regression analysis, you will be able to better understand the regression output in the example below. This is an example of the regression model ln(*effort*) as a function of ln(*size*) using software project data. Figure 12.7 shows the regression line fit to the data.

In the upper left corner of the output, we have a table. This is known as the analysis of variance (ANOVA) table. The column headings are defined as follows: *SS* = sum of squares, *df* = degrees of freedom, and *MS* = mean square. In this example, the total sum of squares (*Total SS*) is 34.86. The sum of squares accounted for by the model is 22.69 (*Model SS*), and *12.17* is left unexplained (*Residual SS*). There are 33 total degrees of freedom (34 observations – 1 for mean removal), of which 1 is used by the model (one variable, *lsize*), leaving 32 for the residual. The mean square error (*Residual MS*) is defined as the sum of squares (*Residual SS*) divided by the corresponding degrees of freedom (*Residual df*). Here, 12.17/32 = 0.38.

Example

```
. regress leffort lsize

  Source |       SS       df       MS              Number of obs =      34
---------+------------------------------           F(  1,     32) =   59.67
   Model |  22.6919055     1  22.6919055           Prob > F      =  0.0000
Residual |  12.1687291    32  .380272786           R-squared     =  0.6509
---------+------------------------------           Adj R-squared =  0.6400
   Total |  34.8606346    33  1.05638287           Root MSE      =  .61666

------------------------------------------------------------------------
 leffort |      Coef.   Std. Err.     t     P>|t|  [95% Conf. Interval]
---------+--------------------------------------------------------------
   lsize |   .9297666   .1203611   7.725   0.000 .6845991     1.174934
   _cons |   3.007431   .7201766   4.176   0.000  1.54048     4.474383
------------------------------------------------------------------------
```

In the upper right corner of the output, we have other summary statistics. The number of observations is 34. The *F* statistic associated with the ANOVA table (1 and 32 refer to the degrees of freedom of the model and the residual, respectively) is 59.67. The *F* statistic is calculated with the following equation:

$$F = \frac{\textit{Model SS/Model df}}{\textit{Residual SS/Residual df}} = \frac{22.6919/1}{12.1687/32} = 59.67 \qquad (12.22)$$

The *F* statistic tests the null hypothesis that all coefficients excluding the constant are zero. *Prob > F* = 0.0000 means that the probability of observing an *F* statistic of 59.67 or greater is 0.0000, which is my statistical analysis package's way of indicating a number smaller than 0.00005. Thus, we can reject the null hypothesis as there is only a 0.005% probability that all the coefficients are zero. This means that there is a 99.995% probability that at least one of them is not zero. In this case, we only have one independent variable, so its coefficient is definitely not zero. The R^2 (*R-squared*) for the regression is 0.6509, and the R^2 adjusted for the degrees of freedom (*Adj R-squared*) is 0.6400. The root mean square error (*Root MSE*) is 0.61666. This is the same as the square root of *MS Residual* in the ANOVA table.

When you interpret the R^2 in the statistical output, you should use the Adjusted R-squared. This is because it is always possible to increase the value of R^2 just by adding more independent variables to the model. This is true even when they are not related to the dependent variable. The number of observations must be significantly greater than the number of variables for the results to be reliable. The Adjusted R-squared is calculated by the following equation:

$$Adjusted\ R^2 = 1 - \frac{(1-R^2)(Total\ df)}{(Residual\ df)} \quad (12.23)$$

The total and residual degrees of freedom (*df*) can be read directly from the statistical output. In regression analysis, the total degrees of freedom are $n-1$ and the residual degrees of freedom are $n-k$, where n is the number of observations and k is the number of independent variables -1 (for the constant term).

At the bottom of the output, we have a table of the estimated coefficients (*Coef.*). The first line of the table tells us that the dependent variable is *leffort*. The estimated model is:

$$leffort = 3.0074 + 0.9298 \times lsize \quad (12.24)$$

At the right of the coefficients in the output are their standard errors (*Std. Err.*), t statistics (*t*), significance of the t statistics ($P>|t|$), and 95% confidence intervals (*95% Conf. Interval*). In this example, the standard error for the coefficient of *lsize* is 0.1203611. The corresponding t statistic is 7.725 (t = *Coef./Std.Err.*), which has a significance level of 0.000. This is my statistical analysis package's way of indicating a number less than 0.0005. Thus, we can be 99.95% sure that the coefficient of *lsize* is not really 0. That is, we can be confident that there really is a relationship between *leffort* and *lsize*. The 95% confidence interval for the coefficient is [–0.6846, 1.1749]. This means that we are 95% confident that the true coefficient of *lsize* in the population lies between –0.6896 and 1.1749. Confidence intervals are explained in Sect. 12.3.

Analysis of Residual Errors

If the assumptions of the regression model are met, then the plot of the residuals vs. fitted values (predicted values) should look like a random array of dots. If there is a pattern, this indicates that we have a problem. Figure 12.12 shows this plot for our regression output.

The assumptions of regression are:

1. A linear relationship exists.
2. The residuals have a constant variance. (This is called homoscedasticity.)
3. The residuals are independent.
4. The residuals are normally distributed.

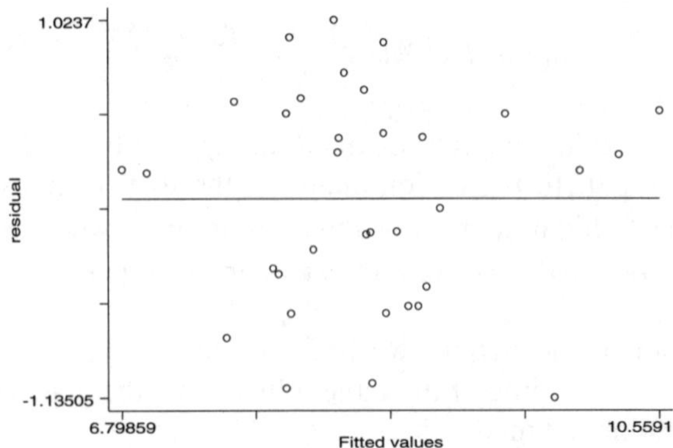

Fig. 12.12. Plot of residuals vs. fitted values

We can check Assumptions 1–3 by looking out for the following patterns in the residuals (Figs. 12.13 to 12.15):

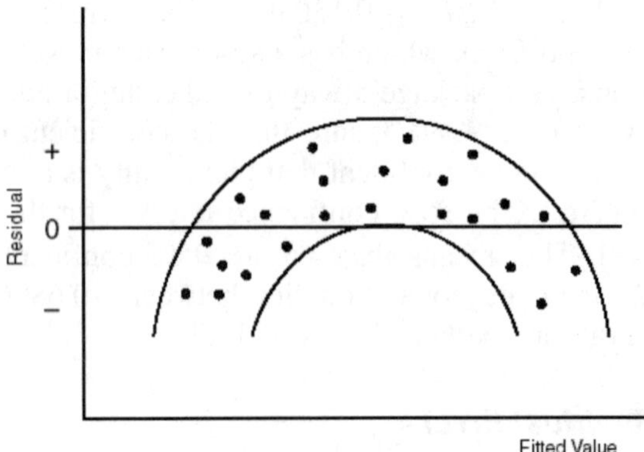

Fig. 12.13. Violation of Assumption 1

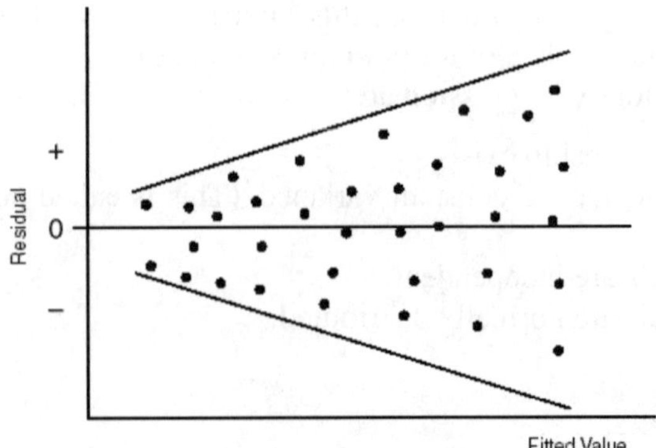

Fig. 12.14. Violation of Assumption 2

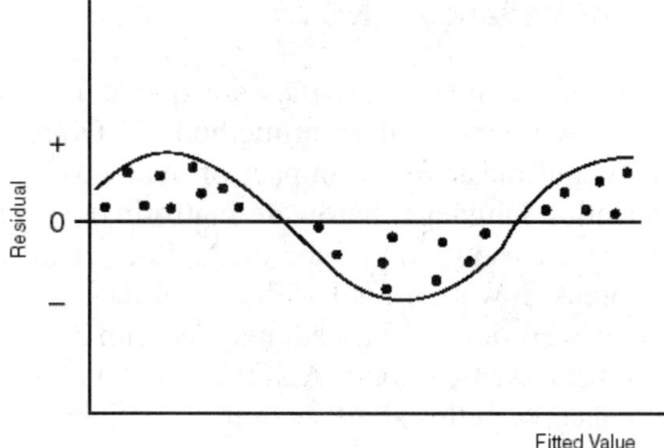

Fig. 12.15. Possible violation of Assumption 3

The residuals in Fig. 12.13 indicate that the relationship is not linear (violation of Assumption 1). Figure 12.14 shows an example where the errors increase with increasing values of x. This is a violation of Assumption 2. A residual pattern like Fig. 12.15 could mean that Assumption 3 has been violated. Assumption 4 is the easiest to check. We simply plot the distribution of the residuals. Figure 12.16 shows the residual distribution for our example.

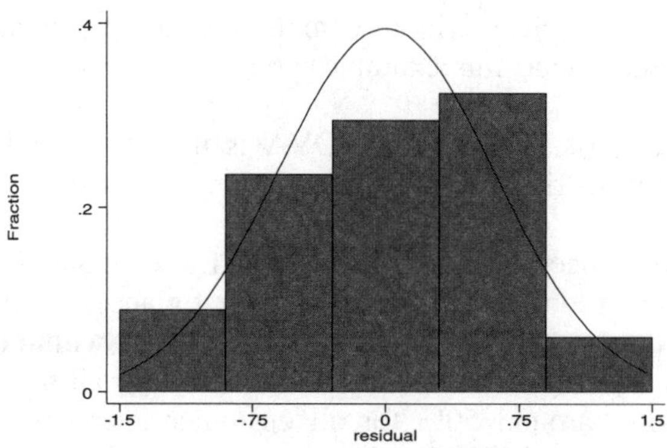

Fig. 12.16. Checking Assumption 4: distribution of the residuals

This distribution of residuals is not too far from a normal distribution. If the assumption of a normal distribution is not met, the tests of significance and the confidence intervals developed from them may be incorrect.

12.5.4 Analysis of Variance (ANOVA)

When many of the independent variables are qualitative, we cannot use regression analysis. We need a different method. ANOVA techniques can be used to identify and measure the impact of qualitative variables (business sector, application language, hardware platform, etc.) on a dependent variable (effort, productivity, duration, etc.). Like regression analysis, these techniques break down the total variation of the data into its various parts using a set of well-defined procedures. As with regression analysis, entire books have been written about ANOVA methods. I've summarised the fundamental concepts in this short section.

Simple ANOVA

Let's say that we want to know if the percentage of JCL (Job Control Language used for programming and controlling batch processing in an IBM mainframe environment) used is related to application type. We will study this relationship using some of the maintenance data from industrial software projects. I have chosen to illustrate the ANOVA method with a subset of the data that contains an equal number of observations in each category. In practice, the number of observations in each category will not be the same because software project data is inherently unbalanced. However, although the calculations are more complicated, the principal remains the same. If you understand this example, you will understand the basics of ANOVA.

One important assumption of ANOVA is that the sample is selected from a normally distributed parent population, which is the case for our example data.

Is there a difference in the percentage of JCL use among the three application types? Let's look at Table 12.17. At first glance, I would say no. It looks like the percentage of JCL use varies quite a lot within each application type. It is not as if we see values around 30% for all back office database applications, around 50% for all customer interconnection service applications, and around 70% for all core banking business system applications. However, it is impossible to make any conclusion by just looking at the data.

Table 12.17. Percentage of JCL use data and some ANOVA calculations

	Back office database	Customer interconnection service	Core banking business system	
	38	54	12	
	24	0	52	
	2	90	90	
	43	0	74	
	60	30	64	
	100	33	55	
	63	21	13	
	55	68	49	
	9	58	12	
	62	56	31	
	55	89	39	
	37	84	49	
	37	96	31	
	35	79	35	
	95	31	53	
GM	47.67	52.60	43.93	Sample Mean = 48.07
GV	737.38	1033.11	513.21	Mean of GV = 761.23

GM = Group Means GV = Group Variances

Our ANOVA example will test the following null hypothesis:

The mean percentage of JCL use is the same (in the population) for each of the three application types.

Of course, we do not know what the means in the population are. But, we can use our sample to estimate the means. If the means of percentage of JCL use for each application type in our sample are very close together, we will be more willing to accept that the null hypothesis is true. Our group means are 47.67%, 52.60%, and 43.93%. These group means do not seem that close to me. But are they significantly different given the size of our sample?[11]

We can get a better idea of any relationship that exists by calculating two variances, the variance between the groups and the variance within the groups, and comparing them. Both of these are estimates of the population variance. We can use their ratio to accept or reject the null hypothesis. The larger the variance in JCL use between application types and the smaller

[11] In practice, a software manager would probably not consider a 9% difference in percentage of JCL use to be that important, even if it was significant.

the variance within the application types, the more likely it is that percentage of JCL use really does differ among application types.

Between-Groups Variance

The between-groups variance calculates the variation between the mean percentage of JCL use of the three application types (47.67, 52.60, 43.93) measured about the mean JCL use of all 45 applications in our sample (48.07). The sample variance of the group means is a function of the squared differences of each group mean and the overall sample mean divided by the number of groups (application types) minus one:

$$s_{\bar{x}}^2 = \frac{(47.67-48.07)^2 + (52.60-48.07)^2 + (43.93-48.07)^2}{2} = 18.91 \quad (12.25)$$

As this is the sample variance of the group mean, we must multiply it by the number of observations in the group (15) to calculate the between groups variance:

$$s_{bg}^2 = ns_{\bar{x}}^2 = 15(18.91) = 283.65 \quad (12.26)$$

Within-Groups Variance

The group variance for each application type tells us how close the actual values of JCL use are to the mean values for that application type; that is, how much the data varies within each group. This is known as the within-groups variance. For example, the variance of JCL use for back office database applications is:

$$s_{backoffice}^2 = \frac{(38-47.67)^2 + (24-47.67)^2 + (2-47.67)^2 + \ldots + (95-47.67)^2}{14} = 737.38 \quad (12.27)$$

We have three application types and thus three estimates of population variance (737.38, 1033.11, and 513.21). Since none of these estimates is any better than the others, we combine them to create a single estimate of the population variance based on the average "within"-groups variation:

$$s_{wg}^2 = \frac{737.38 + 1033.11 + 513.21}{3} = 761.23 \quad (12.28)$$

F Ratio

Now we can calculate the ratio of the between-groups variance and the within-groups variance. This is known as the *F* ratio:

$$F = \frac{s_{bg}^2}{s_{wg}^2} = \frac{283.65}{761.23} = 0.37 \qquad (12.29)$$

The within groups variance can be thought of as the variance due to random differences among applications. The between-groups variance can be thought of as the variance due to random differences among applications plus differences in application type. Thus, the extent to which *F* exceeds 1 is indicative of a possible real effect of application type on JCL use. However, even if *F* exceeds 1, it is possible that it could be by chance alone. The probability of this occurring by chance is given by the F-distribution and is calculated automatically by your statistical analysis package. In our example, *F* is less than 1, and we can conclude that there is no relationship between application type and the percentage of JCL use.

How To Interpret ANOVA Output

Now that you know some basics of ANOVA, you will be able to better understand the ANOVA output in the example below. This is the output from my statistical analysis package for our ANOVA example: percentage of JCL use (*rperjcl*) as a function of application type (*apptype*).

Example

```
. anova rperjcl apptype

    Number of obs =      45      R-squared     =  0.0174
    Root MSE      = 27.5905      Adj R-squared = -0.0294

    Source |  Partial SS    df       MS          F     Prob > F
-----------+----------------------------------------------------
    Model  | 566.933333      2  283.466667   0.37    0.6913
  apptype  | 566.933333      2  283.466667   0.37    0.6913
 Residual  | 31971.8667     42  761.234921
-----------+----------------------------------------------------
    Total  |   32538.80     44  739.518182
```

At the top of the ANOVA output is a summary of the underlying regression. The model was estimated using 45 observations, and the root mean square error (*Root MSE*) is 27.59. The *R-squared* for the model is 0.0174, and the R-squared adjusted for the number of degrees of freedom (*Adj R-squared*) is –0.0294. (See the regression output in the previous section for a discussion of Adjusted R-squared.) Obviously, this model is pretty bad.

The first line of the table summarises the model. The sum of squares (*Model SS*) for the model is 566.9 with 2 degrees of freedom (*Model df*). This results in a mean square (*Model MS*) of 566.9/2 ≅ 283.5. This is our between groups variance, s_{bg}^2. (Once again, there is a small difference between the computer's between-groups variance and my calculation due to rounding errors.)

$$F = \frac{Model\ SS/Model\ df}{Residual\ SS/Residual\ df} = \frac{s_{bg}^2}{s_{wg}^2} \qquad (12.30)$$

The corresponding F ratio has a value of 0.37 and a significance level of 0.6913. Thus, the model is not significant. We cannot reject the null hypothesis and say that there is no difference in the mean percentage of JCL use of different application types.[12]

The next line summarises the first (and only) term in the model, *apptype*. Since there is only one variable, this line is the same as the previous line.

The third line summarises the residual. The residual sum of squares (*Residual SS*) is 31,971.87, with 42 degrees of freedom (*Residual df*), resulting in a mean square error of 761.23 (*Residual MS*). This is our within-groups variance, s_{wg}^2. The *Root MSE* is the square root of this number.

The *Model SS* plus the *Residual SS* equals the *Total SS*. The *Model df* plus the *Residual df* equals the *Total df*, 44. As there are 45 observations, and we must subtract 1 degree of freedom for the mean, we are left with 44 total degrees of freedom.

Multi-variable ANOVA

ANOVA can also be used to produce regression estimates for models with numerous quantitative and qualitative variables. ANOVA uses the method of least squares to fit linear models to the quantitative data. Thus, you can think of it as a combination of multiple regression analysis and the simple ANOVA I just explained. This is not so strange as you can see that the underlying principle in both methods is that we compare values to a mean value. In both methods, we also compare the variation explained by the model to the total variation of the data to measure its accuracy.

---

12 Had we been able to reject the null hypothesis in this example, it might not have been because of the differences in the population means, but because of the differences in their variances. When the sample variances for the different groups are very different, as they are in this example, then reject with caution. The ANOVA approach assumes that the population variances are similar.

12.5.5 Comparing Two Estimation Models

I recommend that non-statistical experts use the Wilcoxon signed-rank test with matched pairs to determine if there is a statistically significant difference between two estimation models. This is a non-parametric statistic. As such, it is free from the often unrealistic assumptions underlying parametric statistics.[13] For example, one of the assumptions of the parametric paired t-test is that the paired data has equal variances. This may not be the case with your data and you do not want to have to worry about it. Non-parametric tests can always be used instead of parametric tests; however, the opposite is not true.

The Wilcoxon Signed-Rank Test Applied to Matched Pairs

The Wilcoxon signed-rank test is based on the sign and rank of the absolute values of pair differences and is done automatically by most statistical analysis packages. What does this actually mean and how can we apply it to effort estimation models? Table 12.18 shows the *estimation error* (i.e. *actual – estimate*) and the *absolute estimation error* (i.e. |*actual – estimate*|) of two hypothetical effort estimation models used on three projects. We use the *absolute estimation error* in our calculations because we are interested only in the magnitude of the estimation error and not if it is over or under the estimate. The *pair difference*, then, is the difference in the absolute values of the estimation errors of the two models, C and D, for each project. The *sign* is negative if Model D's error is greater than Model C's for that project. The *sign* is positive if Model C's error is greater than Model D's for that project. The *rank* is based on the comparison of absolute values of the pair differences for each project. The smallest absolute pair difference of all three projects gets a rank of 1, the second smallest gets a rank of 2, and so on. The computer uses the information in the last two columns to compute the Wilcoxon signed-rank test statistic. From this test, we can determine if either Model C or Model D has consistently smaller errors.

Let's look at the statistical output for this test in the next example to try to understand what is going on. The example compares two models – Model A and Model B.

In the statistical output, *aModel_A* refers to Model A's absolute errors and *aModel_B* refers to Model B's absolute errors. The null hypothesis is that the distribution of the paired differences has a median of 0 and is symmetric. This implies that for approximately half the projects, Model A

13 Parametric statistics are only suitable for data measured on interval and ratio scales, where parameters such as the mean of the distribution can be defined.

has a smaller error, and for half the projects, Model B has a smaller error. Thus neither model is better. If this were the case, then we would expect the sum of the ranks to be the same for positive and negative differences. These are the *expected* values, 976.5, in the statistical output.

Table 12.18. How to Rank Differences for Wilcoxon Signed-Rank Tests on Matched Pairs

Id	OB1	OB2	OB3
Estimation error (hours) Model C	–200	50	150
Estimation error (hours) Model D	300	100	–20
Absolute estimation error (hours) Model C	200	50	150
Absolute estimation error (hours) Model D	300	100	20
Pair difference	–100	-50	130
Sign	–	–	+
Rank of absolute differences	2	1	3

Example

```
. signrank aModel_A=aModel_B

Wilcoxon signed-rank test

     sign |      obs   sum ranks    expected
----------+---------------------------------
 positive |       26         798       976.5
 negative |       36        1155       976.5
     zero |        0           0           0
----------+---------------------------------
      all |       62        1953        1953

unadjusted variance    20343.75
adjustment for ties        0.00
adjustment for zeros       0.00
                     ----------
adjusted variance      20343.75

Ho: aModel_A = aModel_B
             z =  -1.251
    Prob > |z| =   0.2108
```

What we find, however, is that the rank sum of the *positive* differences is 798 and the rank sum of the *negative* differences is 1155. This means that Model B's absolute error is ranked higher than Model A's absolute error for more projects (remember that the difference = Model A – Model B). However, we only have a sample and this may have happened by chance. So, we need to check the probability that this happened by chance.

The statistic computed by the Wilcoxon test, the z value, is –1.251. If –1.96 > z > 1.96, there is no difference between the models. If z is less than –1.96, then Model A has a significantly lower absolute error. If z is greater than 1.96, then Model A has a significantly higher absolute error. As –1.251 is between –1.96 and 1.96, this means that there is no statistically significant difference between the models. Our significance level is 21% ($Pr > |z| = 0.2108$). This means that if we reject the null hypothesis, there is a 21% probability of being wrong (i.e. rejecting the null hypothesis when it is in fact true). It is typical in statistical studies to accept only a 5% chance of being wrong. Thus, there is no statistically significant difference between the two models.

Does this z value, 1.96, seem familiar? In fact, it comes from the 95% confidence interval of the normal curve. There is a 5% chance of getting a value higher than |1.96|. This means there is a 2.5% chance of getting a value lower than –1.96 and a 2.5% chance of getting a value higher than 1.96. This is what is meant by a two-sided (or two-tailed) test. A one-sided test checks only the chance of a value being lower or higher.

12.5.6 Final Comments

In this chapter, you learned some of the basic concepts of statistics and developed a deeper understanding of multivariate statistical analysis. I'll end with one final word of advice: Remember to be reasonable with your inferences. If you find some interesting results based on 30 projects in your company, you can say something about what is going on in your company. This does not mean that this is true for all software projects in the world. Only if people in different companies keep finding the same results can you start to believe that you have found a fundamental truth. For example, enough studies have now been published that we can be certain that there is a real relationship between software effort and size. However, the exact equation describing the relationship varies by study. This is why it is often necessary to calibrate software cost estimation tools using your company's data.

Author's Biography

Katrina Maxwell is an expert in the area of software development productivity and cost estimation. Her research has been published in *IEEE Transactions on Software Engineering*, *IEEE Software, Management Science* and Academic Press's prestigious "*Advances in Computers*" series. She is the author of *Applied Statistics for Software Managers* published by Prentice Hall PTR. She has taught at the University of Illinois, INSEAD, and the Ecole Supérieure de Commerce de Paris, and was Programme Chair of the ESCOM-SCOPE 2000 and 2001 conferences. Between 1988 and 1997 she was a Research Fellow at INSEAD where she undertook research in the areas of economics, business policy, marketing, operations research and technology management. In particular, she worked for four years on a research project, funded by the cost analysis division of the European Space Agency, to develop a better understanding of software development costs in order to improve the evaluation of subcontractor bids. As the manager of the ESA software metrics database, she improved the data collection methodology, collected and validated data from subcontractors, analysed the data, and communicated the results via research papers, conference presentations and workshops. In 1997, she created Datamax, which specializes in consulting, research, and training in software metrics and data analysis. She is also a Senior Research Fellow at INSEAD.

13 Empirical Research Methods in Web and Software Engineering[1]

Claes Wohlin, Martin Höst, Kennet Henningsson

Abstract: Web and software engineering are not only about technical solutions. They are to a large extent also concerned with organisational issues, project management and human behaviour. For disciplines like Web and software engineering, empirical methods are crucial, since they allow for incorporating human behaviour into the research approach taken. Empirical methods are common practice in many other disciplines. This chapter provides a motivation for the use of empirical methods in Web and software engineering research. The main motivation is that it is needed from an engineering perspective to allow for informed and well-grounded decisions. The chapter continues with a brief introduction to four research methods: controlled experiments, case studies, surveys and post-mortem analyses. These methods are then put into an improvement context. The four methods are presented with the objective to introduce the reader to the methods to a level where it is possible to select the most suitable method at a specific instance. The methods have in common that they all are concerned with quantitative data. However, several of them are also suitable for qualitative data. Finally, it is concluded that the methods are not competing. On the contrary, the different research methods can preferably be used together to obtain more sources of information that hopefully lead to more informed engineering decisions in Web and software engineering.

Keywords: Case study, Controlled experiment, Survey, Post-mortem ana–lysis, Empirical investigation, Engineering discipline.

13.1 Introduction

To become a true engineering discipline Web and software engineering have to adopt and adapt research methods from other disciplines. Engineering means, among other things, that we should be able to understand, plan, monitor, control, estimate, predict and improve the way we engineer our products. One enabler for doing this is measurement. Web and software

[1] A previous version of this chapter has been published in Empirical Methods and Studies in Software Engineering: Experiences from ESERNET, pp 7–23, editors Reidar Conradi and Alf Inge Wang, Lecture Notes in Computer Science Springer-Verlag, Germany, 2765, 2003. This chapter has been adapted by Emilia Mendes.

measurement form the basis, but they are not sufficient. Empirical methods such as controlled experiments, case studies, surveys and post-mortem analyses are needed to help us evaluate and validate the research results. These methods are needed so that it is possible to scientifically state whether something is better than something else. Thus, empirical methods provide one important scientific basis for both Web and software engineering. For some types of problems other methods, e.g. the use of mathematical models for predicting software reliability, are better suited, but in most cases the best method is to apply empiricism. The main reason is that Web and software development are human intensive, and hence they do not lend themselves to analytical approaches. This means that empirical methods are essential to the researcher.

The empirical methods are, however, also crucial from an industrial point of view. Companies aspiring to become learning organisations have to consider the following definition of a learning organisation:

> *"A learning organisation is an organisation skilled at creating, acquiring, and transferring knowledge, and at modifying its behavior to reflect new knowledge and insights." [1]*

Garvin continues by stating that learning organisations are good at five activities: systematic problem solving, experimentation, learning from past experiences, learning from others, and transferring knowledge. This includes relying on scientific methods rather than guesswork. From the perspective of this chapter, the key issue is the application of a scientific method and the use of empirical methods as a vehicle for systematic improvement when engineering Web applications and software. The quote from Garvin is inline with the concepts of the Quality Improvement Paradigm and the Experience Factory [2] that are often used in a software engineering context.

In summary, the above means that Web and software engineering researchers and learning organisations both have a need to embrace empirical methods. The main objective of this chapter is to provide an introduction to four empirical research methods and to put them into an engineering context.

The remainder of this chapter is outlined as follows. Four empirical methods are briefly introduced in Sect. 13.2 to provide the reader with a reference framework to better understand the differences and similarities between the methods presented later. In Sect. 13.3, the four empirical methods are put into an improvement context before presenting the methods in some more detail in Sects. 13.4 to 13.7. The chapter is concluded with a short summary in Sect. 13.8.

13.2 Overview of Empirical Methods

There are two main types of research paradigms having different approaches to empirical studies. *Qualitative research* is concerned with studying objects in their natural setting. A qualitative researcher attempts to interpret a phenomenon based on explanations that people bring to them [3]. Qualitative research begins with accepting that there is a range of different ways of interpretation. It is concerned with discovering causes noticed by the subjects in the study, and understanding their view of the problem at hand. The subject is the person who is taking part in a study in order to evaluate an object.

Quantitative research is mainly concerned with quantifying a relationship or comparing two or more groups [4]. The aim is to identify a cause effect relationship. The quantitative research is often conducted through setting up controlled experiments or collecting data through case studies. Quantitative investigations are appropriate when testing the effect of some manipulation or activity. An advantage is that quantitative data promotes comparisons and statistical analysis. The use of quantitative research methods is dependent on the application of measurement, which is further discussed in [5].

It is possible for qualitative and quantitative research to investigate the same topics but each of them will address a different type of question. For example, a quantitative investigation could be launched to investigate how much a new inspection method decreases the number of faults found in a test. To answer questions about the sources of variations between different inspection groups, we need a qualitative investigation.

As mentioned earlier, quantitative strategies, such as controlled experiments, are appropriate when testing the effects of a treatment, while a qualitative study of beliefs and understandings is appropriate to find out *why* the results from a quantitative investigation are as they are. The two approaches should be regarded as complementary rather than competitive.

In general, any empirical study can be mapped to the following main research steps: Definition, Planning, Operation, Analysis & interpretation, Conclusions and Presentation & packaging. The work within the steps differs considerably depending on the type of empirical study. However, instead of trying to present four different research methods according to this general process, we have chosen to highlight the main aspects of interest for the different types of studies.

Depending on the purpose of the evaluation, whether it is techniques, methods or tools, and depending on the conditions for the empirical investigation, there are four major different types of investigations (strategies) that are addressed here:

- *Experiment.* Experiments are sometimes referred to as research-in-the-small [6], since they are concerned with a limited scope and most often are run in a laboratory setting. They are often highly controlled and hence also occasionally referred to as controlled experiments, which is used hereafter. When experimenting, subjects are assigned to different treatments at random. The objective is to manipulate one or more variables and control all other variables at fixed levels. The effect of the manipulation is measured, and based on this a statistical analysis can be performed. In some cases it may be impossible to use true experimentation; we may have to use quasi-experiments. The latter term is often used when it is impossible to perform random assignment of the subjects to the different treatments. An example of a controlled experiment in Web engineering is to compare two different methods for developing web applications (e.g. OOHDM vs. W2000). For this type of study, methods for statistical inference are applied with the purpose of showing with statistical significance that one method is better than the other [7, 8, 9].
- *Case study.* Case study research is sometimes referred to as research-in-the-typical [6]. It is described in this way because a case study normally studies a real project and hence the situation is "typical". Case studies are used for monitoring projects, activities or assignments. Data is collected for a specific purpose throughout the study. Based on the data collection, statistical analyses can be carried out. The case study is normally aimed at tracking a specific attribute or establishing relationships between different attributes. The level of control is lower in a case study than in an experiment. A case study is an observational study while the experiment is a controlled study [10]. A case study may, for example, be aimed at building a model to predict the number of faults in testing. Multivariate statistical analysis is often applied in this type of study. The analysis methods include linear regression and principal component analysis [11]. Case study research is further discussed in [9, 12, 13, 14].

The following two methods are both concerned with research-in-the-past, although they have different approaches to studying the past:

- *Survey.* The survey is referred to by [6] as research-in-the-large (and past), since it is possible to send a questionnaire to or interview a large number people covering whatever target population we have. Thus, a survey is often an investigation performed in retrospect, when a tool or technique, say, has been in use for a while [13]. The primary means of gathering qualitative or quantitative data are interviews or questionnaires. These are done by taking a sample that is representative of the population to be studied. The results from the survey are then analysed to derive descriptive and explanatory conclusions. They are thengeneralised to the population from which the sample was taken. Surveys are discussed further in [9, 15].

- *Post-mortem analysis*. This type of analysis is also conducted on the past as indicated by the name. However, it should be interpreted a little broader than literally as a post-mortem. For example, a project does not have to be finished to launch a post-mortem analysis. It should be possible to study any part of a project retrospectively using this type of analysis. Thus, this type of analysis may, in the descriptive way used by [6], be described as being research-in-the-past-and-typical. It can hence be viewed as related to both the survey and the case study. The post-mortem may be conducted by looking at project documentation (e.g. archival analysis [9]) or by interviewing people, individually or as a group, who have participated in the object that is being analysed in the post-mortem analysis.

An experiment is a formal, rigorous and controlled investigation. In an experiment the key factors are identified and manipulated. The separation between case studies and experiments can be represented by the notion of a state variable [13]. In an experiment, the state variable can assume different values and the objective is normally to distinguish between two situations: for example, a control situation and the situation under investigation. Examples of a state variable could be, for example, the inspection method or experience of the Web developers. In a case study, the state variable only assumes one value, governed by the actual project under study.

Case study research is a technique where key factors that may have any effect on the outcome are identified and then the activity is documented [12, 14]. Case study research is an observational method, i.e. it is done by observation of an on-going project or activity.

Surveys are very common within social sciences where, for example, attitudes are polled to determine how a population will vote in the next election. A survey provides no control of the execution or the measurement, though it is possible to compare it with similar ones, but it is not possible to manipulate variables as in the other investigation methods [15].

Finally, a post-mortem analysis may be viewed as inheriting properties from both surveys and case studies. A post-mortem may contain survey elements, but it is normally concerned with a case. The latter could be either a full Web project or a specific targeted activity.

For all four methods, it is important to consider the population of interest. It is from the population that a sample should be found. The sample should preferably be chosen randomly from the population. The sample should consist of a number of subjects: for example, in many cases individuals participating in a study. The actual population may vary from an ambition to have a general population, as is normally the objective in experiments where we would like to generalise the results, to a more narrow view, which may be the case in post-mortem analyses and case studies.

Some of the research strategies could be classified as both qualitative and quantitative, depending on the design of the investigation, as shown in Table 13.1. The classification of a survey depends on the design of the questionnaires, i.e. which data is collected and if it is possible to apply any statistical methods. Also, this is true for case studies, but the difference is that a survey is done in retrospect while a case study is done when a project is executed. A survey could also be launched before the execution of a project. In the latter case, the survey is based on previous experiences and hence conducted in retrospect to these experiences, although the objective is to get some ideas of the outcome of the forthcoming project. A post-mortem is normally conducted close to the end of an activity or project. It is important to conduct it close in time to the actual finish so that people are still available and the experiences fresh.

Experiments are purely quantitative since they have a focus on measuring different variables, change them and measure them again. During these investigations quantitative data is collected and then statistical methods are applied. Sections 13.4 to 13.7 give introductions to each empirical strategy, but before this the empirical methods are put into an improvement context in the following section. The introduction to controlled experiments is longer than for the other empirical methods. The main reason is that the procedure for running controlled experiments is more formal, i.e. it is sometimes referred to as a fixed design [9]. The other methods are more flexible and it is hence not possible to describe the actual research process in the same depth. Table 13.1 indicates this, where the qualitative and quantitative nature of the methods are indicated. Methods with a less fixed design are sometimes referred to as flexible design [9], which also indicates that the design may change during the execution of the study due to events happening during the study.

Table 13.1. Qualitative vs. quantitative in empirical strategies

Strategy	Qualitative/quantitative
Experiment	Quantitative
Case study	Both
Survey	Both
Post-mortem	Both

13.3 Empirical Methods in an Improvement Context

Systematic improvement includes using a generic improvement cycle such as the Quality Improvement Paradigm (QIP) [2]. This improvement cycle is generic in the sense that it can both be viewed as a recommended way to work with improvement of Web and software development, and also be used as a framework for conducting empirical studies. For simplicity, it is primarily viewed here as a way of improving Web development, and complemented with a simple three-step approach on how the empirical methods can be used as a vehicle for systematic engineering-based improvement.

The QIP consists of six steps that are repeated iteratively:

1. *Characterise*. The objective is to understand the current situation and establish a baseline.
2. *Set goals*. Quantifiable goals are set and given in terms of improvement.
3. *Choose process/method/technique*. Based on the characterisation and the goals, the part to improve is identified and a suitable improvement candidate is identified.
4. *Execute*. The study or project is performed and the results are collected for evaluation purposes.
5. *Analyse*. The outcome is studied and future possible improvements are identified.
6. *Package*. The experiences are packaged so that they can form the basis for further improvements.

It is in most cases impossible to start improving directly. The first step is normally to understand the current situation and then improvement opportunities are identified and they need to be evaluated before being introduced into an industrial process as an improvement. Thus, systematic improvement is based on the following steps:

- Understand,
- Evaluate, and
- Improve.

As a scenario, it is possible to imagine that one or both of the two methods looking at the past are used for understanding and baselining, i.e. a survey or a post-mortem analysis may be conducted to get a picture of the current situation. The objectives of a survey and a post-mortem analysis are slightly different as discussed in Sect. 13.2. The evaluation step may be executed using either a controlled experiment or a case study. It will most likely be a controlled experiment if the identified improvement candidate is evaluated in a laboratory setting and compared with another method, preferably the existing method or a method that may be used for benchmarking. It may be a case study if it is judged that the improvement candidate can be introduced in a pilot project directly. This pilot Web project ought to be studied and a suitable method is to use a case study. In the actual improvement in an industrial setting (normally initially in one project), it is probably better to use a case study approach, which then may be compared with the situation found when creating the understanding. Finally, if the evaluation comes out positive, the improvement is incorporated in the standard Web or software development process.

The above means that the four methods presented here should be viewed as complementary and not competing. They all have their benefits and drawbacks. The scenario above should be viewed as one possible way of using the methods as complementary in improving the way Web applications and software are engineered.

Next, the four methods are presented in more detail to provide an introduction and understanding of them. The objective is to provide sufficient information so that a researcher intending to conduct an empirical study in Web or software engineering can select an appropriate method given the situation at hand.

13.4 Controlled Experiments

13.4.1 Introduction

In an experiment the researcher has control over the study and how the participants carry out the tasks that they are assigned to. This can be compared to a typical case study, see below, where the researcher is more of an observer. The advantage of the experiment is, of course, that the study can be planned and designed to ensure high validity, although the drawback is that the scope of the study often gets smaller. For example, it sould be possible to view a complete Web development project as a case study, but a typical experiment does not include all the activities of such a project.

Experiments are often conducted to compare a number of different techniques, methods, working procedures, etc. For example, an experiment could be carried out with the objective of comparing two different reading techniques for inspections. In this example two groups of people could independently perform a task with one reading technique each. That is, if there are two reading techniques, R1 and R2, and two groups, G1 and G2, then people in group G1 could use technique R1 and people in group G2 could use technique R2. This small example is used in the following subsections to illustrate some of the concepts for controlled experiments.

13.4.2 Design

Before the experiment can be carried out it must be planned in detail. This plan is often referred to as the experiment's design.

In an experiment we wish to draw conclusions that are valid for a large population. For example, we wish to investigate whether reading technique R1 is more effective than reading technique R2 in general for any developer, project, organization, etc. However, it is, of course, impossible to involve every developer in the study. Therefore, a sample of the entire population is used in the experiment. Ideally, it should be possible to randomly choose a sample from the population to include in the study, but this is for obvious reasons almost impossible. Often, we end up trying to determine to which population we can generalise the results from a certain set of participants.

The main reason for the above is that the relation between sample and population is intricate and difficult to handle. In the Web and software engineering domains, it is mostly desirable to sample from all Web or software developers, or a subset of them, e.g. all Web designers using a specific programming language. For practical reasons this is impossible. Thus, in the best case it is possible to choose from Web developers in the vicinity of the researcher. This means that the sample is not a true sample from the population, although it may be fairly good. In many cases, it is impossible to have professional developers and students are used, and in particular we have to settle for students on a specific course. The latter is referred to as convenience sampling [9]. This situation means that in most cases we must go from subjects to population when the preferred situation is to go from population to subjects through random sampling. This should not necessarily be seen as a failure. It may be a complementary approach. However, it is important to be aware of the difference and also to consider how this affects the statistical analysis, since most statistical methods have developed based on the assumption of a random sample from the population of interest. The challenge of representative samples is also discussed in Chap. 12.

Another important principle of experiments is randomisation. With this we mean that when it is decided which treatment every participant should be subject to, this is done by random. For example, if 20 people participate in the study where the two reading techniques R1 and R2 are compared, it is decided at random which 10 people should use R1 and which 10 people should use R2.

In experiments a number of variables are often defined. Two important types of variables are:

- Independent variables: These variables describe the treatments in the experiment. In the above example, the choice of reading technique is an independent variable that can take one of the two values R1 or R2.
- Dependent variables: These variables are studied to investigate whether they are influenced by the independent variables. For example, the number of defects can be a dependent variable that we believe is dependent on whether R1 or R2 is used. The objective of the experiment is to determine if and how much the dependent variables are affected by the independent variables.

The independent and dependent variables are formulated to cover one or several hypotheses that we have with respect to the experiment. For example, we may hypothesise that the number of defects is dependent on the two reading techniques in the example. Hypothesis testing is discussed further in relation to the analysis.

The independent and dependent variables are illustrated in Fig. 13.1 together with the confounding factors. Confounding factors are variables that may affect the dependent variables without the knowledge of the researcher. It is hence crucial to try to identify the factors that otherwise may affect the outcome in an undesirable way. These factors are closely related to the threats about the validity of the empirical study. Thus, it is important to consider confounding factors and the threats to the study throughout the performance of any empirical study. The threats to empirical studies are discussed in Sect. 13.4. One objective of the design is to minimise the effect of these factors.

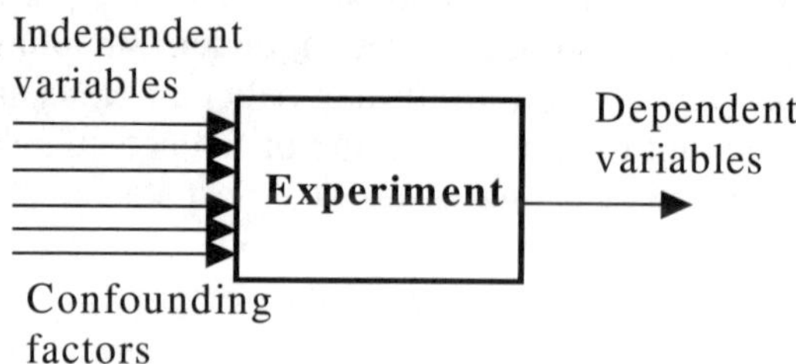

Fig. 13.1. Variables in an experiment

Often one of several available standard designs is used. Some examples of standard designs are:

- *Standard design 1:* One independent variable with two values. For example, two techniques should be compared and each participant uses one of the techniques.
- *Standard design 2:* One independent variable with two values, paired design. The difference between this design and *standard design 1* is

that each person in this design is subject to both treatments. The order in which each participant should apply the treatments is decided at random. For example, if the two reading techniques are to be evaluated, half of the participants first use R1 and then R2, and the other half first use R2 and then R1. The reason for using the treatments in different order is that effects of the order should be ruled out.

- *Standard design 3:* One independent variable with more than two values. The difference between this design and *standard design 1* is that more than two treatments are compared. For example, three reading techniques may be compared.
- *Standard design 4:* More than one independent variable. With this design more than one aspect can be evaluated in an experiment. For example, the choice of both reading technique and requirements notation may be compared in one experiment.

The designs that are presented here are a summary of some of the most commonly used designs. There are alternatives and more complicated designs. For example, sometimes experiments are carried out as a combination of a pre-study and a main experiment.

13.4.3 Operation

In the operation of an experiment a number of parts can be included. These include both parts that have to be done when starting the experiment and when actually running the experiment. Three key parts are:

- Commit participants: It is important that every participant is committed to the tasks. There are a number of factors to consider: for example, if the experiment concerns sensitive material, it will be difficult to get committed people.
- Prepare instrumentation: All the material that should be used during the experiment must be prepared. This may include written instructions to the participants, forms that should be used by the participants during the tests, etc. The instrumentation should be developed according to the design of the experiment. In most cases different participants should be given different sets of instructions and forms. In many cases paper-based forms are used during an experiment. It is, however, possible to collect data in a number of other ways, e.g. Web-based forms, interviews, etc.
- Execution: The actual execution denotes the part of the experiment where the participants, subject to their treatment, carry out the task that they are assigned to. For example, it may mean that some participants solve a development assignment with one development tool and the

other participants solve the same assignment with another tool. During this task the participants use the prepared instrumentation to receive instructions and to record data that can be used later in the analysis.

13.4.4 Analysis and Interpretation

Before actually doing any analysis, it is important to validate that the data is correct, and that the instruments used (e.g. forms) have been filled out correctly. This activity may also be sorted under execution of the experiment, and hence be carried out before the actual analysis.

The first part in the actual analysis is normally to apply descriptive statistics. This includes plotting the data in some way to obtain an overview of the data. Part of this analysis is done to identify and handle outliers. An outlier denotes a value that is atypical and unexpected in the data set. Outliers may, for example, be identified through boxplots [16] or scatterplots. Every outlier must be investigated and handled separately. It may be that the value is simply wrong. Then it may be corrected or discarded. It may also, of course, be the case that the value is correct. In that case it can be included in the analysis or, if the reason for the atypical value can be identified, it may be handled separately.

When we have made sure that the data is correct and obtained a good understanding of the data from the descriptive statistics then the analysis related to testing one or several hypotheses can start. In most cases the objective here is to decide whether there is an effect of the value of the independent variable(s) on the value of the dependent variable(s). This is in most cases analysed through hypothesis testing. To understand hypothesis testing some important definitions must be understood:

- The null hypothesis H_0 denotes that there is no effect of the independent variable on the dependent variable. The objective of the hypothesis test is to reject this hypothesis with a known significance.
- P(type-I error) = P(reject H_0 | H_0 is true). This probability may also be called the significance of a hypothesis test.
- P(type-II error) = P(not reject H_0 | H_0 is false).
- Power = 1 - P(type-II error) = P(reject H_0 | H_0 is false).

When the test is carried out, a maximum P(type-I error) is first decided. Then a test is used in order to decide whether it is possible to reject the null hypothesis or not. When choosing a test, it must be decided whether to use parametric or non-parametric tests. Generally, there are harder requirements on the data for parametric tests. They are, for example, based on the assumption that the data is normally distributed. However, parametric tests generally have higher power than non-parametric tests, i.e. less data is needed to obtain significant results when using parametric tests. The difference is not large. It is, of course, impossible to provide any exact figure, but it is in most cases of the order of 10%. For every design there are a number of tests that may be used. Some examples of tests are given in Table 13.2.

The tests in Table 13.2 are all described in a number of basic statistical references. More information on parametric tests can be found in [7], and information on the non-parametric tests can be found in [8] and [17].

Table 13.2. Examples of tests

Standard design (see above)	Parametric tests	Non-parametric tests
Standard design 1	t-test	Mann–Whitney
Standard design 2	Paired t-test	Wilcoxon, Sign–test
Standard design 3	ANOVA	Kruskal–Wallis
Standard design 4	ANOVA	

Before the results are presented it is important to assess how valid the results are. Basically there are four categories of validity concerns, which are discussed in a software engineering context in [18]:

- *Internal*: The internal validity is concerned with factors that may affect the dependent variables without the researcher's knowledge. An example of an issue is whether the history of the participants affects the result of an experiment. For example, the result may not be the same if the experiment is carried out directly after a complicated fault in the code has caused the participant a lot of problem compared to a more normal situation. A good example of how confounding factors may threaten the internal validity in a study is presented in [19].
- *External*: The external validity is related to the ability to generalise the results of the experiments. Examples of issues are whether the problem that the participants have been working on is representative and whether the participants are representative of the target population.
- *Conclusion*: The conclusion validity is concerned with the possibility to draw correct conclusions regarding the relationship between treatments and the outcome of an experiment. Examples of issues to consider are whether the statistical power of the tests is too low, or if the reliability of the measurements is high enough.
- *Construct*: The construct validity is related to the relationship between the concepts and theories behind the experiment and what is measured and affected. Examples of issues are whether the concepts are defined clearly enough before measurements are defined, and interaction of different treatments when persons are involved in more than one study.

Obviously, it is important to have these validity concerns already in mind when designing the experiment and in particular when using a specific design type. In the analysis phase it is too late to change the experiment in order to obtain better validity. The different validity threats should also be considered for the other types of empirical studies discussed in the following sections.

When the analysis is completed the next step is to draw conclusions and take actions based on the conclusions.

More in-depth descriptions of controlled experiments can be found in [18] and [20].

13.5 Case Study

13.5.1 Introduction

A case study is conducted to investigate a single entity or phenomenon within a specific time space. The researcher collects detailed information on, for example, one single project for a sustained period of time. During the performance of a case study, a variety of different data collection procedures may be applied [4].

If we want to compare two methods, it may be necessary to organise the study as a case study or an experiment. The choice depends on the scale of the evaluation. An example can be to use a pilot project to evaluate the effects of a change compared to some baseline [6].

Case studies are very suitable for the industrial evaluation of Web and software engineering methods and tools because they can avoid scale-up problems. The difference between case studies and experiments is that experiments sample over the variables that are being manipulated, while case studies sample from the variables representing the typical situation. An advantage of case studies is that they are easier to plan but the disadvantages are that the results are difficult to generalise and harder to interpret, i.e. it is possible to show the effects in a typical situation, but they cannot be generalised to every situation [14].

If the effect of a process change is very widespread, a case study is more suitable. The effect of the change can only be assessed at a high level of abstraction because the process change includes smaller and more detailed changes throughout the development process [6]. Also, the effects of the change cannot be identified immediately. For example, if we want to know if a new design tool increases the reliability, it may be necessary to wait until after delivery of the developed product to assess the effects on operational failures.

Case study research is a standard method used for empirical studies in various sciences such as sociology, medicine and psychology. Within Web and software engineering, case studies should be used not only to evaluate how or why certain phenomena occur, but also to evaluate the differences between, for example, two design methods. This means, in other words, to determine "which is best" of the two methods [14]. An example of a case study might be to assess whether the use of perspective-based reading increases the quality of requirements specifications. A study like this cannot verify that perspective-based reading reduces the number of faults that reaches test, since this requires a reference group that does not use perspective-based techniques.

13.5.2 Case Study Arrangements

A case study can be applied as a comparative research strategy, comparing the results of using one method or some form of manipulation to the results of using another approach. To avoid bias and to ensure internal validity, it is necessary to create a solid base for assessing the results of the case study. There are three ways to arrange the study to facilitate this [6].

A comparison of the results of using the new method against a company baseline is one solution. The company should gather data from standard projects and calculate characteristics like average productivity and defect rate. Then it is possible to compare the results from the case study with the figures from the baseline.

A sister project can be chosen as a baseline. The project under study uses the new method and the sister project the current one. Both projects should have the same characteristics, i.e. the projects must be comparable.

If the method applies to individual product components, it could be applied at random to some components and not to others. This is very similar to an experiment, but since the projects are not drawn at random from the population of all projects, it is not an experiment.

13.5.3 Confounding Factors and Other Aspects

When performing case studies it is necessary to minimise the effects of confounding factors. A confounding factor is, as described in Sect. 13.4, a factor that makes it impossible to distinguish the effects of two factors from each other. This is important since we do not have the same control over a case study as in an experiment. For example, it may be difficult to tell if a better result depends on the tool or the experience of the user of the tool. Confounding effects could involve problems with learning how to use a tool or method when trying to assess its benefits, or using very enthusiastic or sceptical staff.

There are both pros and cons with case studies. Case studies are valuable because they incorporate qualities that an experiment cannot visualise, e.g. scale, complexity, unpredictability and dynamism. Some potential problems with case studies are as follows.

A small or simplified case study is seldom a good instrument for discovering Web and software engineering principles and techniques. Increases in scale lead to changes in the type of problems that become most indicative. In other words, the problem may be different in a small case study and in a large case study, although the objective is to study the same issues. For example, in a small case study the main problem may be the actual technique being studied, and in a large case study the major problem may be the number of people involved and hence also the communication between people.

Researchers are not completely in control of a case study situation. This is good, from one perspective, because unpredictable changes frequently tell them much about the problems being studied. The problem is that we cannot be sure about the effects due to confounding factors.

More information on case study research can be found in [12] and [14].

13.6 Survey

Surveys are conducted when the use of a technique or tool has already taken place [13] or before it is introduced. It could be seen as a snapshot of the situation to capture the current status. Surveys could, for example, be used for opinion polls and market research.

When performing survey research the interest may be, for example, in studying how a new Web development process has improved the developer's attitudes towards quality assurance. Then a sample of developers is selected from all the developers at the company. A questionnaire is constructed to obtain information needed for the research. The questionnaires are answered by the sample of developers. The information collected is then arranged into a form that can be handled in a quantitative or qualitative manner.

13.6.1 Survey Characteristics

Sample surveys are almost never conducted to create an understanding of the particular sample. Instead, the purpose is to understand the population, from which the sample was drawn [15]. For example, by interviewing 25 developers on what they think about a new process, the opinion of the larger population of 100 developers in the company can be predicted. Surveys aim at the development of generalised suggestions.

Surveys have the ability to provide a large number of variables to evaluate, but it is necessary to aim at obtaining the largest amount of understanding from the smallest number of variables since this reduction also eases the analysis work.

It is not necessary to guess which are the most relevant variables in the initial design of the study. The survey format allows the collection of many variables, which in many cases may be quantified and processed by computers. This makes it is possible to construct a variety of explanatory models and then select the one that best fits the purposes of the investigation.

13.6.2 Survey Purposes

The general objective for conducting a survey is one of the following [15]:

- Descriptive.
- Explanatory.
- Explorative.

Descriptive surveys can be conducted to enable assertions about some population. This could be determining the distribution of certain characteristics or attributes. The concern is not about why the observed distribution exists, rather what it is.

Explanatory surveys aim at making explanatory claims about the population. For example, when studying how developers use a certain inspection technique, we might want to explain why some developers prefer one technique while others prefer another. By examining the relationships between different candidate techniques and several explanatory variables, we may try to explain why developers choose one of the techniques.

Finally, explorative surveys are used as a pre-study to a more thorough investigation to ensure that important issues are not foreseen. Creating a loosely structured questionnaire and letting a sample from the population answer it could do this. The information is gathered and analysed, and the results are used to improve the full investigation. In other words, the explorative survey does not answer the basic research question, but it may provide new possibilities that could be analysed and should therefore be followed up in the more focused or thorough survey.

13.6.3 Data Collection

The two most common means for data collection are questionnaires and interviews [15]. Questionnaires could be provided both in paper form or in some electronic form, e.g. e-mail or Web pages. The basic method for data collection through questionnaires is to send out the questionnaire together with instructions on how to fill it in. The responding person answers the questionnaire and then returns it to the researcher.

Letting interviewers handle the questionnaires (by telephone or face-to-face), instead of the respondents themselves, offers a number of advantages:

- Interview surveys typically achieve higher response rates than, for example, mail surveys.
- An interviewer generally decreases the number of "do not know" and "no answer" responses, because (s)he can answer questions about the questionnaire.
- It is possible for the interviewer to observe and ask questions.

The disadvantage is the cost and time, which depend on the size of the sample, and they are also related to the intentions of the investigation.

13.7 Post-mortem Analysis

Post-mortem analysis is a research method studying the past, but also focusing on the typical situation that has occurred. Thus, a post-mortem analysis is similar to the case study in terms of scope and to the survey in that it looks at the past. The basic idea behind post-mortem analysis is to capture the knowledge and experience from a specific case or activity after it has been finished. In [21] two types of post-mortem analysis are identified: a general post-mortem analysis capturing all available information from an activity or a focused post-mortem analysis for a specific activity, e.g. cost estimation.

According to [21], post-mortem analysis has mainly been targeted at large Web and software projects to learn from their success or recovery from a failure. An example of such a process is proposed by [22]. The steps are:

1. *Project survey.*
   The objective is to use a survey to collect information about the project from the participants. The use of a survey ensures that confidentiality can be guaranteed.
2. *Collect objective information.*
   In the second step, objective information that reveals the health of the project is collected. This includes defect data, person hours spent and so forth.

3. *Debriefing meeting.*
   A meeting is held to capture issues that were not covered by the survey. In addition, it provides the project participants with an opportunity to express their views.
4. *Project history day.*
   The history day is conducted with a selected subset of the people involved to review project events and project data.
5. *Publish the results.*
   Finally, a report is published. The report is focused on the lessons-learned and is used to guide organisational improvement.

To support small- and medium-sized companies, [21] discusses a lightweight approach to post-mortem analysis, which focuses on a few vital activities and highlights that:

- Post-mortem analyses should be open to participation by all team members and other stakeholders.
- Goals may be used to focus the discussions, but this is not necessary.
- The post-mortem process consists of three main phases: preparation, data collection and analysis. These phases are further discussed in [21].

Post-mortem analyses are a flexible type of analysis method. The actual object to be studied (a whole project or specific activity) and the type of questions posed are very much dependent on the actual situation and the objectives of the analysis.

The referenced articles or the book by Whitten [23] provide more information on post-mortem analysis/review.

Finally, it should be noted that empirical methods also provide positive side effects such as knowledge sharing, which is an added value of conducting an empirical study. This is true for all types of empirical studies. In an experiment, the subjects learn from comparing competing methods or techniques. This is in particular true if the subjects are debriefed afterwards in terms of obtaining information about the objective and the outcome of the experiment. In case studies and post-mortem analyses the persons participating obtain a new perspective of their work and they often reflect on their way of working through the participation in the empirical study. Finally, in the survey the learning comes from comparing the answers given with the general outcome of the survey. This allows individuals to put their own answers into a more general context.

13.8 Summary

This chapter has provided a brief overview of four empirical research methods with a primary focus on methods that contain some quantitative part. The four methods are: controlled experiments, case studies, surveys and post-mortem analyses. The main objective has been to introduce them so that people intending to conduct empirical studies can make an appropriate selection of an empirical research method in a Web or software engineering context.

Moreover, the presented methods must be seen as complementary in that they can be applied at different stages in the research process. This means that they can, together in a suitable combination, support each other and hence provide a good basis for sustainable improvement in Web and software development.

References

1 Garvin DA (1998) Building a Learning Organization. Harvard Business Review on Knowledge Management, 47–80, Harvard Business School Press, Boston, USA

2 Basili VR, Caldiera G, Rombach HD (2002) Experience Factory. In: Marciniak JJ (ed.) Encyclopaedia of Software Engineering, John Wiley & Sons, Hoboken, NJ, USA

3 Creswell JW (1994) Research Design, Qualitative and Quantitative Approaches, Sage Publications, London, UK

4 Denzin NK, Lincoln YS (1994) Handbook of Qualitative Research, Sage Publications, London, UK

5 Fenton N, Pfleeger SL (1996) Software Metrics: A Rigorous & Practical Approach, 2nd edition, International Thomson Computer Press, London, UK

6 Kitchenham B, Pickard L, Pfleeger SL (1995) Case Studies for Method and Tool Evaluation. IEEE Software, July, 52–62

7 Montgomery DC (1997) Design and Analysis of Experiments, 4th edition, John Wiley & Sons, New York, USA

8 Siegel S, Castellan J (1998) Nonparametric Statistics for the Behavioral Sciences, 2nd edition, McGraw-Hill International, New York, USA

9 Robson C (2002) Real World Research, 2nd edition, Blackwell, Oxford, UK

10 Zelkowitz MV, Wallace DR (1998) Experimental Models for Validating Technology. IEEE Computer, 31(5):23–31

11 Manly BFJ (1994) Multivariate Statistical Methods - A Primer, 2nd edition, Chapman & Hall, London

12 Stake RE (1995) The Art of Case Study Research, SAGE Publications, London, UK

13 Pfleeger S (1994–1995) Experimental Design and Analysis in Software Engineering Parts 1–5. ACM Sigsoft, Software Engineering Notes, 19(4):16–20; 20(1):22–26; 20(2):14–16; 20(3):13–15; 20(4):14–17

14 Yin RK (1994) Case Study Research Design and Methods, Sage Publications, Beverly Hills, CA, USA

15 Babbie E (1990) Survey Research Methods, Wadsworth, Monterey, CA, USA

16 Tukey JW (1977) Exploratory Data Analysis, Addison-Wesley, Reading, MA, USA

17 Robson C (1994) Design and Statistics in Psychology, 3rd edition, Penguin Books, London, UK

18 Wohlin C, Runeson P, Höst M, Ohlsson MC, Regnell B, Wesslén A (1999) Experimentation in Software Engineering – An Introduction, Kluwer Academic Publishers, Boston, MA, USA

19 Judd CM, Smith ER, Kidder LH (1991) Research Methods in Social Relations, Harcourt Brace Jovanovich College Publishers, Forth Worth, TX, USA, 6th edition

20 Juristo N, Moreno A (2001) Basics of Software Engineering Experimentation, Kluwer Academic Publishers, Boston, MA, USA

21 Birk A, Dingsøyr T, Stålhane T (2002) Postmortem: Never Leave a Project without It. IEEE Software, May/June, 43–45

22 Collier B, DeMarco T, Fearey P (1996) A Defined Process for Project Postmortem Review. IEEE Software, July, 65–72

23 Whitten N (1995) Managing Software Development Projects - Formula for Success, John Wiley & Sons, NY, USA

Authors Biographies

Dr. **Claes Wohlin** is a Professor of Software Engineering at Blekinge Institute of Technology in Sweden and also Pro Vice Chancellor of the Institute. Prior to this, he held chairs at Lund University and Linköping University. He has a PhD in Communication Systems from Lund University and five years of industrial experience. His research interests include empirical methods in software engineering, software metrics, software quality and systematic improvement in software engineering. Claes Wohlin is the principal author of the book "Experimentation in Software Engineering – An Introduction" published by Kluwer Academic Publishers in 1999. He is co-editor-in-chief of the Journal of Information and Software Technology published by Elsevier. Dr. Wohlin is on the editorial boards of Empirical Software Engineering: An International Journal, Software Quality Journal and Requirements Engineering Journal. He was the recipient of Telenor's Nordic Research Prize in 2004 for his achievements in software engineering and improvement of reliability in telecommunication systems. He is a Visiting Pro–fessor at Chalmers University of Technology working at the IT-University in Göteborg.

Dr. **Martin Höst** is an Associate Professor in Software Engineering in the Software Engineering Research Group at the Department of Communication Systems, Lund University, Sweden. He received a MSc from Lund University in 1992 and a PhD in Software Engineering from the same university in 1999. His main research interests include Software Process Improvement, Empirical Software Engineering, Software Performance Engineering, and Computer simulation of Software development processes. The research is conducted through empirical methods such as controlled experiments, surveys and case studies. Martin Höst has published more than 40 papers in international journals, conference proceedings and workshop proceedings.

Kennet Henningsson is a Ph.D. student in Software Engineering at Blekinge Institute of Technology in Sweden. He received his MSc in Software Engineering, with a focus on Management, in 2001 from Blekinge Institute of Technology and a Licentiate degree in Software Engineering in 2005 from the same university. His research interests are Fault-based software process improvement, Project Management, and Monitoring of Effort and Software Quality.

Index

D

E

H

I

L

M

N

O

T

U